GRANT MANAGEMENT

Funding for Public and Nonprofit Programs

Jeremy L. Hall, PhD

Department of Public Affairs
School of Economic, Political, and Policy Sciences
University of Texas at Dallas

JONES AND BARTLETT PUBLISHERS

Sudbury, Massachusetts

BOSTON   TORONTO   LONDON   SINGAPORE

World Headquarters

Jones and Bartlett Publishers
40 Tall Pine Drive
Sudbury, MA 01776
978-443-5000
info@jbpub.com
www.jbpub.com

Jones and Bartlett Publishers
Canada
6339 Ormindale Way
Mississauga, Ontario L5V 1J2
Canada

Jones and Bartlett Publishers
International
Barb House, Barb Mews
London W6 7PA
United Kingdom

Jones and Bartlett's books and products are available through most bookstores and online booksellers. To contact Jones and Bartlett Publishers directly, call 800-832-0034, fax 978-443-8000, or visit our website www.jbpub.com.

Production Credits
Publisher: Cathleen Sether
Acquisitions Editor: Jeremy Spiegel
Production Manager: Julie Champagne Bolduc
Production Assistant: Jessica Steele Newfell
Senior Marketing Manager: Barb Bartoszek
Associate Marketing Manager: Lisa Gordon
Manufacturing and Inventory Control Supervisor: Amy Bacus
Composition: Cape Cod Compositors, Inc.
Cover Design: Kristin E. Parker
Cover Image: © L00ky/Dreamstime.com
Printing and Binding: Malloy, Inc.
Cover Printing: Malloy, Inc.

Library of Congress Cataloging-in-Publication Data
Hall, Jeremy L.
    Grant management : funding for public and nonprofit programs / Jeremy L. Hall—1st ed.
        p. cm.
    Includes index.
    ISBN 978-0-7637-5527-0 (pbk. : alk. paper)
    1. Research grants. 2. Proposal writing for grants. I. Title.
HG177.H355 2009
658.15'224—dc22
                                                                    2008048848

6048

Printed in the United States of America
13 12 11 10 09   10 9 8 7 6 5 4 3 2 1

To Roger, Mary, Amanda, Homer, Jewell, and Maggie.

CONTENTS

PREFACE

This text is the culmination of convenience. Having written and managed grants now for several years and having experienced the process as both administrator and academician, I was called upon to develop a grant writing course for students in my university's Master of Public Administration program. After much contemplation, I arrived at the conclusion that the skill of grant managing may come naturally or may be learned. In either case, the subject matter can make for a mundane lecture. I ultimately decided that if I were a student of public administration looking for valuable grant skills—knowing what I now know—I would ask for something different than a course in basic grant writing. I would want someone to help me better understand the process of developing programs, organizing partners successfully, identifying funding sources, applying for grants, managing awarded grants effectively, and developing relationships and systems that would facilitate ongoing success. In short, I would ask for a lesson in intergovernmental public management with grant writing and grant management as a focal point.

Given these sentiments, I agreed to teach the course with what I thought was a fairly novel approach. In my search for an appropriate text for such a course I came to the realization that my approach was not only novel, but it was unique. I could not bear to subject professional students to what I would call a "bells and whistles" book with nifty tricks and pointers for writing proposals that might be more useful to individuals who have basic familiarity with the grant-seeking enterprise. Even the best books on the market fell short of the demands I had conceptually formulated because they dealt only with the steps leading up to and including the application process but said nothing of how to organize for community development programs or what to do after receipt of the formal notice of an award. Finding the available books lacking for my purpose, I began to sketch an outline of course content. Very quickly I realized that my course outline bore striking resemblance to a table of contents. That initial stroke of conceptual creativity now manifests itself physically in this book.

In fleshing out the details that made up the content of the outline I kept three interconnected purposes in mind. First, the liberal arts mentality I carry with me insists that, even in a very practical course, students should develop theoretical understanding of the concepts discussed. In that regard, I provide fairly academic treatments of the enterprise of grant making as a policy tool (introduction) and the role organizations play and the impact grants have on their recipient organizations (conclusion). Second, the teacher in me believes that the text should be suitable to train inexperienced students in a classroom setting and should facilitate their learning experience. Third, I have always held that the work performed in ivory towers is beneficial only to the extent it has practical utility on the ground for street-level professionals. To this end, the text should be straightforward enough that practicing professionals in nonprofit and public organizations can utilize it as a reference guide or to self-teach without the benefit of structured, direct faculty supervision. The result of these perspectives is a book that bridges conceptual and applied topics in an effort to bring greater knowledge and understanding to the pursuit of external funding by public and nonprofit agency managers.

This text takes a comprehensive approach to external funding for public and nonprofit agencies, beginning with the search for funding and developing programs, through the technical steps of preparing an application, and then explaining the process used to make decisions, key aspects of grant management, and concluding with an examination of grant making practice from the funder's perspective. The prose is geared toward individuals pursuing graduate study in public administration or nonprofit management. The target audience is assumed to be novice with regard to the subject matter, so the text also provides accessible appeal to public and nonprofit managers—especially those in organizations that lack a professional development division. The majority of the text maintains an extremely applied focus although the introductory and concluding chapters address overarching theoretical issues of relevance to public management more generally, but with an applied perspective with regard to grant funding and management specifically.

Although I wish each reader of this book the very best of luck in his or her pursuit of external funding, I also must caution that success improves with experience, and some things are probably only learned through hands-on repetitive experience. This text should significantly shorten that learning curve, but it cannot eliminate it. My greater desire is not that readers would receive plenteous grant awards, but rather that they would receive the wisdom to make sound decisions about which awards to seek and to utilize grants as a small but significant component of building more lasting and meaningful public programs. This general attitude will reduce the likelihood of dependency, debt, overextension, and other pitfalls that accrue to those who greedily seek funds without regard for their purpose or their effects.

In the way of disclaimers, all grants are not alike, and neither are all organizations. My background, although not narrow, is primarily focused in the field of community and economic development, and you will find that I draw heavily on this background for examples. This means that your setting, your field, or the agencies from which you seek funds will differ tremendously from my own. In that case, the contents of this book should still be relevant from the conceptual standpoint, though the specific details will often differ. Because community programming is seldom conducted in isolation, most programs involve collaboration among several partnering community organizations. The organizing component is essential to successful program development and directly affects the quality of grant proposals and their resulting programs, so you will find that I address this component explicitly. Also, it has been my experience that very few grants are written by a lone individual, but rather are the product of team efforts. Working together in developing a grant proposal, whether within an organization or across organizations, can be challenging but also rewarding. I provide some discussion of my approach to managing multiparty collaborative arrangements in the grant writing process as well.

ACKNOWLEDGMENTS

I am extremely grateful for the support of my current colleagues at the University of Texas at Dallas and previous colleagues at the University of Alabama at Birmingham, my research assistants, and my friends as I have compiled the contents of this text. Most of my gratitude, however, is directed toward three key groups of people—and they know who they are. First are those individuals who saw in me the potential to become a successful grant writer and who gave me opportunities to try my hand at it again and again. Second are those who provided my public administration education at the University of Kentucky. They shaped my understanding and perspective of a series of overlapping literatures that are combined in various ways in my approach to this text. Finally, those students who tolerated the initial test of this text in the classroom as it was being written—quite literally hot off the press—deserve a special thanks.

CHAPTER 1

Introduction

TANSTAAFL. As a doctoral student studying public administration, I was introduced to that elusive acronym by a well-known economist, and I have kept it within close mental reach since that time. TANSTAAFL stands for a variation on the age-old expression popularized by Milton Friedman: "There Ain't No Such Thing As A Free Lunch." Many hear the word *grant* only to have their mind immediately turn to thoughts of free money—a loan that never has to be repaid. We think of grants as generous, charitable outpourings of funds from those who have them to those who need them. These perceptions, though common throughout the population at large, are incorrect. In the way of introduction, allow me a bit of space to dispel that rumor more thoroughly.

Michael Rich (2006b) defines grants-in-aid as "the transfer of money from one level of government to another for a specific purpose and subject to substantive and procedural considerations found in the authorizing legislation and administrative regulations" (p. 294). I characterize grants more broadly to incorporate the fact that, increasingly, nonprofit organizations and, under the George W. Bush administration, faith-based organizations are eligible recipients of federal funds. It is also important to observe that governments are not the only entities engaged in providing grants. Corporations make grant awards as do private foundations. Moreover, grants do not always take the form of a cash payment.

Grants are policy instruments intended to leverage particular desired behaviors on the part of recipients. What behaviors? Naturally, the character of the expectations present in any particular grant is tied directly to the political principals' ideals, the institutions' missions, and to some extent the discretion afforded to agency bureaucrats. In the case of government grants (whether federal, state, or local), politics and bureaucratic discretion may be more important; for nonprofit grant making foundations, the mission and specific interests will be more important when funding requests are funneled through program officers and board committees. Regardless of the source of grant funds, differing in their purposes and expectations as they may, there is simply no such thing as free money.

In the first place, recipients' proposals must meet objectives previously established by the grantors. These objectives represent government and foundation efforts to create public value through change (Moore 1995). That is, they have perceptions about the way things should be, and they make grants for efforts that further those objectives. For example, the mission of the W. K. Kellogg Foundation is "To help people help themselves through the practical application of knowledge and resources to improve their quality of life and that of future generations" (W. K. Kellogg Foundation n.d.). The goals of the Ford Foundation are to "Strengthen democratic values, reduce poverty and injustice, promote international cooperation and advance human achievement" (Ford Foundation 2008b). The Office of University Partnerships (OUP)—a federal agency within the U.S. Department of Housing and Urban Development (HUD)—indicates that "OUP is committed to helping colleges and universities join with their neighbors to address urban problems—partnerships that enable students, faculty, and neighborhood organizations to work together to revitalize the economy, generate jobs, and rebuild healthy communities" (Office of University Partnerships 2008). And the Rural Utilities Service focuses on "helping rural utilities expand and keep their technology up to date, helping establish new and vital services such as distance learning and telemedicine" (Rural Utilities Service 2002).

These goal and mission statements convey the general objectives of the grant making organizations, but their operational objectives are almost always much more specific. For example, under one of the Ford Foundation's programs—Asset Building and Community Development—the specific objectives are as follows:

> In Environment and Development we help people and groups acquire, protect, improve and manage land, water, forests, wildlife and other natural assets in ways that help reduce poverty and injustice.
>
> In Community Development we seek to improve the quality of life and opportunities for positive change in urban and rural communities. We support community-based institutions that mobilize and leverage philanthropic capital, investment capital, social capital and natural resources in a responsible and fair manner.
>
> In Sexuality and Reproductive Health, a field addressed in all three of the foundation's programs, we focus on the social, cultural and economic factors that affect sexuality and reproductive health. Grant making emphasizes community-based responses to growing needs for prevention strategies and appropriate policies. It also focuses on empowering women and youth to participate in improving reproductive health and related policies.
>
> In all these units, grant making also helps to establish and fortify organizations and institutions that support asset building and the expansion of livelihood options through research, practical innovation, training, policy analysis and advocacy.
>
> Grant making aims to help low-income people and communities build the financial, human, social and natural assets they need to overcome poverty and injustice. By supporting and building strong fields, we will be able to help generate strategies appropriate to new situations. (Ford Foundation 2008a)

Or consider the objective of OUP's Hispanic-Serving Institutions Assisting Communities (HSIAC) program: "To assist Hispanic-Serving institutions (HSIs) of higher education expand their role and effectiveness in addressing community development needs in their localities, including neighborhood revitalization, housing and economic development, principally for persons of low- and moderate-income consistent with the purposes of Title I of the Housing and Community Development Act of 1974, as amended" (HSIAC 2008). Suffice it to say that the objectives inherent in the Community Development Act of 1974 add specificity to this statement.

Why make grants rather than directly provide services, you may ask. Some organizations or government agencies are too centralized to realize an impact at the broader state, national, or global level. Furthermore, upon examining their strengths and weaknesses, some organizations find that they lack comparative advantage over other performers

(Bryson 2004). Grant making is one type of policy mechanism that may be used to realize a policy's purposes. Directly providing services is another. Policymakers decide which mechanism best serves their goals in terms of political rationality, administrative feasibility, and substantive rationality. In other words, when comparing policy alternatives, the preferred policy choice must be expected to work in solving some public problem, it has to be able to garner support from enough decision makers to be deemed politically acceptable, and it must be administratively workable enough to be implemented (Bryson & Crosby 1992; Birkland 2005).

One of the features of a hierarchical bureaucracy that makes it appealing is the ability to specialize. Bureaucratic specialization means that an agency or unit is able to focus on a narrow set of activities, resulting in familiarity with those activities and enhancing operational efficiency as a result. Specialization often, though not always, means that an agency is either engaged in service provision or grant making, but not both. Economies of scale make it easy to efficiently distribute grant awards, whereas decentralized administration of numerous local projects can be more daunting. Following Paul Peterson's (1995) functional and legislative theories, it makes good sense for federal agencies to distribute funds while local implementers carry out projects on their own familiar territory.

Foundations face similar decisions. Some are explicitly grant making foundations while others are operating foundations, meaning that they are deeply involved in the programs they support, which usually means that they provide services directly rather than through grants. The Amherst H. Wilder Foundation is a sound example of the operating foundation model. Serving the Minneapolis, Minnesota, area, the foundation employs hundreds of individuals who provide various community services. The foundation feels that it can best serve its purposes and ensure quality services by maintaining control over them itself. Partnerships in which they have been engaged in the past were seen as detracting from their comparative advantage (Bryson 2003).

So, proposed programs have to first meet the basic objectives the grant maker desires. That is the easy part. After awarding a grant, the government or foundation very rarely mails the check, and if they do, it is not without first executing certain contractual documents. In this age of enhanced accountability, grant funds are more often disbursed on a reimbursement basis as costs are incurred. In other words, receiving a grant implies that you will make good faith efforts to perform those activities you proposed. Carrying out the specific activities promised in the proposal or meeting other conditional criteria associated with the grant award is the second manifestation of grantor purposes through recipient activities.

Third, the performance of those activities is expected to change the organization, the community, the state, or the world in some meaningful way. The new public management places attention on performance and outcomes rather than inputs, which have been the primary focus of traditional public administration. As public administration and management continue to focus attention not on inputs but on results and achievement of objectives, there will be increased pressure for grantees to demonstrate that their efforts, utilizing grant funds, have been successful. Federal agencies have already begun to force grantees to focus on the outcomes their proposed projects will yield. HUD has implemented agency-wide use of a logic model form in grant applications that link program activities specifically to agency goals and priorities, and then requires the applicant to spell out the short-, intermediate-, and long-term objectives and the logic by which the activities should lead to those results.

The federal Program Assessment Rating Tool (PART) initiative under the George W. Bush administration follows efforts initiated during the Clinton administration, and more directly by Vice President Gore, to focus federal government agencies on performance (outcomes) rather than budgets (inputs). It is an accountability mechanism that requires agencies to specify their performance objectives and measure progress toward them. How does one measure progress toward grant making? It is actually quite logical and straightforward. Agencies are able to focus on their internal process activities—such as the extent to which they award all funds in a timely fashion only to eligible recipients. They can also focus on the purpose of the grant programs more generally and pass the accountability buck to the recipients to specify objectives and measure performance. The agency can then report on the extent to which implemented programs meet the desired objectives. For example, the U.S. Department of Agriculture's Grants for Economic Opportunities and Quality of Life for Rural America initiative received the highest PART rating—effective (PART n.d.). In the way of assessing the grant making process, the PART review notes, "This program includes a significant number [of] projects (earmarks) added to the Budget by the Congress. Within the limitations of total funding, the inclusion of any unrequested projects reduces funding that could be used for high priority national programs" (PART n.d.). With regard to program outcomes, "The program addresses the problems faced by the fifty-five million Americans who live in rural areas, where in many cases population has been declining. Program efforts are directed toward improving rural communities" (PART n.d.). And in the way of efforts for improvement, PART reports that the agency is "Improving the efficiency of the grants review process by using 'Grants.gov' (a web based peer review system), as well as virtual panels when appropriate" and "Ensuring that all interested parties have the necessary access to grant information, as well as to continue to emphasize grant capacity building as appropriate" (PART n.d.).

So far, out of a grant we see expectations that program objectives meet grantor objectives, that the grantee performs a series of activities or implements certain programs in exchange for those funds, and that grantors will have increasing expectations for accountability in producing outcomes more than simply spending money where they said it would be spent. If only that were the limit to the burdens grant awards create for their recipients.

On rare occasions grants come without strings. Sometimes the expectation is implicit rather than explicit, and the award is made with trust that the recipient will do with the funds what it promised to do. More common is the use of matching requirements—what are often referred to in the fiscal federalism literature as "strings" that come attached to awards. For example, federal grant programs provide only a portion of project expenses; that means that nonprofit organizations, states, and local governments that wish to receive federal funds must provide a significant portion of project costs from their own source revenues—usually as much as 50% of total project costs. Table 1.1 presents a distribution of local match requirements based on various project costs and match amounts with match requirements based on total project costs. Also, observe how match requirements differ when they are based not on the total project costs, but on the federal funding amount (Table 1.2). We revisit this issue in later chapters.

TABLE 1.1   Distribution of Local Match Requirements Based on Total Project Costs

Total Project Cost	Match Requirement Based on Total Project Costs	Federal Funds	Local Funds Required
$1,000,000	25%	$750,000	$250,000
$ 500,000	50% (1 to 1)	$250,000	$250,000
$ 500,000	75%	$125,000	$375,000
$ 500,000	100%	n/a	$500,000

TABLE 1.2   Distribution of Local Match Requirements Based on Federal Grant Amount

Total Project Cost	Match Requirement Based on Federal Amount	Federal Funds	Local Funds Required
$1,000,000	25%	$800,000.00	$200,000.00
$ 500,000	50%	$333,333.33	$166,666.67
$ 500,000	75%	$285,714.28	$214,285.71
$ 500,000	100% (1 to 1)	$250,000.00	$250,000.00

In the case of governments, these match funds may come from new tax revenues, from debt, or movement from other programs. For nonprofit organizations, the funds must be reallocated from existing programs and projects or new funds must be raised in support of the grant-funded program. The point is that there are important financial tradeoffs within organizations that managers must make as they decide to pursue grant funding.

Financial decisions provide the substance of policy decisions. V. O. Key (1940) raised the quintessential question: "On what basis shall it be decided to allocate *x* dollars to activity A instead of activity B?" (p. 1137). Budget choices are policy choices. This is where the grant seeker must become keenly aware of the grant's effect on the organization in light of the organization's overall mission and goals. If the purpose of the grant is not a high priority for the local government, then allocating resources to it may detract from programs of higher priority. The great paradox of grant seeking is that those organizations or governments with the least resources (i.e., the greatest need) find grant funding to be very appealing, often valuing production of something over doing nothing and thus allowing grantor priorities to overwhelm local values and priorities. This is a significant burden to bear.

If, however, the grant's purpose is a high priority for the recipient organization or jurisdiction, then the grant actually provides relief rather than burden. It reduces the recipient's marginal cost of providing high-priority activities that it most likely would have undertaken anyway. **Figure 1.1** demonstrates the effect of a decrease in marginal cost on the efficient quantity of the good consumed. By reducing marginal cost, the efficient price level declines as long as the marginal benefit remains stable, thereby allowing the purchase of a greater quantity of the public good for a lower price. The type of grant instrument utilized

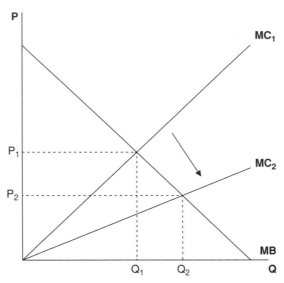

FIGURE 1.1   Effect of a Decline in Marginal Cost on Price/Quantity Relationship

has a great deal to do with how it affects local government spending through the grant's perceived effect on marginal cost of public goods. I return to this discussion near the end of the chapter.

Fiscal illusion occurs when a jurisdiction's citizens do not have perfect information about the grants they receive. The citizens perceive the services the government provides and the taxes they pay and assume a lower than actual marginal price for grant-funded public goods. The result is that more grant-funded public goods are provided as a result of the grant than as a result of the same increase in local income. A dollar of lump-sum grants increases local spending by more than a dollar increase in local income, meaning grant funds "stick where they hit" rather than substituting for local tax revenue (Boadway & Wildasin 1984). This condition is referred to as the flypaper effect.

So, where the grant's purpose matches the values and priorities of the local government or organization, a grant is a value. Where it does not, a grant becomes a burden. The systematic process of seeking and receiving grant funds for projects that are not local priorities can cause dependency on external funding and can lead to significant financial strain for recipients. Knowledgeable decision making, and especially strategic thought and action (Bryson 2004) can aid organizations by helping them to determine which grants to pursue and which to ignore.

Financial strings are one burden grants create. And the value of the almighty dollar is very powerful to citizens who do not understand the tradeoffs that grant funds may imply for their governments. Non-monetary strings are often attached to grants to ensure that other public purposes are being served—and recipients are willing to accept these terms because the value of the financial reward is so significant. Take, for example, higher education. The U.S. Department of Education awards billions of dollars to institutions of higher learning each year—including private colleges. Most of these funds benefit students through loans, grants, or work study programs. However, in agreeing to accept federal funds that assist their students, private colleges agree to a variety of additional federal policies to which they are not otherwise subject. The U.S. Department of Transportation induced state after state to adopt laws requiring use of seatbelts in automobiles by attaching that provision to highway transportation grant funds. They then persuaded states with only secondary enforcement to adopt primary enforcement using the same technique. State highway speed limits are left to the discretion of the states, but for a quarter of a century following the energy crisis of the 1970s they were not. The federal government imposed a restriction on funding that required states to adopt maximum speed limits of 65 miles per hour on limited access highways and 55 miles per hour on other state highways. This requirement was subsequently dropped when automotive technology caught up to our standards for energy consumption. Highway funds were used to leverage states to raise the legal drinking age to 21. Tennessee's open alcoholic beverage container law allows passengers, but not drivers, to possess open alcoholic beverages while traveling in automobiles. But again, by withholding several million dollars in grant funds, the federal government agency caused the Tennessee state legislature to take up the issue in the 2007 legislative session.

Federalism provides the opportunity for granting. Paul Peterson's (1995) functional and legislative theories of governments suggest that development should take place at the local level—where governments understand local needs and values—but that funding should come from higher-order governments (state and federal) that have greater tax bases and ability to raise funds (or in the case of the federal government, print money). In this framework, the federal government should raise revenue and distribute it to the states to use as they see fit. Federalism means states get to set their own policies in all areas not specifically afforded to the federal government by the Constitution. However, the federal government's monetary incentive has been powerful enough to convince state legislatures to convene, consider bills, and pass laws that adopt the federally prescribed policies. In the post-Depression era, the relationship expanded beyond federalism to reflect greater direct vertical integration between the federal government and local governments, special districts, and nonprofit organizations. The thought of losing "free" money seems almost too much to bear. States with traditional conservative values have been the slowest to adopt the federal government's expected provisions, but they have adopted. If only the money were free; TANSTAAFL.

From this introductory consideration, you might be wondering why you have decided to explore the possibility of grant funding or of entering a career that may require you to engage in grant seeking and management activities. Indeed, I have painted a fairly negative image of the entire enterprise. Nonetheless, grants are valuable resources that can assist organizations in accomplishing their goals. The key is that the tradeoffs must be understood in advance, and the price must be one that recipients are willing to pay. And even if the price is seemingly high, public value can still be created. It would be difficult to challenge the benefits to public health and safety that seatbelt use and speed limits help to ensure each day. Now that I have unrung your enthusiasm toward the grant bell, so to speak, and perhaps dampened your expectations of receiving external grant funds en masse, I turn attention to the history of grants, and to the various forms and consistencies grants may take.

FOUNDATION GRANTS: A BRIEF HISTORY

"Philanthropy has strong roots in religious beliefs, in the history of mutual assistance, in democratic principles of civic participation, in pluralistic approaches to problem solving and in American traditions of individual autonomy and limited government" (Council on Foundations 2008). These roots notwithstanding, philanthropy is not a uniquely American creation, and neither is the foundation (Dowie 2001). Small trust funds for charitable purposes were used in ancient Persia, numerous large foundations existed in prerevolutionary France, and in 15th-century England a charity was even created to purchase firewood for burning heretics (Dowie 2001, p. 1). American philanthropy is an imported, not an indigenous, phenomenon; our philanthropic institutions were brought here by Europeans, and they received support from abroad for many years (Bremner 1987). Our philanthropic institutions are copied from early European models, but they grew into a uniquely American enterprise far greater and more powerful than their European predecessors.

The earliest examples of American philanthropy date to colonial times. In 1638, John Harvard donated his personal library of 400 volumes and a sum of £375 to a newly authorized college in the Massachusetts Bay Colony (Nielsen 1996). That seemingly small gift was substantial enough at the time that the institution was named in his honor, and Harvard University carries his name to this day. Somewhat later, individuals like Benjamin Franklin helped to establish civic organizations such as volunteer fire departments, hospitals, universities, and libraries—institutions necessary for the well-being of local communities and their residents. Upon his death in 1829, John Smithson bequeathed $500,000 to the U.S. government to establish an institution that continues to bear his name—the Smithsonian (Bremner 1987). Congress extensively debated the legality of accepting this gift because it previously had never been done. Countless examples could be given, but the system in place today developed much later.

The Peabody Fund is considered the first of modern foundations; it was established by George Peabody in 1867 to support southern education (Bremner 1987). Near the end of the 19th century, American industrialists were faced with a unique challenge—individuals like John D. Rockefeller, Sr. (Standard Oil Corporation) and Andrew Carnegie (Carnegie Steel Corporation) had accumulated such great wealth that they could not ever hope to spend it. As Joel Fleishman (2007) notes, "Enough is enough," so they began to give their fortunes away (p. 2). Andrew Carnegie's *Gospel of Wealth* (1889) argued that the rich should administer their wealth as a public trust during life rather than leaving it to their families (Public Broadcasting Service 1999). Andrew Carnegie sold out Carnegie Steel to J. P. Morgan in 1901 for a sum of $480 million, making him the wealthiest man in the world at the time (Public Broadcasting Service 1999). Leaders such as Carnegie began to turn their attention to philanthropic purposes with the same ardor and tenacity that made them successful in business. They used their resources to give back to society. The Carnegie Foundation is commonly recognized for its work building libraries in communities across the nation—a goal undertaken to help the poor and illiterate to gain the skills they needed to rise up out of poverty into better paying jobs that would enable them to provide for themselves. It turned out to be a substantial task, so much so that John D. Rockefeller hired professional staff to manage his philanthropic efforts in 1891 (Dowie 2001). Making money more quickly than it could be given away became a burden, with early philanthropists opting to institutionally, rather than personally, distribute their charitable contributions. A *philanthropoid* is someone given the responsibility of giving away someone else's money. The first philanthropoid was probably Frederick T. Gates—a Baptist preacher chosen by John D. Rockefeller (himself a devout Baptist) to manage his philanthropic efforts (Fleishman 2007).

During this time, philanthropy was institutionalized in a new corporate form: the foundation. The Rockefeller Foundation was created June 29, 1909 (Fleishman 2007). Business leaders of the day transitioned their philanthropic resources from charitable private trusts (traditional to English law) into these new, more flexible, private foundations. The early 20th century saw philanthropy rise to a new level, being increasingly used to combat problems, conduct research, and promote science (Council on Foundations 2008). With the establishment of the Carnegie Corporation in 1911 (endowed with $125 million), Andrew Carnegie had managed to give away 90% of his personal fortune (Public Broadcasting Service 1999). The Kellogg Foundation was organized in 1930 with an interest in health and education for rural areas (Bremner 1987). In 1943, Frederick Douglas Patterson organized the United Negro College Fund to raise funds for 27 four-year colleges (Bremner 1987). The federal government established the National Science Foundation—the nation's preeminent funder of scientific research—in 1950 (Bremner 1987).

An additional important point should be made about philanthropy and foundations and their development more generally. Unlike governments and their grants, which lack a face and a personality, foundations are extensions of people. Philanthropy has often been looked back on as a "boys' club" with prominent businessmen at the forefront. However, many prominent women have been actively engaged in philanthropy—of most recent note, Melinda Gates comes to mind. The Sage Foundation was the first major American foundation incorporated by a woman (Margaret Olivia Slocum Sage), in 1906, and it was named in honor of her late husband Russell, who himself did not believe in charity (Nielsen 1996). The Annie E. Casey Foundation, the Sarah Scaife Foundation, the Scripps Foundation—each of these foundations reflects the central role of women in the development of American philanthropy. Their actions and leadership have given shape to the programs and activities foundations undertake and the missions they seek to achieve in so doing.

Many philanthropic efforts began as a singular cause or goal such as advancing science, curing disease, or promoting a religious denomination—causes tied to a concern for general human welfare. Philanthropy has undergone considerable shifts today as change has become the impetus for these organizations rather than mere charity (Dowie 2001)—they do not simply give for giving's sake; rather they give to cause some significant change in the world. This distinction is used to separate *expressive* giving from *instrumental* giving. Expressive giving is intended only to show support for an organization or a cause with no expectation of a noticeable impact as a result of the grant whereas instrumental giving is meant to achieve a specific policy objective with a significant impact on a societal problem (Fleishman 2007). Carnegie is responsible for the notion of instrumental giving; he described his own philanthropic goal as systemic change through systematic philanthropy (Fleishman 2007). Foundations and their philanthropist founders are often guilty of thinking that their wealth gives them unlimited power to change the world. Wooster (2006) documents eight case studies where foundations' efforts failed in such key areas as medical education, the war on cancer, public television, and school decentralization.

Today, private foundations carry out various efforts that serve the public interest, though oftentimes the specific activities' and purposes' worth could easily be debated. The reasons people choose to hand their wealth over to foundations for philanthropic purposes is not clearly understood. It has been argued that favorable tax laws make it advantageous to give away wealth, but that argument lacks substance insomuch as tax deductions are always significantly less than the amount donated. Both the Rockefeller Foundation and the Carnegie Corporation were founded prior to the establishment of tax benefits for such activity. Some have argued the purpose is notoriety and recognition—allowing their name to live on in perpetuity—and that sometimes may be the case. But it certainly is not always the case. In fact, John D. Rockefeller distanced himself from his foundation and even refused to serve on the board of trustees (Fleishman 2007). Even so, five of America's "highest-impact foundations" (the Commonwealth Fund, the Alfred P. Sloan Foundation, the Andrew W. Mellon Foundation, the Robert Wood Johnson Foundation, and the Carnegie Corporation of New York) show strong evidence of founder influence (Fleishman 2007). Even when the founder is closely tied to the foundation or provides explicit description of purpose and intent, it is not easy to maintain the instrumental programmatic focus. In very short order after a founder dies, the control of the foundation is typically passed to a spouse or surviving family member, to close business associates, and within the space of a generation to trustees with little or no connection to the founder whatsoever (Dowie 2001). In other words, the founder's goals and philanthropic purposes will fade and the foundation's activities will cease to reflect the founder's purposes. As Nielsen (1996) describes it, "the distribution of power and control within foundations shifts greatly and repeatedly with the passage of time. . . . Depending on circumstances, personalities, and even chance, the locus or distribution of controlling influence over the policies and programs of a foundation—especially a larger one—can shift greatly and repeatedly over the years" (p. 254).

Time has continued to create more super-rich individuals, and they have continued to engage in foundation building. In June 2006, Warren Buffett took an unprecedented step in announcing his intent to contribute $31 billion to a foundation over a span of years. Part of a very elite class of multibillionaires, Buffett, like Carnegie and others before him, saw an opportunity to give back to society. Unlike his predecessors, however, Buffett chose not to invest the time or money building a new foundation but opted instead to donate the funds to the Bill and Melinda Gates Foundation in exchange for becoming the foundation's third trustee. Buffett gave away more than twice (in real dollars) the contributions of Carnegie and Rockefeller combined (Fleishman 2007).

In all, today there are more than 71,000 grant making foundations of various types and sizes (up from 40,100 in 1995), and with many varied purposes, operating in the United States (Lawrence, Austin, & Mukai 2007). They control assets of more than half a trillion dollars and donate approximately $40 billion in grants each year (Fleishman 2007). Foundation giving in 2006 was $40.7 billion, with a total foundation asset base of nearly $551 billion; the Bill and Melinda Gates Foundation tops the list in assets (with $29.1 billion in total assets in 2005) and giving ($1.4 billion in 2005) (Lawrence et al. 2007). More telling is the fact that 70% of foundation assets are controlled by 2% of foundations (Fleishman 2007). Just as in the modern economy, where the wealthiest few individuals hold most of the assets and pay most of the taxes, foundations come in many shapes and sizes. **Figure 1.2** shows the trend in foundation giving over the past decade in real 2000 dollars (adjusted for inflation

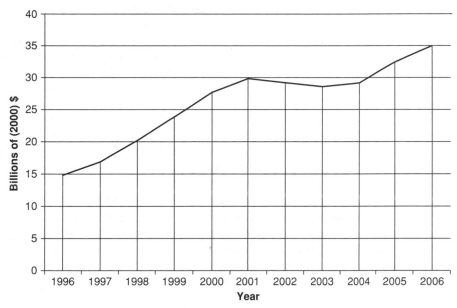

FIGURE 1.2   Trend in Foundation Giving 1996–2006

Source: Lawrence et al. 2007. And U.S. Budget Historical Tables: Table 10.1.

using the standard GDP deflator). Note the impact of the events of September 11, 2001, on foundation giving: the loss of value in the market reduced foundation assets and precipitated a period of retracted growth that has only recently been remedied. A similar result can be expected from the financial crisis of 2008. As markets lose value, foundations' asset bases contract, and their giving must be curtailed to adjust for decreases in investment income. Such catastrophic events will always cause concern for foundations and the organizations they support.

Foundations are constantly engaged in the effort to create public or societal value by working to strengthen and guide grant-receiving organizations (Fleishman 2007). What does that public value look like? No two foundations are alike, so neither are any two conceptualizations of public value. Foundations have supported scientific exploration and development of knowledge, they have supported social program innovation, and they have sought to change the world through grassroots movements at the individual level (Dowie 2001). Foundations can lay to their credit establishment of many successful programs that make our lives better every day, such as the 9-1-1 emergency telephone system. The first 9-1-1 system was established in 1968 in Alabama with support of a grant from the Robert Wood Johnson Foundation (Fleishman 2007). Its success was replicated and is now enjoyed nationwide as the model for effective emergency response. Other "1-1" systems are now being developed as well, such as the 5-1-1 travel information system. The Robert Wood Johnson Foundation (RWJF) has recently generated great attention with a social program geared toward improving Medicaid. Rather than offer strict state-provided services to individuals with disabilities, RWJF felt that such individuals could make decisions about the services they wish to receive, and that the exercise of such choice would increase satisfaction with services and overall quality of life. They put their money behind the idea with pilot programs in New York, Arkansas, New Jersey, and Florida and with a thorough evaluation plan. Subsequent smaller grants have been used to encourage 11 additional states to adopt what is known as the Cash and Counseling program (Cash and Counseling 2007).

How do foundations create public value? Fleishman (2007) identifies three roles that foundations commonly play: driver, partner, and catalyst. As a *driver*, the foundation plans and guides the efforts by making grants to organizations to simply carry out its bidding. As a *partner*, a foundation shares strategy development and decision making with partner organizations, making grants to them to support that effort and carry out the strategy. Finally, as a *catalyst*, the foundation lacks a clear or certain strategy for combating an identified problem and distributes resources broadly with the hope that although most programs are likely to fail, some will turn out to be successful and contribute to our knowledge and understanding of the problem and its solution. Catalyst role is best suited to situations where the problem is not yet ripe for solution (Fleishman 2007). As a catalyst, foundations become particularly entrepreneurial, investing resources and staking their reputation on programs with substantial risk in search of one success that yields significant returns.

Do foundations make grants outright without strings or conditions attached? Very rarely, and then most commonly to organizations they already know support their values. As indicated earlier, foundations are most likely to make grants that support a general purpose, and sometimes a very specific program. Foundations are cognizant that even the vast resources they bring to the table are minute given the magnitude of society and its problems. The result is that foundations have adopted resource leveraging as a means of stretching their dollars. Simply put, foundation dollars are used in the same fashion as a mechanical lever—more can be accomplished with less work by the performing organization when the lever is applied. So, foundations utilize matching grants in much the same fashion as governments, and they may also put money on the table to attract other foundations to join in a project or program to leverage resources from other foundation sources as well as the performing organization (Fleishman 2007). Fleishman notes, "There is nothing wrong with matching requirements, so long as the undertakings being supported are of high priority for the grantee organizations. When they are not, the foundation that imposes a challenge/matching requirement is using its philanthropic dollars to push a grantee in a direction that may conflict with its own priorities" (2007, p. 183). Just as is the case with government grants, foundation grants can be dangerous when they persuade grantees to abandon their own priorities in exchange for those of the grantor institution.

Another form of foundation leveraging is the challenge grant. Challenge grants require the recipient to raise additional funds from other sources as a condition to receiving the gift (Nielsen 1996). Challenge grants give local organizations a very powerful incentive to raise funds for a project or program. The promise of a very large foundation donation often constitutes more than half of a project's costs. Foundations use challenge grants to stretch the value of their dollars. Matching grants serve the same purpose, though both means often have the additional impact of generating local citizen involvement essential for a program's sustained success.

GRANTS IN AMERICAN GOVERNMENT: A BRIEF HISTORY

Operating under the Articles of Confederation, Congress provided for grants of land as early as 1785, and as such, the institution of grant making in the United States predates the Constitution itself. The Land Ordinance of 1785 provided that each township incorporated from federal lands was required to set aside one lot for public schools (Canada 2003). These earliest grants were not made through systematic competitive programs as they are today, but rather ad hoc authorizations of payments to states, local governments, and even to private corporations (Canada 2003). As often as not, these grants were in the form of land rather than cash. And as can be clearly seen in the Land Ordinance example, strings that served federal purposes were attached to even the earliest grants. One might argue that although education has its basis at the local and state levels, much is owed to the national government for its early establishment.

In 1790, the newly formed federal government provided financial assistance to the states by assuming debts incurred during the Revolutionary War. Grants were made to railroads to stimulate infrastructure development. The federal government provided land and technical assistance—in the form of surveying services—for the intracoastal waterway (Canada 2003). All grants are not in the form of monetary awards, as these examples demonstrate. In fact, grants can be characterized as the exchange of any item or service of value, including land, equipment, or technical assistance.

In 1835, with the national debt paid in full, and with future year budget surpluses forecast indefinitely, Congress took the unique step of distributing leftover funds to the states (Hines & Thaler 1995). The funds were distributed on the basis of state population and were expected to be utilized for public works projects—building critical infrastructure in a fledgling but growing nation. The great statesman Henry Clay anticipated that this surplus distribution would stimulate state spending by more than what economic theory suggested (Hines & Thaler 1995). Thus, just as in the earliest grants of land, the first cash outlay by the federal government to the states was also with an express federal purpose in mind, and with an explicit expectation that states would invest the federal funds toward those purposes and supplement expenditures with their own resources. This is in line with the characterization I have developed that grants first serve the purposes of the grantor and then those of the grantee.

The federal government gave large tracts of land to the states under the Morrill Act (1862) for the purpose of establishing state institutions of higher education—hence the term *land grant university* (Nathan 1983). Every state that remained in the union received 30,000 acres for each member of its congressional delegation (Morrill Act 1862). Hence, the grants provided a minimum amount (based on the common number of senators in each state) as well as a marginal increase based on population (which determines the number of U.S. Representatives). These grants, though not even monetary in nature, were provided with federal government priorities in mind—namely, education and support of agriculture. In the way of explicit requirements, the Morrill Act of 1862 required states to invest proceeds from these land sales in "safe stocks, yielding not less than five per centum upon the par value of the said stocks" to support "the endowment, support, and maintenance at least one college where the leading objective shall be ... to teach such branches of learning as are related to agriculture and mechanic arts" (Morrill Act 1862). These grants, in whatever form they take, are given with federal purposes in mind, and with explicit performance requirements attached.

These early examples provide the framework for future development in federal intergovernmental transfers, but growth in such transfers was relatively slow over time. It was not really until the mid-20th century that intergovernmental transfers came into their own right. The Weeks Act of 1911 provides the prototype for the modern grant with its inclusion of several key mechanisms: conditions requiring approval of state plans, matching funds, and giving federal officials a clear oversight role (Canada 2003). Grants to the states expanded significantly over the next decade.

Events of war (WWI), economic distress (Great Depression), and a number of key U.S. Supreme Court rulings based in the Commerce Clause of the Constitution enabled the federal government to gain in power vis-à-vis the states. The ratification of the Sixteenth Amendment in 1913 permitted the federal government to levy a tax on individual incomes. Adoption of the federal income tax in 1913 provided further impetus for this shift as the federal government had then obtained a powerful means of revenue generation not available at the state level. Roosevelt's New Deal and Johnson's Great Society catapulted fiscal federalism to the center of federal efforts as grants became the policy tool of choice for producing desired goods and services (Kettl 1983)—from infrastructure projects in the New Deal to social programs in the Great Society. The increased federal involvement during this time led to a more significant national policy role in various areas where states had previously dominated. Grant outlays tripled during the Eisenhower administration (from $2.4 billion to $6.8 billion), and during the Johnson administration, more grant programs were enacted than all previous years combined (Canada 2003).

Growth in federal grant outlays continued through 1981 when the Omnibus Budget Reconciliation Act (OBRA) of 1981 was passed under the Reagan administration. That year federal grant outlays to state and local governments were curtailed by $6 billion, and grant growth remained slow during the Reagan years (Canada 2003). Reagan took aggressive actions to limit federal spending (Rich 2006b). The general trend of federal grant spending from 1940 to present is presented in **Figure 1.3**. The trend line in Figure 1.3 forms a distinct trough followed by slow growth during the Reagan administration.

Moreover, Reagan is often credited with devolution of authority back to the states from the federal government. Reagan certainly had a clear agenda on federalism, as demonstrated by his issuance of Executive Order 12372 in July 1982. The Order provided for establishment of an intergovernmental review process at the state level that involved actors at the local and regional government levels to ensure that local feedback would be incorporated into federal agency funding decisions. **Figure 1.4** demonstrates the flow of the decision-making process E.O. 12372 was intended to initiate. The Reagan Executive Order ensured a local role in federal decision making. We revisit E.O. 12372 in later chapters.

In 2001, federal grants to state and local governments topped $317 billion and made up 17% of federal spending (Canada 2002); in 2004, federal grant outlays totaled $406 billion—18% of federal outlays, or the equivalent of 25% of all state and local government expenditures (Rich 2006b). To put this in perspective, federal grants to state and local governments constituted only 8% of federal spending in 1960, but grew to 17% by 1978 (Rivlin 1981). The growth rate disguises increases in real terms because during this period the federal

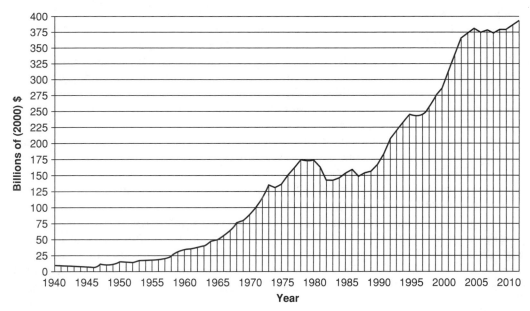

FIGURE 1.3 Total Federal Grant Outlays to State and Local Governments 1940–2012 in Constant (2000) Dollars

Note: Data for years 2007–2012 are estimates.

Source: U.S. Budget Historical Tables: Tables 10.1 and 12.2.

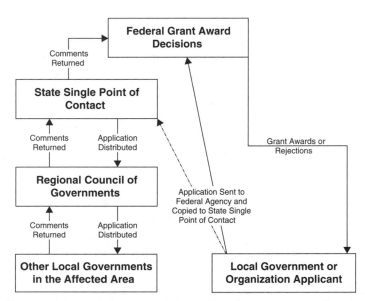

FIGURE 1.4 The Local Comment Process Initiated by E.O. 12372 as Related to Federal Funding Decisions

budget has also grown rapidly, caused in no small part by entitlement spending. "Grants-in-aid have been the primary means through which the federal government has pursued its domestic policy objectives for the past fifty years" (Rich 2006b, p. 295).

A reasonable observer might ask: What are the federal government's purposes in distributing grant monies? What sort of things is the federal government spending money on in the states? To provide some idea of the distribution of funds, **Table 1.3** provides spending levels for various functional categories in 5-year intervals from 1980 to 2005. **Table 1.4** provides the same data in constant 2000 dollars to demonstrate real spending by category.

Whereas in 1980 federal spending for education outpaced health, transportation, and income security programs, the tables have turned significantly. Priorities have clearly shifted by 2005, where spending for health exceeds transportation, education, and income security programs combined (see Table 1.3) and very nearly exceeds their combined total in constant 2000 dollars (Table 1.4).

Grants-in-aid have also been used extensively to influence foreign policy. The "global gag rule" originally known as the Mexico City Policy conditions receipt of foreign aid through the U.S. Aid program on the assurance that recipients do not carry out—or even promote—abortions. "The Mexico City Policy announced by President Reagan in 1984 required nongovernmental organizations to agree as a condition of their receipt of

TABLE 1.3   Total Federal Grants to State and Local Governments by Function (in millions of dollars)

Functional Group	1980	1985	1990	1995	2000	2005
National Defense	$ 93	$ 157	$ 241	$ 68	$ 2	$ 2
Energy	499	529	461	492	433	636
Natural Resources and Environment	5,363	4,069	3,745	3,985	4,595	5,858
Agriculture	569	2,420	1,285	780	724	933
Commercial and Housing Credit	3	2	0	5	1,218	1,364
Transportation	13,022	17,009	19,174	25,787	32,222	43,370
Community and Regional Development	6,486	5,221	4,965	7,230	8,665	20,167
Education, Training, Employment, and Social Services	21,862	17,080	21,780	30,881	36,672	57,247
Health	15,758	24,451	43,890	93,587	124,843	197,848
Income Security	18,495	27,890	36,768	58,366	68,853	90,885
Veterans Benefits and Services	90	91	134	253	434	552
Administration of Justice	529	95	574	1,222	5,263	4,784
General Government	8,616	6,838	2,309	2,335	2,144	4,370

Source: U.S. Budget Historical Tables: Table 12.2.

TABLE 1.4 Total Grants to State and Local Governments by Function (in millions of constant 2000 dollars)

Functional Group	1980	1985	1990	1995	2000	2005
National Defense	$ 175	$ 225	$ 297	$ 74	$ 2	$ 2
Energy	940	760	567	534	433	565
Natural Resources and Environment	10,100	5,844	4,609	4,323	4,595	5,207
Agriculture	1,072	3,476	1,582	846	724	829
Commercial and Housing Credit	6	3	0	5	1,218	1,212
Transportation	24,524	24,428	23,599	27,975	32,222	38,548
Community and Regional Development	12,215	7,498	6,111	7,843	8,665	17,925
Education, Training, Employment, and Social Services	41,171	24,530	26,806	33,501	36,672	50,882
Health	29,676	35,116	54,018	101,526	124,843	175,849
Income Security	34,831	40,055	45,253	63,317	68,853	80,779
Veterans Benefits and Services	169	131	165	274	434	491
Administration of Justice	996	136	706	1,326	5,263	4,252
General Government	16,226	9,820	2,842	2,533	2,144	3,884

Source: U.S. Budget Historical Tables: Tables 12.2 and 10.1.

Federal funds that such organizations would neither perform nor actively promote abortion as a method of family planning in other nations" (Bush 2001). President Clinton rescinded the rule in 1993, and President George W. Bush reinstated it upon assuming office January 22, 2001. We see early on that conditions on government grants can be derived from both legislative and executive sources, and affect both domestic and foreign policy. Grants play a significant role in federal policy today, but to better understand their role and their potential effects, it is valuable to briefly review differences in the form and function grants may take.

As already mentioned, grants can take a number of forms. The federal government makes grants of decommissioned equipment to worthy causes. It offers technical assistance for economic development efforts, and it has made grants of land to the states and even to individuals through the Homestead Act (1862). Although most value exchanged through grants today is in the form of cash payments, it is worthy to note these other forms because they highlight the manner in which many organizations approach grants. "What do I want with technical assistance? What do I want with old equipment?" Many organizations would readily ignore such offers if they didn't have a direct need for that which is being offered. Few would turn down a cash grant, though the provisions attached to a cash grant may make it no more appealing than these alternatives.

TYPES OF GRANTS: CONCEPTUAL DISTINCTIONS

Perhaps the most important distinction among grant types is the designation of conditionality. A conditional grant is one to which the grantor attaches explicit and specific strings or requirements; as you probably suspect, unconditional grants imply the lack of such specific strings. Conditions may be either financial or substantive in nature (Hall & Hail 2006). Rich (2006b) distinguishes recipient discretion from duties and responsibilities of recipients. This distinction is relevant and is a fair way to evaluate a grant. I prefer to view recipient discretion as a function of conditionality, which is premised on the duties and responsibilities attached to the grant. **Figure 1.5** shows the inverse relationship between federal award conditions and local spending discretion. As conditions increase, local discretion declines.

The responsibilities derived from grant conditions may be directly related to the substantive focus of the grant (such as building highways) or may be related only indirectly (such as adopting a higher drinking age). Strings take the form of requirements as to the type of expenditures that may be made, requirements for local matching expenditures, or other mandates accepted as a contingency of funding (Hall 2008). More strings means the grant is more conditional, and the more conditions, the less recipient discretion. What we observe is not a clear distinction between two categories, but a spectrum wherein conditionality may be increased or decreased (**Figure 1.6**).

In other words, we would say that a grant with no matching requirements and no restrictions on expenditure would be considered an unconditional grant. Unconditional grants are certainly not the norm. As I mentioned previously, even the earliest grants contained explicit and implicit conditions on the use of funds. When grants lack explicit

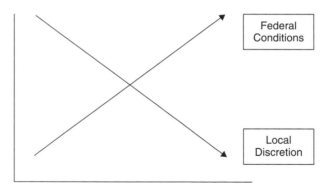

FIGURE 1.5   The Inverse Relationship Between Federal Conditions and Local Discretion

FIGURE 1.6   Grant Conditionality as a Spectrum

requirements, there are almost always some implicit expectations. So, movement from no expectations to implicit expectations, and on to explicit expectations and outright restrictions represents an increase in conditionality, or movement from left to right on the preceding spectrum. Similarly, grants that have no matching requirements are the most unconditional, and adding requirements for expenditure of own-source revenues or in-kind contribution of organizational resources makes them more conditional. "Matching grants require the recipient government to expend own-source revenue on the funded program. The greater the matching requirement, the greater the conditionality of the grant, other things being equal" (Hall 2008). So, a grant requiring a 1:1 match of local funds to federal would be more conditional than a grant requiring a 1:2 matching ratio.

The conceptual problem associated with describing grants as conditional or unconditional is that matching requirements (financial conditions) and expenditure restrictions (non-financial conditions) do not always move in the same direction. In other words, both expenditure restrictions and matching requirements add to the conditionality of the grant. A grant with no matching requirements but explicit expenditure restrictions is still a conditional grant, but less conditional than a grant with both. The Federal Aid Highway Act of 1916 expanded the federal role by attaching a series of conditions and controls to ensure that the states adhered to federal goals and objectives; conditions included project applications, reporting requirements, audits, and project closeouts (Rich 2006a). Conditionality has generally increased in incidence and severity over time (with the exception of New Federalism endeavors under Presidents Nixon and Reagan). In fact, Martha Derthick (1996) observes that by the 1970s the national government had made state and local governments "agents of its purposes through aggressive use of grant-in-aid conditions and partial preemptions" (p. 75–76).

Is it fair to condition grant funds on particular behaviors? Is it legal? The legality of federal grant conditionality was upheld by the U.S. Supreme Court (U.S. Supreme Court, *South Dakota v. Dole*, 483 U.S. 203, 1987). The Court was asked whether the federal government could withhold highway funds from the state because its legal drinking age was not 21; the Court's response was that Congress could use its spending power to influence states when it was in the general public interest (Canada 2003). Other cases have limited absolute use of this power (U.S. Supreme Court, *New York v. United States*, 505 U.S. 144, 1992). The dividing line on legality is crossed when federal efforts leave the realm of encouragement and begin to constitute coercion. Whether or not it is fair constitutes a value judgment based on the reader's views concerning states' rights vis-à-vis the federal government.

Conditionality is important to our understanding of grants not because it affects the application process, but because it changes the effects grants have on our organizations. There is an ongoing debate among fiscal federalism scholars as to the real effects grants have on their recipients. The most recent research demonstrates that the grant type—based on these notions of conditionality—is one of the key determinants of these effects (Hall 2008; Martell & Smith 2004 examine the effects of declines in matching and non-matching grants on state debt). As I have noted, "Conditional grants should not foster dependency, whereas block grants or other unconditional funds may lead to long-term dependency on the federal government" (Hall 2008). On the other hand, it has also been argued that the grant type is not as important as the manner in which the recipient treats it (Nathan 1983). If the funds are treated as separate, and not lumped into local funds or used to offset local expenditures, negative effects would be minimized. We will revisit this issue in later discussions of grant management.

Negative effects include growing dependent on external aid (more common for unconditional grants), which is exacerbated during periods of declining external revenue, and taking on debt to replace declining federal funds. Moreover, conditions have another significant effect on local governments—administration. Administrative requirements associated with federal grants are not light, and for programs with many conditions and explicit requirements, monitoring, recordkeeping, and other administrative duties can pose quite a burden. Given the drastic spending cuts proposed by President Reagan, the Director of the Congressional Budget Office recommended that Congress consider simplifying these administrative requirements to help recipient governments save money (Rivlin 1981). The notion of conditionality is very useful in distinguishing the most commonly used grant types.

Grants need not be distributed equally, and the method of allocation is an additional core dimension in the structure of grants. Equal distribution refers to a division of funds so that each state or citizen receives the same amount of federal funding. Equality and equalization do not mean the same thing. *Equalization* refers to the process of targeting funds to places with the greatest level of need to help bring them up to national standards. The intended result is *equality*; the method of distribution is targeting. Targeting can be performed with an eye toward places or groups of people. Rural places were targeted for highway funds by the Federal Highway Act of 1916, for example (Canada 2003). Today, grants are targeted to geographic areas through agency missions—such as the Appalachian Regional Commission or the Rural Utilities Service of the U.S. Department of Agriculture. They are also targeted on the basis of need by taking into consideration poverty levels and other socioeconomic measures. Targeting is a very important dimension in describing types of grants because it categorizes the method of allocation and provides guidance to agency administrators as they seek to determine rules to govern distribution of federal awards.

Grant Types

Grants can be best understood by breaking them down into dichotomies. There are non-categorical and categorical grants, matching grants and non-matching grants, block grants and project grants. **Figure 1.7** shows the relationships among these constructs. This typology pertains to intergovernmental grants in particular. There are two primary types of grants—categorical and non-categorical. Non-categorical grants are essentially a thing of the past in the United States. They were grants transferred to states from the federal government with no strings, conditions, match requirements, or even expectations as to the type of expenditures for which they would be used. In fact, as I discuss later, they could even be used to offset local tax revenues.

Categorical grants are for specific purposes, such as education or community development. They take two common forms—project grants and block grants. Project grants have explicit performance expectations whereas block grants are broader in nature—providing lump sum funding for projects in a general functional area. Both block and project grants may or may not have matching requirements associated with them. Foundation grants have similar relationships in that they are either for projects (like project categorical grants) or

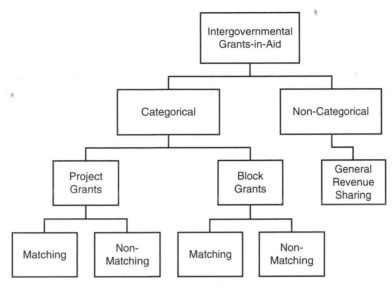

FIGURE 1.7   General Grant Types and Relationships

for general operating support (like general revenue sharing as a non-categorical grant). They may be used for specific projects (like project grants) or for programming in a general area (like block grants), though the former is more common. They may or may not require a match, and there may be other conditions attached to awards as well. In all, categorical grants make up about 95% of federal programs and 80% of federal outlays (Rich 2006a).

Project Grants

Categorical grants provide funding for a very narrow range of eligible activities; funding provided through categorical programs can only be expended on specific and narrowly defined purposes (Canada 2002). Project grants are the primary type of categorical grant. Project grants are awards made, as the name implies, to carry out specific projects. They are the most popular form of federal aid, and they will continue to dominate the grant enterprise because of special interests' strong support for them with Congress (Hale & Palley 1981). Project grants are one type of categorical grant, and they are the oldest form of grant-in-aid program (Hail & Hall 2006). Project grants apply strict conditions on use of funds, and as such significantly limit local discretion in spending. Project grants strongly favor federal (grantor) priorities over local ones (grantee) because they so limit the acceptable use of funds to specific purposes. They are specific not only in terms of projects and related activities, but also for specific periods of time. As grants go, project grants "have the narrowest range of eligible activities of all grant types" (Canada 2002). Project grants entail the most stringent reporting requirements and are subject to audit upon project completion.

Block Grants

Block grants are the second form of categorical grant. Block grants are large sums of funding delivered in lump sum chunks, or "blocks," to states or cities to carry out various programming in a general policy area. Urban Action Grants, Community Development Block Grants, and Temporary Assistance to Needy Families Grants are delivered in block form. Block grants often come about as a result of consolidating numerous individual project grant programs. Consequently, they are also one common policy mechanism through which spending cuts are implemented. By consolidating individual grants into one large lump sum transfer, the federal government is able to trade off increased discretion for less money. Republican administrations have usually favored block grants to more restrictive project grants because, on whole, they afford greater discretion to the states, and because they reduce reporting and recordkeeping requirements and lower total federal spending on a policy area. Consequently, the largest consolidations of categorical project grants into block grants occurred during the Nixon and Reagan administrations (Rich 2006a), though some took place during the Carter administration as well.

The Reagan administration not only reduced federal spending for grants to state and local governments, but also expressly set out to restructure those programs that remained to "lessen federal control and increase state and local flexibility" (Rivlin 1981, p. 4). This was achieved primarily through major consolidations of individual categorical grants into block grants. Block grants are still categorical in nature, in that they are grouped by substantive policy area and are to be used for "categories" of expenditure. However, they lose the explicit project orientation and the highly ordered and specified details of implementation found in project grants. Block grants have a broad range of eligible activities focused on a topical program area expressed in general rather than specific terms (Canada 2002). Block grants have, in the past, been developed through the consolidation of a number of categorical programs under a new unified auspice. Both Nixon and Reagan favored this grant form because it was seen as a tool for returning discretion to state and local governments where the federal government had increased in prominence over time.

George W. Bush proposed consolidating numerous federal community development programs into one large block grant known as the Strengthening America's Communities Initiative (SACI). President Bush's proposal would have cut the total amount of available federal funds for community development from $5.31 billion in fiscal year (FY) 2005 to $3.71 billion in FY 2006—a reduction of approximately 34% (U.S. Department of Commerce 2005). This program would have eliminated the Community Development Block Grant Program through consolidation as well. Block grants are distributed on a formulaic basis, and recipients, rather than the grantor agency, exercises discretion in developing programs aimed at problems of their own identification. State governments and large cities are the usual recipients of federal block grant funds, which they then sub-grant in pieces to other actors within their jurisdiction in the form of project grants. So, block grants essentially move spending discretion, but also administrative burden, to the state and local government recipients. As noted earlier, Temporary Assistance to Needy Families (TANF) and Community Development Block Grants (CDBG) are examples of block grant programs; CDBG funds are commonly redistributed whereas TANF funds are generally managed through state programs. Although it is more difficult for the grantor to exercise control and discretion over block grant spending, the administrative requirements associated with these grants pose substantially less burden for recipient jurisdictions (Canada 2002).

This is not always the case. The general trend in federal grant programs—including block grants—has been to increase conditionality. The Republican majority in the U.S.

House in 1995 put forward a welfare reform package that included consolidating categorical programs into a new block grant program, in part to devolve authority to the states. As Derthick (1996) notes, it was a "strange form of devolution" in that it included "national prescriptions of such force and specificity in a grant-in-aid program [that] would have been unthinkable prior to the 1960s" (p. 78).

Methods of Allocating Grant Funds

A formula grant differs from a discretionary grant in its method of allocation. The method of allocation may be either formula-based or based on the agency's discretion. *Discretionary awards* mean that Congress, in designing the program, set out particular goals and objectives or allowable activities, but left the decision of awarding funds up to the funding agency and its bureaucracy. Discretionary programs are competitive in nature, requiring would-be recipients to justify their requests through competitive applications. Different agencies evaluate discretionary award applications differently, and we discuss that in greater detail in a later chapter. The act of writing federal grant applications is an administrative matter for formula-based programs, but it is a combination of art and science for competitive programs. Sometimes Congress makes funding decisions in the authorizing legislation by specifying a formula that is to be used in distributing available funds among eligible recipients. In other cases the specific formula is left to agency administrators to determine. Formula grants comprise nearly 85% of federal government grants-in-aid to state and local governments, and they are unique in that governments do not have to compete with each other to receive them (Williams 2006).

Whereas discretionary grants are awarded in specific amounts based on anticipated project costs, formula grants are allocated on the basis of a predetermined formula (Canada 2002). The formula factors and the weights assigned to each are either prescribed in the authorizing legislation or determined by agency administrators (Rich 2006a). Education funding, for example, weighs a number of demographic variables—most important, the number of students—in determining funding levels. Other examples of formula components include population, poverty, per capita personal income, and unemployment (Rich 2006a). Such grants are like the tax code in that they leave little or no discretion to bureaucrats and administrators in determining funding levels. These programs have tremendous automaticity—they are awarded nearly automatically year after year on the basis of computational distributions across recipients out of a total grant pool. These programs leave no discretion to agency professionals to evaluate need or worthiness of any given project; they simply divvy up available funds according to Congress's intent. The three most expensive formula grant programs in 2002 included Medicaid, Highway Planning and Construction, and Welfare (Williams 2006).

New grant programs typically assume the categorical grant form, whether allocated by formula or competition. In the way of conditionality, categorical grants "typically include administrative and reporting requirements that help ensure both financial and programmatic accountability" (Canada 2002).

As director of the Congressional Budget Office at the time President Reagan took office, Alice Rivlin (1981) made a series of suggestions to Congress regarding ways in which grants to state and local governments could be restructured. Among her suggestions was to modify current allocation formulas to direct the smallest reductions in funding to the most distressed jurisdictions. This example demonstrates quite clearly the role formulas can play in targeting efforts. It would be incorrect to assume that only project grants can be used for equalization purposes. Project grants may be more precise instruments, but they are not the only instrument that can serve an equalization purpose. **Figure 1.8** presents a general characterization of grant types according to their degree of conditionality.

Table 1.5 provides a general overview of the progression of grants throughout the history of the United States. During the founding era, while the fledgling nation was developing critical infrastructure, defending itself, adding new states and territories, and expanding westward, grants were often made on an ad hoc basis. Land was distributed systematically to states or individuals as noted earlier, but for explicit purposes. Beginning with the New Deal era, the federal government stepped up its fiscal efforts with a series of categorical programs aimed at lifting the nation out of the weak economic state in which it found itself. The War on Poverty was an expansion of these efforts, but the vast growth of the federal government led to a backlash with programs beginning to return (or attempting to return) discretion to the states. Following the Reagan administration, the trend of categorical project grants has returned, but in an era of increased targeting. Programs remain systematic, but requirements are purposed to result in equalization by granting to the neediest areas.

The federal government today classifies the assistance it provides into 15 categories, and, as noted earlier, cash grants constitute only a few of those categories. **Table 1.6** provides the description of these 15 types of assistance as listed in the Catalog of Federal Domestic Assistance.

Unconditional Grants				Conditional Grants
No Conditions				Many Conditions
(General Revenue Sharing)	(Special Revenue Sharing)	(Block Grants)	(Categorical Grants)	(Targeted Project Grants)

FIGURE 1.8   Grant Types Arrayed on the Conditionality Spectrum

TABLE 1.5   General Overview of Grant Types and Structures in U.S. History

Grant Description	*Grant Type*	*General Time Frame*
Land Grants and Ad Hoc Expenditures	Project Grants (Categorical)	Founding to the New Deal
Systematized Categorical Programs	Project Grants (Categorical)	New Deal through War on Poverty
General Revenue Sharing	Non-Categorical	Nixon through early Reagan
Program Consolidation	Block Grants (Categorical)	Nixon through late Reagan
Targeted Project Funding	Project Grants (Categorical)	G. H. W. Bush to Present

TABLE 1.6 Types of Assistance Available Through Federal Programs

Types of Assistance	Description
(A) Formula Grants	Allocations of money to states or their subdivisions in accordance with distribution formulas prescribed by law or administrative regulation, for activities of a continuing nature not confined to a specific project.
(B) Project Grants	The funding, for fixed or known periods, of specific projects. Project grants can include fellowships, scholarships, research grants, training grants, traineeships, experimental and demonstration grants, evaluation grants, planning grants, technical assistance grants, survey grants, and construction grants.
(C) Direct Payments for Specified Use	Financial assistance from the federal government provided directly to individuals, private firms, and other private institutions to encourage or subsidize a particular activity by conditioning the receipt of the assistance on a particular performance by the recipient. This does not include solicited contracts for the procurement of goods and services for the federal government.
(D) Direct Payments with Unrestricted Use	Financial assistance from the federal government provided directly to beneficiaries who satisfy federal eligibility requirements with no restrictions being imposed on the recipient as to how the money is spent. Included are payments under retirement, pension, and compensatory programs.
(E) Direct Loans	Financial assistance provided through the lending of federal monies for a specific period of time, with a reasonable expectation of repayment. Such loans may or may not require the payment of interest.
(F) Guaranteed/ Insured Loans	Programs in which the federal government makes an arrangement to indemnify a lender against part or all of any defaults by those responsible for repayment of loans.
(G) Insurance	Financial assistance provided to assure reimbursement for losses sustained under specified conditions. Coverage may be provided directly by the federal government or through private carriers and may or may not involve the payment of premiums.
(H) Sale, Exchange, or Donation of Property and Goods	Programs that provide for the sale, exchange, or donation of federal real property, personal property, commodities, and other goods including land, buildings, equipment, food, and drugs. This does not include the loan of, use of, or access to federal facilities or property.

TABLE 1.6   (Continued)

Types of Assistance	Description
(I) Use of Property, Facilities, and Equipment	Programs that provide for the loan of, use of, or access to federal facilities or property wherein the federally owned facilities or property do not remain in the possession of the recipient of the assistance.
(J) Provision of Specialized Services	Programs that provide federal personnel directly to perform certain tasks for the benefit of communities or individuals. These services may be performed in conjunction with nonfederal personnel, but they involve more than consultation, advice, or counseling.
(K) Advisory Services and Counseling	Programs that provide federal specialists to consult, advise, or counsel communities or individuals to include conferences, workshops, or personal contacts. This may involve the use of published information, but only in a secondary capacity.
(L) Dissemination of Technical Information	Programs that provide for the publication and distribution of information or data of a specialized or technical nature frequently through clearinghouses or libraries. This does not include conventional public information services designed for general public consumption.
(M) Training	Programs that provide instructional activities conducted directly by a federal agency for individuals not employed by the federal government.
(N) Investigation of Complaints	Federal administrative agency activities that are initiated in response to requests, either formal or informal, to examine or investigate claims of violations of federal statutes, policies, or procedure. The origination of such claims must come from outside the federal government.
(O) Federal Employment	Programs that reflect the government-wide responsibilities of the Office of Personnel Management in the recruitment and hiring of federal civilian agency personnel.

Note: Currently, programs in the Catalog are being classified by GSA into 15 types of assistance. (Cooperative Agreements as a type of assistance is used for programs administered under that mechanism. However, the definition does not appear in this section.) Benefits and services of the programs are provided through seven financial types of assistance and eight non-financial types of assistance. The list defines the types of assistance that are available through the programs. Code letters (A through O), which identify the type of assistance, follow program titles in the Agency Index, Applicant Eligibility Index, the Functional Index, Deadlines Index, and the list of added programs.

Source: U.S. Government Printing Office n.d.

WHY CONDITIONS AND ALLOCATION METHOD MATTER: RECIPIENT RESPONSE TO GRANT TYPES

Now that we have an understanding of the distinctions among grant types, we should return to my earlier observation that different grant types elicit different spending responses based on the features of their design. Boadway and Wildasin (1984) explain that "the appropriate type of grant from a higher level of government to a lower level will depend upon the purpose for which the grant is being given" (p. 527). Looking at grants from the economics perspective, we can diagram the expected effect different grants will have on local collective budget constraints and utility. Let us first consider the effect of non-categorical grants. These grants, such as general revenue sharing, are outright lump sum transfers and have no restrictions, conditions, or matching requirements associated with them. Essentially, they are the same as providing an increase to local income because the funds can either be used to fund public goods or to reduce local taxes that enable citizens to consume more private goods. **Figure 1.9** shows the effect of a non-categorical grant of "A" dollars. The grant shifts the local budget constraint outward and increases spending on both public goods (shown as G_0 to G_1) and private goods (shown as C_0 to C_1), thereby raising utility from E_0 to E_1, which is on a higher indifference curve. This type of grant is most effective if the goal is to simply transfer spending power from one level of government to another with the least interference in local priorities (Boadway & Wildasin 1984). The grant affects the consumption of both public and private goods in the local economy, but the exact distribution depends on local and individual preferences.

Moving on to categorical grants, block grants restrict spending to a specific (categorical) purpose. A block grant with no matching requirement results in the budget constraint

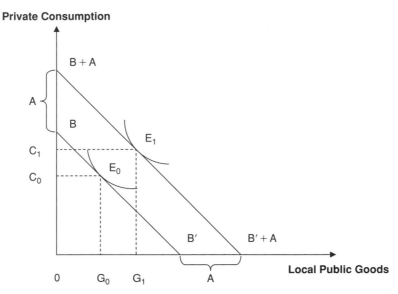

FIGURE 1.9   Effects of a Non-Categorical Grant on Local Budget Constraints (Revenue Sharing: No Restrictions)

shown as the kinked line BRS in **Figure 1.10**. Because the grant increases spending only on the public good, points falling within the area BRN are not possible as they were with an unrestricted non-categorical grant. In other words, the grant cannot substitute for local taxes that would affect local private consumption.

Continuing on, consider the budget constraint facing a local government in receipt of an open-ended matching grant; that is, a grant that increases with the amount of local match spending and that has no upper spending limitation or cap (shown in **Figure 1.11**).

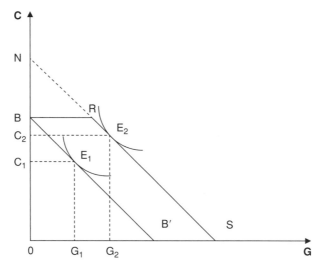

FIGURE 1.10   Effect of Non-Matching Block Grant on Local Budget Constraints

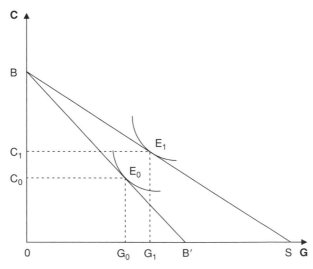

FIGURE 1.11   Effect of Open-Ended Matching Grant on Local Budget Constraints

The matching grant increases the budget by a greater amount as local spending for the grant-supported public good increases. Note that a matching grant lowers the marginal cost of the public good to the jurisdiction, so the budget line with the grant (BS) is flatter than the budget line preceding the grant award (BB'). This grant doesn't have the kinked shape we observed with non-matching block grants because there is no lump sum payment, but rather incremental increases according to the amount of match the local government spends. This type of conditional matching grant is appropriate if the purpose is to encourage a particular type of expenditure by the local government (Boadway & Wildasin 1984).

Of course, the federal government is wise to the fact that open-ended grants add substantial difficulty to budgeting and planning, and even the federal government faces resource scarcity. So, the final example is of a matching grant that includes a spending cap (**Figure 1.12**). Note that the shape of the new budget line is the same as in Figure 1.11 until the local government reaches the maximum grant amount, and then the budget line turns to run parallel to the previous line of the original local budget—just as in the non-matching categorical block grant example (Figure 1.10).

CONCLUSION

Grants can be valuable tools to organizations and governments seeking to provide services, infrastructure, or other value to their constituents. There is a long history of grants in this country, brought about in large part by the federal system of government we have in place. The shape of grants, their form and function, has changed a great deal over time, but there has always been a public purpose at heart, and as such grants have always been intended as an incentive to undertake specific activities or types of activities. Over time grants have become more restrictive, and an emphasis on accountability has heightened our attention to

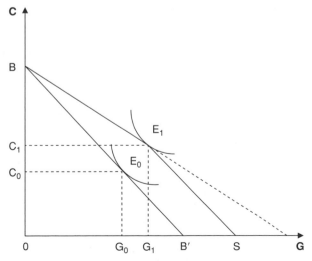

FIGURE 1.12 Effect of Capped Matching Grant on Local Budget Constraints

outcomes as well as procedural accountability stemming from implementation. The enterprise upon which you are about to embark is a highly competitive one; as the saying goes, many are called, but few are chosen. You should not come to expect phenomenal grant writing success without first anticipating a significant number of failures. Your efforts will pay off as you submit, revise, and resubmit proposals for projects and programs important to your government or organization. You will receive grants, and as you develop experience and your organization develops capacity, you will receive more and more. No matter how many grants you receive or how much external funding you raise, never forget the principal lesson of this introductory chapter: TANSTAAFL.

REFERENCES

Birkland, Thomas A. 2005. *An Introduction to the Policy Process: Theories, Concepts, and Models of Public Policymaking, 2nd Edition.* Armonk, NY: M. E. Sharpe.

Boadway, Robin W. and David E. Wildasin. 1984. *Public Sector Economics, 2nd Edition.* Boston: Little, Brown and Company.

Bremner, Robert H. 1987. *American Philanthropy, 2nd Edition.* Chicago: University of Chicago Press.

Bryson, John. 2003. The Amherst H. Wilder Foundation case: January 1, 1985–December 31, 1997. *Journal of Public Affairs Education* 9(3): 193–213.

Bryson, John M. 2004. *Strategic Planning for Public and Nonprofit Organizations: A Guide to Strengthening and Sustaining Organizational Achievement, 3rd Edition.* San Francisco: Jossey-Bass Publishers.

Bryson, John M. and Barbara Crosby. 1992. *Leadership for the Common Good: Tackling Public Problems in a Shared Power World.* San Francisco: Jossey-Bass Publishers.

Bush, George W. January 22, 2001. Memorandum for the Administrator of the United States Agency for International Development. Accessed April 15, 2007. Available at: http://www.whitehouse.gov/news/releases/20010123-5.html.

Canada, Ben. 2002. *Federal Grants to State and Local Governments: Overview and Characteristics.* CRS Report RS20669. Washington, DC: Congressional Research Service.

Canada, Ben. 2003. *Federal Grants to State and Local Governments: A Brief History.* CRS Report RL30705.

Cash and Counseling. 2007. Program Overview. Accessed May 2, 2007. Available at: http://www.cashandcounseling.org/about.

Council on Foundations. 2008. An Abbreviated History of the Philanthropic Tradition of the United States. Accessed April 9, 2007. Available at: http://www.cof.org/Learn/content.cfm?ItemNumber=730.

Derthick, Martha. 1996. Crossing thresholds: Federalism in the 1960s. *Journal of Policy History* 8: 64–80.

Dowie, Mark. 2001. *American Foundations: An Investigative History.* Cambridge, MA: MIT Press.

Fleishman, Joel L. 2007. *The Foundation: A Great American Secret.* New York: Public Affairs.

Ford Foundation. 2008a. Asset Building and Community Development. Accessed April 15, 2007. Available at: http://www.fordfound.org/program/community.cfm.

Ford Foundation. 2008b. Our Mission. Accessed April 15, 2007. Available at: http://www.fordfound.org/about.

Hail, Michael and Jeremy L. Hall. 2006. Project Grants. In *Federalism in America: An Encyclopedia, Volume 2,* Joseph Marbach, Ellis Katz, and Troy Smith, Eds. Westport, CT: Greenwood Press.

Hale, George E. and Marian Lief Palley. 1981. *The Politics of Federal Grants.* Washington, DC: CQ Press.

Hall, Jeremy L. 2008. The changing federal grant structure and its potential effects on state/local community development efforts. *Journal of Public Budgeting, Accounting, and Financial Management* n.d.

Hall, Jeremy L. and Michael Hail. 2006. Conditional Grants. In *Federalism in America: An Encyclopedia, Volume 1,* Joseph Marbach, Ellis Katz, and Troy Smith, Eds. Westport, CT: Greenwood Press.

Hines, J. and R. Thaler. 1995. Anomalies: The flypaper effect. *Journal of Economic Perspectives* 9(4): 217–226.

Hispanic-Serving Institutions Assisting Communities (HSIAC) NOFA. 2008. Accessed April 15, 2007. Available at: http://www.oup.org/funding/nofa_HSIAC.asp.

Kettl, D. 1983. *The Regulation of American Federalism.* Baton Rouge: Louisiana State University Press.

Key, V. O. 1940. The lack of a budgetary theory. *American Political Science Review* 34(6): 1137–1144.

Lawrence, Steven, Algernon Austin, and Reina Mukai. 2007. *Foundation Growth and Giving Estimates Current Outlook, 2007 Edition.* New York: The Foundation Center.

Martell, C. and B. Smith. 2004. Grant levels and debt issuance: Is there a relationship? Is there symmetry? *Public Budgeting & Finance* 24(3): 65–81.

Moore, Mark. 1995. *Creating Public Value.* Cambridge, MA: Harvard University Press.

Morrill Act of 1862. *U.S. Statutes at Large 12 (1862): 503.*

Nathan, R. 1983. State and local governments under federal grants: Toward a predictive theory. *Political Science Quarterly* 98(1): 47–57.

Nielsen, Waldemar A. 1996. *Inside American Philanthropy: The Dramas of Donorship.* Norman: University of Oklahoma Press.

Office of University Partnerships. 2008. Welcome to the Office of University Partnerships. Accessed April 15, 2007. Available at: http://www.oup.org.

Peterson, P. 1995. Functional and Legislative Theories of Federalism. In *The Price of Federalism*, Paul Peterson, Ed. Washington, DC: Brookings.

Performance Assessment Rating Tool (PART). n.d. USDA Grants for Economic Opportunities and Quality of Life for Rural America. Accessed April 18, 2007. Available at: http://www.whitehouse.gov/omb/expectmore/summary/10003021.2006.html.

Public Broadcasting Service. 1999. Andrew Carnegie: Rags to Riches Timeline. Accessed May 2, 2007. Available at: http://www.pbs.org/wgbh/amex/carnegie/timeline/timeline2.html.

Rich, Michael J. 2006a. Categorical Grants. In *Federalism in America: An Encyclopedia, Volume 1*, Joseph Marbach, Ellis Katz, and Troy Smith, Eds. Westport, CT: Greenwood Press.

Rich, Michael J. 2006b. Grants-in-Aid. In *Federalism in America: An Encyclopedia, Volume 1*, Joseph Marbach, Ellis Katz, and Troy Smith, Eds. Westport, CT: Greenwood Press.

Rivlin, Alice M. April 7, 1981. Statement of Alice M. Rivlin, Director, Congressional Budget Office, Before the Subcommittee on Intergovernmental Relations of the Committee on Government Operations, U.S. House of Representatives. Accessed October 15, 2008. Available at: http://www.cbo.gov/ftpdocs/52xx/doc5283/doc04.pdf.

Rural Utilities Service. 2002. Connecting Rural America. Accessed April 15, 2007. Available at: http://www.usda.gov/rus/index2/aboutus.htm.

U.S. Department of Commerce. 2005. Strengthening America's Communities Initiative: An Overview. Accessed November 1, 2005. Available at: http://www.commerce.gov/SACI/SACI_Overview.pdf.

U.S. Government, Office of Management and Budget. n.d. Budget of the United States Government. Accessed December 30, 2008. Available at: http://www.whitehouse.gov/omb/budget/fy2009.

U.S. Government Printing Office. n.d. Catalog of Federal Domestic Assistance. Accessed December 30, 2008. Available at: http://12.46.245.173/pls/portal30/CATALOG.TYP_ASSISTANCE_DYN.show.

U.S. Supreme Court, *New York v. United States*, 505 U.S. 144, 1992.

U.S. Supreme Court, *South Dakota v. Dole*, 483 U.S. 203, 1987.

W. K. Kellogg Foundation. n.d. Who We Are: Mission Vision Values. Accessed April 15, 2007. Available at: http://www.wkkf.org/default.aspx?tabid=63&ItemID=1&NID=34&LanguageID=0.

Williams, Elizabeth G. 2006. Formula Grants. In *Federalism in America: An Encyclopedia, Volume 1*, Joseph Marbach, Ellis Katz, and Troy Smith, Eds. Westport, CT: Greenwood Press.

Wooster, Martin Morse. 2006. *Great Philanthropic Mistakes.* Washington, DC: Hudson Institute.

CHAPTER 2

The Search for Funding

Now that we have a common understanding of grant types and important distinctions among them, it is possible to approach the grant seeking process from an informed perspective and in an informed manner. How does one begin the search for available grant funding? It is important to specify important criteria on which to judge available grants before beginning the search because this adds structure and rationality to what can be a daunting process. So, for example, if your organization is seeking start-up funds and has no source of available match funds, matching grants can be eliminated from the equation. Similarly, if you are seeking funding that will enable flexible programming, grants with significant conditions that do not directly relate to program activities will prove to be less desirable because of the imposition they create for the organization's administration and management. The prerequisite information that should be considered prior to embarking on the search includes the following: eligibility, conditions, match requirements, allowable costs, program area, and the funding amount. I review each of these topics conceptually and then address their practical application near the end of the chapter. The overarching theme of this chapter is learning to work smart rather than work hard. Smart work will save endless hours of application work, disappointing rejection letters, and strenuous efforts managing programs with conditions that would bite off more than feasibly could be chewed.

This chapter is based on the principle of developing and using a rubric to evaluate the viability of any particular funding source or opportunity. A wise search would not categorize all funding opportunities or announcements into only two categories—the "go" and "no go" alternatives. Rather, to save a great deal of frustration along the way, it is best to identify those opportunities that are absolutely acceptable (viable), those that are absolutely unacceptable (not viable), and those that might be acceptable (possibly viable). This third category can become very useful when an exhaustive search has identified no acceptable grant programs to which to apply. The rubric is best executed in stages based on the set of prerequisite key evaluative criteria identified earlier. I turn first to the most important of those criteria—what is almost always a threshold consideration—eligibility.

EVALUATIVE CRITERIA

Eligibility

Does the funding agency provide support to the type of organization I represent? That is the central question of concern in determining eligibility. A second, though equally important

33

concern is whether the funding agency supports the proposed activities for which funding is being sought. Ineligibility means grant requests will not be approved, and making such requests is a waste of time for grant seekers and their organizations. It is the first quality that should be considered in seeking funding.

The federal government designates who or which organizations are and are not eligible for grant funds under each program. For example, some funding is available to researchers and scientists in universities and research institutes (such as research funding from the National Science Foundation's Social, Behavioral and Economic Sciences Program). Some funding is available only to universities that are designated Historically Black Colleges and Universities (HBCUs) by the U.S. Department of Education (such as the HUD HBCU program). Eligibility for that program is limited to "Historically Black Colleges and Universities as determined by the Department of Education in 34 CFR 608.2 pursuant to that Department's responsibilities under Executive Order 13256, dated February 12, 2002" (Catalog of Federal Domestic Assistance [CFDA] 14.520 Historically Black Colleges and Universities Program). Funding is available for doctoral students and graduate students engaged in research on certain topics, such as the Department of Education's Overseas Doctoral Dissertation program, which provides funds "to enable doctoral candidates to complete field research for their dissertations" (CFDA, 84.022 Overseas Doctoral Dissertation). Some funding is restricted to not-for-profit organizations generally or specifically, such as the U.S. Department of Education's Centers for Independent Living Program. Eligible recipients under that program are "the private nonprofit agencies that received funding . . . under the Centers for Independent Living program in fiscal year 1992" (CFDA, 84.132 Centers for Independent Living). Some funding is restricted to the states (such as Medicaid). Other funding is available for community development organizations or local governments. (In the way of terminology, local governments and special districts are sometimes referred to as instrumentalities of the states because they are technically the corporate creations of sovereign states.) The point is that federal programs specify which organizations are and are not eligible to receive grant funding. What is not always clear is whether the government's definition of the organization type and your own are exactly the same.

When there is doubt about whether your organization is eligible for funding, the wise thing to do is simply to contact the program officer or other agency representative and ask. Getting in the habit of maintaining open communication with agency personnel is a very valuable technique to facilitating funding. A word of caution, however: when asking for any sort of official determination, it is essential to get the responses in writing. Agency personnel are fallible too, and asking someone to certify something in writing usually stimulates that person to take extra precaution in ensuring its accuracy. Not to mention you will have the written evidence in response to your question. It is important to understand that calling someone you don't know and asking them to make an official written determination is not a good approach to building rapport. When it is necessary to do so, it must be pursued with a tremendous deal of tact, and it will always be easiest if rapport has already been established in previous conversations. Organization eligibility is the first consideration in determining whether your organization is permitted to receive funding.

Thinking beyond organization type alone, federal grants specify a range of eligible and ineligible activities. For example, construction is not permitted through many categorical programs. One example is the Fund for Rural America program, which states outright that

"Funds provided under the CSREES Fund for Rural America competitive grants program may not be used for the construction of a new building or for the acquisition, expansion, remodeling, or alteration of an existing building (including site grading and improvement and architect fees), or for the purchase of fixed equipment" (CFDA, 10.224). Interestingly enough, the definition of what is and is not construction may vary by agency and program. You may very well be able to undertake renovations or minor construction activities that are part of a larger non-construction project under some grants. Learning the details of the program requirement is an absolute necessity.

Construction versus non-construction is a very common distinction among federally funded grant activities. Other common categories of activities include start-up costs, operating expenses, planning, programming, and indirect costs. There are other examples that may be less clear if you lack familiarity with a program and its purposes. For example, the HUD Community Outreach Partnership Center program (which Congress has presently defunded) has long held a requirement that funds may be spent for research or outreach activities, but that research activities may constitute no more than 25% of the project costs. "Research and outreach activities funded under this program must focus on problems associated with housing, economic development, neighborhood revitalization, infrastructure, health care, job training, education, crime prevention, planning, community organizing and other areas deemed appropriate by the Secretary" (CFDA, 14.511 Community Outreach Partnership Center Program). The Rural Business Opportunity Grant (RBOG) Program limits the use of grant funds to activities that "assist in the economic development of rural areas by providing technical assistance, training, and planning for business and economic development" (CFDA, 10.773 Rural Business Opportunity Grants). The RBOG's less restrictive counterpart program, the Rural Business Enterprise Grant, may be used for the following sorts of activities:

> Rural business enterprise grant (RBEG) funds may be used to create, expand or operate rural distance learning networks or programs that provide educational or job training instruction related to potential employment or job advancement to adult students; develop, construct or acquisition land, buildings, plants, equipment, access streets and roads, parking areas, utility extensions, necessary water supply and waste disposal facilities; refinancing; services and fees; and to establish a revolving loan fund. Television demonstration grant (TDG) funds may be used for television programming to demonstrate the effectiveness of providing information on agriculture and other issues of importance to farmers and other rural residents. All uses must assist a small and emerging private business enterprise except for the TDG Program. (CFDA, 10.769 Rural Business Enterprise Grants)

So, in addition to the type of applicant organization, the second eligibility consideration is eligibility of the activities proposed to be considered for grant funding.

The third facet of eligibility is location—either of the applicant or of the proposed project. Is the applicant located in an urban or rural service area? Alternatively, is the proposed activity to be undertaken located in an eligible area? Both may be used to ascertain eligibility for a given proposal. The HUD Rural Housing and Economic Development program (CFDA, 14.250) and the Department of Homeland Security Urban Areas Security Initiative (CFDA, 97.008) programs represent two federal efforts where location matters. One interesting observation regarding the "urban" designation is that not all definitions of urban are the same. Some agencies consider urban to mean any incorporated place with a Census population of 2,500 or more whereas others have a large city model in mind. Regional differences matter as well. The Appalachian Regional Commission funds projects in those counties designated as Appalachian, for example. The Alaska Native/Native Hawaiian Institutions Assisting Communities program in HUD limits funds to institutions in those states (CFDA, 14.515). A more extreme example is the Alaska Coastal Marine Institute program (CFDA, 15.421), which restricts funding to one eligible recipient—the University of Alaska. In the case of the Overseas Doctoral Dissertation program identified previously, both applicant type and project location matter: only institutions of higher education may apply, and "awards will not be available for projects focusing primarily on Western Europe or countries where the United States has no diplomatic representation" (CFDA, 84.022 Overseas Doctoral Dissertation).

Place may clearly be used to determine eligibility of the applicant or of the applicant's proposed project if it is to be conducted in a location other than that of the proposing organization. It is actually quite common for large organizations or organizations with a broad service area to undertake projects significant distances from their headquarters. Consider briefly two Kentucky organizations dedicated to outreach across a large service area: the Center for Rural Development and the Institute for Regional Analysis and Public Policy (IRAPP). Both are public nonprofit organizations that rely heavily upon external funding to fulfill their missions. The Center for Rural Development (www.centertech.com) is headquartered in non-metropolitan Pulaski County, Kentucky, in a facility that serves 42 counties in southern and eastern Kentucky—primarily the Commonwealth's Appalachian counties (**Figure 2.1**). Although many programs and services administered by the Center are region-wide, and some are specific to the county in which it is located, many projects and services are carried out away from the headquarters.

IRAPP (http://irapp.moreheadstate.edu) is a university-based research and outreach center (and a state program of distinction) of Morehead State University, a regional 4-year public university in Rowan County, located in northeastern Kentucky. IRAPP designates four conceptual service areas including the university's service area (**Figure 2.2**), the 51 Kentucky

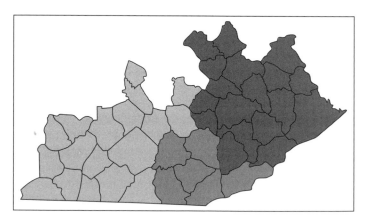

FIGURE 2.1   The Center for Rural Development 42-County Service Area in Southern and Eastern Kentucky

Adapted from: Center for Rural Development n.d.

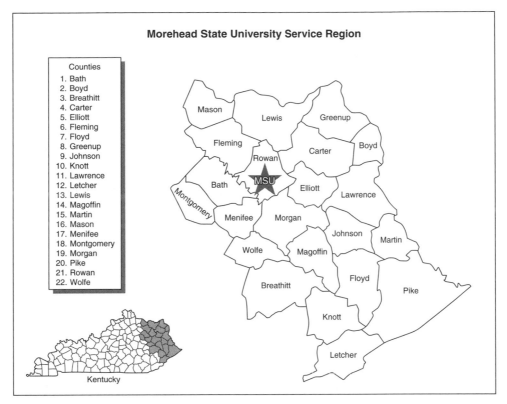

FIGURE 2.2   The Institute for Regional Analysis and Public Policy University Service Area
Source: Courtesy of Morehead State University.

Appalachian counties, the 410 federally defined counties of Appalachia (**Figure 2.3**), and similar rural regions of national or global scope. This may seem relatively complex, but the reality is that most of IRAPP's funded projects and programs are carried out in the university and Kentucky Appalachian service areas, while funded research and other activities extend to consider the broader global scope. Projects IRAPP seeks to undertake may be eligible or ineligible on the basis of the university's location or the project location.

The fourth and final eligibility dimension considers character of the place or the organization. It is through this dimension that targeting efforts can be best realized. For example, basic demographic information may be used to determine eligibility. High rates of poverty, unemployment, and other characteristics may demonstrate greater need, so programs may use such characteristics as the basis for explicit eligibility criteria. The federal Empowerment Zone program provides an excellent example of how local character is used to determine eligibility, and thus fulfill the targeting expectations:

Each renewal Community must have a continuous boundary and a population not exceeding 200,000 residents. A rural nominated RC must have a minimum population of 1,000 and an

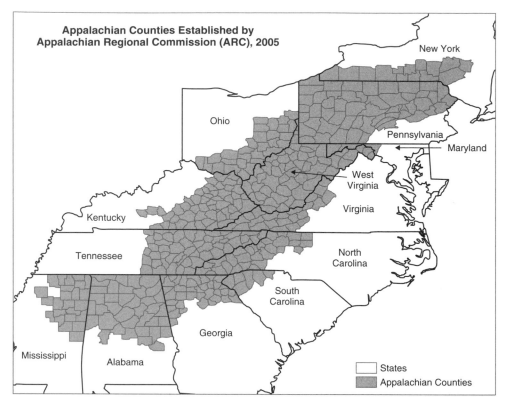

FIGURE 2.3   Appalachian Counties Established by Appalachian Regional Commission (ARC), 2005

Source: Courtesy of Morehead State Univeristy.

urban nominated RC must have a minimum population of 4,000. The unemployment rate of each urban and rural nominated RC must be 150% of the national unemployment rate. Each census tract of a nominated RC must have a poverty rate of at least 20%. Also, at least 70% of area households for an urban nominated RC as a whole must have incomes below 80% of the Household Adjusted Median Family Income. There is no requirement for rural areas. Both urban and rural nominated areas must also submit a certification of economic distress with their application. A nominated Empowerment Zone cannot be larger than 20 square miles, but also may include developable sites consisting of no more than 2,000 acres. These sites must be used for commercial and industrial purposes and need not meet the poverty rate criteria in other areas of the EZ. No urban EZ may have a population greater than 200,000. The poverty rate for each census tract within the nominated urban area must be at least 20% and the poverty rate for at least 90% of the area's census tracts must be at least 25%. (CFDA 14.244)

Other programs may look at race—proportion of the population that is of Hispanic origin may be used. Social characteristics such as crime rates, HIV or teen pregnancy rates, and other conditions may be used in determining eligibility in numerous programs. The Local

Law Enforcement Block Grant program uses crime rates as the basis of the formula used to determine award amounts to jurisdictions. The use of the crime rate criterion in this program is as follows:

> Each unit of local government must report Uniform Crime Report (UCR) data so as to determine amounts of allocation. These data must reflect Part I violent crimes, which are murder, aggravated assault, rape, and robbery, that have been reported in each eligible jurisdiction. Data for the three most recent available years reported to the FBI will be averaged and used to compute allocations. The amount of the award is proportionate to each local jurisdiction's average annual amount of Part I violent crimes compared to that for all other local jurisdictions in the State. Jurisdictions whose reported crime rates would yield an award of less than $10,000 will not receive a grant. (CFDA, 16.592)

Another example is the AIDS Education and Training Centers program, which does not look to the character of the locality or impacted region but rather at the character of the organization's expertise and experience. It stipulates that "Applicants must have extensive experience in the field of health professional training and adult learning, HIV disease and disease management, and program administration and monitoring. Applicants that fail to show experience in all three areas will not be considered" (CFDA, 93.145). It should be fairly obvious by now that local or organization character matters in the allocation of grant awards and may variously be used to determine eligibility.

To provide one last example that demonstrates the relative complexity associated with determining eligibility, consider the eligibility requirements for the USDA Rural Housing Preservation Grant Program (CFDA, 10.433), which follows:

> [The applicant m]ust be a State or political subdivision, public nonprofit corporation, Indian tribal corporations, authorized to receive and administer housing preservation grants, private nonprofit corporation, or a consortium of such eligible entities. Applicants must provide assistance under this program to persons residing in open country and communities with a population of 10,000 that are rural in character and places with a population of up to 20,000 under certain conditions. Applicants in towns with population of 10,000 to 20,000 should check with local Rural Development office to determine if the Agency can serve them. Assistance is authorized for eligible applicants in the United States, Puerto Rico, Virgin Islands, and the territories and possessions of the United States. (CFDA, 10.433 Rural Housing Preservation Grants)

This program description demonstrates that eligibility is not always clear or discernable from the program description alone. USDA has a decentralized structure with state and local offices throughout the country; the program description clearly indicates that speaking with the appropriate agency representative is a wise initial step.

To briefly review, eligibility for federal funding takes four shapes: organization type, location, proposed activities, and character of place or of the organization. This combination of eligibility criteria should make it easy to determine whether your organization or your intended program is likely to be deemed eligible for funding by the federal agency. In other cases, it is still necessary to seek additional insight from program officials who are well-equipped to respond to such inquiries. Using these questions to formulate a basic rubric for considering various funding opportunities should be relatively straightforward, though it admittedly can become a very complex enterprise when looking at a broad array of potential programs. Still, it is best to sort possibilities into viable, not viable, and possibly viable categories. The same basic rubric can also be used to evaluate non-government foundation grants.

The case of non-federal foundation funding is much the same. Most foundations are forthright about the sorts of organizations they fund. Like federal grant funds, foundation funding may be limited by any of the four factors identified earlier: organization type, activity type, location, and character. Some foundations restrict funding to researchers inside or outside institutions (the IBM Center for the Business of Government, for example). Others limit their activities to states or cities where they have a corporate presence, such as the Clorox Company Foundation, which notes that it "makes grants primarily in its headquarters community of Oakland, California" but that "Clorox manufacturing plants operate small giving programs in their local communities" (Clorox Company 2006). Some foundations limit funding on the basis of religious affiliation, and some prohibit funding start-up costs or other specific activities.

A good example of a common eligibility statement comes from the Sarah Scaife Foundation:

> The Sarah Scaife Foundation's grant program is primarily directed toward public policy programs that address major domestic and international issues. There are no geographical restrictions. The Foundation does not make grants to individuals for any purpose or to nationally-organized fundraising groups. Proposals for the following are usually declined: event sponsorships, endowments, capital campaigns, renovations, or government agencies. (Scaife Foundations n.d.)

From this statement, it should be fairly clear whether your proposed project is deemed eligible, but only to a certain degree of generality. To be absolutely certain, it is again best to inquire personally.

The Carnegie Corporation of New York similarly specifies that "The Corporation accepts requests for funding at all times of the year and welcomes inquiries from potential grantees whose work fits our strategic guidelines" (Carnegie Corporation 2007a). To make it easier to understand, they have also compiled a quiz for interested grant seekers that helps to determine whether their activities are eligible (Carnegie Corporation 2007b). With each quiz question, a statement of the corporation's position on funding is also provided. As do most foundations, the Carnegie Corporation specifies those applicants and activities that they do not fund:

> Carnegie Corporation does not make grants for construction or maintenance of facilities or endowments. The Corporation does not generally make grants to individuals except through the Carnegie Scholars Program, that supports the work of select scholars and experts conducting research in the foundation's fields of interest. In addition to these general restrictions, there are, other than those indicated in the program statement, specific criteria for the acceptance of proposals pertaining to three of the program areas.
>
> *Education:* The foundation does not review requests from individual preschools, elementary schools, middle schools or junior high schools or high schools.
> *International Peace and Security:* With some exceptions, grants made in this program are to U.S. institutions. No curriculum projects within individual schools or colleges are supported. Proposals for media-related grants are only occasionally supported.

International Development: Geographic focus is restricted to African countries that are or have been members of the British Commonwealth as of 1948.

Strengthening U.S. Democracy: This program focus is restricted to the following areas: Civic education/engagement of young people; Integrating immigrants and new citizens into U.S. civic life; Addressing structural barriers to civic participation; Strengthening and encouraging civil society through the nonprofit/philanthropic sectors. (Carnegie Corporation 2007c)

You probably notice a distinct difference in character between the Sarah Scaife Foundation and the Carnegie Corporation of New York from these brief excerpts. The Scaife Foundation is a family foundation, still tied closely to its intended purposes and aligned to conservative ideals, whereas the Carnegie Corporation is a more general mission-focused foundation in search of somewhat broader goals in specific program areas. There is an important difference in magnitude and resources between the two foundations as well. Not to belittle the Scaife Foundation in any way, the Carnegie Corporation simply has more notoriety, more resources, and hence more requests for funding—the demands of which probably necessitated developing more sophisticated mechanisms for helping grant seekers understand their purpose and expectations.

Table 2.1 shows how a basic rubric looking only at eligibility might appear. Eligibility is the first dimension to be considered because it constitutes a preliminary threshold review. That is, we eliminate all grant programs and funding sources from which we know we will not be eligible to receive funds for our proposed activity. This step, if conducted carefully, can serve as a basis for future search efforts and tremendously reduce information-seeking activities in the future. Here's how. By distinguishing among funding programs on the basis of whether or not they are viable for a particular program, your outcome will be based on your mission. That is, the resulting list of programs you compile will only tell you whether or not they are appropriate for that program, but not whether they might be appropriate for future projects or programs. For this reason I strongly recommend using a rubric with multiple categories that can be reviewed in the future to ascertain not only whether but also why a program was deemed appropriate or inappropriate. Table 2.2 demonstrates this more useful rubric. An additional variation (Table 2.3) might include more categories; for example, under the organization type, you either are or are not eligible without wiggle room. But under activities, you can designate several regular activity types that might shed additional light on the funding source for the next time you revisit the list in a new search. This means working smarter rather than harder; for an additional investment of up-front time, lots of time can be saved later on. Of course, this

TABLE 2.1 Format of a Basic Rubric for Threshold Review Based on Eligibility

Program Title/ Funding Source	Viable/ Appropriate	Not Viable/ Inappropriate	Possibly Viable/ Appropriate
Foundation A	✔		
Agency 1		✔	
Foundation B			✔

TABLE 2.2   Categories of Eligibility for the Threshold Review

Agency/ Foundation Name	Program Title	Organization Type	Location	Proposed Activities	Character	Viability (+, -, ?)
Foundation A	n/a	–	+	+	+	–
Agency 1	Economic Development Planning	+	+	+	+	+
Foundation B	Community Activism Program	+	+	?	+	?

doesn't eliminate the need to be cautious. One still needs to consider the possibility that funding agencies may change focus over time.

Eligibility is a threshold review that should precede evaluation based on the remaining evaluative criteria. After all, if the organization is not eligible for a particular agency's funding, there is no point in spending time to look further into the nature of that funding agency's programs. The remaining criteria should be prioritized based on the applicant organization's purposes and expectations to determine the most feasible order in which to proceed. Those remaining evaluative criteria are funding conditions, match requirements, allowable costs, program purpose, and funding amount; I consider each in turn.

Conditions

The second evaluative criterion of importance is the degree of conditionality associated with the grant. For the purpose of this chapter, I consider non-financial conditions and match requirements separately. As noted in the introductory chapter of the text, conditions may be substantively related to the proposed activities, or they may be unrelated to the proposed program activities. In considering the importance of conditions, a prospective applicant has to evaluate the possible effects—both positive and negative—that may result.

Let's consider conditions related to the proposed activities first. Conditions of this nature impact what you are expected to do with the awarded grant money, and hence pose important restrictions on activities and spending. Suppose you are undertaking a construction project to install a new facility. The conditions of award stipulate that you must follow the provisions of NEPA—the National Environmental Protection Act—pertaining to environmental impact. A savvy grant seeker becomes aware of these conditions prior to developing and submitting an application. This condition adds both time and expense to a project, but the foreknowledge allows the applicant to plan accordingly. If time is not a concern, then the same savvy grant writer will build the cost of environmental review into the proposal and inflate budget estimates to accommodate unexpected environmental concerns that necessitate changing plans or approach during implementation. If time is a concern, then

TABLE 2.3   A More Specific Threshold Rubric Can Be Useful for Future Searches

Agency/ Foundation Name	Program Title				Eligibility Criteria							
						Eligible Activities						
		Organization Type	Location: Applicant	Location: Project	Construction	Start-Up Costs	Planning	Operating Expenses	Indirect Costs	Character of the Applicant	Character of the Program	Viability (+, −, ?)
Foundation A	n/a	−	+		−	+	+	−	−	+	+	−
Agency 1	Economic Development Planning	+	+		+	−	+	+	+	+	+	+
Foundation B	Community Activism Program	+	+		−	+	+	+	−	+	+	?

the opportunity cost associated with waiting may be too great to bear, and the applicant may seek funds from other non-federal sources.

Other conditions related to the award can also impose costs; these are administrative conditions. Maintaining reporting requirements, audits, and other mandates that are associated with federal funding can be time consuming and expensive as well. These conditions should be considered in pursuing grant funds. For example, a small organization might conscientiously avoid crossing the threshold of $500,000 per year in federal grant awards to avoid undergoing mandatory audit. Administrative conditions affect our organizations. Having administered large federal awards, I can attest to the stress they create from time to time. I once took part in an administrative meeting to iron out some disputes over conditions associated with a federal grant project jointly funded by the Small Business Administration and the National Aeronautics and Space Administration to support a new research facility. Among the concerns was whether or not the project constituted a "construction project." Although the grant as a whole was designated non-construction, it included components that clearly looked like construction, such as building a concrete platform and installing an antenna. Ultimately we determined that component to constitute "assembly of a pre-fabricated device" rather than construction, but developing a road to the site was designated "construction."

A seemingly minor distinction was actually a tremendous administrative nightmare because the construction designation by one agency affected whether or not NEPA was applicable, as well as whether or not a prevailing wage clause had to be inserted into a request for proposals to carry out parts of the project—not only to the agency in question, but to the other federal agency supporting different components of the overall project. Prevailing wage and environmental impact are conditions of award—sometimes they apply and sometimes they do not. The project underwent significant delays awaiting completion of an environmental impact statement, and additional approval delays upon learning of the presence of the endangered Indiana Big-Eared Bat in the affected habitat. There are obviously two ways to look at this example: for one, the requirement spared an endangered species potential harm; for the other, non-federal funding would not have required the additional attention or expense and the project could have proceeded on schedule, with a possible cost to bats that probably would not have been discovered. I could spend endless pages documenting conditions to watch out for, but the fact remains they are specific to agencies, to funding sources, to activities, and will be unique for each proposal. The important thing to take away is that there are conditions associated with program activities. Knowing them and subjecting them to a legitimate cost-benefit analysis is a good way to determine the real value of the grant assistance.

There are also costs associated with unrelated conditions. As I mentioned in Chapter 1, the federal government has increasingly burdened local governments with requirements and expectations through federal grant instruments (Derthick 1996). We have seen states amend their drinking age, highway speed limits, accommodations for individuals with disabilities, and various other changes as a result of conditions on federal aid. Much like preserving the Indiana Big-Eared Bats, one would be hard pressed to say that these conditions don't have some value. Indeed, they usually do. The question here should be twofold: do we value the potential conditions locally, or do local political and social context mean that we value them far less? And, what will the new conditions cost? Each time states acquiesce to the federal government we move one step closer to homogenization. We become more uniform and lose the distinctive local character that makes a place or an organization unique. The basic question is whether our values at the local, state, or organization level differ enough from those imposed by grant conditions to cause us to incur a cost—financial or psychological—and if so, whether that cost is worth the discount the grant provides for other meaningful activities.

Non-financial conditions directly related to project activities as well as those not directly related to project activities impose costs on our organizations. We must be proactive in assessing these costs and taking them into consideration as we determine which grants to pursue and which to let pass by.

Match Requirements

Besides non-financial conditions, we have also discussed financial conditions intended to stimulate local spending for designated purposes. When seeking grant funds it is useful to know whether local match is even available. If your organization is strapped for cash, such as most start-up organizations are, then grants that require cash match in any amount are certain to be problematic. Most grant programs allow some flexibility in what constitutes local match. Whereas cash match is a financial expenditure from the applicant's own funds or from partner organizations' financial contributions to the project, in-kind match is a bit easier to come by. It is not necessary for match funds to be new funding. For example, an agency executive director is being paid from existing organization resources. The salary and time the director spends managing and implementing a grant program (assuming the time is not billed to the grant) counts as a cash contribution because it is expended from organizational resources for the grant program's purposes. So, a director earning $50,000 per year who will invest 25% of her time on the project over 2 years represents a $25,000 cash match, plus associated fringe benefit expenses (fringe benefits range upward from 8.65% of salary but are usually around 20% of salary costs).

An in-kind match refers to the donation of time or services that have a financial value but that do not actually involve an exchange of money between organizations. For example, a team of volunteers may canvass local parks to promote services available through a grant program managed by a local social services organization. To the organization, the volunteers are playing a valuable role—recruitment—and their time can be documented and given an estimated value. A team of 10 volunteers working 100 hours each with an imputed hourly wage of $10/hour is equivalent to $10,000 worth of in-kind contributions that can be counted toward match requirements where in-kind match is permitted. A local business may allow the use of a billboard to support program advertising purposes. If the billboard's market rental rate per month is $980, then that is an additional $980 per month worth of in-kind match. An example of the calculation of these match contributions appears as **Table 2.4**.

In part, then, ascertaining whether a program is suitable for your organization's needs depends a great deal on what match requirements are associated with the program, and whether those requirements are cash or in-kind. Naturally, at this point it helps to have some idea of your organization's available resources as well as those available from potential partner organizations. Match requirements are an important evaluative criterion to use in determining appropriate funding opportunities.

TABLE 2.4   Calculation of Cash and In-Kind Match

Object Description	Cost Basis	Project Contribution	Match		
			Year 1	Year 2	Total Project
Salary					
Director	$50,000/year	25%	$12,500	$12,500	$25,000
Fringe	20% of salary		2,500	2,500	5,000
In-Kind Contributions					
Volunteer Labor	$10/hour	1,000 hours (10 vol × 100 hours)	5,000	5,000	10,000
Billboard	$980/month	12 months	11,760	0	11,760
Total Match			$31,760	$20,000	$51,760

Allowable Costs

There are certain things you simply cannot do with federal grant money if the program in question designates those activities to be unallowable costs. For example, the HUD COPC program discussed earlier prohibits the use of funds for construction or rehabilitation. This becomes a problem if one of your primary partners in a project is planning to use their share of the grant receipts to finance the refurbishment of a downtown storefront facility into office and meeting space. For a much more detailed explanation, OMB Circular A-21 specifies at length the process used to determine cost standards to be applied to universities in federal grant award programs. If you are a university applicant, then the rules specified in A-21 determine how to account for certain costs, and what happens when your activities drift beyond the realm of allowable costs and unallowable costs as specified in statutory provisions. We revisit the OMB Circulars later in the discussion of budgeting.

It is fair to make room for an exception here. Grant accounting is a tricky occupation, but one where many grant problems can be solved with a creative and cooperative accountant. Let me introduce you to the concept of *fungibility*. Fungibility simply means that a dollar is a dollar, and its spending power is the same no matter what you call it. So, if you have a dollar tucked away to use to purchase lunch, but a colleague asks you to donate to her child's scout troop, that dollar can be used for that alternative purpose and you can buy lunch with another dollar you had set aside for unforeseen costs. The dollar has the same buying power no matter what it is called. So, in the organizational context, federal grant funds may be restricted in their use, but they are still fungible if the organization has other funding sources. An example will explain.

Suppose that a grant award prohibits purchasing fixed capital equipment, but fixed equipment is the one piece of your program that is most essential. Table 2.5 shows the preferred strategy of receiving grant funds to purchase the needed equipment. $15,000 is debited from the grant account and credited to the equipment account. If there are no available

TABLE 2.5　Account Ledger Under Preferred Strategy: Grant Pays for Necessary Equipment

	Account Ledger: When Capital Expenses Are Eligible for Grant			
	Debit Accounts		Credit Accounts	
	General Fund	Grant Fund	Payroll Fund	Capital Fund
Salary	$-50,000	$ 0	$50,000	$ 0
Fringe	-10,000	0	10,000	0
Equipment	0	-15,000	0	15,000
Total	$-60,000	$-15,000	$60,000	$15,000

funding alternatives that will support equipment purchases, you can request funding for a different, equally legitimate purpose knowing that the funds are fungible once in the organization's budget. Here's how: Our executive director mentioned previously is contributing salary and fringe benefits by working on the project. Even though equipment is the goal, you request funding for a feasibility study and planning efforts. The director has $75,000 in salary that is not allocated to the project over the course of the 2-year period. The grant can be billed for an additional 25% of her time (or more, but we will discuss this later in Chapter 4, "Developing the Grant Budget and Budget Narrative"). Thus, she is contributing 25% of her time as a cash match, and another 25% is billed to the grant, so she spends 50% of her total time working on this important project.

The organization already had funding to cover her salary, hence the source of the 25% match amount. This means that the director's direct non-match time on the grant project will be reimbursed by the grant program. And because that portion of her salary was grant-funded, the funds in the organization budget that were originally dedicated to her salary remain unexpended. Because they are from the organization's own sources, those funds can be used to purchase the desired equipment or anything else that is needed. **Table 2.6** shows this relationship. You will notice that the general fund and the grant fund are debited the same amount as in the last example, but in different budget lines. Now the grant is paying for salary and fringe and leaving the excess funds in the general fund to purchase the needed equipment.

Grant funds open a plethora of opportunities if they are carefully managed and accounted for. This exchange is neither unlawful nor unethical so long as the director

TABLE 2.6　Account Ledger Under Alternative Strategy: Grant Pays for Salary

	Account Ledger: When Capital Expenses Are Ineligible for Grant			
	Debit Accounts		Credit Accounts	
	General Fund	Grant Fund	Payroll Fund	Capital Fund
Salary	$-37,500	$-12,500	$50,000	$ 0
Fringe	-7,500	-2,500	10,000	0
Equipment	-15,000	0	0	15,000
Total	$-60,000	$-15,000	$60,000	$15,000

legitimately spent the documented time administering the requirements of the grant. Again, a good accountant or budget director goes a long way—particularly one with past grants experience.

Or consider the COPC storefront example. There are two ways to circumvent the limitation on construction and renovation costs. One is that the grant recipient—in this case a university—can use their fungible resources to support the partner's efforts and retain the grant funds to be used for some other project purpose. Another alternative would be that the program could strike a deal with the partner to pay rent on a portion of the facility for the duration of the project. The grant program doesn't prohibit leasing office space, and the guarantee of grant-funded rental income may allow the partner to finance the refurbishment up-front from other funds or financing sources.

So, even when the organization is not permitted to expend funds for certain things, grants should not always be ignored. If the grant can contribute to the organization's purpose or mission, it should be considered. Obviously, in developing our rubric, we want to assign greater weight to those programs that do allow the expenses and activities that are most important to us than to those that are secondary or tangential. Even so, their value should be assessed carefully as one of the important evaluative criteria.

Program Purpose

What is the organization's goal or purpose? What is the grantor's goal or purpose? Do they match? Our goal may be to prevent teenage pregnancy, but with intent to do so through abstinence-based programming based on religious beliefs. Our goal to reduce teenage pregnancy might be shared equally by various funding agencies and foundations. One in particular, hypothetically speaking, offers $25,000 grants for programs to reduce pregnancy, but they advocate this reduction through methods that include use of birth control and abortion. Although the direct goal is the same—to reduce teenage pregnancy—the purpose and values driving the grantor organization do not mesh with those of the programming our organization has embraced. To what extent do the goals and purposes of our organization coincide with those of the funding agency, and are there deeper values or core beliefs that otherwise set us apart? This question spares wasted time writing applications that are unlikely to be funded, it spares the rejection letters, and it spares strife between the grant giver and the grant receiver where differences were covered up to facilitate grant awards. Comparing organizational purpose, goals, and values must be a component of the evaluative criteria considered in your rubric for grant seeking.

Funding Amount

How much money do you need? If you are trying to establish a community recycling program that will cost $17,000 to initiate and operate in its first year, then a federal program with an average award amount of $250,000 and a low award amount of $100,000 is probably not going to have great interest in your proposal. Similarly, if you need $250,000 to build critical organization infrastructure, then requesting grants from foundations whose average grant amount is $10,000 is not helpful, in spite of the success you may have in obtaining that funding. The effort associated with writing 50 grant proposals (assuming a generous 50% success rate) for $10,000 each is too great for the task at hand. Moreover, to facilitate the project, you need the money to be committed at the same time—something that is fairly difficult to ensure from multiple funding partners. The point here is that you should match your funding needs and expectations to the grant making needs and expectations of the granting agencies. Funding amount is the final component of the evaluative rubric I recommend for assessing grant programs for their potential as sources of funding for your programs and organizations. Although I have included it last, it may very well be the highest priority consideration as you make your exclusionary decisions using the rubric for funding viability.

OTHER CONSIDERATIONS

There are other considerations to keep in mind as you develop your assessment rubric, though they may be secondary to those already identified. First of all, if the program is a multiorganizational collaboration, it is possible that either cash or in-kind matching resources would be available from prospective partners. A strategy commonly used among community development programs is for the lead organization to recruit other community organizations whose distinctive competencies (Bryson 2004) match the proposed project or program. By recruiting public or nonprofit organizations to do those things they would already do absent the grant is a win-win situation. Their involvement provides expertise to the proposed program and it ensures the partner a stream of participants or a venue to carry out their mission. But most important, such organizations usually already have funding to support the key activities that will be undertaken—a source of in-kind match. Although they would not likely spend their resources to take on unrelated efforts, such as a less-needy category of clients, most will be receptive when the requested participation is closely aligned with their existing mission.

Second, appearances matter. Some grant making foundations have ideological leanings as well as preferences for particular methods of service provision. A ready example is the Smith Richardson Foundation, which supports a range of programs that have a generally conservative appeal. A funding source's perspective has important implications for the funding search because it means informed outsiders will associate the grant-receiving organization and program with the ideology or perspective of the funding organization. If a grant seeking organization accepts funds from a known liberal foundation, conservative foundations may be reluctant to support its future endeavors. Moreover, should the grant seeker successfully write a proposal to a foundation whose core values conflict with those of the grant seeking agency, it is likely that the differences will impede formation of a positive relationship as the organizations interact over time—something that can be very important to an organization's long-term success. So, although not a deal-breaker, asking funds of or accepting funds from sources with values that do not align with the prospective grantee can be a hazardous endeavor. These conditions reflect the situational characteristics your organization and project may face, and they should be kept in mind informally if not formally as you embark on and proceed with your funding search.

With this checklist in place, you have developed what is essentially a rubric for evaluating each available grant opportunity that comes to your attention, whether in a formal search or on an ad hoc basis. **Table 2.7** presents an example of a complete rubric including

TABLE 2.7 Complete Rubric Including All Prerequisite Considerations

Agency/ Foundation Name	Program Title	Organization Type	Location: Applicant	Location: Project	Construction	Start-Up Costs	Planning	Operating Expenses	Indirect Costs	Character of the Applicant	Character of the Program	Conditions	Match Requirement	Expenses Are Allowable Costs	Program Purpose Is Appropriate	Low Grant Amount	High Grant Amount	Average Grant Amount	Total Available Program Funding	Viability (+, −, ?)
						Eligible Activities														
Foundation A	n/a	−	+	−	−	+	+	−	+	+	+	NO	50%	NO	NO	2,000	15,000	2,500	300,000	−
Agency 1	Economic Development Planning	+	+	+	+	−	+	+	+	+	+	NO	25%	YES	YES	50,000	1,000,000	360,000	45,000,000	+
Foundation B	Community Activism Program	+	+	+	−	+	+	+	−	+	+	NO	25%	?	YES	40,000	200,000	75,000	2,500,000	?

Eligibility Criteria

50

each of these prerequisite considerations. You can easily ignore programs that fail to meet your core criteria. As I mentioned in the introduction to this chapter, a wise search would use three alternative categories—viable, not viable, and possibly viable. This process saves frustration along the way, particularly at the stage when you realize there are no perfectly viable funding sources for your desired program. The third category, possibly viable, can become very useful when an exhaustive search has identified no acceptable grant programs to which to apply. The uncertainty in this category can come from two sources: (1) a lack of information about what is and is not eligible for funding by the source including vague description of purpose and goals of the grant program, and (2) from considerations on the part of the prospective grantee about how much match funding would be available for the program or whether the organization's stakeholders would view new conditions on activities as a worthy tradeoff for the requested grant funding.

APPLIED ORGANIZATIONAL EXAMPLE: ESTABLISHING CRITERIA

To organize the criteria effectively requires a reasonable understanding of your organization and proposed program. Let us formulate a hypothetical example. Our organization is a not-for-profit community development corporation with tax exemption under section 501(c)(3) of the Internal Revenue Code (otherwise known as a 501(c)(3) organization). We are located in a non-metropolitan Appalachian county, and we are not classified as economically distressed. The development corporation receives revenue flows from a county occupational tax, a portion of which is set aside to fund the corporation's mission to recruit industry and create jobs in the county. We are in the process of developing an innovative industrial park that will cater to high-tech industries by providing inducements such as Internet bandwidth, telecommunications accessibility, and so on. We have acquired land, and we are now seeking grant funds to improve the site and construct a 30,000-square-foot speculative facility to lure potential businesses. We are able to accommodate this plan in one phase (development and construction) or two (development, then construction). Our anticipated project costs are $200,000 for site development and improvements and $800,000 for construction (total project costs of $1 million).

So, how do we set up our criteria and our rubric? We have identified our organization type: a 501(c)(3) public nonprofit corporation. That is the first category of interest as we assess organization eligibility. We must also consider whether our proposed activities are eligible, whether our location is eligible for funding, and whether the character of our organization and project are appropriate for the grant maker.

In terms of activity eligibility, the proposed activities are both construction related, so non-construction programs will not be useful. If there is a distinction between site preparation and construction, some programs may be willing to fund our site development efforts while others may be willing to fund the building construction effort. Others still may be willing and able to fund both. As location is concerned, we need a program that funds projects in rural counties, Appalachian counties, or both. Our character is not unique, which means foundations are not likely to be interested in our project. We focus on economic development activities and have a high-tech focus. The population we are serving is economically stable, with unemployment and poverty rates below or near the national average.

So, we will be looking for programs that do not specifically target distressed regions or that at least do not indicate they restrict their funding to distressed regions. With this understanding of our own organization and goal in mind, using the evaluative rubric, we are able to begin reviewing programs and funding sources in the threshold eligibility evaluation.

With eligibility covered, we must also clarify our status with regard to the remaining criteria: funding conditions, match requirements, allowable costs, program purpose, and funding amount. Funding conditions are unique to each combination of program, agency, and grantor. In our case, we are building a facility with the intent to recruit industry. We would welcome start-up businesses of a home-grown nature, but that is secondary to our purpose. Hence, if the award was conditioned upon restricting competitive recruitment efforts, we would not be able to accept it. Alternatively, if the award were to include as a condition that we develop concurrent programming to stimulate entrepreneurial training, we might be able to accept the condition although it is secondary to our real purpose. This is a question that may require input from directors and stakeholders to properly define. A grant writer will not always know and understand which conditions are acceptable and which are not.

Match requirements are always important. In the case of our organization, we have a stream of local tax revenue to support our operational costs, debt service on any bonds issued for past projects, and any new projects to be undertaken. Let's assume that we have, after deducting operating expenses and debt service, $250,000 per year to contribute to new projects. That means if we pursue no other projects this year, we would be able to provide up to $250,000 in match funds to support the project. If we purposefully spread the project over 2 years, we would have $500,000 in available cash match. Of course, most organizations have multiple projects and goals to pursue, so it is difficult to assume that we are willing to devote all of this discretionary revenue to a single project unless it is our very top priority. If it is such a high priority, and if we have favorable credit ratings, we may additionally be able to issue debt to cover a greater portion of the expenses. So, in our search we desire a combination of grants that demands no more than $250,000 this year or $500,000 over this year and the next, with greater amounts being less desirable. We might be willing to accept something greater only if we give this project our full attention.

Allowable costs must include site preparation and construction. These components are absolute necessities. But remember, we could break the project into phases, so we want to keep any program that funds one or the other or both. Also, as part of the site preparation effort we will need to install utilities. This may or may not be an eligible activity covered by the preceding categories. If it is not, we know that we must also keep our eyes open for programs that explicitly include these costs and that we will probably need to consider the project in three phases rather than two. Are we willing to accept site preparation and construction without utilities? Our answer is probably going to be affirmative because in this case having something is better than nothing.

In regard to program purpose, our general goal corresponds closely to the consideration made for eligibility of the proposed activities mentioned previously. We are engaged in the effort to stimulate economic development. This should be a clue that we want to begin our search in agencies that play an economic development role. At the federal level this is not as straightforward as you might think. Economic development activities are carried out by the Economic Development Administration, the Small Business Administration, the Department of Commerce more generally, the Appalachian Regional Commission, the Department of Agriculture, the Department of Housing and Urban Development, just to name the primary sources. What is important is that the character of economic development differs for each of these agencies, and so may their purpose differ from ours. Whereas the Rural Utilities Service may be able to support utility infrastructure for our project, they would not be interested in the site preparation or the building effort. The Economic Development Administration regularly funds large-scale project-based efforts like ours. HUD has a more urban and community development focus that reflects a different goal or purpose. It becomes clear that we need to have a solid idea about how our project's purpose is defined so that we may adequately compare it to the purpose of the funding sources we consider.

We conclude our example with a consideration of the desired funding amount. We need $1 million to complete the project, of which $800,000 is in the form of construction, and $200,000 is in the form of site preparation (of this amount we will assume that $75,000 is needed to install utilities). We either need a grant that will provide $1 million and cover all eligible activities, or some combination of funding that includes a construction grant of $800,000 and a site preparation grant that includes utilities of $200,000 or a site preparation grant excluding utilities of $125,000 and a grant for utilities of $75,000.

Two thoughts are justified in being mentioned here. First, the either/or approach does not work. If we are not able to attain the full $1 million grant, then we can't seek utility funding or construction funding. We must begin with site preparation because without it the other components cannot proceed. With a site prepared, we have justification for utilities and then for the building. So, if we are forced to split the project into pieces, our approach must be all the more methodical and planned. Second, it may require an investment of local funds to stimulate the project. For example, if a grant program will not fund site preparation, but they will provide the building, then it may be possible to apply for the building grant using own-source resources to provide the site preparation and utilities. It is necessary, of course, to ensure that these are eligible match activities for the grant in question.

This section has developed a hypothetical example for how to take organization and program needs into consideration in developing and preparing to use a rubric for assessing potential funding sources for viability. The remainder of the chapter explores where to find available funding and how to locate it.

WHERE TO LOOK: COMMON APPROACHES TO FUNDING

With three categories and a checklist in hand, you are anxious to initiate your search. Where do you begin looking? Funding proposals may be either solicited, meaning the funding agency asks that funding proposals be sent to them, or unsolicited, meaning that you propose a project for funding for which the funding agency has issued no specific indication of their desire to fund it. There are two basic ways to search for funds, and the most successful approach is to combine the two. First, funding agencies and foundations issue requests for proposals (RFPs); an RFP is a formal document advising the public that the organization has funds available for a specific purpose or cause. A response to an RFP would be considered a solicited proposal. The document will include a program description, guidelines for preparing proposals, eligibility requirements, and so forth. RFPs take nearly all of the guesswork out of the funding search. The concerns raised in your checklist are almost certain to be addressed in an RFP document. In my experience, RFPs communicate most of the useful information, but a follow-up call to the program officer or official is usually necessary to obtain the fullest possible understanding of the agency's intentions and expectations. Many times programs have unofficial norms that dictate how funding decisions are made in which some program types may be favored over others. Informal discussions with program officers about your project prior to the application may yield insight into how realistic it is to pursue the grant. You shouldn't expect them to put their responses to such issues in writing—informal norms or personal observations about the type of programs that have been the most successful in the past obviously don't have to be disclosed and bear no official status. Still, they can be very helpful.

As I continue to mention the importance of communicating with program officers, it is useful to point out that communication should be well-organized and limited to avoid frustrating otherwise busy professionals. It is important to be respectful of these individuals' time constraints, which means first taking significant time to review all publicly available documents for guidance. When working as a team, communication with the potential funding organization should be organized through a single individual—preferably a manager—to prevent duplication and confusion among team members. Also, it is more likely that a designated contact person will become more familiar to the program officer. Disorganized communication can portray the applicant organization poorly.

The second method for seeking funding is to search by funding source according to the criteria noted previously hoping to find an eligible recipient for an unsolicited proposal. This technique is most useful for foundations that either do not issue RFPs or make substantial awards outside of RFP processes. Most federal agencies issue RFPs because Congress appropriates funding that must be given away within an established time frame. Moreover, the federal government often justifies its actions and decisions in terms of process equity rather than substantive equity. This simply means that it is so difficult to distribute scarce resources in such a way that the outcomes are equitable or fair (substantive equity) that the only legitimate distribution is a competitive one where the rules are fair—that is, each potential applicant has the same opportunity to apply and they are evaluated fairly (process equity). Still, there are federal programs that expend funds exclusively through discretionary programs with no formal solicitation. These processes are often initiated through local, regional, or state offices that have been allocated a portion of program funds to be used on projects they deem to be necessary. On the other hand, foundations are much more likely to award funding on the basis of a general purpose without specific calls for proposals. Some will divide their spending into categories or priorities, with an indication of what they will or will not support, but RFPs are seldom used by foundations except in cases where they have a clear objective to incite a very specific type of change. In this case, competitive proposals ensure they will receive a pool of applications most closely related to their intended purpose.

Many foundations do not solicit proposals at all, but simply provide instructions for proposals to be submitted to a board or program officer. To save time and energy, it is very common for foundations to request a brief letter of interest rather than a full proposal. If the topic seems viable, they would then request that a full proposal be developed. Other foundations support activities within broad topics and have an established process for handling proposals. Foundations typically provide instructions on how to formally request funding, but they are often very broad. To really understand a foundation's intent and the feasibility of your proposed activity given their interests, it is almost always necessary to have a conversation with the appropriate program official. It saves you time in preparing a proposal that is unlikely to succeed, and it spares them endless hours of reading and evaluating proposals that are doomed to fail because they do not match the foundation's purpose or goals.

In reviewing foundation funding opportunities, a common discovery is that the foundation does not accept unsolicited proposals. This is a good indication that you should continue your search elsewhere. Many foundations do not have the vast resources of the Bill and Melinda Gates Foundation or the Ford Foundation, and they have to invest their scarce resources very carefully. More often than not, these foundations have a select list of local organizations and causes that they support on an annual basis—perhaps organizations of the founder's choosing—and they lack a pool of discretionary funds from which to draw for support in addition to these preferred recipients. Other times, the foundation lacks a large professional staff and prefers to negotiate proposals in advance of submitting them. In this case, the "no unsolicited proposals" gesture is intended to dissuade shotgun applicants from submitting random proposals that are not tailored to the foundation's interests. In this case, it is again very useful to contact and engage the program officer. This individual will almost certainly be forthright about the foundation's position and obtaining a clear answer will take far less time than developing an unsuccessful proposal.

TARGETING: LEARNING TO THINK LIKE A GRANTOR

We have already discussed the role targeting plays in funding decisions. Agencies specify clear targets to try to get the most bang from their grant buck. They want to fund projects that will have the greatest effect or make the greatest difference. Rather than make virtually meaningless small awards to every eligible recipient, they make a few large awards with enough substance to realize genuine effects. The same approach can be applied to grant writing endeavors as well. There are two common approaches to grant seeking. Both can be successful, though one has a clear advantage in terms of efficiency.

These approaches are what I refer to as the shotgun approach and the targeted approach. A shotgun blast may pepper a general area with pellets, without actually bringing down the target (a fortunate fact for Mr. Cheney's hunting companions). The metaphorical comparison is looking at a general area of funding with many grant making organizations, pulling out a broad, general proposal, and sending it to as many funding agencies as possible in hopes that it will fit one of their expectations well enough to merit a grant award. As I stated earlier, this approach maximizes your exposure and may lead to some funding success. However, it is a very inefficient way to work. There is an old adage that says it is better to work smart than to work hard. Indeed, this approach may increase exposure, but the quality of that exposure can have significant negative ramifications for the organization. Many grantors that would consider a sound proposal would be turned off by a half-baked one not clearly targeted to their interests.

Turning to the targeted approach, a poison-tipped blow dart is a precision instrument tailor-made to its target, and its use requires caution and tact. To compare it to the grants process, think about one ideal target that is valued above all others—the ideal grant award. Lots of preparation goes into developing a sound proposal—an appropriate dart is crafted and the appropriate amount and quality of poison is applied—and it is delivered at the ideal moment to ensure the greatest probability of success. It is tailored to the target—the grant maker's interests, purpose, and conditions. The target is identified, but then studied, pursued, and invested with lots of preparation before the attack. So, a well-developed proposal, specifically tailored to the grantor's interests, and delivered at the beginning of a funding cycle when plenty of award money is available will stand the greatest chance of bringing down the target—receiving that one ideal grant award that best fits your program and organization goals. A targeted weapon, though more costly, yields superior results. To extrapolate, shooting a tank with a shotgun only prolongs your demise; targeting wild game with a poison dart yields the desired victory. Grantors are trying to target their funds to affect their areas and organizations of interest. Grant writers should keep this in mind as they develop proposals to these grantors and ensure that the proposals are clearly and specifically targeted to the agency and its goals.

GRANT SEEKING TOOLS

You know what you're looking for. You have developed a list and with a rubric in hand or in mind, you set out to find the grant program(s) or granting agency that best fits what you have in mind. Where do you turn for this information? The distinction between government and foundation grants is fairly important here because they are commonly aggregated in different places. To set out on a search for foundation funding, you will need to become familiar with the Foundation Center and its resources—most important, the Foundation Directory.

Seeking funding in the electronic age is simple compared to the days of books and paper. Among other tools is the Community of Science database, which specializes in funding for research-related activities. Other search tools come and go. A membership in the Association of Public Policy and Management (APPAM) once included a subscription to a regular funding announcement service distributed via e-mail that has since been discontinued. Other websites provide links to funding organizations and funding information, including Foundations.org (www.foundations.org; Northern California Community Foundation, Inc. 2007), the Grantsmanship Center (www.tgci.com), GuideStar (www.guidestar.org), the Council on Foundations (www.cof.org), or if Europe is your territory, Funders Online (www.fundersonline.org; European Foundation Centre 2007). Be aware that some of these services are available only for a fee.

Most foundation funding information can be obtained free of charge, though regular trips to the library might exceed the cost of an annual subscription to the Foundation Center's Foundation Directory online (https://fcsecure.fdncenter.org/fdo_signup_prof/register.php?setplan=start; presently as little as $195/year for the basic or up to $1,295/year for the professional). A good deal of information can also be obtained using more general Internet searches such as Google (www.google.com) if you have enough information to develop a productive search.

If federal funding is more in line with your expectations, the place to begin is the Catalog of Federal Domestic Assistance (www.cfda.gov; General Services Administration 2007a). The CFDA is a catalog of every federal assistance program available (you will notice the references to federal programs throughout the first half of this chapter are mostly drawn from the catalog). CFDA will help you to identify agencies and programs that fit your needs, but it is not sufficient by itself to help you develop and submit a proposal. This is because the CFDA is a permanent catalog of authorized programs, whereas programs are supported through annual appropriations from Congress. The federal budget cycle is rarely completed on time, so award periods often vary considerably from year to year for many programs. Notices of Funding Availability (NOFAs) appear in the *Federal Register* (www.gpoaccess.gov/fr/index.html; Government Printing Office 2007), which is the federal government's daily newspaper that communicates all matters of policy, rulemaking, and other announcements, including funding announcements. NOFAs in the *Federal Register* provide explicit requirements and application instructions for federal award programs, and users should note that administrative rulemaking leads to changes from year to year. You should never expect the previous year's NOFA or application packet to be accurate for the present year. Deadlines, program purpose, allowable costs, and funding ceilings frequently change. Other federal resources include agency websites, which often communicate valuable information, and the new electronic web portal for the federal grants system—Grants.gov (www.grants.gov; U.S. Department of Health and Human Services 2007). There are also more specialized federal funding databases, such as CRISP (http://crisp.cit.nih.gov; National Institutes of Health 2007), which includes information on funding for biomedical research.

Many aggregators differentiate by field rather than funding source, such as IRIS—the Illinois Researcher Information Service (www.library.uiuc.edu/iris; University of Illinois at Urbana Champaign Library 2007). The New York Foundation for the Arts (NYFA) provides information about grant funding opportunities for artists (www.nyfa.org/nyfa_source.asp?id=47&fid=1). The HUD Office of University Partnerships provides links to agency funding, government funding, and foundation funding, with their foundation database in a searchable format (www.oup.org/funding/upcfoundation/PubSearch.asp; U.S. Department of Housing and Urban Development, Office of University Partnerships, 2007).

I have, to this point, purposely ignored non-federal government grants. The reality is that state governments frequently make grants (or contracts) through their various agencies, although most do not have a comprehensive database of funding opportunities like the federal government does. It is safe to say that state government grant funding searches should be agency focused. In other words, the grant purpose should direct you to the agency that serves that purpose. For our economic development corporation, the state's Economic Development Cabinet is the place to begin. For tourism-based development, programs may be found in the Department of Travel and Tourism. For environmental grants, environmental protection agencies are an appropriate place to start the search. Some state agencies have very effective websites that advertise their available programs, such as California (http://getgrants.ca.gov; State of California 2007) and Wyoming (http://www-wsl.state.wy.us/sis/grants; Wyoming State Library 2007), whereas others have moved more slowly into the information age and do not provide that information across the board. Some state agencies include databases of their own programs, such as the Texas Department of

State Health Services through its Funding Alert Grant Database (www.dshs.state.tx.us/fic/search.asp). What this should tell you, as with foundations and federal grants, is that the best way to learn about state programs is to call and inquire in person.

A beginning grant seeker should focus on the most comprehensive sources and rely on their own knowledge to identify potential funding sources before relying on secondary databases that have been compiled by others who may have used different criteria to decide which programs to include and which to exclude. To that end, for foundation funding, the Foundation Center resources are the place to begin, and users interested in foundation funding should become familiar with the information included so as to formulate more effective searches. On the federal government side, learning how to use the CFDA and the *Federal Register* to search for funding opportunities will prove most valuable. The next section provides a description of the contents of these search tools and how to use them to facilitate your funding search.

USING THE TOOLS

The Foundation Directory

The Foundation Center operates in partnership with libraries in each state that act as local repositories for Foundation Center research materials. (A list of these libraries can be found at http://foundationcenter.org/collections.) Through this relationship they provide access to print copies of the Foundation Directory and its supplements as they are updated. They also provide access in electronic format, either online or on compact disc, so that researchers can conduct electronic keyword searches based on their topics of interest. If you write grants sporadically or on an ad hoc basis and are located close to one of the repository libraries, these resources may prove to be sufficient for your needs. However, if you are a professional grant writer and come to rely on the resource on a daily basis, you would be well advised to encourage your organization to purchase the print directory or subscribe to the online directory to facilitate that regular use.

Each foundation has an entry in the print directory, and the complete information is available in the electronic formats as well. It is useful to review the anatomy of these entries to become familiar with the information that is available before beginning your search. The key components of a Foundation Directory entry are the foundation's contact information, characteristic and giving data, giving interests and limitations, application information, and information about the foundation and its officers and directors. The content headings for a typical directory entry appear as in **Table 2.8**. Let's review each one in turn.

The contact information component of a foundation's entry includes its official name, its physical address, telephone number, website, fax number, e-mail address, and the name of the official contact person—essentially everything one needs to know to learn more about the foundation or initiate contact. This is important because it enables you to formalize a letter of inquiry with appropriate contact information among other things. A foundation's website information may prove to be very useful, or not useful at all; one never knows until accessing it. By useful, I mean the foundation may more clearly define its interests, or address current program interests that change from year to year, or that

TABLE 2.8　Contents of Foundation
Directory Entries

Entry Number
Foundation Name
Contact Information
　Contact Person and Title
　Street Address
　Telephone, Fax, E-mail, Website
Establishment Data
　Establishment Date and Location
　Foundation Type
Financial Data
　Fiscal Year End Date
　Assets (Market or Ledger)
　Total Expenditures
　Total Grant Expenditures and Numbers
　Low, High, and Average Grant Amount Data
Giving Interests
Purpose and Activities
Fields of Interest (Keywords)
Types of Support
Limitations
Publications
Application Information
　Application Form Requirement
　Initial Approach
　Deadlines
　Board Meeting Dates
　Final Notification Dates
Information About Foundation and Officers
Officers and Director
Number of Staff
EIN (IRS Identification Number)

Source: Jacobs 2002.

highlight specific components and projects on a yearly basis. By not useful, as you can imagine, some websites provide less information than is already available in the Foundation Directory entry.

　A foundation's characteristic data include when and where it was established and what type of foundation it represents (i.e., community, grant making). A community foundation is going to have a narrow interest in the community it serves and should be considered only if your organization or the project of interest is located in the community. Remember our concern for location as an eligibility criterion. This is a very appropriate way to determine the likelihood that a foundation will have interest in your organization's proposal.

Perhaps the information of greatest interest to grant seekers is the foundation's giving data. The Foundation Directory includes the foundation's accounting period, its total market or ledger assets at the end of the most recent fiscal year, the amount of gifts it received, its total expenditures, the total annual amount of giving for grants, and the high, low, and average amount of grants given. One can readily see how this information is relevant to a funding search. Knowing the foundation's fiscal year determines when it begins and ends a new giving cycle, and hence when money is likely to be available or already expended. Requests should always target the beginning of funding cycles to garner the greatest likelihood of success. Keep in mind, however, that foundations may spread their intended contributions over quarterly funding cycles, leading to four opportunities per year rather than only one.

Total assets give a good indication of the foundation's magnitude and its available spending power. Larger foundations (in terms of assets) tend to have more available resources and are able to make larger awards. Of course, no foundation will make an award greater than perceived to be necessary for a given project, but if your project happens to call for a large investment, small foundations may not be viable sources.

The grant expenditure information is probably the most important target for your consideration. Let's take two examples to demonstrate this point. Assume there are two foundations, each of which gave $1 million in grants during their most recent fiscal year (see **Table 2.9**). Foundation 1 had a high grant amount of $500,000 and a low amount of $100,000, whereas Foundation 2 had a high grant amount of $200,000 and a low amount of $250. Clearly, Foundation 1 concentrates its efforts on large projects with major impact while Foundation 2 funds numerous smaller projects and an occasional large project with significant impact. Although either foundation might be interested in your $400,000 proposal, the probability is higher that an award would come from Foundation 1 unless it was an absolute slam dunk match for Foundation 2's interests. The rationale is that Foundation 2 clearly enjoys being able to spread its influence broadly among many worthy projects, and making such a substantial award would limit its ability to do so because the award consumes such a large portion of the foundation's annual giving. This is also born out more clearly in the average grant data. Foundation 1 averages $250,000/grant while Foundation 2 averages $5,000/grant. By dividing the total grant giving ($1 million) by the average grant amount ($250,000 and $5,000), we can determine how many awards the foundation made. Foundation 1 awarded four grants ($1,000,000 ÷ $250,000 = 4) while Foundation 2 awarded 200 ($1,000,000 ÷ $5,000 = 200). Your $10,000 proposal to develop a local pilot program stands a much greater chance of receiving an award from Foundation 2.

TABLE 2.9   Comparing Foundation Grant Giving Data

	Foundation 1	*Foundation 2*
Total Grant Giving	$1,000,000	$1,000,000
High Grant Amount	$ 500,000	$ 200,000
Low Grant Amount	$ 100,000	$ 250
Average Grant Amount	$ 250,000	$ 5,000

With some idea of the foundation's general approach to funding in mind, we proceed to consider their funding interests. A foundation's giving interests are provided in the directory in three divisions: purpose and activities, fields of interest, and types of support. The purpose and activities will tell you what the foundation's overall goal or mission is—the purpose for which it was founded, and hence the purpose it has in mind when making grant awards. A good grant proposal will show the foundation how the proposed activities will further its own purpose. The foundation's activities give you a general idea about the sorts of efforts the foundation takes in pursuit of its purpose or mission. The foundation's field of interest will be composed of a set of keywords. Keywords are very useful as you narrow your search, but alone they do not reveal the foundation's true interest and your idea's correlation with it. Fields of interest may include education, community development, environment, agriculture, and so forth. Examining the foundation's fields of interest in light of its purpose will give you some appreciation for the scope of the foundation's activities, though a review of its website and publications will be far more informative.

A foundation's support types describe general categories of funding that they are willing to support. Types of support include emergency funds, capital campaigns, scholarships, endowments, seed money, program development, operating expenses, building funds, debt reduction, scholarly research, fund drives, and other similar categories. This category spills over into the limitations category in the Foundation Directory entry because one of the first things a foundation will tell you is the types of support they do not provide. Other limitations are based on location, including places the foundation will and will not give, and restrictions on organization type and character. For example, many foundations do not contribute to religious organizations or organizations affiliated with a religion, whereas others limit their giving to such organizations. Some foundations may restrict their funding to grassroots efforts, some to nonprofit organizations, and some to colleges and universities. The foundation's giving limitations are derived from its purpose—not necessarily the one listed in the Foundation Directory so much as the purpose given it by its founder(s).

Application information is only important when you determine a foundation is a good match for your funding interests, and then it is essential. You never want to approach a foundation with a funding request in a manner that differs from their explicit requirements. Doing so would indicate failure to do your homework and is an indication of poor quality workmanship. In other words, it reflects poorly on you and your organization when the application procedure is available and you fail to follow it. The information in this section includes whether or not an application form is needed, whether there are specific proposal format and length requirements, how the initial approach should be made, application deadlines (usually annually, biannually, or quarterly), and the dates of final notification. If an applicant requires initial approach, you can be assured that this is a screening mechanism to reduce the number of unfit proposals they have to consider. Some foundations may only accept invited proposals—another clearing mechanism. Some will base an invitation to submit a proposal on the initial telephone or letter contact, and if they require an application form, they may only provide the form and instructions for the complete proposal upon determining your proposal's appropriateness.

Information about the foundation and its officers and directors is always useful. In the way of information about the foundation, the Directory provides a list of the publications that the foundation makes available. Common among them are annual reports, strategic plans, application guidelines, financial statements, lists and partial lists of grant awards, brochures, newsletters, and so forth. These documents hold a treasure trove of knowledge about the foundation, its interests, and its past giving activity. Financial statements give a picture of the organization's financial status. Are its earnings increasing or decreasing? Is it receiving donations or in the process of de-funding? Grants lists may be organized by amount, recipient, topic, or they may be abridged to demonstrate the foundation's interests. In some cases, they are annotated, and in some cases foundations provide examples of successful past projects carried out by grant awards. Information about directors and officers may be very useful. Are they community representatives? Are they corporate executives? Are they politically affiliated? What are their personal interests? The amount of information that can be derived from these lists is limited in part by how publicly or privately the referenced individuals carry out their lives and their charitable activities. You should at least be familiar with the composition of the board because it is the living breathing apparatus that guides the foundation and its funding decisions. All of this information—about the foundation and its officers—is available and knowable. A successful grant seeker should know this information before initiating contact, but certainly before submitting an application; in these actions the grant seeker can and should demonstrate to the foundation that it has a good working knowledge of who it is and what it does.

I have discussed the information collected and presented in the Foundation Directory generally, but the electronic versions provide a greater degree of simplicity in use. Keyword searches can significantly reduce your search time. Of course, as is always the case, such searches are only as good as the searcher's creativity and familiarity with common terminology. It is well worth the time for beginning grant seekers to spend some time browsing directory entries to become more familiar with the terminology used. The directory is a superb resource to narrow your search. It is insufficient to determine with absolute certainty whether or not your proposal fits the interests and scope of a foundation's giving interests. To ascertain this relationship, you must always read the foundation's website, seek out annual reports and other publications that may include a list or selection of grant awards, and consult with foundation representatives to be certain. It is best to be sure before preparing a formal solicitation. To summarize, the Foundation Directory narrows the search, but it is only the beginning of a more careful search to learn and understand a foundation's interests.

The Catalog of Federal Domestic Assistance

The federal government catalogs each assistance program it provides in the Catalog of Federal Domestic Assistance (CFDA) according to the awarding agency and the program title using a unique five-digit identifying code for each program. These program codes and titles are persistent over time, although Congress and the agency may make changes to funding priorities and program descriptions from time to time. The CFDA is still available in print form at many government document repository libraries, though it is readily accessible via the Internet (www.cfda.gov). The catalog is an excellent place to begin your search for federal funding because it carefully categorizes federal programs by assistance type (such as grants, which is our particular type of interest), by agency, by eligibility requirements, and by other considerations.

As was the case with the Foundation Directory, it is helpful to understand the anatomy of a CFDA Program Description entry before attempting to utilize the resource. Each program description includes the following categories of information: program number, title, and popular name; federal agency; authorization information; program objectives; types of assistance; uses and use restrictions; eligibility requirements (applicant and beneficiary); application and award process; assistance considerations (conditions); financial information; and contact information. **Table 2.10** shows the contents of a CFDA entry. Let's consider each component individually.

The program number, as indicated, is used to distinguish catalog entries. The first two-digit sequence designates the funding agency and the remaining three digits identify programs in numerical sequence. For example, program 10.500 is a program administered by the U.S. Department of Agriculture, program 11.500 is administered by the Department of Commerce, and program 12.500 is administered by the Department of Defense. The complete listing of federal programs is far too extensive to replicate here. The program title is the descriptive name given to the program by law or administrative decision. Often programs are known by a common name that is less technical than the program title; these names are given where applicable.

The federal agency section indicates which federal agency, department, commission, or other functional unit has operational authority for the program and its administration. The program authorization information provides references to the law or statutes from which the program is based and obtains its authority. Program objectives state the specific intent of the program—what it is supposed to do and any goals toward which it is directed. Program objectives provide a good basis for keyword searches. This section corresponds, more or less, to the "purpose and activities" section of entries in the Foundation Directory, though the focus is at the program level, not at the organization or agency level. With this information in hand it begins to become apparent whether a given grant program is in line with your project objectives.

The type of assistance classification differentiates among 15 separate assistance types that the federal government provides (this list was provided in Chapter 1 in Table 1.6). It distinguishes grant funds from other types of assistance such as technical assistance, and it also classifies programs according to their method of allocation—block grant, formula grant, or project grants. The uses and use restrictions category should sound familiar; it partially corresponds to the "types of support" and "limitations" categories we observed in the Foundation Directory. This category describes the sorts of things that are allowable and that are not allowable under program funding. Unlike foundations, which are somewhat flexible with regard to the things they can fund, federal agencies are bound by law or administrative regulation. What you see is what you get for a program cycle—a restricted use will not be permitted for funding. This section provides a much clearer understanding of a program's purpose than the statement of objectives alone can. Much like combining the fields of interest with the statement of purpose and activities in the Foundation Directory, combining uses and objectives in the CFDA gives a much clearer picture of what programs are trying to do and how.

Eligibility requirements in the catalog are divided into two components—applicant eligibility and beneficiary eligibility. It is often the case that federal funds are not intended to benefit the recipient organization, but some group of individuals or entities that the recipient

TABLE 2.10   CFDA Program Description Entry Outline

Program Number, Title, Popular Name
Federal Agency
Authorization
Objectives
Types of Assistance
Uses and Use Restrictions
Eligibility Requirements
   Applicant Eligibility
   Beneficiary Eligibility
   Credentials/Documentation
Application and Award Process
   Preapplication Coordination
   Application Procedure
   Award Procedure
   Deadlines
   Range of Approval/Disapproval Time
   Appeals
   Renewals
Assistance Considerations
   Formula and Matching Requirements
   Length and Time Phasing of Assistance
Post Assistance Considerations
   Reports
   Audits
   Records
Financial Information
   Account Identification
   Obligations
   Range and Average of Financial Assistance
Program Accomplishments
Regulations, Guidelines, and Literature
Information Contacts
   Regional or Local Office
   Headquarters Office
Related Programs
Examples of Funded Projects
Criteria for Selecting Proposals

Source: General Services Administration 2007b.

serves. This section clearly states the eligibility requirements for each. This section is similar to the "limitations" section of a Foundation Directory entry.

The application and award process section specifies the procedure through which funding determinations are made, and hence how to proceed in applying for funding. Preapplication coordination describes the type of initial contact that is required prior to submitting an application. Some programs require a preapplication; some require intergovernmental review (under Executive Order 12372, which was previously discussed in Chapter 1); some do not require either. The application procedure indicates whether applications are made directly to the federal agency or to local or state divisions that process applications on their way to the federal agency-level decision. Some programs require submission of approved federal forms, some require a statement of need, and some require a formal response to a notification of funding availability that appears in the *Federal Register* (which I discuss in the next section). The award procedure simply indicates how the agency makes awards to recipients. This section also includes useful information about program deadlines, the range of time for award approval/disapproval, appeals, and renewals (if applicable).

If you heed my observations and warnings about the potential effects of grants on the recipient organizations presented throughout Chapter 1, then the section of the CFDA on considerations should be of particular interest to you. For formula grants, this section describes the basis of the formula; for project grants, it discusses financial conditions such as match requirements (either cash or in-kind) and the source of match. It is very common for programs to disallow consideration of match funds that come from other federal sources. The length of assistance is defined in this section—it is almost universal for grant funds to be expended within a given time frame, though that time is usually expandable by 12 months through a no-fault extension (I discuss this further in Chapter 9). This section also describes administrative requirements and non-financial conditions that are placed on the grant funds. These include reporting and audit requirements and record-keeping information.

Financial information is always key to understanding a federal program just as it tells us much more about the type of grants a foundation gives. This section reports on agency obligations—the amount it has had, has, or will have available in the past year, current year, and budget year as indicated by current documents. The range of grant amounts and average grant amount are also provided to assist grant seekers in determining program appropriateness.

The final section of the CFDA reports contact information for program and agency officials at the local, state, and federal levels whom you may need to contact to obtain program information, application packets, or even information about when NOFAs are expected in the *Federal Register.*

The CFDA is the best place to begin familiarizing yourself with available federal programs. As with the Foundation Directory, CFDA program information can easily be browsed or searched online. The catalog may be browsed by agency, subagency, program title, by programs that require/do not require intergovernmental review, and by type of support; it may be searched by keyword. As with the Foundation Directory, it is almost always a good idea for beginning grant seekers to browse relevant sections of the catalog to become familiar with common terminology and the range of programs available. Over time, given the incremental stability of federal programs even through times of political change, grant seekers working in an organizational context (i.e., not consultants) become intimately familiar with the available federal programs, their purposes, and restrictions. It is very common for organizations to receive federal grants in a given program many times for unique projects, so over time grant writing efforts become more familiar and the search becomes obsolete.

From time to time, however, the federal government still creates new programs. For example, new programs were created to examine community design following Hurricane Katrina (HUD, URAP). Sometimes familiarity with new programs is provided through networking, agency listservs, and newsletters, but the value of a new search from time to time should be clear. As indicated previously, the CFDA is not sufficient, by itself, to provide all necessary program and application information. It is often useful to peruse agency websites, but it is necessary to search the *Federal Register* for program announcements and NOFAs. The *Federal Register* announcements include all of the information you need to prepare and submit an application, except as usual, contacting program officers for clarification. I discuss it next.

The Federal Register

The *Federal Register*, as indicated previously, is the government's daily newspaper announcing hearings, program changes, funding competitions, and lots of other information. It is probably not feasible to read the *Federal Register* in its entirety each day unless you are a very quick reader with a high tolerance for administrative announcements. More useful and realistic is the search feature available at the main Federal Register website (www.gpoaccess.gov/fr/index.html). From here searchers can perform a quick search of the current volume, or they can access search pages for advanced search functions on current and past volumes. Using the advanced search function, grant seekers are able to specify a search based only on notices by volume, date, and keyword (www.gpoaccess.gov/fr/advanced.html). Also, to stay abreast of updates, changes, and announcements, you can also subscribe to have the *Federal Register*'s table of contents sent to you daily via e-mail. Of the available government tools, this one has the greatest capacity to frustrate because of the sheer volume of information that must be reviewed and sorted. Nonetheless, it is a valuable resource with which you should become familiar.

Grants.gov

In the search for federal funding, systems have finally matured to meet their task. The previous two tools discussed (the CFDA and the *Federal Register*) are comprehensive with regard to grant information. However, a relatively new shared system spearheaded by the Department of Health and Human Services—Grants.gov—has changed the way people search for and apply for grants. This system is a one-stop shop for grant seekers and applicants. Information regarding grant opportunities from all 26 federal grant making agencies is readily available through the Grants.gov portal, complete with program links and deadline information. Most federal programs now use the Grants.gov portal for application submission, so it is a resource that will become familiar if you regularly submit federal proposals.

Searching the Grants.gov portal is quite simple. Applicants are able to browse available programs by agency—much like in the CFDA. Simple and advanced search options are also available. The basic search engine allows the grant seeker to search by funding opportunity number (unique to Grants.gov), by keyword, or by CFDA number, which you should now be familiar with (www.grants.gov/search/basic.do). The advanced search permits searches of open, closed, and archived funding opportunities within user-defined time constraints by keyword, opportunity number, CFDA number, agency, eligibility, funding category, or the type of funding instrument. Finally, it is possible to browse by category, including the following options: Arts; Community Development Disaster Prevention and Relief; Employment, Labor and Training; Environment; Health; Humanities; Income Security and Social Services; Natural Resources; Regional Development; Transportation; Agriculture; Business and Commerce; Consumer Protection; Education; Energy; Food and Nutrition; Housing; Information and Statistics; Law, Justice and Legal Services; Science and Technology and other Research and Development; Other; and All Categories (www.grants.gov/search/category.do).

Another system feature that aids professional grant seekers is the ability to receive e-mailed funding notices tailored to their particular needs: all notices, notices based on specified criteria, or notices based on funding opportunity number (www.grants.gov/applicants/email_subscription.asp). None of the search features or e-mail features require registration with the system. We discuss registering with Grants.gov in detail in a later chapter.

We have discussed the tools most commonly used to identify and search for grant funding opportunities—the Foundation Directory, the CFDA, the *Federal Register*, and Grants.gov. Your grant seeking tool kit is now complete and ready to be exercised using the criteria-based rubric developed earlier in the chapter. To conclude the chapter, I provide a brief example of a simple initial search for government grants to support economic development projects requiring construction.

APPLICATION OF THE SEARCH TOOLS

This concluding section provides a brief example of a search for economic development funds to be used for construction projects. By first opening the CFDA web page (www.cfda.gov) and clicking the link to "Search for assistance programs," one arrives at the search options page. From this page, using the "Browse the Catalog by Functional Category" feature takes you to a list of functional categories. "Business and Commerce" most closely approximates the object of our search, so clicking the link takes you to a final list of subcategories that include small business, economic development (the topic of interest), economic injury and natural disaster, commercial fisheries, maritime, international, statistics, special technical services, and minority business enterprises. Clicking on the economic development link takes us to the list of all federal programs that include economic development as a stated purpose. The stated purpose is an important distinction because other programs may fit into a broad economic development effort though not be classified as economic development per se. This browsing effort netted 63 potential programs to consider, presented in **Table 2.11**.

TABLE 2.11   CFDA Browse Results: Business and Commerce, Economic Development

Subcategory	CFDA No.	Agency	Program Title
Economic	10.056	USDA	Farm Storage Facility Loans
Development	10.24	USDA	Alternative Agricultural Research and Commercialization Program
	10.404	USDA	Emergency Loans
	10.406	USDA	Farm Operating Loans
	10.67	USDA	National Forest_Dependent Rural Communities
	10.766	USDA	Community Facilities Loans and Grants
	10.767	USDA	Intermediary Relending Program
	10.768	USDA	Business and Industry Loans
	10.769	USDA	Rural Business Enterprise Grants
	10.773	USDA	Rural Business Opportunity Grants
	10.86	USDA	Rural Business Investment Program
	11.111	DOC	Foreign-Trade Zones in the United States
	11.113	DOC	ITA Special Projects
	11.3	DOC	Grants for Public Works and Economic Development Facilities
	11.302	DOC	Economic Development_Support for Planning Organizations
	11.303	DOC	Economic Development_Technical Assistance
	11.304	DOC	Economic Development_Public Works Impact Program
	11.305	DOC	Economic Development_State and Local Economic Development Planning
	11.462	DOC	Hydrologic Research
	11.614	DOC	Experimental Program to Stimulate Competitive Technology
	11.8	DOC	Minority Business Enterprise Centers
	12.002	DOD	Procurement Technical Assistance for Business Firms
	12.6	DOD	Community Economic Adjustment
	12.607	DOD	Community Economic Adjustment Planning Assistance
	12.61	DOD	Community Economic Adjustment Planning Assistance for Joint Land Use Studies
	12.612	DOD	Community Base Reuse Plans
	12.613	DOD	Growth Management Planning Assistance
	14.218	HUD	Community Development Block Grants/Entitlement Grants
	14.219	HUD	Community Development Block Grants/Small Cities Program
	14.225	HUD	Community Development Block Grants/Special Purpose Grants/Insular Areas
	14.227	HUD	Community Development Block Grants/Technical Assistance Program

TABLE 2.11   (Continued)

Subcategory	CFDA No.	Agency	Program Title
	14.228	HUD	Community Development Block Grants/State's Program
	14.246	HUD	Community Development Block Grants/ Brownfields Economic Development Initiative
	14.412	HUD	Employment Opportunities for Lower Income Persons and Businesses
	14.862	HUD	Indian Community Development Block Grant Program
	15.02	DOI	Aid to Tribal Governments
	15.021	DOI	Consolidated Tribal Government Program
	15.022	DOI	Tribal Self-Governance
	15.023	DOI	Tribal Self-Governance Grants
	15.024	DOI	Indian Self-Determination Contract Support
	15.032	DOI	Indian Economic Development
	15.124	DOI	Indian Loans_Economic Development
	15.875	DOI	Economic, Social, and Political Development of the Territories
	20.507	DOT	Federal Transit_Formula Grants
	21.02	TREAS	Community Development Financial Institutions Program
	21.021	TREAS	Bank Enterprise Award Program
	23.001	ARC	Appalachian Regional Development (See individual Appalachian Programs)
	23.002	ARC	Appalachian Area Development
	23.011	ARC	Appalachian Research, Technical Assistance, and Demonstration Projects
	39.011	GSA	Election Reform Payments
	44.002	NCUA	Community Development Revolving Loan Fund Program for Credit Unions
	45.301	IMLS	Museums for America
	45.302	IMLS	Museum Assessment Program
	45.303	IMLS	Conservation Project Support
	45.304	IMLS	Conservation Assessment Program
	45.305	IMLS	Professional Services Program
	45.306	IMLS	Museum Leadership Initiatives
	59.041	SBA	Certified Development Company Loans (504 Loans)
	59.052	SBA	Native American Economic Development Assistance
	90.1	DRC	Denali Commission Program
	90.2	DC	Delta Regional Development
	90.201	DC	Delta Area Economic Development
	93.57	HHS	Community Services Block Grant_ Discretionary Awards

Source: General Services Administration 2007a.

TABLE 2.12   Results of Advanced CFDA Search for Economic Development
Construction Programs

11.300—Grants for Public Works and Economic Development Facilities
11.307—Economic Adjustment Assistance

Source: General Services Administration 2007a.

The browse function provides the most comprehensive list, but if we know more details about our planned project and have working familiarity with the CFDA and its categories, it is possible to narrow the search considerably using the CFDA's advanced search feature. Browsing to the advanced search feature provides the opportunity to provide up to five limitations on the search. For this example, three were used. First, the Types of Assistance category was selected and the term "grants" was typed into the search box. Second, the Uses and Use Restrictions category was selected and "construction" was typed into the search box. Finally, the Objectives category was selected and "economic development" was typed into the search box. The result is a list of two programs that fit the specified criteria, displayed in **Table 2.12**.

As can be seen, the quality of a search improves as familiarity with CFDA increases. These two programs may not be the only two federal grants that could be used for the stated purpose, but they do provide funds for the stated purpose. Reviewing their program descriptions provides the necessary information to begin the application process.

CONCLUSION

This chapter has presented a conceptual method that can be used to evaluate funding opportunities. For beginners, use of such a decision rubric will be useful to make habitual the important concepts that should be considered. For more experienced writers, the rubric provides a checklist that may be kept mentally rather than on paper. In either case, the purpose and utility is the same—to use a systematic method of evaluating opportunities to determine appropriateness or viability for a given organization or program. The second half of the chapter presented the key tools that are used to identify funding sources and locate information on funding opportunities. Using the conceptual rubric in conjunction with these applied tools will provide solid search results on which to base the next steps leading up to an application. Chapter 3 continues the quest with discussions of how to build effective grant teams and partnerships to strengthen and sustain programs.

REFERENCES

Bryson, John M. 2004. *Strategic Planning for Public and Nonprofit Organizations: A Guide to Strengthening and Sustaining Organizational Achievement, 3rd Edition.* San Francisco: Jossey-Bass Publishers.

Carnegie Corporation of New York. 2007a. The Corporation's Program: How to Apply for a Grant. Accessed May 5, 2007. Available at: http://www.carnegie.org/sub/program/grant.html.

Carnegie Corporation of New York. 2007b. How to Apply for a Grant: Grantseeker Quiz. Accessed May 5, 2007. Available at: http://www.carnegie.org/sub/program/grantquiz.html.

Carnegie Corporation of New York. 2007c. How to Apply for a Grant: General and Specific Funding Restrictions. Accessed May 5, 2007. Available at: http://www.carnegie.org/sub/program/grantrestrictions.html.

Center for Rural Development. n.d. 42 County Service Area. Accessed May 5, 2007. Available at: http://www.centertech.com/42counties.

Clorox Company. 2006. The Clorox Company Foundation: Guidelines and Priorities. Accessed May 5, 2007. Available at: http://www.thecloroxcompany.com/community/guidelines.html.

Derthick, Martha. 1996. Crossing thresholds: Federalism in the 1960s. *Journal of Policy History* 8: 64–80.

European Foundation Centre. 2007. Funders Online. Accessed May 10, 2007. Available at: http://www.fundersonline.org.

Foundation Center. 2007. Foundation Directory Online. Accessed May 5, 2007. Available at: https://fcsecure.fdncenter.org/fdo_signup_prof/register.php?setplan=start.

General Services Administration. 2007a. Catalog of Federal Domestic Assistance. Available at: http://www.cfda.gov.

General Services Administration. 2007b. The Catalog of Federal Domestic Assistance: Anatomy of a Program Description. Accessed April 1, 2007. Available at: http://12.46.245.173/pls/portal30/catalog.ANATOMY_OF_PROG_DESC_RPT.show.

Government Printing Office. 2007. *The Federal Register.* Accessed April 1, 2007. Available at: http://www.gpoaccess.gov/fr/index.html.

Institute for Regional Analysis and Public Policy. Morehead State University Service Region. Accessed May 5, 2007. Available at: http://irap.moreheadstate.edu/images/svc_reg_05.jpg.

Institute for Regional Analysis and Public Policy. Appalachian Counties Established by the Appalachian Regional Commission, 2005. Accessed May 5, 2007. Available at: http://irapp.moreheadstate.edu/images/app_map_lg.jpg.

Jacobs, David G., Ed. 2002. *The Foundation Directory.* New York: The Foundation Center.

National Institutes of Health. 2007. ERA Commons: Computer Retrieval of Information on Scientific Projects. Accessed May 5, 2007. Available at: http://crisp.cit.nih.gov.

New York Foundation for the Arts (NYFA). 2007. NYFA Source: Grants and Resources for all Artists. Accessed May 10, 2007. Available at: http://www.nyfa.org/nyfa_source.asp?id=47&fid=1.

Northern California Community Foundation, Inc. 2007. Foundations.Org. Accessed May 10, 2007. Available at: http://www.foundations.org.

Scaife Foundations. n.d. Sarah Scaife Foundation. Accessed May 5, 2007. Available at: http://www.scaife.com/sarah.html.

State of California. 2007. Getgrants. Accessed May 10, 2007. Available at: http://getgrants.ca.gov.

Texas Department of State Health Services. 2007. Funding Alert Grant Database. Accessed May 10, 2007. Available at: http://www.dshs.state.tx.us/fic/search.asp.

University of Illinois at Urbana Champaign Library. 2007. Illinois Researcher Information Service (IRIS). Accessed May 10, 2007. Available at: http://www.library.uiuc.edu/iris.

U.S. Department of Health and Human Services. 2007. Grants.gov. Accessed May 10, 2007. Available at: http://www.grants.gov.

U.S. Department of Housing and Urban Development, Office of University Partnerships. 2007. Foundations Database. Accessed May 10, 2007. Available at: http://www.oup.org/funding/upcfoundation/PubSearch.asp.

Wyoming State Library. 2007. Wyoming Grants Information. Accessed May 10, 2007. Available at: http://www-wsl.state.wy.us/sis/grants.

CHAPTER 3

Planning and Preparation

In the first chapter of this book, I explored what grants are, including their purpose, their effect on recipient organizations, and the differential effects that grants of different types can have on local organization or government efforts. I also discussed the process of developing mechanisms to aid in the search for funds through use of a conceptual rubric to assess each program's standing with regard to a number of core criteria. And I presented the primary sources of grant information available for foundation and government funding. With this basic conceptual understanding and an accompanying applied understanding of the search tools and techniques, a grant seeker can embark on the search for appropriate funding sources in both the federal and foundation arenas. This chapter discusses the preliminary work that must take place to build sustainable partnerships that will enhance program success and achieve greater success with funding requests.

The process I discuss in this chapter is summative to a certain degree (Bryson 2004). That is to say that it doesn't take place outright, but it is dependent on the result of your search for funding opportunities. What is the character of the funding source? What do they expect to see in an application? What did previous applicants do correctly that helped them to secure grant awards from each funding source? And the key question becomes, as you probably suspect: What steps can I take to enhance my probability of success? The process may also be seen as iterative to a degree. Many times we begin with an ideal program approach or idea that we would like to have funded, and then seek the most appropriate funding source for that idea. If an ideal funding source is identified, the program must still be adapted and tailored to the grantor's interests, values, and requirements. If a suitable funding source is not identified, we have to revisit the basics of our approach to determine how it might be amended to become suitable for one or more funding agencies.

Building on our previous discussion about targeting grant proposals to fit funding agencies' desires, this chapter elaborates a series of key steps and techniques that will aid in the process of program and application development. I begin by considering how to assemble the best possible team to develop the program and prepare the application for funding. Following that, I move into the more detailed aspects of developing the program idea and partnerships that lead to program success. Because each situation is different and fact-dependent, these steps may be more or less useful in different settings and under different conditions. I have found them to be very effective in community-based projects across a number of subject areas including development, the arts, environment, and education and training.

Partnerships provide unique opportunities because they enable the lead organization to focus on its core and distinctive competencies (Bryson 2004) without expanding into or developing new areas of expertise that detract from its core mission and values. Drawing on other organizations that have distinctive competencies that are different from your own, but that add significant utility to the proposed program, makes for a richer programmatic idea that shows greater strength and likelihood of success than does a proposed approach that involves either applicant going it alone. As Lasker, Weiss, and Miller (2001) have observed, the desired benefits that lead partners into collaborative arrangements include "the acquisition of additional funds, new competencies, and useful knowledge to support their own activities" (p. 191). This certainly sounds like the purpose collaboration serves for organizations seeking new grant funding—funding, specific competencies, and knowledge.

It also is true that partners seek out collaboration because it enables them to better share the risk inherent in new projects and programs (Boschken 1998). Among the reasons for collaboration is improved effectiveness or efficiency derived from some combination of economy of scale, non-duplication of effort, and collaborative advantage. Collaboratives that increase benefits for each partner while reducing costs are more likely to form and succeed (Lubell, Schneider, Scholz, & Mete 2002). Collaboration can also be beneficial to agencies under conditions of increased competition for limited funding because it provides a viable opportunity for organizational growth when it is least likely for any of the partners individually (Boschken 1998).

The reasons for undertaking collaborative arrangements are numerous. These benefits notwithstanding, there are also challenges associated with forming and operating effective collaborations. Networks have collaborative costs as well as collaborative benefits, with the most common cost being the relinquishment of agency turf, authority, and resources (Agranoff 2006). "Collaboration for collaboration's sake or to achieve only individual goals is likely to result in failure given the complexity of the collaboration process" (Thomson & Perry 2006, p. 28). In other words, collaborating for show and not substance is not beneficial. For collaboration to be effective, each agency must both contribute something significant that was not otherwise available and benefit in ways it would not have outside the collaborative. There is an information asymmetry problem here that provides a disincentive to genuine collaboration. It is easy to demonstrate to a funding source on paper that a collaborative effort has been formed and will jointly carry out a proposed grant project. The partners' genuineness toward collaborating with one another may be less resolved than a grant application makes it appear. On the other hand, one cannot control every uncertainty, and lead agencies may not have received genuine support from the partners they believe to have squarely on board with the project.

The capacity needed to work in networks is different from what an organization needs to work alone. Multiple partners mean that multiple goals will be present (Agranoff & McGuire 1998), and to be successful these goal differences will have to be reconciled. To arrive at joint strategy, managers in collaborative partnerships will be forced to rely on team building, conflict resolution, and problem-solving skills (Agranoff & McGuire 1998). Collaborative efforts created with proper motives and mutual benefit to all participants will prove to be beneficial.

The concept expands beyond simple community projects as well. Many federal programs require, and many foundation programs desire, an evaluation component to demonstrate program effects. Most community organizations, nonprofit organizations, and even local and state government agencies lack professional staff equipped with the knowledge and skill to execute a comprehensive program evaluation. Managers who may have some evaluation skills certainly will lack the necessary time to dedicate to such efforts. So, even in programs and projects where the substance of the program can be carried out in-house, there is still call for collaboration with organizations (usually universities and their public administration faculty) that bring such core competencies as program evaluation to the table. Although I discuss evaluation in greater detail in Chapter 10, I add here that bringing an evaluator on board in advance of program design has significant advantages.

The management point here is that grant seekers should soberly confront their purpose, and that of their organization, in pursuing extramural funding. Is it to create public value (Moore 1995), or is it to enhance organizational budgets? The corollary question, in lay terms, is whether we are being greedy and simply trying to sustain our organization (which is an acceptable goal in certain settings), or we are trying to maximize the benefit to a community or a group of individuals that would be directly affected by the proposed program. Knowing the answer to this question indicates how an organization is likely to view and approach partnership arrangements. There are three models here. First is the organization with altruistic motives focused on the effect of the project; they will embrace partnership opportunities and treat partners fairly. Second is the self-serving or egocentric organization concerned only with budget resources; this organization will disregard partners altogether because their inclusion means diffusion of the benefits attained through grant seeking. And third is the conniving organization that realizes its success is greatest if it shows strong partnerships and community support in its application but gives those partners short shrift when funding is awarded.

The first organization serves as our model, in consideration of the fact that not all programs require partnerships, and thus organizations "going it alone" are not necessarily greedy or self-serving. The second organization harms no one but itself in carrying out its grant seeking activities. However, the third organization runs the risk of harming partners that invest it with their trust. If the partners understand that their support is symbolic, no harm is done because they aren't expecting anything in return. On the other hand, if partners have been promised a substantive role in the project in exchange for a portion of the grant proceeds, they may be harmed if the lead organization finds ways to work without them upon receiving the grant award. This has long-term ramifications for our example organization—our available partners become alienated and distrustful, which reduces the prospect of future collaborations. Studies of collaboration success have observed that collaboration has proven beneficial "when a history of dyadic working relationships makes intergovernmental exchange familiar and more predictable" (Boschken 1998, p. 606). In other words, collaboratives that have the foundation of mutual trust among partners prove more successful than do those tainted with suspicion.

If you had planned on being a solo operator, planning, seeking, and managing grant programs alone, it should be becoming clear that that is rarely possible, and even less advisable. Sometimes we have no choice. Many of you are employed or will find yourselves employed in small organizations that lack staff and financial resources, and in these settings one must learn to cope and wear many hats. I argue that there are significant advantages to working collaboratively as a team in planning and preparing a program and its associated grant application. With these thoughts in mind, let us begin our consideration of program preparation and planning with a discussion of how to create a winning grants team, from both an ongoing operational standpoint as well as for a specific project.

BUILD THE GRANTS TEAM

To begin the process of program development and application preparation, an organization needs to know strengths and weaknesses of its team and understand how individual strengths may be exploited to yield superior programs and applications, and thus greater results. A grants team is preferred to an individual because it reduces the workload under significant time constraints, but more important because different individuals bring unique perspectives to the process. The most significant difference among participating individuals is the way they process information and interact with the world. To assess these differences, a personality type indicator is a straightforward and quite simple technique for learning who in your organization has which strengths. To proceed most efficiently, some time must be dedicated to learning and analyzing individual preferences in the organizational context. Again, sometimes organizations do not have the scale to be able to assemble and draw on a team of grant seekers. Although not members of the grants team per se, other organization members or outsiders may be able to contribute in meaningful ways throughout the process using this technique. I discuss the Myers-Briggs Type Indicator cognitive style preferences as the framework for assessing individual strengths and applying them to both program development and to the grant seeking venture.

Cognitive Style Characteristics

The Myers-Briggs Type Indicator is a self-administered indicator of cognitive style preferences that categorizes individuals into one of 16 possible four-letter categories (**Figure** 3.1).

ISTJ	**ISTP**	**ISFJ**	**ISFP**
INTJ	**INTP**	**INFJ**	**INFP**
ESTJ	**ESTP**	**ESFJ**	**ESFP**
ENTJ	**ENTP**	**ENFJ**	**ENFP**

FIGURE 3.1   The 16 MBTI Style Preferences

The four dimensions assessed are introversion/extraversion (source of energy; **Figure** 3.2), sensing/intuiting (information gathering preference; **Figure** 3.3), thinking/feeling (decision making style; **Figure** 3.4), and judging/perceiving (preference for ordering the outside world; **Figure** 3.5). There is nothing inherently good or bad about either type or an individual's score on either dimension. However, these four categories do present some strengths and weaknesses in approaching particular tasks. These differences provide a reasonable justification for assigning certain individuals to perform particular tasks in the process—the reality is that certain styles predispose individuals to confront such tasks with greater ease.

Before we embark on a deeper analysis of the types and their most suitable activities, you should be aware that no certain type makes someone a good or a bad grant writer. In fact, individuals can readily perform tasks that cross from one end of a dimension's spectrum to another; they are simply less comfortable performing those tasks that do not correspond to their type preference. So, the nature of the tasks used in the planning and application process and their correspondence with the features of each type dimension provide fodder for examining how best to assign individuals to maximize their performance in completing grant seeking activities. The four-letter type is less important than the strength of each individual's directional preference on each dimension's spectrum.

The dimensions of the MBTI are best presented as a scale or spectrum pitting two extremes against each other. Differences among individuals on any given scale can be the source of tension and conflict, and similarity can be the source of agreement. Our goal is not to achieve agreement, but to stimulate positive dissonance—disagreement that can be negotiated to arrive at a product that appeals to persons of all types. How the team is

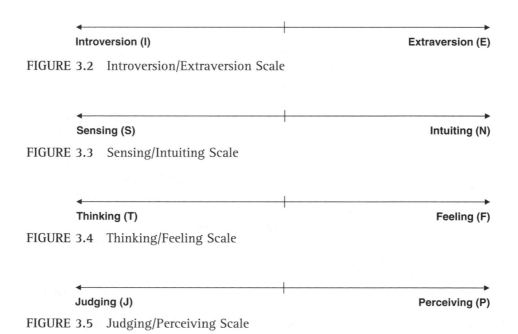

Introversion (I)   **Extraversion (E)**

FIGURE 3.2   Introversion/Extraversion Scale

Sensing (S)   **Intuiting (N)**

FIGURE 3.3   Sensing/Intuiting Scale

Thinking (T)   **Feeling (F)**

FIGURE 3.4   Thinking/Feeling Scale

Judging (J)   **Perceiving (P)**

FIGURE 3.5   Judging/Perceiving Scale

constructed and how tasks are assigned determine how effectively this conflict is managed, and hence how successful the effort will be.

Assessing your type is quite simple. You can always pay a consultant to administer the official MBTI assessment, or there are assorted Internet sites where sufficient assessments are available. So, what do the types signify? A thorough discussion is not warranted in this text, but I briefly interpret and describe each letter's meaning. Extraversion (E) and Introversion (I) refer to the way a person interacts with the world. This difference is the most commonly understood of the four and probably needs little explanation. Introverts tend to be reserved and quiet; they take their energy from inside, and they develop energy best during alone time. Introverts consider their response to questions before responding, and often only respond when questioned directly. These are the individuals who sit in the corner in a chair at office parties. Extraverts receive their energy from outside. They require constant interaction with others to sustain their energy. Hence, they always seem to be talking, often loudly, interrupting others. Extraverts blurt out answers to questions without thinking. They are usually found in the center of the room at the office party vying for others' conversational attention.

The Sensing (S) and Intuiting (N) dimension is the most important for the grants enterprise. Most people are familiar with the term *intuitive* but have not had the opportunity to consider it as a personality trait. Intuitives are big picture thinkers who see the forest and not the trees. They have a ready grasp of concepts and the relationships that link things together and make them work, but specifics and details escape them. Sensors focus on details and minutia—the very things that Intuitives find to be so mundane. The trees hold the most interest for Sensors, and they easily become lost in the forest as they move from tree to tree without considering the big picture relationships among them. Because of their acuity for detail, Sensors seldom make errors of fact.

The dimension separating Thinking (T) and Feeling (F) gets at whether a person is driven by logic and rational analysis or by emotion. As you may have guessed, Thinkers are highly analytical individuals who seek rationality in arguments. Feelers are driven by emotion and instead rely on emotion to make decisions. Whereas a Thinker is more apt to demand a rational justification for action, Feelers act on instinct, often on the basis of a "gut feeling."

Finally, Judging (J) is distinguished from Perceiving (P). Judgers are tremendous planners who think things out in advance and use lists and checklists to guide their process. They thrive on organization. Judging individuals approach their tasks with a preconceived notion of the way things are supposed to be, and they can be particularly stubborn or closed-minded about changing the status quo. Perceivers thrive on flexibility. They need no guidelines, they are disorganized, but they tend to be very open minded and flexible in dealing with unanticipated problems or questions. Perceivers have a genuine knack for "winging it" that enables them to respond calmly and fluidly in urgent situations.

With this brief description in mind, and even without having assessed your own personality profile, you can probably picture various individuals in your personal and professional lives who characterize each of the letters discussed. To the extent that you are able to read peoples' styles and preferences, no formal assessment may be necessary. You should also keep in mind, however, that many people are balanced evenly between the styles on some dimensions, and thus are able to function comfortably on either side of the spectrum.

And as I noted earlier, these are neither good nor bad traits, though some are more useful than others in certain situations. Do not forget: we are not constrained by our type in any way, it is simply a measure of our comfort level with different settings. Whereas a Sensor is able to look for big picture relationships, this person is more comfortable sorting through details. Days without details are difficult for Sensors; days with lots of details are difficult for their Intuitive counterparts.

Use Cognitive Style to Determine Roles

With an understanding of how the preference dimensions differ, consider program development and grant seeking roles where each is most useful. Introverts dislike meetings whereas extraverts thrive on interaction. Planning meetings with potential partners and stakeholders should be led by or at least include an Extravert. While we are on the topic of meetings, this is a good time to consider Perceivers' and Judgers' preferred contributions. Judgers, as noted, will be well organized, with meeting plans and agendas. (You can always tell Intuitive Judgers [NJ] from Sensor Judgers [SJ] by the level of detail included in their meeting agendas.) Judgers will have already mapped out roles, financial contributions, and various other items in advance of the meeting. Perceivers are good to have on hand at planning meetings because they work well in the face of adversity. When something that isn't on the agenda comes up, or when someone takes variance with their planned role or contribution, perceivers are able to respond and iron out such unforeseen difficulties.

Project planning and organization can be handled best by a Judger. As I noted earlier in reference to meeting agendas, it may be good to balance Intuitive Judgers and Sensor Judgers to ensure that all of the big picture elements are included in the plan along with a sufficient level of detail. As I discuss in Chapter 5, planning the proposal is a very important step. When, at the last minute before submitting an application, you realize that some component was left out of the plan, the Perceiver is the go-to person to fill in the gaps.

Thinking and Feeling individuals differ so considerably it is difficult to discuss their potential roles in the same context. The analytical approach of Thinkers is essential in proposal development—especially budgeting—because they rely on logic and rationality. Thinkers will write descriptions that put the pieces together, adequately explaining what is to happen at each stage in a proposed project and how the proposed project will generate its desired outcomes. Budgets require logical justification, and Thinkers with budgeting skills will embrace the task of developing budgets and budget justifications. As before, Sensing Thinkers will develop more detailed budgets with more categories, line items, and more specific explanations than will Intuitive Thinkers. Feelers provide the balance of emotion to an overly analytical description. Allowing a Feeler involvement in the proposal will make it more human and thus more appealing to readers through the emotion Feelers draw on to make the proposal more convincing. Feelers will likely be better able to draw on their ability to effectively emphasize the benefits the program will have on its intended beneficiaries.

I turn, finally, to the Intuitive/Sensing dimension. As you can probably tell from the way I intertwined these elements with the other dimensions already described, this dimension is the most important in planning and writing a proposal. Sensing individuals (and particularly Thinking ones) are ideal persons to read and understand RFPs and submission requirements, and then write a grant narrative that responds to each specific requirement. The Sensor's attention to detail is most valuable in these endeavors. However, the Intuitive's role is equally significant. Without the Intuitive perspective to see and describe the big picture of the program—how it works and how the partners relate to one another—the proposal will read like a television repair manual: full of useful information, but a dry read missing both theme and plot. It is probably best to approach a proposal narrative through an iterative and interactive process whereby an Intuitive lays out the basic program (this can even be done verbally or in notes) that the Sensor then uses to craft the complete program narrative in response to the application requirements. When the document seems too free-flowing and open, you might guess it was written by a Perceiver. By asking a Judger to review it and add structure (such as section headings and subheadings), you can help shape an application that is strong, complete, and easily understandable and readable by reviewers who may be any of the types themselves.

Although cognitive style preferences may seem somewhat complicated and confusing now, the more you interact with your own grants team—if you are fortunate enough to have a team—you will find that each member excels at some components and settles into particular roles that are reassumed with each new project or proposal. This may be the result of individuals naturally selecting those tasks with which they are most comfortable. If you find your team has particular weaknesses, or your completed proposals have obvious deficiencies, you might rely on the cognitive style descriptions to identify the cause of your problem.

I noted earlier that I would discuss options for making use of this information when your work is performed alone, either because you are the only grant writer or because you are the only organizational staff person whatsoever. In these cases, it is a good idea to exploit your family and friends, or even members of partner organizations whose cognitive styles differ from your own. You have often heard the advice that you should ask someone else to review your work before submitting it. That is true, and the differences I have pointed out here are the reason for doing so. When you hand your work to someone else to criticize, especially if that person's style differs from your own, he can point out those things that he doesn't understand or that are too detailed or not detailed enough. Knowing and understanding your own style can help you to come to terms with your own preferences, and knowing your own predispositions can help you to watch out for manifestations of those preferences that may cloud the information your proposal intends to convey.

As I have pointed out, the best way to build a grants team is to exploit individual preferences for project tasks to which each person is best suited while striving to achieve balance in the proposal document itself. With this understanding, I now turn to the steps involved in developing your program idea and forming partnerships that will enable you to develop more successful applications in the next stage—proposal development.

DEVELOP A PROGRAM IDEA

When should you begin developing a program idea and putting together partnerships needed to supplement your application's attractiveness to potential funders? It is never too early to develop an idea. I have written grants where the program idea has been the cart, and those where it has been the horse. Should one come before the other? Shouldn't we develop program ideas before seeking funding and applying for grants? Not necessarily. Organizations tend to have scopes or missions with sufficient breadth to enable them to undertake a variety of programs. Sometimes the program idea does come first. Sometimes a program idea will be drummed up as a strategy to address some key organizational issue in a strategic planning process. But it is fairly regular for organizations to familiarize themselves with funding agencies whose scope corresponds with their own and monitor available grant opportunities on an ongoing basis. When programs are open or new RFPs are issued, the agency snaps into action to develop an idea that corresponds to the call for proposals. In the case of federal grant programs, most are issued on a recurring basis, and failure to receive funding in one year leads to proposal modification and reapplication in subsequent years. The important consideration to maintain at all times is what a given program does to further an organization's mission.

When program ideas are developed in response to a call for proposals, the application must be developed rapidly to meet upcoming deadlines. Knowing this, it is never too early to begin developing the program structure and the partnership arrangements needed to fulfill it. There are tradeoffs with beginning too soon. One is the proclivity to become immersed in the application process and allow it to absorb more time than necessary. A grant application, in my experience, can be tweaked and modified indefinitely if you allow it to be. In the interest of other applications and other organization goals, it is usually a good idea to begin early while not becoming wholly devoted to one proposal. The tradeoff in starting too early with regard to partnership developments is the declining quality of both individual and organizational memory over time. When we make arrangements and negotiate agreements too soon, people forget what they promised. Sometimes our program idea changes during the proposal process and our arrangements need to be modified. Sometimes partner organizations go through changes that require them to alter their participation in the negotiated arrangement. Each of these considerations suggests the value of frequent repeated contact.

A program idea in an ideal world would be developed in light of the organization's mission, vision, mandates, and constraints. Are there things it has to do? Are there things it must not do? If such a process is followed, the organization will produce programs that mesh with its core values and that are tailored to create the sort of public value the organization is charged with generating. From this standpoint, the program idea becomes the guideline for using the rubric developed in Chapter 2. Are the activities eligible? Are the costs allowable? Is the beneficiary group fundable by the proposal? And so on. The program idea becomes the constraint used to select potentially viable grants in the search. Those grant programs that do not seem viable would be ignored while those that are viable would be pursued further.

This is not an ideal world, however. In all likelihood the program idea developed will need to be changed—either broadened to include a more heterogeneous target group, or narrowed to limit attention to a particular homogeneous target group, for example. It is very uncommon for our organizational goals to perfectly align with the goals a foundation or agency is pursuing with their available grant funding. So, in those cases where the program idea was the impetus for a funding search, it is a good idea to make sure the idea is flexible. Here lies the problem: if the program goals become too flexible, then the organization runs the risk of pursuing the funding agency's mission rather than its own. This is precisely the sort of adverse effect Chapter 1 was intended to dissuade. Sometimes the desire for funding can interfere with rational mission-oriented thinking.

Program ideas may lead a funding search, they may be modified as a result of a funding search, and finally, they may follow a funding search. Oftentimes, I have set out to identify grant programs for which my organization has attained basic eligibility, and then crafted a program idea and a grant proposal in response to particular funding sources I identified. This is also perfectly acceptable as an approach and should be used if generating funding to support an organization is a priority. Responding to requests for proposals with program ideas can be very challenging because they require creative thinking, action within a limited time frame, and rapid mobilization of partner organizations for resource commitments and letters of support. Nonetheless, these programs can have rewarding results.

This third approach is easiest to pursue when the organization has a fairly broad mission, such as "advancing economic development" or "improving quality of life." Both economic development and quality of life have different meanings for different people. It is easy to craft a program that fits the objectives of these broad missions. Of course, broad missions usually lead an organization down a path of diffuse impact and benefit. They risk becoming generalists with no core focus. Agencies with specific missions may find it more challenging to respond to RFPs with proposals that fit their mission. For example, if the organization's mission, rather than economic development generally, is to "stimulate entrepreneurship in rural County X through microcredit revolving loan programs," then finding funding opportunities to which you can respond with a program idea and proposal will be an uphill battle. As was the case with the modification approach, generating program ideas in response to an opportunity runs the risk of elevating the grantor's goals and purposes to a higher status than the organization's own goals. All is not lost; creative grant writers can often generate innovative program ideas that serve both organizations' purposes simultaneously.

DEVELOP A WORKGROUP OR ADVISORY COMMITTEE

One approach to developing a program idea is to use collaboration. As I have noted, collaboration can be very useful and can lead to rewards for all participants, but it can also be a great challenge to manage effectively. Shared decision making means shared power, and shared power means loss of control over the program and its direction. This can be frustrating to an organization seeking to lead an effort as each additional partner dilutes the core idea with their own perspective. Logrolling among participants to garner support may be necessary to arrive at a program that is suitable for all. As is the case with legislation in Congress, this usually means the resulting idea is watered down from its initial draft.

For these reasons—loss of control and declining program quality—it is a bad idea to invite a broad array of potential participants to your first meeting. An advisable approach is to first sit down internally with organization staff and devise a framework or approach. Then, take the idea to four or five organizations that could play a substantive role in the project and invite them to participate in the project, its planning, and the proposal process.

Again, at this stage unnecessary adversity is harmful, so selecting members of organizations with whom you have positive working relationships or with whom you have worked successfully in the past is a necessity. These four or five key participants form the basis of a workgroup or advisory committee. It is a good idea to give the group a name and send each participant a formal letter of invitation. Formalizing the group helps to secure confidence from its participants as well as outsiders—namely, funding organizations. When looking at submitted grant proposals, an agency or foundation that sees a formal planning effort leading up to the proposal will have greater confidence in the organization's capacity to implement the proposed project or program successfully, and will in turn rate the application more favorably. For example, the advisory committee can be referenced in the proposal narrative, or meeting minutes could be included in an appendix, if allowed.

What if you need additional support or more partners that aren't represented in the program workgroup? This is also a common problem for organizations operating in a community setting. There could always be more partnership involvement than what is represented on the advisory committee. Should you invite these needed additional participants to join the group? Doing so is generally a bad idea. If they had been trusted partners, they would have been included in the initial advisory group. So, how do you facilitate participation by other community partners without giving them full decision-making power? Let's discuss the reasons for keeping these partners at arm's length during the planning stages while still garnering their support and involvement with the application and program implementation.

SOLICIT PARTNERSHIPS

Two important types of partnerships appear in grant proposals: symbolic partners and substantive partners. Both have value. The following subsections discuss each type of partner.

Symbolic Partners

Symbolic partnerships are essentially expressions of support from community organizations that have particular importance to the project at hand. These partnerships can be very beneficial to funding applications if they are used appropriately. Symbolic partners are organizations or groups that are not actively involved in the project's key activities. They do not provide either cash or in-kind match. Their purpose is essentially to produce letters of support for the proposed project. A letter of support is a one- or two-page letter from the symbolic partner to the applicant that is to be included in the application packet. Letters of support often are also addressed to the funding agency rather than the applicant organization. These letters should be carefully crafted to convey important information about the community, the applicant, and the proposed program.

A consort of well-composed letters can paint a picture that the application narrative cannot. It can show the degree of community involvement and awareness of the organization and its proposed program. Seeing that community organizations are aware of the grant application is a solid indication that the applicant has done its homework, consulted with relevant actors, and sought community input into the planned program. These letters can substantiate claims that are to be made in the proposal. A grant proposal is a formal proposal to help bring resolution to some identified problem, either organizational or community. One of the first components of a program narrative in a grant application is a statement of need, or a problem statement. These symbolic letters of support can help to explain the identified need from perspectives other than the applicant's. They can discuss the applicant's role in the community, its history of successfully completing projects, and its effective interaction with other community groups and organizations on past projects as well as the current proposal. One could call these letters testimonials, and that is essentially one of their most important roles: they convey a sense of confidence in the applicant and its proposed effort.

Finally, symbolic letters of support can provide an additional description of the proposed program, how it will benefit the community (from the partner's standpoint), and how it fits with the shared community vision for change. What many grant writers fail to realize is that letters of support are very powerful instruments. They should always appear on the official letterhead of the supporting organization and should bear the signature of that organization's responsible party. Of course, letters of support should never appear in application packets that prohibit their inclusion. However, they should be included in all applications that expressly provide for their use as well as applications that do not explicitly prohibit them. For example, an application packet may allow for a section of appendices and supporting documentation without specifying letters of support as one of those components. Applicants should include symbolic letters when conditions permit.

Substantive Partners

Symbolic partners are important; substantive partners are essential. Substantive partners are integrally involved in the project and its key activities. They contribute something of value to the program or are playing a role that is to be funded by the proposed grant. Their letters follow all of the same rules as symbolic letters but with one key addition—they must communicate their role and their commitment to the proposed program or project. To this end, they should state what grant funds they will receive through subcontracts from the applicant, what they will do with the money, and who in the organization will participate in what role. In other words, their roles must be clearly stated, not only for grant funds, but also for any match (cash or in-kind) they have agreed to provide. The match contribution can be counted toward federal match requirements in most cases, so these letters should be detailed. A poorly crafted letter would state, "We will provide $10,000 of in-kind match contributions to the proposed project." On the contrary, a solid letter of substantive support would state something like the following:

> Community Counseling Services has committed $10,000 of in-kind match to the proposed program. The executive director (Ms. Wilson) will contribute 5% of her time for project coordination activities over the 24-month implementation period ($50,000 × 5% = $2,500 × 2 years = $5,000). Additionally, two project coordinators (Mr. Holmes and Ms. Schmidt) will each invest

10 hours per week in career counseling for program participants (10 hours × 2 coordinators = 20 hours/week. 20 hours/week × $15.00/hour = $300/week. $300/week × 40 weeks = $12,000). This counseling has a value of $12,000, $5,000 of which will be contributed as in-kind match funds and $7,000 of which will be funded through grant funds, if awarded.

So, a good substantive letter communicates information not only about the program, the applicant, and the need for the program in the community but also the partner's role in the project. It goes without saying that the partner's letter of support should match the budget included with the grant as well as the program description provided in the grant narrative.

Soliciting Letters

The other common mistake that grant seekers and writers frequently make is to ask for letters of support without providing guidance to the organization on what the letter should include. The most successful method to generate effective letters (especially on a short time line) is to provide a template letter with boilerplate language that clearly communicates information about need for the program, the applicant's reputation and ability, and the benefits the proposed program will create. This should always be provided electronically so that it can be edited and given the author's personal touch, and the template should be appropriately addressed to the funding agency using the address included in the RFP or application packet. At bare minimum, an outline of the letter should be provided to these partners so that they will be sure to draft letters that will be meaningful in the grant decision process. An example of a template letter I once generated and provided to a city official is provided in Figure 3.6. The letter underwent minor edits, and the lack of specificity was overcome by delineating the city's contribution in the grant budget and narrative.

In the past, the boilerplate technique has resulted in similar or verbatim letters from partners; this could be considered suspect by funders, so it may be wise to draft different templates to provide each respective symbolic partner. Of course, some partners will want to edit the letter or draft their own, and this should always be encouraged so long as the key information is communicated. If the applicant has established strong working relationships with the partner, the partner organization may advise the grant writer to draft the letter and bring it to the partner to sign. I have had numerous community organizations provide me with their official letterhead so that I could draft the letters and fax, e-mail, or hand deliver letters to them for signature prior to submitting the application. These working relationships truly take trust and commitment and are invaluable to an organization integrally involved in grant seeking on the community's behalf.

External Partners

It was mentioned that some partners should be kept out of planning activities. The reasons are clear. Allowing too many chiefs and no workers in a planning group can devolve into disputes over roles and program direction such that no agreement can be reached. These external partners should be approached for their symbolic support if there is no role for

---

May 29, 2003

Processing and Control Branch
Office of Community Planning and Development
451 Seventh Street SW
Room 7255
Washington, DC 20410
Ladies and Gentlemen:

We are writing to convey enthusiastic support for the [Applicant Name] proposal for a HUD YouthBuild 2003 grant. We have participated in planning meetings with [Applicant Name] representatives and are committed to serve in an advisory capacity to assist and support the project. This initiative has great potential for the youth of the region for a program that will integrate education, technical assistance, and affordable housing programming.

A partnership between educators and housing providers in the region that will provide youth with the skills necessary to favorably direct their long-term career development strategy, as well as an opportunity to be responsive to the basic needs of their community for shelter, has extensive support across this county.

The combined efforts of the University and its partners, in support of personal development, leadership, and entrepreneurial education, along with on-site, direct construction work, will promote a comprehensive system designed to maximize outcomes for this at-risk population in our county.

The City of [City Name], through its nonprofit Housing Authority, pledges the support of three properties to allow YouthBuild students to participate in rehabilitation activities: [Property Names and Addresses]. Students will be granted access to these sites for rehabilitation work required by their half-time practicum. The appraised value of these properties is $7,500,000. Additionally, the City of [City Name] pledges in-kind support of staff time and associated fringe benefits to support marketing, recruitment, participant selection, project advisement, and on-site supervision of students. These services are valued at $107,000 over the 24-month period of the grant.

I strongly support this program and look forward to a favorable review by HUD. Thank you for your consideration of this proposal.

Sincerely,

[Name]
Mayor

FIGURE 3.6   Template Letter of Substantive Support to a City Official

them to play in the project as conceived. On the other hand, if there is a role for them to play, they must be approached delicately. A grant writer never wants a prospective partner to feel second rate as a result of knowledge that they were not invited to the advisory group. It is usually best to approach them with a program plan already in place, including an invitation to participate and an explanation of their role, but without an indication that the program idea is up for discussion. The benefits to them should have been thought out in advance, and the importance of their role should be communicated to persuade them to participate. The strategy employed in negotiation can be helpful here. Presenting the role, the benefits, and a request for in-kind match contributions may result in their participation. It is a good idea to keep some of the grant budget available to ply these partners if they are reluctant.

Sometimes it is best to keep program details in hat so as to prevent tipping off the prospective partner to the opportunity. Because so many funding programs are so highly competitive, tipping off another local organization to the funding that is available may lead to detrimental competition, not only from the applicant in the grant pool, but related competition for support from local partners.

Of course, the way these partners are treated in the present proposal will determine what role they will play in future projects, whether they will want to participate in future collaborations, whether they will become part of the core advisory group for future programs, and how successfully the program implementation will be carried out. Sometimes partners are reluctant, and sometimes existing partners pull out of the core group of participatory community organizations. The following example demonstrates each case.

Example: Developing Partnerships for a Housing Grant Program

Several years ago, while working in Appalachian Kentucky on community development projects, I found myself developing a housing program in a community where only two housing organizations existed—one was public (the city housing department) and the other was a private nonprofit corporation. The applicant organization I represented had no housing expertise or housing construction sites that could be drawn on to fulfill the grant requirements, so at least one community organization was absolutely essential to the application going forward. Two roadblocks were encountered, one anticipated and the other unanticipated.

The private nonprofit housing agency realized that its impact was being diffused as a result of collaboration on community projects. Grant programs that did not directly fund housing construction were seen as detracting from the organization's mission. As a result, they indicated to all community partners with which they had worked in the past that they would no longer be willing to participate in grant programs where they were not the applicant organization. This setback indicated two things: first, they had reengaged their mission and strategized about how to best achieve it; second, they had developed a lack of confidence and trust in their community partners—perhaps as a result of feeling cheated on past collaborative grant projects. This organization's abrupt withdrawal was a truly unanticipated setback in my organization's grant seeking endeavors.

The second organization, the city housing authority, was led by a local individual who had what might be the least appealing personality I have ever encountered. A political appointee, the Housing Director was loyal to the mayor and carried out his function in a no-nonsense, straightforward manner. He had to agree to participate in our project or the project could not proceed. Having not yet worked with or even met the Housing Director, our grants team first met with the city mayor, who was a regular symbolic and substantive partner on a wide variety of local development projects, to iron out the city's role. Because we anticipated problems from a relatively unsophisticated housing manager, we first presented the details of the arrangement to the mayor and received clear support from the city. Then, the Housing Authority was approached directly by the team of three grants team members—one a local whose name was known in the community, one who had drafted the program idea and proposal, and one who was a representative of the applicant organization with authority to commit to details of any arrangement that needed to be worked out in advance. This meeting was the most memorable of my grants career.

The Housing Director emphasized that he would not tolerate any problems in his operation, and that our proposal seemed to represent numerous opportunities for significant problems, including liability issues. He was generally an adversarial participant in the meeting, and his words still echo in my mind: "I don't want no problems here." As he made it clear that our project was an unnecessary inconvenience to his regular operations and that he could not agree to participate, the applicant's representative offered assurance that the applicant's insurance policy would enable them to assume liability for the project. Still reluctant, we then produced the letter of support from the city mayor—including its statement about the role of the city Housing Authority in the proposed project. Upon seeing that document, the Housing Director explained that he would sign our letter, but that he "didn't want no problems" and that the first time there was a problem, the project was finished as far as he was concerned. Reluctant partners can be difficult to persuade.

If this individual had been included in program planning activities, the project would never have come to fruition. In fact, it wasn't funded during that grant cycle anyway, but a slight revision the following year paid off. This brings up another important thought: it is always easier to negotiate partnership roles and to facilitate letters of support when you can produce the letters that state those roles and match amounts from the previous application cycle. As noted, having the responsible party's signature on the letter certainly helps to eliminate the problem of diminishing memory capacity over a year's time. An example of a request for support for such a resubmission appears as **Figure 3.7**.

There is a need for some secrecy in the grants enterprise to prevent losing a competitive advantage, but there is not room for outright dishonesty. Being forward and forthcoming with all potential partners about the program details will lead to stronger relationships and working arrangements among community organizations that require each other's support and assistance from time to time in most effectively pursuing their missions.

AGREE ON ROLES

There is no easy way to go about identifying and assigning program roles and responsibilities. This is why it is best to begin with an internal program approach that is filled out with amicable partners, and then nuanced to fit those partners' individual needs, desires, and available contributions. Involving external partners almost always involves a lot of work explaining the program, conveying the expected benefits to the partners, and negotiating roles and match contributions as well as share of the grant funds to be requested.

One thing remains constant, and you can expect it to be true in a great percentage of your own grant seeking efforts: each participant wants the greatest benefit with the least cost, and they will resist participation unless that ratio seems appropriate to them. Involving organizations that understand grants and the process of collaboration on grant projects will always be easier to do than involving organizations that lack such experience because these organizations will be less certain and hence less trusting about what they are being asked to do.

April 3, 2003

[Name], Director
[Organization Name]
[Address]
[City, State Zip Code]

Dear [Name]:

I write to express my sincere appreciation for your partnership in our previous application to HUD for a YouthBuild grant to serve high school dropouts in the [Community Name] area. As you may recall, this program seeks to identify, recruit, and assist high school dropouts to obtain their GED while simultaneously providing them with instruction and on-site construction training to improve low-income housing in the service area. Unfortunately, our previous application was not selected for funding in 2002; however, we have received encouraging feedback on reapplication, and we intend to resubmit the proposal in the 2003 funding cycle.

HUD has not yet released the 2003 Notice of Funding Availability, but the deadline was mid-May last year, and we anticipate a similar deadline this year. To resubmit the application and develop a successful program, we depend on your continued partnership and support. As such, we request that you provide a letter of support and financial commitment, just as you did last year, to the proposed YouthBuild project. Because our comments were favorable in the previous funding cycle, we ask that you contribute at the same level and type of support as before. To facilitate this process, I am enclosing a photocopy of the letter your organization provided last year. Please feel free to change the date and leave the letter exactly as it was written.

Please send your revised letter of support to:
  [Name, Title]
  [Address]
  [Organization]
  [City, State Zip Code]

Feel free to contact me at [Telephone Number] if you have any questions or concerns. Thank you for your continued support of this meaningful community service project. We will be in touch as the project develops.

Sincerely,

Jeremy L. Hall
Program Coordinator

FIGURE 3.7   Request for Revised Letter of Support in Subsequent Funding Cycle

AGREE ON CONTRIBUTIONS

The contributions a partner organization makes to a proposed grant project take several forms. They may be human resources, financial resources, or other in-kind contributions. Volunteer support can be given a value, as can participation by agency staff supported by own-source revenues. The expense of the time the partner organization invests in the project should be counted as match. If the purpose of the program is to create some public value or benefit through an innovative approach, then the only way to assess project effectiveness is to accurately measure costs and benefits to arrive at an estimate of the net benefit of the program. Partners' participation is a cost, even if it is not directly borne by the applicant organization. Contributions must be allowable under the conditions of the particular grant. Many would-be partners feel rejected when told that they are not allowed to contribute the support they have offered. This can hurt feelings and damage working relationships, so these negotiations require more than a little tact.

Another problem is incorporating what partners are willing to contribute even if it does not mesh perfectly with the program plan. Willingness to be flexible in accepting these contribution offers should extend to the point at which the offer is not reconcilable with the program purpose. That is, it either conflicts with the intended program, or it cannot be logically justified in the planned grant program. Another problem is the offer of services that are not novel or new. In essence, existing programs contributing to a proposed grant program, if of sufficient quantity, may give the proposal a stale flavor that could make it less appealing to the grant making agency or organization.

Finding ways to accommodate partners is a necessity, but grant writers should always be cautious to ensure that the perceived value of the proposal is as great as possible. Sometimes this may mean declining offers, negotiating with partners to offer something that is of greater value, or seeking additional external partners that seem to fit more closely with the proposed program and its goals.

OTHER PLANNING CONSIDERATIONS

Depending on an organization's mission and scope, along with agency submission limitations, it is sometimes possible to apply to the same federal program more than once on behalf of different beneficiaries or service areas. This means that a proposal developed for funding in one year for a 3-year project in County A can be recycled during the next funding cycle as the framework for a proposal to fund a 3-year project in County B. A good proposal—good in this case is measurable by its past success—should never be wasted.

The quality of the partnership arrangements you develop in your region or service area may also help you to circumnavigate requirements that limit the number of applications any single organization can submit in a given year. My project team and I were once able to facilitate just such an arrangement for a housing and youth training program. The university where I worked had a broad service area, portions of which were also served by regional community colleges that also happened to be eligible applicants for the program in question. Building on our unique, distinctive competencies, we were able to facilitate a plan that called for each organization to provide the same service roles in the program, with the same match contributions, at three different sites. My university was the lead applicant for one proposal and two community colleges served as lead applicants for each of the other two, although both of those proposals were written entirely in-house by myself and my project team. As it happened, one of the off-site projects was funded the first year, and the on-site project was funded within 2 years after some minor modifications to the original proposal. The lesson here is that quality material should never be wasted.

CONCLUSION

This chapter has investigated the approach to assembling an internal grants team for applicant organizations, suggesting a set of techniques to ensure that grant proposals are of the highest quality. It has also focused on the role of partner organizations in developing program ideas and in contributing significantly to proposals and program implementation when funded. These external roles are realized through workgroups or advisory committees as well as through other symbolic and substantive partnership agreements.

Partnership and partner roles, though tricky to negotiate, are essential to leveraging grant awards in many cases. These roles and agreements between the lead (applicant) organization and the various partners are manifested in the form of letters of support. Letters of support should always communicate as much information as possible about local need, the applicant, the proposed program and its expected benefits, and the capacity of the grant partnership to implement the proposed program successfully. Although few novice grant writers realize it, this essential piece of the puzzle can be strengthened through increased planning and preparation of template letters to assist the partners in providing the most useful information possible.

Chapter 4 and Chapter 5 turn to developing program proposals in a formal sense, beginning with the program budget and continuing with the program narrative. You should now have a clear understanding of grant types, where to find grants, how to assemble effective partnerships, and how to compile a grants team that will be most effective at generating winning proposals. The result of the steps to be covered in the following chapters can only be as strong as the foundation upon which they are built. So, as has been pointed out, an excellently written proposal for which the applicant is not eligible would be a complete waste. The same is true for a solid proposal with weak partnership arrangements to support and sustain the proposed implementation effort. Becoming a smart grant writer is much more important than becoming proficient at writing compelling proposals.

REFERENCES

Agranoff, Robert. 2006. Inside collaborative networks: Ten lessons for public managers. *Public Administration Review* 66(6 supplement): 56–65.

Agranoff, Robert and Michael McGuire. 1998. Multinetwork management: Collaboration and the hollow state in local economic policy. *Journal of Public Administration Research and Theory* 8(1): 67–91.

Boschken, Herman L. 1998. Institutionalism: Intergovernmental exchange, administration-centered behavior, and policy outcomes in urban agencies. *Journal of Public Administration Research and Theory* 8(4): 585–614.

Bryson, John M. 2004. *Strategic Planning for Public and Nonprofit Organizations: A Guide to Strengthening and Sustaining Organizational Achievement, 3rd Edition.* San Francisco: Jossey-Bass Publishers.

Lasker, Roz D., Elisa S. Weiss, and Rebecca Miller. 2001. Partnership synergy: A practical framework for studying and strengthening the collaborative advantage. *Milbank Quarterly* 79(2): 179–205.

Lubell, Mark, Mark Schneider, John T. Scholz, and Mihriye Mete. 2002. Watershed partnerships and the emergence of collective action institutions. *American Journal of Political Science* 46(1): 148–163.

Moore, Mark. 1995. *Creating Public Value.* Cambridge, MA: Harvard University Press.

Thomson, Ann Marie and James L. Perry. 2006. Collaboration processes: Inside the black box. *Public Administration Review* 66(6 supplement): 20–32.

CHAPTER 4

Developing the Grant Budget
and Budget Narrative

How important is the budget, anyway? In reality, it is central to the proposal and the reader's ability to understand the proposed program. How does your organization create its annual operating budget? Generally, existing programs are evaluated and increased or decreased, and new programs are considered alongside available revenues. Decisions are made about the best way to distribute the organization's scarce resources across departments, programs, or functions. For a grant making agency, the exercise extends into implementation. It is easy to determine how much will be needed for salaries and wages, supplies, and the usual expenses, and the agency can even estimate the amount of grant funding to be offered. A grant making agency can determine how much to spend on each grant program, but it has no way to anticipate what proposals it might receive, how many, or of what quality.

Consider grant making as a budgeting exercise taking place within the grant making agency. Why are granting agencies concerned with the quality of proposals they receive? They use program information supplied by the applicant to assess which proposal(s) will give them the greatest results with their available resources. This assessment necessarily combines the level of need, the quality of the proposed plan, the applicant's resources (human, financial, network, and so forth), and increasingly the likelihood of success determined by applicant capacity and past evidence of success. This is not unlike the goals inherent in the 1912 Taft Commission on Economy and Efficiency—those of obtaining the best return in program terms for the resources expended (Lee, Johnson, & Joyce 2008, p. 134). And V. O. Key (1940) called for comparing alternative program options on their merits. The First Hoover Commission argued that budgeting should be expressed in terms of the work to be completed (Lee et al. 2008, p. 135). Grant making is inherently a budgeting activity.

BUDGET: THE GRANT PROPOSAL'S CORE COMPONENT

Budgets have been an afterthought for many grant writers who invest long hours developing partnerships and writing narratives in striking prose. Unfortunately, this approach is usually met with failure in the funding process. The practice of hastily compiling a budget just before the submission deadline is irresponsible. It necessarily overlooks the fact that a budget embodies the proposed project and serves as a rubric against which to judge the proposal's realism and likelihood of success.

A more responsible approach is to draft the budget alongside the narrative, such that the cost of various activities and objects of expenditure can be weighed and prioritized as the proposal develops. The enterprise of grant budgeting is similar to any public/nonprofit budget process; there are various actors with interests in the proposed program and in the financial resources it may provide. As such, V. O. Key's (1940) question has substantial applicability: "On what basis shall it be decided to allocate x resources to activity A rather than activity B?"

Organizational complexity determines the facility with which budgets may be developed. In a small organization with little programmatic diversity, the process should be straightforward, involving only the grant writer and the agency director or manager (assuming the same person does not perform both roles, as is likely to be the case in many small nonprofit and government agencies). In an organization as large and complex as a major research university, various academic and applied research departments may be involved or may vie for an active role in the proposed program to ensure their position at the financial trough. Even this seemingly complex setting is fairly simple when compared to a multiorganizational collaboration. Involving multiple actors in the budget negotiation process is complicated not only by the complexity of organizing multiple actors with varied interests, but also by the allocation of required match dollars and the combination of multiple indirect cost rates and fringe benefit rates. Multiple actors in a partnership add sufficient complexity to program planning such that budgetary issues should be resolved as early in the planning process as possible.

Budget requirements vary across grantor organizations, and sometimes across RFPs within a grant making agency or organization. The greater the level of detail required, the greater the level of planning and thought is necessary, and the more mistakes are possible. Grant making organizations have come to rely on budgets as a mechanism of accountability, ensuring that funds are used as planned rather than being absorbed into the recipient's operating budget. Consequently, it is customary for budget forms and narratives to include substantial detail. This is especially true for large programs with large monetary awards.

Experience has taught many grant writers, including the author of this text, that Murphy's law applies to grant budgets—if it can go wrong, it usually will. And when an application is racing the clock for timely completion and submission, the budget is usually the one place where things noticeably fail to add up. (In reality, language is an art and differences in style are expected; math is a universally understood science and mistakes convey inadequacies.) This is exacerbated by the fact that multiple budget forms, narrative descriptions, and other documentation require financial information from different perspectives. Familiarity with spreadsheet programs such as Microsoft Excel is an absolute necessity for any grant writer. A team member with an affinity for detail and precision will be a true asset to budget development. Most of this chapter examines the components and construction of the grant budget and the budget narrative, but some focuses on using formulas in spreadsheet software programs to ensure accuracy and reduce the likelihood of adverse mistakes.

The budget reflects the planned commitment of resources—personnel, equipment, and supplies—to be used in implementing the proposed activity or activities. And more important, budgets justify the allocation of resources to the project by describing how they will be used and why they are needed. Grant budgeting is a core element of the proposal planning and development process. As with most public budgeting exercises, the planned activities must fall within the bounds of available revenue streams dictated by the funding source's funding cap or funding estimate on one hand and by the applicant's and partners' available resources on the other. As I discuss later, budgets can be compiled according to object code (the traditional line item budget), but they can also be compiled according to project activity (in the manner of program budgeting) and organizational division.

The chapter begins with a discussion of the importance of budgets to grant proposals. Differences in the *functional categories* that comprise the budget are discussed, including methods of computing *indirect cost, fringe benefits*, and travel expenses. The chapter then continues by examining the construction of a *budget template* that can be expanded (or contracted) for use with virtually any grant application. The *budget narrative* is a document whose name often incites confusion; two approaches to constructing the budget narrative are considered. To conclude, the budget is related backward to the planning and preparation stage, and the program narrative and evaluation plan, and also related forward to the performance management and evaluation processes to come.

BUDGET: THE PLAN IN NUMBERS

Why is the grant budget so important? Does the grantor really care how I plan to spend the money, as long as I achieve the proposed results? Although the grant narrative explains the process to be followed during implementation—the program strategy—the budget reflects what will be purchased and how the pieces will come together to generate the desired results.

There are several important things a budget can communicate. First, the grantor probably wants an idea about whether the grant funds are necessary for the program to come to fruition. At one extreme, this means the granting agency wants to ensure that it isn't simply providing duplicative funding for a program that would be carried out even absent the funding assistance. For example, is the grant buying out agency staff time, or is it providing new positions? The academic literature has examined the extent to which grant funds are fungible—that is, the extent to which a dollar of grant money can substitute for a dollar of local revenues (for example, Logan 1986; Nathan 1983; Stein 1984; Volden 1999; and Zampelli 1986). The arguments about fungibility have led researchers to suggest tightening the strings in grant programs. Hence, Federal Revenue Sharing ended in 1986, and categorical project grants largely took the place of such flexible funding streams. These new competitive grant structures have much more stringent limitations on the use of funds to ensure that federal priorities are being met. The requirement of matching funds forces local investment in the project as well, preventing grant funds from substituting for local revenues.

Second, the grantor is probably interested in whether its funds are needed to provide core project activities or if the funding will be "icing the cake" with luxuries such as new office space, excessive conference travel, or laptop computers. Third, the grantor will examine the budget to clearly determine the nature of the program as a sort of check on the narrative description. Program narratives can paint a very compelling picture of the need for a program and its proposed function, but budgets do not lie. The proposed use of budgeted funds will reveal which components of the proposal are truly needed and how any awarded grant funds will truly be used. (As is discussed later, accountability for actual expenditures is maintained through reporting and evaluations.) A grantor may view the proposal holistically without much concern for the role it (and its money) is playing in the program, but many grantors will want to know that their money is the determining element of success. Budgets clearly reveal each participant's role—the requesting agency, the funding agency, and each partner. To this end, many funding agencies may elect to negotiate the features of the proposed budget (often with reductions for seemingly unnecessary items of expenditure) prior to making a grant award.

Fourth, funding agencies place limitations on the objects of expenditure that are allowable, and this is especially true of government agencies. Budgets will be examined to determine whether the proposed project contains any such limitations explicitly delineated and prohibited in the request for proposals or the program guidelines. Incorporating unallowable items in budgets is risky behavior, so it is best to understand the funding limitations before writing the grant budget or the proposal narrative. If an unallowable cost is budgeted, the proposal may be disqualified. If not disqualified, the item will certainly not be allowed to be purchased. If it is purchased, the grant making entity will not make reimbursement if it is made known. And of course, if reimbursement is made inadvertently, the recipient may be forced to repay the funds expended for that item. One example of a common unallowable cost is alcoholic beverages. Most public and nonprofit organizations already disallow such purchases, but if they are purchased with meals during professional travel, they may go unnoticed. A federal grant audit might have cause to examine itemized meal receipts, the effect of which would be discovery of the forbidden expenditure.

Fifth, budgets are program management tools. A budget is almost always segmented by program year or quarter to provide a map of the necessary funding obligations and their timing. Budgets show the intended use of funds, but also when they will be used. A grant application requesting funds for a 3-year program will raise eyebrows if the funds for personnel are all budgeted in the first quarter of the first year. A reviewer or program officer would be led to ask whether the applicant intended a project with questionable sustainability or whether the applicant is inept in budget preparation. Either question is a negative mark on the application quality and lessens the likelihood of program funding. Unlike most public budgeting processes, the majority of grant budgets are not open to revision, negotiation, or explanation during the review process; they are given simple up or down votes by program staff or peer reviewers.

Finally, grant budgets may be used as instruments of accountability. Budgets can be reviewed in proposed-to-actual comparisons to measure implementation, its timeliness, and completeness. They can also indicate important nodes around which to develop the evaluation plan and determine key program evaluation measures to collect. Each of these uses is important independently in that it provides a basis for grantor judgment regarding the quality of a proposal.

Perhaps more important than these independent effects is the interconnected nature of these criteria with other major components of the grant application. All of the pieces must align, and the logic of a proposal must ring true throughout each of its component pieces. It is thus very important to ensure that the budget, in both substance and timing, corresponds directly to the proposal narrative and to the evaluation plan. Those evaluating a proposal will certainly view the pieces collectively, so the project team must be certain that their independent work follows the overarching program strategy to develop a document that leaves no questions in the reviewers' minds as they evaluate the complete proposal.

BUDGET PREPARATION PROCESS

Now that I have introduced the various important roles that budgets play in grant proposals, I turn to budget preparation as a part of the larger proposal development process. I first examine timing of the process and then present the technical features of developing the budget and the budget narrative. Examples of common budget templates are provided and their utility demonstrated. A good starting point, again, is to review the rules in the request for proposals regarding allowable and unallowable costs, maximum amounts, and other limitations that should be adhered to. If the proposal is to a federal agency, the standard federal budget form, SF-424A, provides a template of appropriate categories that should be used. Other funding agencies may elect to use a budget with slightly different categories or labels. For the most part, the federal budget categories are sufficient.

When should the budget be developed? The organization of this text intentionally places budget development prior to the program narrative for rational reasons. Just as the budget is the most important policy document of the federal government, the budget embodies the program strategy for a grant proposal. A quick read of the budget and budget narrative should reveal the program theory that is expected to produce the desired result of the grant. As noted earlier, words are art, but math is science. For that reason, it is usually easier to sketch out a general strategy, build a concrete budget to support it, and then build the narrative around your spending plan. After all, a grant application is all about documenting how the requested funds will be used. The narrative can be adjusted as necessary to better represent the spending plan. The spending plan (budget) itself may be harder to adjust to fit an existing narrative because of the limitations and constraints around which it must be built—and particularly so if grant funds and matching funds are distributed among partner organizations. But the narrative can be used to explain away most any uncertainty resulting from the budget, so long as both are well crafted.

As implied previously, another reason for addressing budgets early in the process is the negotiation that must take place between potential partners. Each partner will be interested in their share of funds as well as their responsibilities regarding effort and match requirements. With a set amount of funding, a potential partner can determine specifically how much service it will provide, and how much match it can contribute in what forms. These can be budgeted firmly, and the proposal narrative can then be written around them. Consider the futility of doing this in reverse: An applicant crafts a lucid proposal narrative describing a magnificent program to be used in the grant application. Into that narrative, the applicant has written proposed roles for each of several important partner organizations (or departments within an organization). A budget is developed, and then partners are consulted. Only now, the partners are displeased with the amount they are expected to provide in match and the level of service they are expected to perform for the budgeted amount. Now the budget must be amended, but the narrative must also be rewritten to elucidate the changes in partner roles from those mapped out in the original draft. It is best to develop the budget first, negotiate any external contributions to the budget, and begin writing the proposal narrative with a relatively firm budget in place.

Does this mean that the draft budget will remain unchanged? Of course it does not. Budgets are often revisited and revised during this process. Negotiations are often required to establish the distribution of funds in a manner that is equitable, or at least agreeable, to all of the partners involved. Usually, the first draft is a bit too idealistic, resulting in proposed spending well above the allowable maximum grant award for the program. Budgeting then becomes a task of cutting excess, trimming back unnecessary components, and manipulating partner roles to fit into the constraints imposed by the granting agency's limitations. On a side note, it is often easy to get partners to agree to perform roles that will be reimbursed from the grant; it is more difficult to obtain commensurate match commitments from them to meet match requirements or expectations.

Another source of budget adjustment is often the market. Prices for some goods may change during the proposal process, requiring an adjustment to particular budgeted amounts. This usually means a price increase for some items and commensurate reduction in other components of the spending plan. For example, a police department may be applying for funds to purchase GIS software to improve their accuracy and response time. The software company may release a new and improved version during the application period. A grant budget needs to accurately reflect the actual price of the goods included, so the amount must be increased for that item, and probably decreased for other items in the proposal. Failure to accurately reflect the price in the proposal will result in frustration if the grant is awarded with the old price listed in the budget. If that were the case, the price difference would have to come from other line items at that time through a budget transfer (to be discussed in Chapter 9) or from other revenue sources.

Some adjustments will occur after the narrative has been written because things can change unexpectedly. Partners sometimes withdraw from projects. Prices change. The budget may need to be adjusted until the final draft is ready to submit. The key point is that several minor changes can be easily accommodated in the narrative, whereas lots of big changes cannot. To develop a superior, clear, concise narrative, it is best to have a workable budget platform on which to build.

A final reason for developing the budget first in the process is the presence of any internal (or external) approval processes that may be required by your organization or your partner organizations. Approval processes are almost always more concerned with anticipated financial contributions your organization will have to provide than they are the specific nature of activities to be performed. The budget approval is the one that counts—it reflects commitments the organization will make in submitting the application. Universities usually require review of grant budgets by grants officers prior to approving the application for submission to the grant making agency. Nonprofit agencies may have a designated director or accounting officer to perform this function, or they may require review and approval by the board of directors or an executive committee thereof. Once again, with an approved budget, the narrative can be perfected over the remaining time. However, a well-written narrative may be a waste of time if the budget it accompanies fails to meet with the approval of internal gatekeepers or external partner organizations' boards and officers. In such a case, the budget would need to be adjusted, but the narrative would again be subject to revision. It is best to nail down the budget prior to investing serious time in the proposal narrative.

THE BUDGET DOCUMENT

Whereas most budgets begin with an estimation of available revenue, the grant budget focuses exclusively on expenditures. After all, a grant is about obtaining money from a single source, right? In fact, this is not generally the case. Grant funding is one revenue source, and the increased requirement for the use of matching funds over time has increased the need to identify own-source revenues to apply as match. Many programs have multiple funding sources of which grant funding is an important part. In essence, then, the budget submitted with a grant proposal communicates two things—the need for and proposed use of requested grant funding, and the combination of all funding sources that will be applied to the program or project and how the requested grant funds fit into the picture. In large organizations, it is the commitment of resources that has led to institutional requirements that grant proposals be approved prior to submittal. The identification of own-source revenues and commitments from partner organizations is a central part of the budget preparation exercise. Often, very large projects combine grant funds from multiple sources across federal and state agencies in addition to local match funds.

An applicant can make two types of commitments to a project that are included in the program budget: cash and in-kind contributions. To avoid complexity associated with multiorganizational partnerships, I refer to these commitments collectively as *local match*. Local match may be in the form of cash—that is, the applicant's expenditure of funds to support the project. Payment of personnel salaries and wages, purchasing supplies, or reimbursement for travel expenses are all examples of cash match when the applicant pays for these resources with its own funds. In-kind match occurs when something of value is provided, but no funds are expended to provide the resource. If either type of match is permitted, it is usually not necessary to distinguish them in the grant budget. If the granting agency permits only cash match, or limits the amount of in-kind match relative to cash match, both types of match contributions should be accounted separately (for example, in separate columns) in the budget document.

A very common source of in-kind match in social and community programs is the value of time contributed by volunteers. Volunteer effort is a valuable component of many public and nonprofit programs, and it takes unique capacity to manage and coordinate volunteers (Frederickson & London 2000). Although it is difficult to estimate how many volunteers will serve, or how much time they will commit, if this resource is to be a component of the program, it should be accounted for. What is volunteer time worth? There are different ways to estimate the value of a volunteer. One way is to estimate what you would pay a regular staff person to perform the tasks for which the volunteer is responsible. Of course, you must include in this computation the fringe benefits a paid person would receive as well. A preferable way is to utilize existing estimates of the average value of volunteer time.

The Independent Sector (www.independentsector.org/programs/research/volunteer _time.html) produces annual estimates of the value of volunteer time by state (**Table 4.1**).

TABLE 4.1   Value of Volunteer Time by State and Rank, 2006

States, Alphabetically	2006	States, Rank Ordered	2006
Alabama	$16.33	Puerto Rico	$10.21
Alaska	$18.65	Montana	$13.51
Arizona	$18.17	South Dakota	$13.72
Arkansas	$14.63	Mississippi	$14.08
California	$21.97	North Dakota	$14.27
Colorado	$20.08	Arkansas	$14.63
Connecticut	$25.75	West Virginia	$14.70
Delaware	$21.28	Virgin Islands	$14.85
District of Columbia	$30.10	Idaho	$14.90
Florida	$17.38	Maine	$15.25
Georgia	$18.77	New Mexico	$15.35
Hawaii	$16.52	Nebraska	$15.37
Idaho	$14.90	South Carolina	$15.52
Illinois	$21.09	Iowa	$15.59
Indiana	$16.83	Oklahoma	$15.68
Iowa	$15.59	Utah	$15.97
Kansas	$16.64	Kentucky	$16.07
Kentucky	$16.07	Vermont	$16.07
Louisiana	$16.95	Alabama	$16.33
Maine	$15.25	Hawaii	$16.52
Maryland	$20.47	Kansas	$16.64
Massachusetts	$24.29	Wyoming	$16.69
Michigan	$19.29	Wisconsin	$16.76
Minnesota	$19.46	Indiana	$16.83
Mississippi	$14.08	Louisiana	$16.95
Missouri	$17.19	North Carolina	$17.14
Montana	$13.51	Missouri	$17.19
Nebraska	$15.37	Tennessee	$17.29
Nevada	$17.98	Oregon	$17.33
New Hampshire	$19.77	Florida	$17.38
New Jersey	$23.62	Ohio	$17.53
New Mexico	$15.35	Rhode Island	$17.81
New York	$26.18	Nevada	$17.98
North Carolina	$17.14	Arizona	$18.17
North Dakota	$14.27	Alaska	$18.65
Ohio	$17.53	Georgia	$18.77
Oklahoma	$15.68	Pennsylvania	$18.86
Oregon	$17.33	Michigan	$19.29
Pennsylvania	$18.86	Minnesota	$19.46
Rhode Island	$17.81	Washington	$19.53
South Carolina	$15.52	New Hampshire	$19.77
South Dakota	$13.72	Texas	$19.89
Tennessee	$17.29	Colorado	$20.08
Texas	$19.89	Virginia	$20.08
Utah	$15.97	Maryland	$20.47
Vermont	$16.07	Illinois	$21.09
Virginia	$20.08	Delaware	$21.28
Washington	$19.53	California	$21.97
West Virginia	$14.70	New Jersey	$23.62
Wisconsin	$16.76	Massachusetts	$24.29
Wyoming	$16.69	Connecticut	$25.75
Puerto Rico	$10.21	New York	$26.18
Virgin Islands	$14.85	District of Columbia	$30.10

Source: Independent Sector 2009. Reprinted with special permission of Independent Sector. A nonprofit, nonpartisan coalition of charities, foundations, and corporate philanthropy programs whose mission is to advance the common good by leading, strengthening, and mobilizing the independent sector. www.independentsector.org.

It employs a relatively straightforward methodology that uses data from the U.S. Bureau of Labor Statistics to calculate the average hourly earnings of all production and nonsupervisory workers on private nonfarm payrolls; it then increases this average by 12% to reflect the value of fringe benefits. The national average in 2007 was $19.51/hour—a substantial amount if the program employs volunteers for a significant amount of service. Although it may be tempting to overestimate in-kind contributions to generate adequate match dollars, this should be avoided in practice. Accurate, or at least realistic, estimates will limit future frustration because actual match must be documented for periodic reports and audit purposes.

In the way of an in-kind match example, the applicant may propose to provide office space for the program in its existing facility free of charge. If the rental value of office space is $10/square foot, then a 10-foot by 10-foot office space (100 square feet) would have a value of $12,000/year (100 feet × $10/foot = $1,000/month; $1,000/month × 12 months = $12,000). This is not a cash contribution but is a valuable resource that should be accounted for as in-kind match in the program budget—particularly if match is required.

As a result of the occupied office space, the program will also be utilizing utilities paid by the applicant organization. Utilities are arguably a cash contribution because funds change hands to provide them. However, calculating the appropriate amount can be tricky. Separate electricity meters or pay toilets seem too great a burden to impose on a temporary program office. A common method of arriving at such costs is to evaluate the total utility usage for a period, and then compute a ratio that reflects the program office's portion of utilities consumed. So, if the office (say, 1,000 square feet) is 10% of the total usable space in the building, a fair estimate of the program's utility usage is 10% of electricity, water, sewer, and gas bills, if applicable. It is not possible to accurately predict utility usage or costs, but sound estimates can be arrived at by comparing similar periods during the previous year. So, if the program office is to be occupied all year, the monthly average is a reasonable estimate. If the office is only to be occupied from January to June, those months' past utility costs should be used as an estimate. (Please note that both office space and utilities customarily are elements included in administrative overhead, otherwise referred to as indirect costs. If your organization has a negotiated indirect cost rate, then these elements only would be budgeted separately under unique circumstances.)

Both cash and in-kind match contributions are included in the grant budget. It is useful to maintain them in distinct columns on the budget spreadsheet so that they can be easily calculated. Some programs require match without regard for its source or type; others limit the amount of in-kind match to ensure that the recipient leverages the grant funds with new expenditure of local funds.

Another consideration to keep in mind in preparing to develop a budget is the timing. All applications require a budget that reflects total project costs, but some also require annual budgets that reflect the actual amount expended in each program year. For short programs, usually up to about 18 months, the program may ask for quarterly or monthly budget estimates to reflect when funds will be used in each functional category. The logical method for developing the budget is to start with the least common denominator, whether month, quarter, or year, and build the total program budget by summing the components. In a case where a great deal of the program effort can be provided through local match resources, it might be feasible to start with an aggregate budget that meets the program requirements, and then dissect it into annual components in a way that better suits the applicant organization's needs.

For example, an applicant may have several ongoing grant programs, some of which will come to an end at different times during the period for the new proposed program. The total requested funds could be allocated to pay staff salaries in later years after the ongoing programs come to an end when the organization has greater need for resources to sustain its workforce. Either way, it is absolutely essential that the budget components sum to the totals, in each category, on the total project budget document. Spreadsheets that link multiple sheets using formulas are a very effective way to avoid mistakes. Of course, complicated formulas can also be the source of the mistake, so budgets should be checked by calculator to ensure their accuracy.

Federal grant awards will generally request an anticipated cash flow for the program by quarter. Obviously, such a request must be based on the budget documents. This further highlights the utility of quarterly budget periods during budget planning, where possible. These estimates are used to facilitate apportionment of federal funds. Congress apportions agency allotments over the quarters of the fiscal year to prohibit agencies from overspending their resources in any particular quarter. Grant making agencies have to turn to their grantees for these estimates because they do not actually control when expenditures are incurred. Quarterly estimates of expenses are used to keep programs on track and to estimate agency cash flow needs.

Table 4.2 demonstrates the relationships between categories and years in the budget documents. Each year's total spending in all functional categories can be summed to arrive at the total grant budget for that year (column relationships). Similarly, the spending in any functional category, such as personnel or travel, can be summed across years to obtain the project total (row relationships). In this way, by using multiple linked budgets, it is possible to compare the amount of spending in each time period to the others, and it is possible to evaluate the distribution of funds across functional spending categories. For example, if the proposed program begins with a pilot study and then a phased implementation, Y1 may

TABLE 4.2   Relationship Between Linked Budget Components and Summaries

Total Personnel	= Y1 Personnel	+ Y2 Personnel	+ Y3 Personnel
Total Fringe Benefits	= Y1 Fringe Benefits	+ Y2 Fringe Benefits	+ Y3 Fringe Benefits
Total Travel	= Y1 Travel	+ Y2 Travel	+ Y3 Travel
Total Equipment	= Y1 Equipment	+ Y2 Equipment	+ Y3 Equipment
Total Supplies	= Y1 Supplies	+ Y2 Supplies	+ Y3 Supplies
Total Contractual	= Y1 Contractual	+ Y2 Contractual	+ Y3 Contractual
Total Construction	= Y1 Construction	+ Y2 Construction	+ Y3 Construction
Total Other	= Y1 Other	+ Y2 Other	+ Y3 Other
Project Subtotal	**= Y1 Subtotal**	**+ Y2 Subtotal**	**+ Y3 Subtotal**
Total Indirect Costs	= Y1 Indirect Costs	+ Y2 Indirect Costs	+ Y3 Indirect Costs
Project Total	**= Year 1 Total**	**+ Year 2 Total**	**+ Year 3 Total**

represent 20% of the total budget, Y2 may represent 30%, and Y3 may represent 50% (notice that the percentages for all budget years sum to 100%). Or, alternatively, a proposed program with immediate implementation and consistent service delivery would see equal 33.3% distributions in each of the three budget years. If we consider the ratio of personnel to total project costs, we can get a picture of the extent to which the proposal emphasizes human resources. So, if personnel and fringe are 95% of the total project costs, it is clear that the program is focused on providing human resources. If travel and supplies are emphasized in the program, they should have a higher proportion of the total project costs across budget years.

Basically, there is no right or wrong proportion of funding across functional budget categories. A good heuristic is to examine whether an outside reviewer might consider the proportion in each category to be logical for the proposed project. Another heuristic is to examine the proportions across functional categories to determine whether any raise red flags that might make the funding agency suspicious or reluctant to fund the project. A well-balanced distribution of funding is usually preferable, unless the agency or program seeks to provide a narrowly focused basket of goods and services. For example, the Clinton administration sought to put more police officers on the street; these programs emphasized personnel. The Bill and Melinda Gates Foundation provided libraries with technology resources, so those program budgets emphasized computing equipment (which may be classified as supplies or equipment, depending on the grant seekers' and grant maker's accounting system and program requirements).

BUDGET BASICS: CATEGORIES AND OBJECTS OF EXPENDITURE

Budget categories are important not only to clearly differentiate what items will be purchased, but for setting up the organization's accounts for the funded program. Budget categories correspond to common objects of expenditure that have unique object codes in operating budgets. Hence, when the federal government or other granting agency provides spending authority through a grant award, the amounts in each category will be loaded into a budget account to provide spending up to the allowed amount. In the case of the federal government, the common budget categories for non-construction programs can be found on form SF-424A under "6. Object Class Categories." They include Personnel, Fringe Benefits, Travel, Equipment, Supplies, Contractual, Construction, Other, and Indirect Costs. These global categories are sufficient to include most all necessary program expenditures. Of course, the specific budget requirements of the funding agency or the program in question should be followed for all budget documents. Some federal programs require additional budget forms that address other requirements unique to the program in question. Construction programs (SF-424C) include a unique set of expenditure classification categories that permit greater specificity and better represent the components that comprise typical construction projects. These categories include Administrative and legal expenses; Land, structures, rights-of-way, appraisals, etc.; Relocation expenses and payments; Architectural and engineering fees; Project inspection fees; Site work; Demolition and removal; Construction; Equipment; and Miscellaneous. These standard functional budget categories are listed in **Figure 4.1.**

Non-Construction Project Object Classifications	**Construction Project Object Classifications**
Personnel	Administrative and Legal Expenses
Fringe Benefits	Land, Structures, Rights-of-Way, Appraisals, etc.
Travel	Relocation Expenses and Payments
Equipment	Architectural and Engineering Fees
Supplies	Project Inspection Fees
Contractual	Site Work
Construction	Demolition and Removal
Other	Construction
Indirect Costs	Equipment
	Miscellaneous

FIGURE 4.1   Standard Federal Functional Budget Categories
Source: SF-424A and SF-424C.

You should always use the budget categories provided by the funding agency as the basis for your detailed program budget. The subtotals from each category in your detailed budget will be transferred to the official budget form(s) used by the agency to which you are applying. In the case of the federal government, the categories discussed in the following section are generally sufficient. It goes without saying that the budget detail information you compile, the budget forms you complete, and the program narrative should match. They should provide identical information in every instance throughout the application.

BUDGETING FOR COMMON COST ITEMS

This section presents methods for estimating the cost items standard to most grant program budgets. The principles are the same for estimating most items' cost, whether the categories are those used in the standard federal budget forms or not. There are two general types of costs that must be confronted in developing a grant budget—those under our control and those that are beyond our control. We are better able to estimate the former than the latter. I consider each of the usual functional categories in turn, providing examples and factors to consider with each.

Personnel

Personnel costs include salaries and wages that are directly associated with the program or project to be funded. This category includes only individuals who will be on the organization's payroll, not those who will be paid for through contract. Direct involvement generally means a meaningful role will be played in managing or implementing the program. Generally, administrators such as accountants and administrative associates are not included because they constitute administrative overhead and are included in the organization's indirect cost rate.

There are two types of payroll expenses—those related to existing staff that will be allocated to the project, and those related to new positions to be created as a result of the grant. For existing positions, we already know the annual salary or hourly wage and can use it as the basis of our budget estimates. It is customary to add from 2% to 5% onto existing salary rates for each future year to account for anticipated merit or cost of living increases. Failure to budget for such increases will result in too little budgeted grant funding available to meet the actual expense. So, if a program director in your institution earns $30,000 annually, and your raise pool is expected to be 5%, you would use $31,500 as the basis for the program director's salary in the first grant program year. The year following, the salary would be $33,075.

The second group of payroll expenses—those for positions that do not currently exist—is subject to estimation. On one hand, you can budget any amount for a position's salary, from very low to very high. On the other hand, the higher the salary budgeted, the more competent the individual you will recruit to fill it. Knowledge of the local labor market is also useful to guide budget estimates. If the market is strong, and unemployment is low, it will take a higher salary to recruit someone to fill the position. If the market is weak and there are large numbers of unemployed or underemployed individuals available for work, lower salaries may be acceptable and sufficient.

It is not necessary to utilize an employee 100% for grant-related duties. That is, employee time can be divided into work on various projects and programs. The proportion of time that will be spent on the grant project by any single person will be difficult to estimate with precision, but an effort should be made to provide a reasonable estimate. In the case of salaried workers, we estimate effort as a percentage of time. A position dedicated to the project full time with no other responsibilities would devote 100% of its time to the grant. This amount could be paid for with grant funds or match funds; the important point is that this position's time is spent only on the funded program. So, 100% of $31,500 is $31,500. If the worker will spend only 50% of her time on the grant program and 50% on other organizational functions, the total budget would be 50% of $31,500, or $15,750. Again, it is not important whether the funds will come from the grant or from the organization as match, so long as 50% of the employee's effort is spent on project activities.

For hourly workers, we use the number of hours dedicated to the project to estimate their cost. There are 2,080 hours in a work year, of which 80 hours (two weeks) are customarily taken as vacation. If an employee is budgeted to work more than 40 hours per week, it may be necessary to use a higher hourly overtime rate for those additional hours. State employment law should be consulted to determine what requirements exist, and what the rate of pay must be. Many states also have minimum wage laws that require hourly wages to be higher than the federal minimum wage. Budgeting for hourly staff should be done with these restrictions and limitations in mind. For a full-time data entry specialist making $12/hour and dedicated only to the program, we would budget $24,960 ($12 × 2,080). An existing specialist who works ad hoc on programs as needed could be budgeted at any amount of hours. Moreover, if there is more than one employee with the same job title, duties, and salary, it is not necessary to budget each employee; instead we can budget for the total hours of services required. So, if we have a data entry division with five such workers, we could budget up to 10,400 hours of service from the same line item for a given year as long as the basis is clearly described in the budget narrative.

These salary and personnel expenses should not be budgeted with the expectation that they can be used to show local match for the program whether or not they are actually used. It is unethical to claim that an employee worked on a project when he did not. In practice, as a grant manager, if you anticipate more than a 5% difference in budgeted time for any employee and her actual expended time, you should probably initiate a budget revision. There are ways of tracking actual effort, such as timesheets and effort reports. Many programs will require you to disclose your management capacity in the application. That capacity includes the ability to track and monitor employee time spent on project activities. No employee should ever be budgeted to spend more than 100% of a 2,080-hour work year on grant projects. In other words, it is not possible to receive three grants that each budget the same employee for 50% effort. (Unless the individual works 60 hours per week, it is not possible to attain 150% effort.) In addition to being unethical, audits could reveal such activities, resulting in legal problems as well as ethical ones.

Fringe Benefits

Fringe benefits include any benefit employees are provided by virtue of their employment at the expense of their employer. Most employees are subject to federal Social Security and Medicare withholding, so their employers pay 7.65% of their wages to the federal government; these are the most basic fringe benefits. (Some states operate pension systems that allow employees to opt out of social security withholding.) Other benefits include health insurance, dental insurance, vision insurance, workers' compensation, accidental death and disability insurance, tuition benefits, day care, and so on. For each of these, the actual amount expended per employee should be used to estimate and budget costs. Of course, from year to year these costs fluctuate—usually upward. So, it is wise to build in an expected increase in premiums or other costs paid by the employer. Fringe may be taken as a percentage of salaries and wages if it is rate-based in the institution. If an institutional fringe rate is not available, one could be estimated by dividing total payroll by total fringe costs for the previous year. So, if the fringe benefit rate is 22.1%, and salaries budgeted for the grant total $1 million, then the fringe benefit cost would be $221,000. Salaries and fringe are usually linked in grant budgets such that a dollar of salaries paid from any source would see the resulting fringe benefit paid from that source as well.

If fringe is calculated on an actual cost basis rather than a percentage, then each component of the fringe cost should be itemized on its own line in the budget. This method becomes much more difficult to calculate when employees spend only a portion of their time on the grant program. It then becomes necessary to calculate each employee's cost by multiplying each fringe cost component by the proportion of annual effort devoted to the grant. So, if an employer pays $1,000 per year for an employee's health insurance and the employee is budgeted to spend 40% of his time on the grant program, then that fringe item for that employee would cost $400. As you will see, the use of formulas in the budget spreadsheet alleviates much of the difficulty with these cost estimations.

Travel

Travel can be itemized in various ways in a grant budget. You could budget for particular trips, estimating the cost for each. That line item might read: "Site Visit Trips | 16 trips @ $400 | $6,400." Using this format, trips of different types or purposes might be listed separately. So, you might also have a line item such as: "Conference Trips | 4 trips @ $750 | $3,000." Although this approach better describes the use of the funds, it lacks functional clarity. What will the money be spent on during each trip? Mileage costs? Food? Lodging? To clarify these questions and add transparency to the budget, I prefer to list objects of expenditure as line items in the travel section. Common categories include mileage, airline tickets, lodging, ground transportation, parking, registration fees, and per diem. Other objects may be applicable depending on the situation in question. I opt for this format because the project narrative should explain the purpose of any budgeted travel. If it is still not sufficient, an additional budget narrative can further clarify and justify the use.

How do you estimate travel expenses? With global energy prices in such dramatic fluctuation, it is often difficult to guess precisely. Of course, it is not prudent to pad the budget with inflated costs either. To estimate mileage, two options are available. First, you can use your organization's official mileage reimbursement rate. If your organization does not have such a rate, the IRS official rate for business travel can be used. Of course, it is subject to change as well. In this case, you may want to estimate a few more trips than necessary or a few more miles per trip to allow for unexpected increases in mileage rates during the life of the project.

Airfares are no different. The prices fluctuate, and in the current environment, they usually increase as well. However, airlines do publish fares between known destinations. The best approach is to use an airline's website, or a travel website, to search for tickets during the period you will be travelling. Tickets may only be booked a year in advance, and prices may change during the period from grant submission to the award notification. It is best to round up the prices by a small percentage to allow for price changes. Or, if you will be buying tickets to several destinations, round up the average price per ticket. So, if I find three tickets for future trips priced at $249, $400, and $540, my budget might read: "Airfare | 3 trips @ $425 | $1,275." Technically, that estimate is higher than the average ticket price ($396.33), but it is still a reasonable estimate because it falls within the range between the lowest- and highest-priced ticket. This estimate leaves some flexibility for price changes, but a keen reviewer checking prices online would find that the price estimate is not exorbitantly high.

Lodging is also straightforward. You can check hotel prices in destinations you know you will visit prior to estimating the price per night. Of course, rates are based on the day of week and season, and they are also subject to change. The same estimation process applies as with airfare. The estimated price for each location multiplied by the number of nights will give you a total cost; you can back into the average rate per night by again dividing by the number of nights. For example, rooms may cost $125/night in city 1, where you will spend three nights; rooms in city 2 are $190/night and you will stay four nights, and rooms in city 3 cost $160/night, and you will stay there five days across two trips. So, we get $375, $760, and $800 (or $1,935 total) for 12 nights. The real average is $161.25/night. A line item in the grant budget might read: "Lodging | 12 nights @ $170 | $2,040." This round estimate leaves about $100 in flexibility while it is still a fair estimate of costs. Again, it falls within the range bracketed by the lowest and highest nightly rates.

Equipment

There is no way to estimate the cost of specialty equipment except to negotiate with its manufacturer. Competing suppliers may be asked to provide bids or estimates. They will respond more favorably if they have adequate time to prepare such an estimate. A midnight request before the grant is to be submitted will not generate an accurate or reasonable price in most cases—if it generates an estimate at all. Non-specialty equipment (off-the-shelf or off-the-lot items) will have a retail market price that can be obtained by checking with the manufacturer's website or a salesperson. In these conversations, it is also a good idea to ask about expected price increases in the next year. In most cases, the lowest price for adequate equipment should be used. In the way of a metaphor, proposing to buy a Cadillac (or Mercedes) with grant funds when a Nissan (or Ford) will do the job is a sure way to see that the grant application is rejected. There must be a clear determining reason with which any informed reviewer would concur when a luxury item is included in a program budget.

Supplies

Supplies are defined differently by differing organizations. There are two things to keep in mind when budgeting supplies for your project. First, make sure the items you are considering aren't included in the administrative overhead charge. Charging your standard indirect cost rate and billing for supplies your rate covers constitutes double dipping, is unethical, and is probably illegal. If it's obvious, it could mean a rejected proposal; if not, it could mean trouble during implementation. Generally, this means the supply items you budget are specifically necessary for your project and will only be used by it—they will not contribute to the overhead of the organization in any other way. Supplies are often thought of as office supplies—paper, pens, and paperclips. In reality, the category is much broader. Supplies are the things needed to make the project work that have a price tag *under* a certain limit and are expendable (they have a short useful life). For example, the federal government generally treats items under $5,000 as supplies, and items $5,000 and higher as equipment (OMB Circular A-21, 60).

The rationale behind this distinction comes from capital budgeting. Any item with a useful life longer than one year and a large price tag should be budgeted as equipment. The federal government is unique among U.S. governments because it has a unified budget, the size of which makes it unnecessary to plan and budget for large capital projects separately. All states and most other municipalities and public entities have capital budgets and engage in capital improvement planning, following Statement 34 of the Government Accounting Standards Board (GASB). The rationale for a price floor for equipment is that big ticket items would place undue burden on the annual operating budget of the organization—they would add lumps to an otherwise incremental system. The large prices mean planning needs to be done to pay for such items over multiple years, either with debt or through a capital investment fund. The second component is inventory control. Items with longer lives and large prices will be cataloged and added to the organization's net assets, depreciated over time, and scheduled for replacement. Inventory procedures, of course, track assets for accounting purposes, but they also seek to prevent valuable items from walking away with the employees responsible for them.

Most entities establish their own capital budgeting policies, and therefore their own definitions of equipment versus supplies. Different organizations have different price thresholds to observe, including applicants and grant making agencies. So, if you work for a public university, you will probably find that the threshold is $5,000 to match OMB Circular A-21. Small cities may have a threshold of $2,000 or $2,500. Smaller budgets mean that lesser amounts create lumps. On the other hand, very large cities may have a $25,000 threshold. (For a thorough discussion of capital budgeting, see Vogt 2004 or Bland 2007.)

What happens when your organization's definition of equipment versus supplies differs from the grant making agency to which you are applying? The general rule is to treat the item according to the rules used by the grant making agency for application purposes. This will streamline the review process and prevent any holdups that might lead to increased scrutiny. Once the funds are awarded, it is a good idea to discuss the issue with the grant program officer—especially if your organization's policies prohibit using the supply account to fund equipment or vice versa.

Once you have established what to include in the supply budget, it is appropriate to group like items in the budget spreadsheet. So, for example, in an application for an environmental study grant you might have line items in the supply category for handheld GPS units, waterproof pens, a tablet laptop PC (if under the equipment price limit), sample containers, and waders. The list is probably incomplete, but this shows the price, number, and total cost for each category, providing transparency to the grant reviewer and a check on accountability for program staff, auditors, and evaluators.

Contractual

The contractual category is simple, once you understand what to include. Any fees to be paid under contract through the grant program should be included as a separate line item within this category. Essentially, contracts cover goods and services not provided by employees of the applicant organization, and usually services, because supplies and equipment cover most tangible items. So, a contract with a surveyor might be charged by the job whereas a contract with a research scientist might be charged by the hour or by the month. Included in the contractual category are all payments made to partner organizations. If you have developed a partnership that involves sharing the grant funds with partner organizations, this is the mechanism through which that will occur. One organization serves as the applicant and administers the award; this gives that organization control over the funds. This also gives it responsibility over the use of funds and requires it to keep partner organizations accountable for the use of grant funds. Contracts can't be given because you want to curry favor with an organization—a service must be provided to the proposed project or program.

A line item in the contractual category might read: "University of _____ |
$5,000 | Evaluation Services." Another might read: "Research Services, Inc. | $125/hour |
100 hours | $12,500." In the latter case, the services are to be provided on an hourly basis.
This means that the grant writer and the contractor should discuss the project in advance to
arrive at a fair estimate of the number of hours. In the former example, it is clear that the
contract is priced by the job or task to be completed. This puts the burden on the evaluator
to do as much as possible for the funds available, but it means the grants team should have
met with the evaluator in advance to estimate a fair price for the services to be rendered.

A grant writer who is not skilled in program evaluation methodologies might estimate
an amount suitable for evaluation based on the price used for a previous grant. This
approach is flawed because no two evaluations are quite the same, and the previous
methodology may not be rigorous enough to determine success of the new program. In this
case, any potential evaluator is likely to decline the contract because he or she cannot provide a good, definitive evaluation with the resources provided. Some may be willing to take
it, but will explain the limitations under which it will be carried out. Most contracts that
appear in grant applications have been worked out prior to the application process, and
often these contracts are included with the application packet as appendices or attachments.
Otherwise, the contractors are named and the services to be provided are explained thoroughly in the program narrative. For any contractual item that has not been previously
established, the narrative would need to explain the services to be provided and the process
to be used in selecting a contractor. In such cases, the budget would simply reflect a generic
entry such as: "Evaluation Services | $5,000."

Construction

This category appears in non-construction budgets because projects that are not primarily
construction in nature may still contain small construction components. It is customary
for non-construction programs to prohibit construction. When this is the case, this line
item should obviously read "0." Otherwise, you should be aware of any limitations on the
amount or percentage of the grant that can be used on construction to ensure that the
amount does not exceed it. An example where construction might come into play is in the
establishment of a new social service program in a historic downtown area. The program
requires a new office, which will be renovated in a historic building owned by the city,
and paid for with grant funds. The renovation requires construction, and a contractor will
need to provide estimates to be used in the budget. Let's assume the contractor estimates
the cost of renovation to be $29,000. The budget item would simply read: "Storefront
Renovation | $29,000."

What if the new office seems to be a necessary project component, but construction
costs are not permitted in the grant? Every dollar is fungible. If construction is prohibited,
it will usually not be permitted as eligible match either. However, the value of office
space could be used as match or paid for with grant funds. In this case, for a 36-month
program, the applicant might negotiate with the city to establish a rent contract for the
space in the amount of $800/month for 36 months ($28,800); if the value of the space at
the market rate is actually $900, then the remaining funds ($3,600) could be listed as a

matching contribution. This expense would be entered in the contractual section of the budget as: "City of _____ | Office Space Rental | 36 months @ $800 | $28,800." When the grant is issued, the applicant can make payment (possibly in full, depending on the contract terms) for the space rental, and the city can hire a contractor to provide the necessary renovations. The city is willing to enter such an agreement because it receives the value of the renovations on its facility (at a true cost of only $200) in addition to the value of the services to be provided to local residents.

Other

The Other category is for budget entries that seem to have no home in the aforementioned categories. If you can't determine where an expense belongs, you may need to think about it differently to determine its purpose and how it fits into the project, or how it will be paid for. If it's a tangible item, it probably belongs in supplies or equipment. If services, it is probably travel, contractual, or construction. If you're paying your own employees, then it belongs in personnel. Usually, things we think of as having no home just need to be thought of differently.

For example, if I proposed to hire two graduate assistants with grant funds, under university policy I might be required to pay their tuition. Where does tuition belong in a grant budget? It isn't a salary or wage, it isn't a tangible item, and it isn't really a contractual item. It is, however, a benefit to the student recipient, so it fits into the fringe benefit category. That placement may require some recalculation, or adjustment of formulas, but the fringe benefit category is its appropriate home. A stipend for participation in a focus group, however, might legitimately fit in the Other category. It isn't a wage because no employment relationship is established. It cannot be a fringe benefit for the same reason. It isn't a supply or equipment because it is intangible. It isn't contractual because no contractual relationship is established. Payments of this nature usually belong in the Other category. It is a good idea to request an opinion from the program officer before submitting the grant, however.

Indirect Costs

Indirect costs cover the vast category of expenses that usually go unmeasured. This category is included to cover the administrative overhead costs of the organization. Most organizations that receive federal grants have negotiated indirect cost agreements with the federal government. First-time applicants may use a provisional rate until a negotiation can be completed. The indirect cost rate includes capital costs, operating costs, and personnel costs that serve purely administrative functions. For example, the building you are sitting in, the chair you are sitting on, and the person who cleans the bathrooms are all components of indirect costs—they are costs that are necessary to allow the organization to function effectively. These expenses are compared to the organization's direct service delivery costs to arrive at a proportion—the indirect cost rate. A great deal of accounting information is required to establish a rate agreement, but it certainly facilitates future grant applications. If no rate agreement exists, then any administrative costs must be itemized to demonstrate how the total was determined. Or you could simply leave them out. But if overhead benefits the project, it should be included for reimbursement.

One of the great advantages of indirect costs is their fungibility. They do not go into the grant budget; rather, they are transferred into the organization's regular operating account as direct grant expenditures are made. The grant essentially reimburses the organization for use of its overhead to administer the program. This means that the funds can be used for any purpose without restriction. They could be allocated to offset future administrative expenses, they could be used to fund new programs or pay for personnel, or they could be put in the bank for a rainy day. Indirect cost reimbursement is payment to the organization for use of its overhead in the funded program. It isn't free money, but it is flexible money. It is to the organization's advantage to recover indirect costs wherever possible.

If you intend to pursue federal funding, it is a good idea to establish an indirect cost agreement as soon as possible. If, however, you deal primarily with foundations and private funding sources, it may not be necessary. Many private funding sources prohibit recovery of indirect costs, usually on very small grants. A grant of $10,000, given an indirect cost rate of 35%, would only leave $7,407 for program activities ($7,407 × 0.35 = $2,592; $7,407 + $2,592 = $9,999). In other cases, indirect/administrative/overhead costs are capped at 10% of program expenses. Again, it is easier to document and establish the amount of overhead if you negotiate an indirect cost rate agreement. These agreements are usually valid for 3 years, and the more complex agreements differentiate between types of program activities, and on-location versus off-location activities. For more information about determining indirect cost rates and agreements with the federal government, consult the appropriate OMB Circular for your organization type. For example, if you represent a nonprofit organization, you will need to consult OMB Circular A-122, Attachment A, Sections D and E (www.whitehouse.gov/omb/circulars/a122/a122_2004.pdf).

BUDGET CALENDARS

Given that the budget categories we utilize correspond to the organizational accounting system, it is also a good idea to understand the relationship of the budget period to the fiscal year of both the grant making agency and the applicant organization. What is a grant budget year? Is it the same as the calendar year, January 1–December 31? Is it July 1–June 30, like most states' fiscal years? Or could it be the federal fiscal year of October 1–September 30? In reality, the grant budget year is an abstract concept.

There are two ways to develop a budget with regard to the time periods. First, you might overlay the budget periods with the organization's or funder's fiscal year. For example, if your organization's fiscal year begins July 1, but the project will not begin until January 15, using this model you would report expenditures for January 15–June 30 as year 1, even though it is less than 6 months. This method is not very common for the proposal budget; because the periods of grant activity are not perfectly uniform, it clouds the reader's perception of the amount of funding to be expended in a given period.

The more commonly accepted approach to grant budgeting is to adopt the period from the proposed start date of the project to one day before in the following year. So, if the proposed start date is September 1, 2009, the budget period for year 1 is September 1, 2009, through August 31, 2010. This approach directly links the budget to the time frame for project implementation; it facilitates program planning and evaluation because the funds to be used match the project calendar, not the organization's calendar. Of course, in linking it to implementation, it de-links it from agency or organization accounting time lines. So, adjustments may have to be made to estimate the funds to be used in each period of the organization's budget as well (this may be monthly or quarterly).

One way to ease tension and confusion when it comes to grant accounting is to link the project itself to either the applicant's or the funding agency's calendar. Linking the project implementation to the federal budget period means that the budget will also be linked to it. The federal fiscal year begins on October 1 each year, and ends on September 30. It is customary for federal agencies to initiate competitions for funding once the federal budget is approved; because the federal budget is often late, funding cycles may also be delayed or compressed. The budget is approved in spring preceding the October 1 fiscal year, and new funds become available on that date.

If you are applying for federal funds, it is a wise move to investigate the agency's award dates and the dates on which funds will be released. For many federal programs, October 1 is a safe bet. Most funding agencies work on a quarterly basis, releasing funds annually, semiannually, or quarterly. Projects that begin in January, April, July, and October will have the greatest chance of coinciding with existing calendars in a more uniform fashion, and they will probably coincide with your organization's quarterly accounting system as well.

Whatever the method or the dates you elect to use to represent budget periods for your proposal, each year's column should be labeled with date range represented. And no dates should be selected without first consulting the program information, RFP, or agency staff in an effort to determine the expected date at which funds will be released for awarded proposals. It is common for them to be delayed, but rarely will they be released early. If your implementation plan and budget start dates match the date funds will be provided, your successful proposal can be implemented without the delay of budget and scope-of-work adjustments needed to synchronize your plans to the funding.

TEMPLATE: USING FORMULAS IN MICROSOFT EXCEL

As mentioned earlier, the use of spreadsheets in writing grant budgets cannot be overemphasized. A set of well-designed templates can facilitate rapid development of grant budgets in the future. To become effective at constructing and editing such templates, you need to obtain a working knowledge of a good spreadsheet program like Microsoft Excel. Formulas prevent mathematical errors as you calculate amounts and aggregate them across functional categories or budget periods. Errors can be made in the formulas themselves, so it is recommended that calculators be used to double-check the mathematics of your budget document.

After you have developed several budgets, you will attain a familiarity with the program that will enable you to copy and paste formulas to save time. You will also become more accustomed to formatting your cells and spreadsheets to make them as clear to read as possible. For example, I prefer to use boldface type for rows or columns that are subtotals and totals. For normal line item entries, I use normal typeface and indent each line item. I typically use boldface capital letters and left-justify cells containing the project grand total. This makes it easier for anyone reading the budget to determine what items are included in any subtotal by row or column on the page.

Using the functional categories previously mentioned (Figure 4.1), and the 3-year budget example in Table 4.2, I have developed a simple template that demonstrates how formulas can be used to compute budget information automatically. **Table 4.3** presents the same information using formulas rather than symbols of the relationships between cells. The amount budgeted should be entered for each category and each year where "[Amount]" is indicated. Other cells with formulas compute amounts and tabulate subtotals and totals automatically. For example, in cell D6, the formula reads "=D5*fringe rate." If your fringe benefits consist only of the common payroll taxes, Social Security and Medicare withholding, your organization's fringe rate is 7.65%, and the correct formula is "=D5*.0765." Many organizations have much higher rates for fringe benefits because they provide insurance or retirement benefits as well. With this formula in place, any personnel salary amount you enter in cell D5 will automatically be used to calculate the correct fringe amount. For any subsequent change to the personnel salary amount in that cell resulting from budget revisions, the fringe benefit amount will be automatically updated. Budget automaticity makes it very easy to craft a project budget that equals the maximum award amount, if that is your goal. The effects of every change are immediately captured and visible when you use formulas to construct your grant budget.

Similar formulas are used to total program costs each year by summing the values in each annual column (such as cell H13). Formulas in column B total the project amount for each functional category and tabulate the total project costs: direct, indirect, and combined direct and indirect. Indirect costs, as discussed earlier, are administrative expenses, often referred to as overhead costs. Indirect costs for federal grant programs are almost exclusively calculated using a negotiated federal indirect cost rate agreed upon in advance by the applicant and a "cognizant" federal agency.

The budget template in Table 4.3 puts the project information of greatest importance—the totals—on the left and bottom of the spreadsheet. Column totals should generally be added at the bottom. Row totals, on the other hand, can be configured from left to right or right to left with the summary information on either side. In grouping time periods, I customarily keep the totals on the left, closest to the category labels. In grouping funding sources, as we consider in a moment, I generally keep the aggregate totals on the right. This keeps the information of greatest importance to the funder in the most accessible location. Total grant funds are more important to the funder than are annual amounts, so I keep the project totals on the left. Likewise, grant funds are usually of greater interest to the funder than applicant match amounts or the total project costs, so I keep the grant funding column on the left, followed by a match column(s) and a project total column on the right for total project budgets. This convention is mostly one of

TABLE 4.3 Using Formulas to Aggregate Multiperiod Budgets

	A	B	C	D	E	F	G	H
4		*Project Total*		*Y1*		*Y2*		*Y3*
5	Personnel	[=D5+F5+H5]		[Amount]		[Amount]		[Amount]
6	Fringe	[=D6+F6+H6]		[=D5*fringe rate]		[=F5*fringe rate]		[=H5*fringe rate]
7	Travel	[=D7+F7+H7]		[Amount]		[Amount]		[Amount]
8	Equipment	[=D8+F8+H8]		[Amount]		[Amount]		[Amount]
9	Supplies	[=D9+F9+H9]		[Amount]		[Amount]		[Amount]
10	Contractual	[=D10+F10+H10]		[Amount]		[Amount]		[Amount]
11	Construction	[=D11+F11+H11]		[Amount]		[Amount]		[Amount]
12	Other	[=D12+F12+H12]		[Amount]		[Amount]		[Amount]
13	Project Subtotal	[=D13+F13+H13]		[=SUM(D5:D12)]		[=SUM(F5:F12)]		[=SUM(H5:H12)]
14								
15	Indirect Costs	[=D15+F15+H15]		[=D13*Indirect Cost Rate]		[=F13*Indirect Cost Rate]		[=H13*Indirect Cost Rate]
16								
17	PROJECT TOTAL	[=D17+F17+H17]		[=D13+D15]		[=F13+F15]		[=H13+H15]

habit, but if it has the effect of conveying information most efficiently, so it serves a valuable purpose.

Table 4.4 shows a more complicated budget model. This template itemizes the costs that go into each category and sums them to estimate total costs of the proposed project. It provides the detail that is used as the basis of the cumulative budget in Table 4.3. This table presents only total project costs without disaggregating them according to the fund source, grants or matching. By including the cost basis and the number or percentage of each line item, this template also serves as a narrative of expenditures. This is a basic line item budget, but it includes information about how each amount was estimated—that is the core purpose of a budget narrative. Budget narratives are discussed later in the chapter.

Although ordinary budget totals are customarily developed by adding components together, I prefer to develop grant budgets in reverse. What appears on the page viewed by the funding agency is components and totals, not the method used to calculate them. The funder's interest will be in making sure the totals are accurate based on the component line items and fund sources; the reviewer will not be able to determine whether the budget was arrived at logically by adding the components, or in reverse by subtracting known amounts from known totals.

Using simple algebra ($a + b = c$), we can simply use the two known quantities to determine a third unknown quantity for each line item in the budget. For complicated grant budgets, I calculate each itemized component amount by subtracting from the total project costs those components that have known match sources or that have components I know will be funded from grant funds rather than local sources. This can be done with match amounts known, with grant amounts known, or a combination of the two.

Now consider a hypothetical situation where the goal is to allocate project costs such that the total grant funding requested is $1,000,000—our hypothetical budget cap. Table 4.5 shows a budget that achieves this goal, coming in right at the $1,000,000 mark. It was arrived at by first inserting the necessary formulas and then adding known information and adjusting flexible areas until the maximum amount of grant funds permitted had been obtained. To demonstrate the efficacy of this method, two additional tables show the formulas used to compute the missing amounts in the grant funds column (Table 4.6) or the matching funds column (Table 4.7). Table 4.8 shows a hybrid model with some known information in each column. This model might be applicable, for instance, when you know expensive equipment will be purchased with grant funds while existing agency personnel will be used as cost match for the project. Each of the templates used in Table 4.6 through Table 4.8 will produce the same results. That is, if we looked at the amounts rather than the formulas used to calculate the amounts, each budget would appear the same as that in Table 4.5.

THE NARRATIVE: TWO APPROACHES

The budget narrative, sometimes also referred to as the budget justification, plays a central role in the grant proposal process. It itemizes the objects of expenditure to be used in the program, documents the basis used to estimate their cost, and even estimates the time in which they will be incurred in some budgets. Two approaches to developing the budget

TABLE 4.4 Budget Template Used to Estimate Total Costs

A	B	C	D	E	F	G	H	I
2	**Budget Template: Estimate of Total Costs**							
4	*Category*	*Basis*	*%*	*Grant Funds*		*Match Funds*		*TOTAL COST*
5	Personnel							
6	Director	$50,000.00	100%					$150,000.00
7	Staff 1	$30,000.00	50%					$45,000.00
8	Staff 2	$25,000.00	25%					$18,750.00
9	Subtotal			$0.00		$0.00		$213,750.00
11	Fringe		22.1%	$0.00		$0.00		$47,238.75
13	Travel							
14	Mileage	12,000	$0.553					$6,636.00
15	Airfare (tickets)	4	$450					$1,800.00
16	Lodging (nights)	12	$150					$1,800.00
17	Per Diem (days)	12	$45					$540.00
18	Subtotal			$0.00		$0.00		$10,776.00
20	Equipment							
21	Item 1 description	$159,345.00	1					$159,345.00
22	Item 2 description	$376,987.00	1					$376,987.00
23	Item 3 description	$50,000.00	3					$150,000.00
24	Subtotal			$0.00		$0.00		$686,332.00
26	Supplies	$2,500.00	3					$7,500.00
28	Contractual							
29	Contractor 1	$35,000.00	1					$35,000.00
30	Contractor 2	$45,000.00	1					$45,000.00
31	Subtotal			$0.00		$0.00		$80,000.00
33	Construction	$0.00						
35	Other	$0.00						
37	**Project Subtotal**			$0.00		$0.00		$1,045,596.75
39	Indirect Costs	Total Direct Costs	45.2%	$0.00		$0.00		$472,609.73
41	**PROJECT TOTAL**			$0.00		$0.00		$1,518,206.48

TABLE 4.5 Budget Model

A	B	C	D	E	F	G	H	I
2	**Budget Template: Estimate of Total Costs**							
4	*Category*	*Basis*	*%*	*Grant Funds*		*Match Funds*		*TOTAL COST*
5	Personnel							
6	Director	$50,000.00	100%	$0.00		$150,000.00		$150,000.00
7	Staff 1	$30,000.00	50%	$0.00		$45,000.00		$45,000.00
8	Staff 2	$25,000.00	25%	$0.00		$18,750.00		$18,750.00
9	Subtotal			$0.00		$213,750.00		$213,750.00
11	Fringe		22.1%	$0.00		$47,238.75		$47,238.75
13	Travel							
14	Mileage	12,000	$0.553	$0.00		$6,636.00		$6,636.00
15	Airfare (tickets)	4	$450	$0.00		$1,800.00		$1,800.00
16	Lodging (nights)	12	$150	$0.00		$1,800.00		$1,800.00
17	Per Diem (days)	12	$45	$0.00		$540.00		$540.00
18	Subtotal			$0.00		$10,776.00		$10,776.00
20	Equipment							
21	Item description	$159,345.00	1	$159,345.00		0		$159,345.00
22	Item 2 description	$376,987.00	1	$376,987.00		0		$376,987.00
23	Item 3 description	$50,000.00	3	$150,000.00		0		$150,000.00
24	Subtotal			$686,332.00		$0.00		$686,332.00
26	Supplies	$2,500.00	3	$2,373.00		$5,127.00		$7,500.00
28	Contractual							
29	Contractor 1	$35,000.00	1	$0.00		$35,000.00		$35,000.00
30	Contractor 2	$45,000.00	1	$0.00		$45,000.00		$45,000.00
31	Subtotal			$0.00		$80,000.00		$80,000.00
33	Construction	$0.00		$0.00		$0.00		$0.00
35	Other	$0.00		$0.00		$0.00		$0.00
37	Project Subtotal			$688,705.00		$356,891.75		$1,045,596.75
39	Indirect Costs	Total Direct Costs	45.2%	$311,294.66		$161,315.07		$472,609.73
41	PROJECT TOTAL			$999,999.66		$518,206.82		$1,518,206.48

TABLE 4.6 Budget Template Using Known Match Amounts (Formulas)

A	B	C	D	E	F	G	H	I
2	Budget Template: Estimate of Total Costs							
4	*Category*	*Basis*	*%*	*Grant Funds*		*Match Funds*		*TOTAL COST*
5	Personnel							
6	Director	50000	1	=I6-G6		150000		=D6*C6*3
7	Staff 1	30000	0.5	=I7-G7		45000		=D7*C7*3
8	Staff 2	25000	0.25	=I8-G8		18750		=D8*C8*3
9	Subtotal			=SUM(E6:E8)		=SUM(G6:G8)		=SUM(I6:I8)
11	Fringe		0.221	=D11*E9		=D11*G9		=I9*0.221
13	Travel							
14	Mileage	12000	0.553	=I14-G14		6636		=C14*D14
15	Airfare (tickets)	4	450	=I15-G15		1800		=C15*D15
16	Lodging (nights)	12	150	=I16-G16		1800		=C16*D16
17	Per Diem (days)	12	45	=I17-G17		540		=C17*D17
18	Subtotal			=SUM(E14:E17)		=SUM(G14:G17)		=SUM(I14:I17)
20	Equipment							
21	Item 1 description	159345	1	=I21-G21		0		=C21*D21
22	Item 2 description	376987	1	=I22-G22		0		=C22*D22
23	Item 3 description	50000	3	=I23-G23		0		=C23*D23
24	Subtotal			=SUM(E21:E23)		=SUM(G21:G23)		=SUM(I21:I23)
26	Supplies	2500	3	=I26-G26		5127		=C26*D26
28	Contractual							
29	Contractor 1	35000	1	=I29-G29		35000		=C29*D29
30	Contractor 2	45000	1	=I30-G30		45000		=C30*D30
31	Subtotal			=SUM(E29:E30)		=SUM(G29:G30)		=SUM(I29:I30)
33	Construction	0		=I33-G33		0		0
35	Other	0		=I35-G35		0		0
37	Project Subtotal			=E35+E33+E31+E26+ E24+E18+E11+E9		=G35+G33+G31+ G26+G24+G18+ G11+G9		=I35+I33+I31+ I26+I24+I18+ I11+I9
39	Indirect Costs	Total Direct Costs	0.452	=E37*D39		=G37*D39		=I37*D39
41	PROJECT TOTAL			=E37+E39		=G37+G39		=I37+I39

TABLE 4.7 Budget Template Using Known Grant Contributions (Formulas)

A	B	C	D	E	F	G	H	I
2	**Budget Template: Estimate of Total Costs**							
4	*Category*	*Basis*	*%*	*Grant Funds*		*Match Funds*		*TOTAL COST*
5	Personnel							
6	Director	50000	1	0		=I6-E6		=D6*C6*3
7	Staff 1	30000	0.5	0		=I7-E7		=D7*C7*3
8	Staff 2	25000	0.25	0		=I8-E8		=D8*C8*3
9	Subtotal			=SUM(E6:E8)		=SUM(G6:G8)		=SUM(I6:I8)
11	Fringe		0.221	0		=D11*G9		=I9*0.221
13	Travel							
14	Mileage	12000	0.553	0		=I14-E14		=C14*D14
15	Airfare (tickets)	4	450	0		=I15-E15		=C15*D15
16	Lodging (nights)	12	150	0		=I16-E16		=C16*D16
17	Per Diem (days)	12	45	0		=I17-E17		=C17*D17
18	Subtotal			=SUM(E14:E17)		=SUM(G14:G17)		=SUM(I14:I17)
20	Equipment							
21	Item 1 description	159345	1	159345		=I21-E21		=C21*D21
22	Item 2 description	376987	1	376987		=I22-E22		=C22*D22
23	Item 3 description	50000	3	150000		=I23-E23		=C23*D23
24	Subtotal			=SUM(E21:E23)		=SUM(G21:G23)		=SUM(I21:I23)
26	Supplies	2500	3	2373		=I26-E26		=C26*D26
28	Contractual							
29	Contractor 1	35000	1	0		=I29-E29		=C29*D29
30	Contractor 2	45000	1	0		=I30-E30		=C30*D30
31	Subtotal			=SUM(E29:E30)		=SUM(G29:G30)		=SUM(I29:I30)
33	Construction	0		0		=I33-E33		0
35	Other	0		0		=I35-E35		0
37	Project Subtotal			=E35+E33+E31+E26+ E24+E18+E11+E9		=G35+G33+G31+ G26+G24+G18+ G11+G9		=I35+I33+I31+ I26+I24+I18+ I11+I9
39	Indirect Costs	Total Direct Costs	0.452	=E37*D39		=G37*D39		=I37*D39
41	PROJECT TOTAL			=E37+E39		=G37+G39		=I37+I39

TABLE 4.8 Hybrid Budget Template Using Known Match and Grant Amounts

A	B	C	D	E	F	G	H	I
2	**Budget Template: Estimate of Total Costs**							
4	Category	Basis	%	Grant Funds		Match Funds		TOTAL COST
5	Personnel							
6	Director	50000	1	=I6-G6		150000		=D6*C6*3
7	Staff 1	30000	0.5	=I7-G7		45000		=D7*C7*3
8	Staff 2	25000	0.25	=I8-G8		18750		=D8*C8*3
9	Subtotal			=SUM(E6:E8)		=SUM(G6:G8)		=SUM(I6:I8)
11	Fringe		0.221	0		=D11*G9		=I9*0.221
13	Travel							
14	Mileage	12000	0.553	0		=I14-E14		=C14*D14
15	Airfare (tickets)	4	450	0		=I15-E15		=C15*D15
16	Lodging (nights)	12	150	0		=I16-E16		=C16*D16
17	Per Diem (days)	12	45	0		=I17-E17		=C17*D17
18	Subtotal			=SUM(E14:E17)		=SUM(G14:G17)		=SUM(I14:I17)
20	Equipment							
21	Item 1 description	159345	1	159345		=I21-E21		=C21*D21
22	Item 2 description	376987	1	376987		=I22-E22		=C22*D22
23	Item 3 description	50000	3	150000		=I23-E23		=C23*D23
24	Subtotal			=SUM(E21:E23)		=SUM(G21:G23)		=SUM(I21:I23)
26	Supplies	2500	3	2373		=I26-E26		=C26*D26
28	Contractual							
29	Contractor 1	35000	1	0		=I29-E29		=C29*D29
30	Contractor 2	45000	1	=I30-G30		45000		=C30*D30
31	Subtotal			=SUM(E29:E30)		=I31-E31		=SUM(I29:I30)
33	Construction	0		0		=I33-E33		0
35	Other	0		0		=I35-E35		0
37	Project Subtotal			=E35+E33+E31+ E26+E24+E18+ E11+E9		=G35+G33+G31+ G26+G24+G18+ G11+G9		=I35+I33+I31+ I26+I24+I18+ I11+I9
39	Indirect Costs	Total Direct Costs	0.452	=E37*D39		=G37*D39		=I37*D39
41	PROJECT TOTAL			=E37+E39		=G37+G39		=I37+I39

narrative can be used. The first approach is the development of the detailed functional line-item budget I have spent most of this chapter exploring. That is, each cost to be incurred is listed, and the information used to calculate the estimate—the cost basis—is provided. Each employee is listed, along with his or her salary and the amount of time or effort the employee will contribute. Each contract is itemized, each piece of equipment is listed. Travel resources are listed by function with rates and price estimates as well as the number of trips or miles. The itemized budget, including the cost basis and matching funds, presents a complete picture of the applicant's spending plan for the proposed project. This approach is the one I use most frequently in my grant proposals.

In some cases, it is necessary to provide explanatory notes in addition to the basic spreadsheet. Though objective, numbers cannot always communicate everything that needs to be said. For example, in a multiyear budget, I typically inflate employee salaries by around 3% (a fairly standard cost of living increase) in each subsequent year. The cost basis in this case is the employee's current salary. An asterisk or footnote may explain that regular cost of living increases are anticipated and budgeted at 3% per annum. A formula in the spreadsheet would calculate these increases automatically. But this fact—that numbers are not enough—leads to a second type of budget narrative, and the one implied by its name: a written description of costs, their basis, and their necessity.

It is not possible to describe the need for a particular expenditure in a budget spreadsheet alone. And the use of explanatory notes for many cost items implies a need for more descriptive explanation. Some funders expect a written description of each expense to be incurred, how it was calculated, an explanation of its purpose or use in the program, and a justification of its necessity. An example of such a budget narrative is provided in **Figure 4.2**. This narrative description may be framed by program or function to be undertaken, or by object of expenditure in the line-item budget spreadsheet, or both.

The key to the budget narrative/justification is that it be as transparent as possible. Every cost should be clear, and there should be no questions about the process used to derive a particular cost or expenditure. In preparing to justify your program budget, it may be a good idea to consult with the granting agency program staff to determine their expectations about the format of the budget justification. For many agencies, the line item spreadsheet will suffice. Others will require further detail in a narrative form. My preference is to provide as much information as succinctly as possible, hence my preference for the spreadsheet format alone. A well-written project description, the proposal narrative itself, should explain how each of the expenses reflected in the budget will fit into the program, and how they all will work together to ensure program success. Describing the use of each expense a second time is redundant and time consuming when the program does not require the more descriptive format.

The budget proposal should be clear and concise. It should precede the development of the program narrative to ensure that the narrative description reflects the use of funds described in the budget as accurately as possible. A grant proposal is usually constructed in pieces, but it is reviewed and evaluated from a holistic perspective. A proposal with its various components in agreement communicates the proposed program and activities clearly. A clear plan is understandable to the funding agency, and it communicates your organization's planning and organization abilities. Your management capacity will often be a factor—stated or unstated—that influences funding decisions. Having a plan that the

---

Budget Narrative: Year 1

Salary:

$49,436 is requested to support the PI for 33% effort during the academic year (Academic Year Salary $52,000 × 1/3 = $17,160), two months summer salary ($52,000 × 2/9 = $11,556), and to support two full-time graduate research assistants (20 hours/week; annual stipend $10,360 each = $20,720).

Fringe:

$20,477 is requested for fringe benefits. 22% of wages ($49,436 × .22 = $11,321), graduate in-state tuition for two graduate research assistants (2 @ 4,578 = $9,156).

Domestic Travel:

$14,261 is requested for domestic travel. Airfare is estimated at an average of $250/trip for 17 person/trips (TL $4,250) for the PI and graduate assistants to attend academic conferences and to visit state economic development or legislative offices as necessary. Lodging is estimated at $150/night, with an average of two nights per person/trip, for a total of 34 nights (34 @ $150 = $5,100). Per diem is requested for 17 trips, averaging 3 days per person/trip, for a total of 51 days (51 days @ $36/day = $1,836). Parking and ground transportation is estimated at $75/trip for 17 trips (17 @ $75 = $1,275). Registration fees for PI and graduate assistants are estimated at an average of $200 each for 9 conferences (TL $1,800).

Supplies:

$7,598 is requested for supplies during year one. This includes one laptop computer and docking station for use in off-site data gathering activities, estimated at $2,500. In addition, one PC and laser printer will be acquired for dedicated project use by the graduate assistants (estimated at $2,000 and $500, respectively, for total $2,500. Software licenses will be purchased, including Intercooled Stata v.9 ($719) and StatTransfer ($179), totaling $898. $1,000 is requested for project-related photocopying at an estimated cost of $0.10/sheet, or 10,000 copies. $550 is requested for a 4GB flash memory storage device ($430) and a supply of recordable CD-Rs ($120) for data transfer, backup, and to provide requested copies of project materials to state officials and other interested parties. $150 is requested for postage to facilitate requests for data or legislative history, submittal of manuscripts to journals, and delivery of project materials to requestors.

Indirect Costs:

The approved on-campus indirect cost rate is 45.5% of total modified direct costs ($91,771 @.455 = $41,756).

Summary:	Salary	49,436
	Fringe	20,477
	Travel	14,261
	Supplies	7,598
	Indirect	41,756
	TOTAL Y1	**$133,528**

FIGURE 4.2　Sample Budget Narrative: Written Explanation of Costs

funder can easily discern from the application is key. If you propose a program plan that is outside the funder's interests, it is no excuse for submitting a vague or confusing proposal. It may be rejected, but it will be rejected because it doesn't fit their goals, not because they can't understand what you propose to do. As a grant reviewer, I have observed many proposals where the pieces don't add up; budgets don't match the narrative or even the budget forms. A big question mark emerges when such details are out of

Budget Narrative: Year 2

Salary:
$49,436 is requested to support the PI for 33% effort during the academic year (Academic Year Salary $52,000 × 1/3 = $17,160), two months summer salary ($52,000 × 2/9 = $11,556), and to support two full-time graduate research assistants (20 hours/week; annual stipend $10,360 each = $20,720).

Fringe:
$20,477 is requested for fringe benefits. 22% of wages ($49,436 × .22 = $11,321), graduate in-state tuition for two graduate research assistants (2 @ 4,578 = $9,156).

Domestic Travel:
$14,261 is requested for domestic travel. Airfare is estimated at an average of $250/trip for 17 person/trips (TL $4,250) for the PI and graduate assistants to attend academic conferences and to visit state economic development or legislative offices as necessary. Lodging is estimated at $150/night, with an average of two nights per person/trip, for a total of 34 nights (34 @ $150 = $5,100). Per diem is requested for 17 trips, averaging 3 days per person/trip, for a total of 51 days (51 days @ $36/day = $1,836). Parking and ground transportation is estimated at $75/trip for 17 trips (17 @ $75 = $1,275). Registration fees for PI and graduate assistants are estimated at an average of $200 each for 9 conferences (TL $1,800).

Supplies:
$2,598 is requested for supplies. Software licenses or updates will be purchased, including Intercooled Stata v.9 ($719) and StatTransfer ($179), totaling $898. $1,000 is requested for project-related photocopying at an estimated cost of $0.10/sheet, or 10,000 copies. $550 is requested for a 4GB flash memory storage device ($430) and a supply of recordable CD-Rs ($120) for data transfer, backup, and to provide requested copies of project materials to state officials and other interested parties. $150 is requested for postage to facilitate requests for data or legislative history, submittal of manuscripts to journals, and delivery of project materials to requestors.

Indirect Costs:
The approved on-campus indirect cost rate is 45.5% of total modified direct costs ($86,772 @ .455 = $39,481).

Summary:	Salary	49,436		Year 1 TL	$133,528
	Fringe	20,477		Year 2 TL	$126,253
	Travel	14,261		**Project TL**	**$259,781**
	Supplies	2,598			
	Indirect	39,481			
	TOTAL Y2	**$126,253**			

FIGURE 4.2   (Continued)

synch. The budget narrative should also be viewed from this perspective—it is one component of many that work together to show the applicant's plan. Redundancy is boring to a grant reviewer, and it may lead them to skip pages and miss important information. The budget narrative should be compiled in the format required, or expected, by the funder, and it should clearly and concisely communicate information that cannot be found elsewhere in the proposal.

After this thorough examination of the budget development process, the following section presents examples of detailed budgets I have developed for grant proposals in recent years.

EXAMPLES FROM PRACTICE

On the following pages, I present four actual detailed grant budgets from two perspectives. First, you will see exactly what the reviewers see—the face of the budget with amounts, explanations, subtotals, and totals—the information that is used to complete forms and to write further narrative or justification. Second, I present the formula view of each budget to demonstrate the approach used to compute or calculate various entries in the budget documents. The method of computation used in each formula may be obvious (such as subtotaling a category), or it may be detailed in an explanatory note. These formula views provide examples of the approach used to develop grant budgets and should clarify the approach you would use in creating a budget template from scratch. In each of the cases presented, the detailed budget spreadsheet was submitted as the budget justification without further explanation. The examples vary in size and complexity as a result of the nature of the programs for which they were prepared and the nature of tasks to be performed. I begin with simple examples and conclude with a fairly complex grant budget.

Tables 4.9 and 4.10 present a fairly simple budget, as is common for small award amounts. In this case, the proposal was to a local community foundation for an applied research project, and the available funding was only $3,000. Two personnel were involved in the grant, and the detail provides information on the salary basis used to determine the amounts. Fringe benefits must be included if salary is billed, so fringe benefits are the only other category on this budget. They are computed using the institution's standard fringe benefit rate (24.4%). Because the funding agency disallows indirect costs, they are not budgeted here, and a note is included for internal institutional review purposes. Only one budget column is provided because there is only one funding source (the foundation, C.F.) and the project lasts significantly less than one year. In Table 4.10, you will see that the salary amounts are entered by hand rather than formula. In this case, the objective was to maximize the grant funds available for salary and to provide equal amounts to each staff member. Because the base salaries are different, the percentage of effort devoted to the

TABLE 4.9   Simple Detailed Budget Example 1

John Doe, PhD, PI; Jane Doe, PhD, CO-PI
[Institution Name]
2007 Community Foundation Grant Proposal Budget

	C. F. *2007*
Summer Salary	
John Doe, Co-Principal Investigator ($5,987/month @ 0.2 months)	$1,205.57
Jane Doe, Co-PI ($6,562/month @ 0.18 months)	$1,206.00
Subtotal	$2,411.57
Fringe	
24.4% of wages	$ 588.42
Total Direct Costs*	$2,999.99

Note: CF prohibits indirect cost recovery on grant awards. See attached letter.

TABLE 4.10   Simple Detailed Budget Example 1, Formulas

John Doe, PhD, PI; Jane Doe, PhD, CO-PI
[Institution Name]
2007 Community Foundation Grant Proposal Budget

		C. F. 2007
12	Summer Salary	
13	John Doe, Co-Principal Investigator ($5,987/month @ 0.2 months)	1205.57
14	Jane Doe, Co-PI ($6,562/month @ 0.18 months)	1206.00
15	Subtotal	=D13+D14
16	Fringe	
17	24.4% of wages	=D15*0.244
18		
19	Total Direct Costs*	=D15+D17

Note: CF prohibits indirect cost recovery on grant awards. See attached letter.

project also had to vary to result in equal amounts of pay. Formulas were not used to compute salaries because the cost basis would require too many decimal points to yield the exact amount.

Table 4.11 provides an example of a slightly more involved budget. This proposal was submitted to a university for a competitive research program, so the funds were explicitly linked to one research project. The program narrative explained the approach to be followed, and the detailed budget provides the basis of the expenses to be incurred. In this

TABLE 4.11   Detailed Budget Example 2

John Doe, PhD
[Institution Name]
2006 Young Investigator Development Grant Proposal Budget

	Grantor 2006–2007
Summer Salary	
John Doe, Principal Investigator ($5,780/month @ 0.519 months)	$3,000
Fringe	
22.9% of wages	$ 687
Travel	
SECOPA 2006 Annual Conference	$ 415
Software	
Intercooled Stata 9	$ 719
Stat/Transfer 8	$ 179
Total*	$5,000

Note: Grantor prohibits indirect cost recovery on grant awards.

case, those expenses include salary, the associated fringe benefits, some funds to help offset travel to a conference, and computer software. In a larger, more complex budget, the budgeted software purchases would not appear in a Software category, but rather they would have been included in the Supplies category. Because software is the only type of supply to be purchased, that label was used. Again, note that indirect costs are prohibited for this award and so noted on the budget for internal review purposes.

In Table 4.12, it is clear that formulas played a greater role. Salary is budgeted using the cost basis for one month, multiplied by the number of months. As in most budgets, this amount was manipulated to maximize the award under the $5,000 limit. Fringe benefits are again calculated by a fringe benefit rate and linked to the amount of salary listed in the budget. In other words, for a given salary, the spreadsheet automatically calculates the correct fringe benefit amount. Other items are entered by hand in that they reflect the market price for software and the expected cost of conference travel.

Table 4.13 presents a fairly complex grant budget with the full consort of federal expenditure categories. It also shows the matching costs to be provided by the applicant or partner organizations in addition to showing the grant funds requested. This budget presents a good picture of the total project costs and how the various components provided by different organizations will work together to achieve the desired result. This budget was for a HUD YouthBuild project. YouthBuild has since moved to the U.S. Department of Labor, and the rules are different from when this budget was drafted.

One downside to the budget displayed in Table 4.13 is that it reflects only 24-month totals, and not annual expenses. Beginning with personnel, several employees are listed, as is their contribution. Percentage effort is reported, but their salaries are not. If one knows the total to be paid and the percentage it reflects, the base salary can be easily determined from the information provided. A clearer budget would report the salary information

TABLE 4.12   Detailed Budget Example 2, Formulas

John Doe, PhD
[Institution Name]
2006 Young Investigator Development Grant Proposal Budget

		Grantor *2006–2007*
	Summer Salary	
12	John Doe, Principal Investigator ($5,780/month @ 0.519 months)	=5780*0.519
13	Fringe	
14	22.9% of wages	=D12*0.229
15	Travel	
16	SECOPA 2006 Annual Conference	415
17	Software	
18	Intercooled Stata 9	719
19	Stat/Transfer 8	179
20	Total*	=SUM(D12:D19)

Note: Grantor prohibits indirect cost recovery on grant awards.

TABLE 4.13   Detailed Budget Example 3

_____ COMMUNITY COLLEGE
In partnership with _____ UNIVERSITY

APPALACHIAN COMMUNITY REDEVELOPMENT PROJECT:
_____ COUNTY YOUTHBUILD PROJECT BUDGET

		(24 MONTH TOTALS)		
BUDGET CATEGORIES		*HUD*	*MATCH*	*TOTAL*
PERSONNEL	%	$	$	$
Project Coordinator	100.00	56,000	10,000	66,000
Counselor	100.00	42,500	10,000	52,500
Youth Advocate	50.00	15,000	2,400	17,400
Construction Curriculum Instructor	25.00	7,500	12,500	20,000
Construction Curriculum On-Site Supervisor	25.00	7,500	12,500	20,000
Grant Administrator	20.00	–	16,000	16,000
Chief Academic Officer	15.00	–	22,500	22,500
President	10.00	–	20,000	20,000
Wages for 15 Participants @$5.50/hr	100.00	85,800	–	85,800
Educational stipends		15,000	–	15,000
PERSONNEL TLS.		229,300	105,900	335,200
FRINGE BENEFITS	32.00%	48,842	20,333	69,175

32% as standard [institution] fringe benefit rate (9% for student participants; excludes educational stipends from calculation)

TRAVEL		11,094	1,025	12,119

All project personnel would average eight trips a month at the standard [partner organization] reimbursement rate of $.32/mi. or $55 per trip for 65 trips, transport cost of students at $10 per day, and one training conference at $4,000.

EQUIPMENT		–	–	–
SUPPLIES		4,400	750	5,150
CONTRACTUAL		70,000	–	70,000

[University partner]: Leadership development, entrepreneurial training, and related courses.

OTHER:
HOUSING RESOURCES

_____ County Habitat for Humanity Inc.		–	125,000	125,000
IN-KIND MATCHING RESOURCES				
_____ County Adult Education		–	500	500
_____ County Judge Executive		–	2,400	2,400
_____ County Schools		–	25,000	25,000
_____University		–	70,000	
TOTAL DIRECT		363,636	350,908	619,544
INDIRECT CHARGES		36,364	130,140	166,504

10% total administrative cost limitation of HUD.

TOTAL PROJECT		$400,000	$481,049	$881,049

directly. More important than the number of employees, this budget has different categories of salaries and wages. Regular employees have different fringe benefit rates than student employees. Stipends technically are not wages, so they are excluded from the fringe benefit cost calculation. These details can be seen in the formulas presented in **Table 4.14**.

The Other category includes housing resources as matching funds. Technically, this reflected the value of properties on which students in the program would work. It is an essential component of the project, and without commitment of those resources, the program would not have been funded. It is technically not contractual because it is based in a letter of support rather than a contract. A stray category has also been added with the label *In-Kind Matching Resources.* As with the housing resources, these line items reflect the in-kind match to be provided by several partner organizations. These amounts are listed in the match column, and the basis for the goods and services they provided is documented in signed letters of support that were included in the grant application packet. If these organizations had also been planned recipients of contracts to provide services under the grant, they would have been listed under the Contractual column and the match amounts would have been listed in the match column there rather than in a separate section.

This program has a maximum award size of $400,000, and as you can see, the budget requests the maximum amount. Matching funds are also required, so the total program cost is more than double the requested amount. In calculating the match amount, a tricky technique was employed. This program, under HUD, limited administrative expenses to 10% of the direct project grant amount, which is significantly lower than the organization's negotiated indirect cost rate of 52% of salaries and wages. The formulas in Table 4.14 reveal the computation used. This organization's indirect cost rate is 52% of salaries and wages, so that rate is first multiplied by the total dollar amount of salaries and wages budgeted in the match column (cell E23). But the total indirect costs are not recoverable under the grant award because there is a 10% limit. The administrative cost limit is based on total project costs, so it is computed by multiplying total direct project costs by 10%. The institution's rate, again, is based on salaries and wages. In other words, these *unrecovered indirect costs* are a real expense to the organization, and they can be used as match. So, along with the first component of indirect matching costs, we include the product of the rate (52%) and the direct salaries and wages (not including stipends) less the amount of indirect costs included.

If you are up for a challenge, try your hand at developing a budget with this level of complexity at the exact amount of $400,000 without using a formula-based template. It will become immediately clear how spreadsheets and formulas save time in the budget process.

Tables 4.15 and 4.16 provide the final budget example. Although there are several items in each category, this grant is actually not very complicated. The time frame is 24 months, so the budget reflects two time periods and the total grant funding over those periods. As before, Table 4.16 reveals the formulas used to tabulate particular entries.

TABLE 4.14 Detailed Budget Example 3, Formulas

			COMMUNITY COLLEGE		
	In partnership with		UNIVERSITY		
	COUNTY YOUTHBUILD PROJECT BUDGET				
	24 MONTH TOTAL BUDGET				
	BUDGET CATEGORIES		HUD	MATCH	TOTAL
A	B	C	D	E	F
		%	$	$	$
10	PERSONNEL				
11	Project Coordinator	100	56000	=(33000*2)-D11	=SUM(D11:E11)
12	Counselor	100	42500	=(26250*2)-D12	=SUM(D12:E12)
13	Youth Advocate	50	15000	=(17400*2)*0.5-D13	=SUM(D13:E13)
14	Construction Curriculum Instructor	25	7500	=(40000*2)*0.25-D14	=SUM(D14:E14)
15	Construction Curriculum On-Site Supervisor	25	7500	=(40000*2)*0.25-D15	=SUM(D15:E15)
16	Grant Administrator	20	0	=40000*2*0.2	=SUM(D16:E16)
17	Chief Academic Officer	15	0	=75000*2*0.15	=SUM(D17:E17)
18	President	10	0	=100000*2*0.1	=SUM(D18:E18)
19					
20	Wages for 15 Participants @$5.50/hr	100	85800	0	=SUM(D20:E20)
21	Educational stipends		15000	0	=SUM(D21:E21)
22					
23	PERSONNEL TLS.		=SUM(D11:D21)	=SUM(E11:E21)	=SUM(D23:E23)
24					
25	FRINGE BENEFITS	0.32	=((D23-(D21+D20))* 0.32)+(D20*0.09)	=E23*0.192	=SUM(D25:E25)
26					
27	32% as standard [institution] fringe benefit rate (9% for student participants; excludes educational stipends from calculation)				
28					
29	TRAVEL		11094	1025.42	=SUM(D29:E29)
30					
31	All project personnel would average eight trips a month at the standard [partner organization] reimbursement rate of $.32/mi.				
32	or $55 per trip for 65 trips, transport cost of students at $10 per day, and one training conference at $4,000.				

(Continued)

TABLE 4.14 (Continued)

			HUD	MATCH	TOTAL
	BUDGET CATEGORIES	C	D	E	F
	B				
33	EQUIPMENT	0	0		0
34					
35	SUPPLIES	4400	750		=SUM(D38:E38)
36					
37	CONTRACTUAL	70000	0		=SUM(D40:E40)
38	[University partner]: Leadership development, entrepreneurial training, and related courses.				
39					
40	OTHER:				
41	HOUSING RESOURCES				
42	___ County Habitat for Humanity Inc.	0	125000		=SUM(D45:E45)
43					
44	IN-KIND MATCHING RESOURCES				
45	___ County Adult Education	0	500		=SUM(D48:E48)
46	___ County Judge Executive	0	2400		=SUM(D49:E49)
47	___ County Schools	0	25000		=SUM(D50:E50)
48	___ University	0	70000		
49					
50	TOTAL DIRECT	=SUM(D23:D50)	=SUM(E23:E51)		=SUM(F23:F49)
51					
52	INDIRECT CHARGES	=0.1*D53	=(E23*0.52)+((SUM(D11: D20)*0.52)-D55)		=SUM(D55:E55)
53	10% total administrative cost limitation of HUD.				
54					
55	TOTAL PROJECT	=SUM(D53:D55)	=SUM(E53:E55)		=SUM(D58+E58)

131

TABLE 4.15   Detailed Budget Example 4

John Doe, PhD
[Institution Name]
NSF 2006 Proposal Budget July 1, 2006–June 30, 2008

	NSF 7/01/2006– 6/30/2007	NSF 7/01/2007– 6/30/2008	NSF Total
Salary	$	$	$
John Doe, Principal Investigator (33% effort, 9-Month Salary)	17160	17160	34320
John Doe, Principal Investigator (Summer Salary @ 2/9 of $52,000)	11556	11556	23111
Research Assistant 12-Month Stipend ($860/month)	10360	10360	20720
Research Assistant 12-Month Stipend ($860/month)	10360	10360	20720
Subtotal	49436	49436	98871
Fringe			
22.9% of wages	11321	11321	22641
RA Tuition allowance (2 @ $4,578/year)	9156	9156	18312
Subtotal	20477	20477	40953
Travel			
Airfare	4250	4250	8500
Lodging	5100	5100	10200
Per Diem	1836	1836	3672
Ground Transportation and Parking	1275	1275	2550
Registration Fees (9 @ $200)	1800	1800	3600
Subtotal	14261	14261	28522
Supplies			
Laptop Computer with docking station	2500	0	2500
PCs and printer	2500	0	2500
Software Licenses and Updates	898	898	1796
Printing and Photocopying	1000	1000	2000
Flash Memory and CD-Rs	550	550	1100
Postage	150	150	300
Subtotal	7598	2598	10196
Total Direct	91772	86772	178544
Indirect Costs (45.5% of Total Modified Direct Costs)	41756	39481	81238
Total Project	$133528	$126253	$259782

TABLE 4.16   Detailed Budget Example 4, Formulas

John Doe, PhD
[Institution Name]
NSF 2006 Proposal Budget July 1, 2006–June 30, 2008

B	C	D NSF 7/01/2006-6/30/2007	E NSF 7/01/2007-6/30/2008	F NSF Total
9		*NSF*	*NSF*	*NSF Total*
10		*7/01/2006-6/30/2007*	*7/01/2007-6/30/2008*	*Total*
11	Salary			
12	John Doe, Principal Investigator (33% effort, 9-Month Salary)	=0.33*52000	=0.33*52000	=SUM(D12:E12)
13	John Doe, Principal Investigator (Summer Salary @ 2/9 of $52,000)	=52000/9*2	=(52000/9*2)	=SUM(D13:E13)
14	Research Assistant 12-Month Stipend ($860/month)	10360	10360	=SUM(D14:E14)
15	Research Assistant 12-Month Stipend ($860/month)	10360	10360	=SUM(D15:E15)
16	Subtotal	=SUM(D12:D15)	=SUM(E12:E15)	=SUM(D16:E16)
17	Fringe			
18	22.9% of wages	=D16*0.229	=E16*0.229	=SUM(D18:E18)
19	RA Tuition allowance (2 @ $4,578/year)	=4578*2	=4578*2	=SUM(D19:E19)
20	Subtotal	=SUM(D18:D19)	=SUM(E18:E19)	=SUM(D20:E20)
21	Travel			
22	Airfare	4250	4250	=SUM(D22:E22)
23	Lodging	5100	5100	=SUM(D23:E23)
24	Per Diem	1836	=D24	=SUM(D24:E24)
25	Ground Transportation and Parking	1275	1275	=SUM(D25:E25)
26	Registration Fees (9 @ $200)	1800	1800	=SUM(D26:E26)
27	Subtotal	=SUM(D22:D26)	=SUM(E22:E26)	=SUM(D27:E27)
28	Supplies			
29	Laptop Computer with docking station	2500	0	=SUM(D29:E29)
30	PCs and printer	2500	0	=SUM(D30:E30)
31	Software Licenses and Updates	=719+179	=719+179	=SUM(D31:E31)
32	Printing and Photocopying	1000	1000	=SUM(D32:E32)
33	Flash Memory and CD-Rs	550	550	=SUM(D33:E33)
34	Postage	150	150	=SUM(D34:E34)
35	Subtotal	=SUM(D29:D34)	=SUM(E29:E34)	=SUM(D35:E35)
36	Total Direct	91772	86772	=SUM(D36:E36)
37	Indirect Costs (45.5% of Total Modified Direct Costs)	=D36*0.455	=E36*0.455	=SUM(D37:E37)
38	Total Project	=SUM(D36:D37)	=SUM(E36:E37)	=SUM(D38:E38)

133

FORWARD AND BACKWARD LINKAGES

This chapter has focused thus far on budget development, but in the context of the larger grant proposal. Budgets do not stand alone. Rather, they relate to other components of the proposal and also to other components of the planning process and to implementation and evaluation. This brief section considers the budget as an outcome of planning and preparation and as an input to implementation through performance management and evaluation.

If we think back to earlier chapters, the focus of planning and preparation has been on organizing resources. The budget is the outcome of partnership negotiations, and is an objective measure of what each participant organization has agreed to provide in services and match and what they will receive in funds from the grant. Planning would have determined which organizational units would be responsible for implementation and which staff would be involved. In doing so, their other responsibilities would also be considered to determine the amount of commitment each staff member would be able to contribute during the life of the grant program. With regard to community needs, the budget should reflect decisions to provide services that are not otherwise available, and that are directly related to fulfilling community needs identified. The budget represents the financial plan that will be used to solidify the rough and sometimes amorphous plans hashed out by partner organizations.

As mentioned several times already, it is easiest to write the proposal narrative after the budget has been established with a degree of certainty because the budget highlights activities that will take place, and those activities have time lines associated with them. The activities relate to one another in important ways, suggesting a sequence of events. In short, the program theory becomes apparent from the proposed components. What we propose to do suggests an implementation approach and sequence that can be used by program managers to ensure that the program is on track. Budgets by year or shorter time periods can be used to keep track of financial goals and progress toward them. Nodes at which program activities shift provide natural points at which information can be collected for program management and program evaluation activities. And all of these components provide a logical framework to follow during the grant reporting process, which includes financial and narrative components. In short, the budget becomes the framework against which all other program components are compared. A good budget will be a valuable tool not only to write the remainder of the proposal, but to successfully manage program implementation. By comparison, a poorly designed budget will lead to a disjointed narrative description. And most likely, if a poorly configured budget did not result in the grant's rejection, it would also create implementation problems and delays. As the adage goes, an ounce of prevention may indeed be worth a pound of cure.

CONCLUSION

This chapter has considered the components of grant budgets, the process of grant budgeting, and the development of detailed budgets and budget instruments. The budget must be considered a key component of the grant proposal—after all, grants are all about the money. It is usually best to draft the budget early in the process, even before the program narrative. This will help to ensure that the various components of the budget come together in a clear, concise, and understandable fashion, but more important, that all of the proposal components are in agreement with one another. A good detailed project budget facilitates completion of required budget forms, and it provides the road map to use in composing the program narrative, which I consider in the next chapter.

REFERENCES

Bland, Robert L. 2007. *A Budgeting Guide for Local Government.* Washington, DC: ICMA.

Frederickson, Patricia and Rosanne London. 2000. Disconnect in the hollow state: The pivotal role of organizational capacity in community-based development organizations. *Public Administration Review* 60(3): 230–239.

Independent Sector. 2008. Research: Value of Volunteer Time. Accessed January 2, 2009. Available at: http://www.independentsector.org/programs/research/volunteer_time.html.

Key, V. O. 1940. The lack of a budgetary theory. *American Political Science Review* 34(6): 1137–1144.

Lee, Robert D., Jr., Ronald W. Johnson, and Philip G. Joyce. 2008. *Public Budgeting Systems, 8th Edition.* Sudbury, MA: Jones and Bartlett Publishers.

Logan, Robert R. December 1986. Fiscal illusion and the grantor government. *Journal of Political Economy* 94(6): 1304–1318.

Nathan, Richard P. Spring 1983. State and local governments under federal grants: Toward a predictive theory. *Political Science Quarterly* 98(1): 47–57.

Stein, Robert M. November 1984. Municipal public employment: An examination of intergovernmental influences. *American Journal of Political Science* 28(4): 636–653.

Vogt, John A. 2004. *Capital Budgeting and Finance: A Guide for Local Governments.* Washington, DC: ICMA.

Volden, Craig. Summer 1999. Asymmetric effects of intergovernmental grants: Analysis and implications for U.S. welfare policy. *Publius: The Journal of Federalism* 29(3): 51.

Zampelli, Ernest M. February 1986. Resource fungibility, the flypaper effect, and the expenditure impact of grants-in-aid. *Review of Economics and Statistics* 68(1): 33–40.

APPENDIX: SAMPLE BUDGET

This appendix presents the budget of a HUD Community Outreach Partnership Center (COPC) grant funded in 2002. COPC funding was eliminated from the federal budget during recent years but may be reinstituted with recent change in control of Congress. It is provided here as an example of a very complex federal grant budget with overlapping requirements. COPC required (1) a maximum award of $400,000, (2) a cap on planning and administration costs in the amount of 20% of total project costs, (3) that the grant should fund activities that are classified as research at no more than 25% of the budget, (4) that the budget should reflect the expenses that constitute each proposed program activity (this latter requirement forces the applicant to generate what more closely resembles a program budget [based on activities], and a functional budget [research/outreach allocations], but alongside the traditional and line item budget), and (5) that the match for research activities should be at least 50% and the match for outreach activities should be at least 25%. (Requirements for the 2002 COPC program application are available in the *Federal Register*, volume 67, issue number 58, Tuesday, March 26, 2002, in the Notices section, pages 13925–13974.)

On a scale of complexity, this budget is one of the most difficult you might expect to encounter. So difficult, in fact, that my project team failed to develop versions of the budget that reconciled with each other prior to the submission deadline on our first attempt. The problem? A combination of rounding errors and formula errors that were subsequently corrected. This grant was awarded on the third application attempt, testifying to the value of perseverance.

Federal Assistance Funding Matrix

OMB Approval No. 2501-0017 (exp. 03/31/2005)

The applicant must provide the funding matrix shown below, listing each program for which Federal funding is being requested, and complete the certifications.

Program*	Applicant Share	Federal Share	State Share	Local	Other	Program Income	Total
HUD COPC	640,060	399,999			222,406	0	1,262,465
Grand Totals	640,060	399,999			222,406	0	1,262,465

*   For FHIPs, show both initiative and component

Instructions for the HUD-424-M

Public reporting burden for this collection of information is estimated to average 45 minutes per response, including the time for reviewing instructions, searching existing data sources, gathering and maintaining the data needed, and completing and reviewing the collection of information. This agency may not conduct or sponsor, and a person is not required to respond to, a collection of information unless that collection displays a valid OMB control number.

This form is to be used by applicants requesting funding from the Department of Housing and Urban Development for application submissions for Federal assistance.

Enter the following information:

Program: The HUD funding program you are applying under.

Applicant Share: Enter the amount of funds or cash equivalent of in-kind contributions you are contributing to your project or program of activities.

Federal Share: Enter the amount of HUD funds you are requesting with your application.

State Share: Enter the amount of funds or cash equivalent of in-kind services the State is contributing to your project or program of activities.

Local Share: Enter the amount of funds or cash equivalent of in-kind services your local government is contributing to your project or program of activities.

Other: Enter the amount of other sources of private, non-profit, or other funds or cash equivalent of in-kind services being contributed to your project or program of activities.

Program Income: Enter the amount of program income you expect to generate and contribute to this program over the life of your award.

Total: Please total all columns and fill in the amounts.

	Type O	HUD TL	TL	Local Partner TL	Project TL	HUD Y1	Y1	Local Partner Y1	TL Y1	HUD Y2	Y2	Local Partner Y2	TL Y2	HUD Y3	Y3	Local Partner Y3	TL Y3
Community Organizing and Planning																	
1. Leadership Training/Public Policy Seminars																	
a. Personnel																	
Project Coordinator		15,000	18,000	0	33,000	5,000	6,000	0	11,000	5,000	6,000	0	11,000	5,000	6,000	0	11,000
Michael		6,000	7,800	0	13,800	2,000	2,600	0	4,600	2,000	2,600	0	4,600	2,000	2,600	0	4,600
Jeremy		3,000	5,000	0	8,000	1,000	1,667	0	2,667	1,000	1,667	0	2,667	1,000	1,667	0	2,687
Ed		3,000	7,980	0	10,980	1,000	2,660	0	3,660	1,000	2,660	0	3,660	1,000	2,660	0	3,660
Greg		1,000	5,001	0	6,001	333	1,667	0	2,000	333	1,667	0	2,000	333	1,667	0	2,000
Suzanne		3,000	3,000	0	6,000	1,000	1,000	0	2,000	1,000	1,000	0	2,000	1,000	1,000	0	2,000
Holly		5,000	5,000	0	10,000	1,667	1,667	0	3,333	1,667	1,667	0	3,333	1,667	1,867	0	3,333
William		1,000	7,500	0	8,500	333	2,500	0	2,833	333	2,500	0	2,833	333	2,500	0	2,833
Total Personnel		37,000	59,281	0	96,281	12,333	19,760	0	32,094	12,333	19,760	0	32,094	12,333	19,760	0	32,094
b. Fringe Benefits		13,505	21,638	0	35,143	4,502	7,213	0	11,714	4,502	7,213	0	11,714	4,502	7,213	0	11,714
c. Travel		1,500	0	0	1,500	500	0	0	500	500	0	0	500	500	0	0	500
d. Equipment		0	0	0	0	0	0	0	0	0	0	0	0	0	0	0	0
e. Supplies		0	0	0	0	0	0	0	0	0	0	0	0	0	0	0	0
f. Contractual		0	0	0	0	0	0	0	0	0	0	0	0	0	0	0	0
g. Other Direct		1,875	0	13,610	15,485	625	0	4,537	5,162	625	0	4,537	5,162	625	0	4,537	5,162
Total Direct Costs		53,880	80,919	13,610	148,409	17,960	26,973	4,537	49,470	17,960	26,973	4,537	49,470	17,960	26,973	4,537	49,470
h. Indirect Costs		14,430	23,120	0	37,550	4,810	7,707	0	12,517	4,810	7,707	0	12,517	4,810	7,707	0	12,517
Project Subtotal		68,310	104,038	13,610	185,958	22,770	34,679	4,537	61,986	22,770	34,679	4,537	61,986	22,770	34,679	4,537	61,986
2. Historical Preservation				Other TL				Other Y1				Other Y2				Other Y3	
a. Personnel																	
Holly		3,000	1,000	0	4,000	1,000	333	0	1,333	1,000	333	0	1,333	1,000	333	0	1,333
Jeremy		1,500	1,500	0	3,000	500	500	0	1,000	500	500	0	1,000	500	500	0	1,000
Michael		3,000	4,000	0	7,000	1,000	1,333	0	2,333	1,000	1,333	0	2,333	1,000	1,333	0	2,333
Kevin		1,500	7,566	0	9,066	500	2,522	0	3,022	500	2,522	0	3,022	500	2,522	0	3,022
Total Personnel		9,000	14,066	0	23,066	3,000	4,689	0	7,689	3,000	4,689	0	7,689	3,000	4,689	0	7,689
b. Fringe Benefits		3,285	5,134	0	8,419	1,095	1,711	0	2,806	1,095	1,711	0	2,806	1,095	1,711	0	2,806
c. Travel		1,500	0	0	1,500	500	0	0	500	500	0	0	500	500	0	0	500
d. Equipment		0	0	0	0	0	0	0	0	0	0	0	0	0	0	0	0
e. Supplies		0	0	0	0	0	0	0	0	0	0	0	0	0	0	0	0
f. Contractual		0	0	0	0	0	0	0	0	0	0	0	0	0	0	0	0
g. Other Direct		750	0	12,361	13,111	250	0	4,120	4,370	250	0	4,120	4,370	250	0	4,120	4,370
Total Direct Costs		14,535	19,200	12,361	46,096	4,845	6,400	4,120	15,365	4,845	6,400	4,120	15,365	4,845	6,400	4,120	15,365
h. Indirect Costs		3,510	5,486	0	8,996	1,170	1,829	0	2,999	1,170	1,829	0	2,999	1,170	1,829	0	2,999
Project Subtotal		18,045	24,686	12,361	55,092	6,015	8,229	4,120	18,364	6,015	8,229	4,120	18,364	6,015	8,229	4,120	18,364

3. GIS-GPS Training — O

	HUD TL	TL	Other TL	Project TL	HUD Y1	Y1	Other Y1	TL Y1	HUD Y2	Y2	Other Y2	TL Y2	HUD Y3	Y3	Other Y3	TL Y3
a. Personnel																
Kevin	4,500	7,569	0	12,069	1,500	2,523	0	4,023	1,500	2,523	0	4,023	1,500	2,523	0	4,023
Steve	4,500	4,500	0	9,000	1,500	1,500	0	3,000	1,500	1,500	0	3,000	1,500	1,500	0	3,000
Total Personnel	9,000	12,069	0	21,069	3,000	4,023	0	7,023	3,000	4,023	0	7,023	3,000	4,023	0	7,023
b. Fringe Benefits	3,285	4,405	0	7,690	1,095	1,468	0	2,563	1,095	1,468	0	2,563	1,095	1,468	0	2,563
c. Travel	0	0	0	0	0	0	0	0	0	0	0	0	0	0	0	0
d. Equipment	0	0	0	0	0	0	0	0	0	0	0	0	0	0	0	0
e. Supplies	0	0	0	0	0	0	0	0	0	0	0	0	0	0	0	0
f. Contractual	0	0	0	0	0	0	0	0	0	0	0	0	0	0	0	0
g. Other Direct	0	0	12,361	12,361	0	0	4,120	4,120	0	0	4,120	4,120	0	0	4,120	4,120
Total Direct Costs	12,285	16,474	12,361	41,120	4,095	5,491	4,120	13,707	4,095	5,491	4,120	13,707	4,085	5,491	4,120	13,707
h. Indirect Costs	3,510	4,707	0	8,217	1,170	1,569	0	2,739	1,170	1,569	0	2,739	1,170	1,569	0	2,739
Project Subtotal	15,795	21,181	12,361	49,337	5,265	7,060	4,120	16,446	5,265	7,060	4,120	16,446	5,265	7,060	4,120	16,446

4. Public Sector Capacity Study — R

	HUD TL	TL	Other TL	Project TL	HUD Y1	Y1	Other Y1	TL Y1	HUD Y2	Y2	Other Y2	TL Y2	HUD Y3	Y3	Other Y3	TL Y3
a. Personnel																
Michael	3,000	8,400	0	11,400	1,000	2,800	0	3,800	1,000	2,800	0	3,800	1,000	2,800	0	3,800
Suzanne	3,000	3,000	0	6,000	1,000	1,000	0	2,000	1,000	1,000	0	2,000	1,000	1,000	0	2,000
Jeremy	3,000	9,000	0	12,000	1,000	3,000	0	4,000	1,000	3,000	0	4,000	1,000	3,000	0	4,000
Total Personnel	9,000	20,400	0	29,400	3,000	6,800	0	9,800	3,000	6,800	0	9,800	3,000	6,800	0	9,800
b. Fringe Benefits	3,285	7,446	0	10,731	1,095	2,482	0	3,577	1,095	2,482	0	3,577	1,095	2,482	0	3,577
c. Travel	2,750	0	0	2,750	917	0	0	917	917	0	0	917	917	0	0	917
d. Equipment	0	0	0	0	0	0	0	0	0	0	0	0	0	0	0	0
e. Supplies	0	0	0	0	0	0	0	0	0	0	0	0	0	0	0	0
f. Contractual	0	0	0	0	0	0	0	0	0	0	0	0	0	0	0	0
g. Other Direct	750	0	10,610	11,360	250	0	3,537	3,787	260	0	3,537	3,787	250	0	3,537	3,787
Total Direct Costs	15,785	27,846	10,610	54,241	5,262	9,282	3,537	18,080	5,262	9,282	3,537	18,080	5,262	9,282	3,537	18,080
h. Indirect Costs	3,510	7,956	0	11,466	1,170	2,652	0	3,822	1,170	2,652	0	3,822	1,170	2,652	0	3,822
Project Subtotal	19,295	35,802	10,610	65,707	6,432	11,934	3,537	21,902	6,432	11,934	3,537	21,902	6,432	11,934	3,537	21,902

Economic Development & Neighborhood Revitalization

1. Entrepreneurial Development & Business Incubator O

	HUD TL	TL	Other TL	Project TL	HUD Y1	Y1	Other Y1	TL Y1	HUD Y2	Y2	Other Y2	TL Y2	HUD Y3	Y3	Other Y3	TL Y3
a. Personnel																
Michael	5,000	3,045	0	8,045	1,667	1,015	0	2,682	1,667	1,015	0	2,682	1,667	1,015	0	2,682
Technology Specialist	2,500	27,669	0	30,169	833	9,223	0	10,056	833	9,223	0	10,056	833	9,223	0	10,056
Project Coordinator	12,000	50,000	0	62,000	4,000	16,667	0	20,667	4,000	16,667	0	20,667	4,000	16,667	0	20,667
Susan	1,000	8,001	0	9,001	333	2,667	0	3,000	333	2,667	0	3,000	333	2,667	0	3,000
David	2,000	9,000	0	11,000	667	3,000	0	3,667	667	3,000	0	3,667	667	3,000	0	3,667
Jeremy	5,000	4,000	0	9,000	1,667	1,333	0	3,000	1,667	1,333	0	3,000	1,667	1,333	0	3,000
Mike	0	4,605	0	4,605	0	1,535	0	1,535	0	1,535	0	1,535	0	1,535	0	1,535
Bob	0	4,284	0	4,284	0	1,428	0	1,428	0	1,428	0	1,428	0	1,428	0	1,428
Tom	0	2,499	0	2,499	0	833	0	833	0	833	0	833	0	833	0	833
Mark	2,000	4,000	0	6,000	667	1,333	0	2,000	667	1,333	0	2,000	667	1,333	0	2,000
Total Personnel	29,500	117,103	0	146,603	9,833	39,034	0	48,868	9,833	39,034	0	48,868	9,833	39,034	0	48,868
b. Fringe Benefits	10,768	42,743	0	53,510	3,589	14,248	0	17,837	3,589	14,248	0	17,837	3,589	14,248	0	17,837
c. Travel	1,500	0	0	1,500	500	0	0	500	500	0	0	500	500	0	0	500
d. Equipment	0	0	0	0	0	0	0	0	0	0	0	0	0	0	0	0
e. Supplies	0	0	0	0	0	0	0	0	0	0	0	0	0	0	0	0
f. Contractual	7,500	0	0	7,500	2,500	0	0	2,500	2,500	0	0	2,500	2,500	0	0	2,500
g. Other Direct	1,550	0	26,694	28,244	517	0	8,898	9,415	517	0	8,898	9,415	517	0	8,898	9,415
Total Direct Costs	50,818	159,846	26,694	237,357	16,939	53,282	8,898	79,119	16,939	53,282	8,898	79,119	16,939	53,282	8,898	79,119
h. Indirect Costs	11,505	45,670	0	57,175	3,835	15,223	0	19,058	3,835	15,223	0	19,058	3,835	15,223	0	19,058
Project Subtotal	62,323	205,516	26,694	294,532	20,774	68,505	8,898	98,177	20,774	68,505	8,898	98,177	20,774	68,505	8,898	98,177

2. Economic Policy Study R

	HUD TL	TL	Other TL	Project TL	HUD Y1	Y1	Other Y1	TL Y1	HUD Y2	Y2	Other Y2	TL Y2	HUD Y3	Y3	Other Y3	TL Y3
a. Personnel																
Suzanne	3,000	3,042	0	6,042	1,000	1,014	0	2,014	1,000	1,014	0	2,014	1,000	1,014	0	2,014
Holly	3,000	2,499	0	5,499	1,000	833	0	1,833	1,000	833	0	1,833	1,000	833	0	1,833
Michael	3,000	1,977	0	4,977	1,000	659	0	1,659	1,000	659	0	1,659	1,000	659	0	1,659
Total Personnel	9,000	7,518	0	16,518	3,000	2,506	0	5,506	3,000	2,506	0	5,506	3,000	2,506	0	5,506
b. Fringe Benefits	3,285	2,744	0	6,029	1,095	915	0	2,010	1,095	915	0	2,010	1,095	915	0	2,010
c. Travel	1,500	0	0	1,500	500	0	0	500	500	0	0	500	500	0	0	500
d. Equipment	0	0	0	0	0	0	0	0	0	0	0	0	0	0	0	0
e. Supplies	0	0	0	0	0	0	0	0	0	0	0	0	0	0	0	0
f. Contractual	0	0	0	0	0	0	0	0	0	0	0	0	0	0	0	0
g. Other Direct	798	0	13,610	14,408	266	0	4,537	4,803	266	0	4,537	4,803	266	0	4,537	4,803
Total Direct Costs	14,583	10,262	13,610	38,455	4,861	3,421	4,537	12,818	4,861	3,421	4,537	12,818	4,861	3,421	4,537	12,818
h. Indirect Costs	3,510	2,932	0	6,442	1,170	977	0	2,147	1,170	977	0	2,147	1,170	977	0	2,147
Project Subtotal	18,093	13,194	13,610	44,897	6,031	4,398	4,537	14,966	6,031	4,398	4,537	14,966	6,031	4,398	4,537	14,966

	O	HUD TL	TL	Other TL	Project TL	HUD Y1	Y1	Other Y1	TL Y1	HUD Y2	Y2	Other Y2	TL Y2	HUD Y3	Y3	Other Y3	TL Y3
Education																	
1. Community History/Oral History Program	O																
a. Personnel																	
Holly		4,500	3,000	0	7,500	1,500	1,000	0	2,500	1,500	1,000	0	2,500	1,500	1,000	0	2,500
Michael		2,500	1,000	0	3,500	833	333	0	1,167	833	333	0	1,167	833	333	0	1,167
Total Personnel		7,000	4,000	0	11,000	2,333	1,333	0	3,667	2,333	1,333	0	3,667	2,333	1,333	0	3,667
b. Fringe Benefits		2,555	1,460	0	4,015	852	487	0	1,338	852	487	0	1,338	852	487	0	1,338
c. Travel		0	0	0	0	0	0	0	0	0	0	0	0	0	0	0	0
d. Equipment		0	0	0	0	0	0	0	0	0	0	0	0	0	0	0	0
e. Supplies		0	0	0	0	0	0	0	0	0	0	0	0	0	0	0	0
f. Contractual		5,250	0	0	5,250	1,750	0	0	1,750	1,750	0	0	1,750	1,750	0	0	1,750
g. Other Direct		3,000	0	17,584	20,584	1,000	0	5,861	6,861	1,000	0	5,861	6,861	1,000	0	5,861	6,861
Total Direct Costs		17,805	5,460	17,584	40,849	5,935	1,820	5,861	13,616	5,935	1,820	5,861	13,616	5,935	1,820	5,861	13,616
h. Indirect Costs		2,730	1,560	0	4,290	910	520	0	1,430	910	520	0	1,430	910	520	0	1,430
Project Subtotal		20,535	7,020	17,584	45,139	6,845	2,340	5,861	15,046	6,845	2,340	5,861	15,046	6,845	2,340	5,861	15,046
2. Literacy/GED Training	O																
a. Personnel																	
William		2,500	5,500	0	8,000	833	1,833	0	2,667	833	1,833	0	2,667	833	1,833	0	2,667
Total Personnel		2,500	5,500	0	8,000	833	1,833	0	2,667	833	1,833	0	2,667	833	1,833	0	2,667
b. Fringe Benefits		913	2,008	0	2,920	304	669	0	973	304	669	0	973	304	669	0	973
c. Travel		0	0	0	0	0	0	0	0	0	0	0	0	0	0	0	0
d. Equipment		0	0	0	0	0	0	0	0	0	0	0	0	0	0	0	0
e. Supplies		0	0	0	0	0	0	0	0	0	0	0	0	0	0	0	0
f. Contractual		3,000	0	0	3,000	1,000	0	0	1,000	1,000	0	0	1,000	1,000	0	0	1,000
g. Other Direct		0	0	14,583	14,583	0	0	4,861	4,861	0	0	4,861	4,861	0	0	4,861	4,861
Total Direct Costs		6,413	7,508	14,583	28,503	2,138	2,503	4,861	9,501	2,138	2,503	4,861	9,501	2,138	2,503	4,861	9,501
h. Indirect Costs		975	2,145	0	3,120	325	715	0	1,040	325	715	0	1,040	325	715	0	1,040
Project Subtotal		7,388	9,653	14,583	31,623	2,463	3,218	4,861	10,541	2,463	3,218	4,861	10,541	2,463	3,218	4,861	10,541

Housing

	HUD TL	TL	Other TL	Project TL	HUD Y1	Y1	Other Y1	TL Y1	HUD Y2	Y2	Other Y2	TL Y2	HUD Y3	Y3	Other Y3	TL Y3
1. Fair Housing Training for Landlords/Tenants (O)																
a. Personnel																
Project Coordinator	2,000	4,000	0	6,000	667	1,333	0	2,000	667	1,333	0	2,000	667	1,333	0	2,000
William	1,500	6,000	0	7,500	500	2,000	0	2,500	500	2,000	0	2,500	500	2,000	0	2,500
Total Personnel	3,500	10,000	0	13,500	1,167	3,333	0	4,500	1,167	3,333	0	4,500	1,167	3,333	0	4,500
b. Fringe Benefits	1,278	3,650	0	4,928	426	1,217	0	1,643	426	1,217	0	1,643	426	1,217	0	1,643
c. Travel	0	0	0	0	0	0	0	0	0	0	0	0	0	0	0	0
d. Equipment	0	0	0	0	0	0	0	0	0	0	0	0	0	0	0	0
e. Supplies	0	0	0	0	0	0	0	0	0	0	0	0	0	0	0	0
f. Contractual	0	0	0	0	0	0	0	0	0	0	0	0	0	0	0	0
g. Other Direct	1,500	0	34,861	36,361	500	0	11,620	12,120	500	0	11,620	12,120	500	0	11,620	12,120
Total Direct Costs	6,278	13,650	34,861	54,789	2,093	4,550	11,620	18,263	2,093	4,550	11,620	18,263	2,093	4,550	11,620	18,263
h. Indirect Costs	1,365	3,900	0	5,265	455	1,300	0	1,755	455	1,300	0	1,755	455	1,300	0	1,755
Project Subtotal	7,643	17,550	34,861	60,054	2,548	5,850	11,620	20,018	2,548	5,850	11,620	20,018	2,548	5,850	11,620	20,018
2. Housing Policy Study (R)																
a. Personnel																
David	3,000	11,472	0	14,472	1,000	3,824	0	4,824	1,000	3,824	0	4,824	1,000	3,82(	0	4,824
Holly	6,000	3,000	0	9,000	2,000	1,000	0	3,000	2,000	1,000	0	3,000	2,000	1,00(	0	3,000
Michael	2,000	3,600	0	5,600	667	1,200	0	1,867	667	1,200	0	1,867	667	1,20(	0	1,867
Suzanne	2,000	1,989	0	3,989	667	663	0	1,330	667	663	0	1,330	667	66(	0	1,330
Jeremy	2,000	3,042	0	5,042	667	1,014	0	1,681	667	1,014	0	1,681	667	1,01(	0	1,681
Steve	3,000	3,000	0	6,000	1,000	1,000	0	2,000	1,000	1,000	0	2,000	1,000	1,00(	0	2,000
Kevin	1,000	7,569	0	8,569	333	2,523	0	2,856	333	2,523	0	2,856	333	2,52(	0	2,856
Bob	1,000	2,034	0	3,034	333	678	0	1,011	333	678	0	1,011	333	67(	0	1,011
Total Personnel	20,000	35,706	0	55,706	6,667	11,902	0	18,569	6,667	11,902	0	18,569	6,667	11,90(	0	18,569
b. Fringe Benefits	7,300	13,033	0	20,333	2,433	4,344	0	6,778	2,433	4,344	0	6,778	2,433	4,34(	0	6,778
c. Travel	1,500	0	0	1,500	500	0	0	500	500	0	0	500	500		0	500
d. Equipment	0	0	0	0	0	0	0	0	0	0	0	0	0		0	0
e. Supplies	0	0	0	0	0	0	0	0	0	0	0	0	0		0	0
f. Contractual	0	0	0	0	0	0	0	0	0	0	0	0	0		0	0
g. Other Direct	189	1,889	34,861	36,939	63	630	11,620	12,313	63	630	11,620	12,313	63	63	11,620	12,313
Total Direct Costs	28,989	50,628	34,861	114,478	9,663	16,876	11,620	38,159	9,663	16,876	11,620	38,159	9,663	16,87	11,620	38,159
h. Indirect Costs	7,800	13,925	0	21,725	2,600	4,642	0	7,242	2,600	4,642	0	7,242	2,600	4,64	0	7,242
Project Subtotal	36,789	64,553	34,861	136,203	12,263	21,518	11,620	45,401	12,263	21,518	11,620	45,401	12,263	21,51	11,620	45,401

	O	HUD TL	TL	Other TL	Project TL	HUD Y1	Y1	Other Y1	TL Y1	HUD Y2	Y2	Other Y2	TL Y2	HUD Y3	Y3	Other Y3	TL Y3
Environment																	
1. Solid Waste Education																	
a. Personnel																	
April		3,000	2,823	0	5,823	1,000	941	0	1,941	1,000	941	0	1,941	1,000	941	0	1,941
Total Personnel		3,000	2,823	0	5,823	1,000	941	0	1,941	1,000	941	0	1,941	1,000	941	0	1,941
b. Fringe Benefits		1,095	1,030	0	2,125	365	343	0	708	365	343	0	708	365	343	0	708
c. Travel		0	0	0	0	0	0	0	0	0	0	0	0	0	0	0	0
d. Equipment		0	0	0	0	0	0	0	0	0	0	0	0	0	0	0	0
e. Supplies		0	0	0	0	0	0	0	0	0	0	0	0	0	0	0	0
f. Contractual		0	0	0	0	0	0	0	0	0	0	0	0	0	0	0	0
g. Other Direct		1,500	0	6,600	8,100	500	0	2,200	2,700	500	0	2,200	2,700	500	0	2,200	2,700
Total Direct Costs		5,595	3,853	6,600	16,048	1,865	1,284	2,200	5,349	1,865	1,284	2,200	5,349	1,865	1,284	2,200	5,349
h. Indirect Costs		1,170	1,101	0	2,271	390	367	0	757	390	367	0	757	390	367	0	757
Project Subtotal		6,765	4,954	6,600	18,319	2,255	1,651	2,200	6,106	2,255	1,651	2,200	6,106	2,255	1,651	2,200	6,106
2. Pollution Monitoring Program																	
a. Personnel																	
Brian		4,500	17,343	0	21,843	1,500	5,781	0	7,281	1,500	5,781	0	7,281	1,500	5,781	0	7,281
April		3,000	2,853	0	5,853	1,000	951	0	1,951	1,000	951	0	1,951	1,000	951	0	1,951
David		2,000	3,034	0	5,034	667	1,011	0	1,678	667	1,011	0	1,678	667	1,011	0	1,678
Total Personnel		9,500	23,230	0	32,730	3,167	7,743	0	10,910	3,167	7,743	0	10,910	3,167	7,743	0	10,910
b. Fringe Benefits		3,468	8,479	0	11,946	1,156	2,826	0	3,982	1,156	2,826	0	3,982	1,156	2,826	0	3,982
c. Travel		0	0	0	0	0	0	0	0	0	0	0	0	0	0	0	0
d. Equipment		0	0	0	0	0	0	0	0	0	0	0	0	0	0	0	0
e. Supplies		0	0	0	0	0	0	0	0	0	0	0	0	0	0	0	0
f. Contractual		0	0	0	0	0	0	0	0	0	0	0	0	0	0	0	0
g. Other Direct		1,750	0	10,210	11,960	583	0	3,403	3,987	583	0	3,403	3,987	583	0	3,403	3,987
Total Direct Costs		14,718	31,709	10,210	56,636	4,906	10,570	3,403	18,879	4,906	10,570	3,403	18,879	4,906	10,570	3,403	18,879
h. Indirect Costs		3,705	9,060	0	12,765	1,235	3,020	0	4,255	1,235	3,020	0	4,255	1,235	3,020	0	4,255
Project Subtotal		18,423	40,769	10,210	69,401	6,141	13,590	3,403	23,134	6,141	13,590	3,403	23,134	6,141	13,590	3,403	23,134

	O	HUD TL	TL	Other TL	Project TL	HUD Y1	Y1	Other Y1	TL Y1	HUD Y2	Y2	Other Y2	TL Y2	HUD Y3	Y3	Other Y3	TL Y3
3. Environmental Academy & Training Institute																	
a. Personnel																	
April		18,000	5,646	0	23,646	6,000	1,882	0	7,882	6,000	1,882	0	7,882	6,000	1,882	0	7,882
Project Coordinator		11,000	12,000	0	23,000	3,667	4,000	0	7,667	3,667	4,000	0	7,667	3,667	4,000	0	7,667
Michael		5,000	5,000	0	10,000	1,667	1,667	0	3,333	1,667	1,667	0	3,333	1,667	1,667	0	3,333
Suzanne		3,000	3,000	0	6,000	1,000	1,000	0	2,000	1,000	1,000	0	2,000	1,000	1,000	0	2,000
Total Personnel		37,000	25,646	0	62,646	12,333	8,549	0	20,882	12,333	8,549	0	20,882	12,333	8,549	0	20,882
b. Fringe Benefits		13,505	9,361	0	22,866	4,502	3,120	0	7,622	4,502	3,120	0	7,622	4,502	3,120	0	7,622
c. Travel		6,000	0	0	6,000	2,000	0	0	2,000	2,000	0	0	2,000	2,000	0	0	2,000
d. Equipment		0	0	0	0	0	0	0	0	0	0	0	0	0	0	0	0
e. Supplies		0	0	0	0	0	0	0	0	0	0	0	0	0	0	0	0
f. Contractual		15,561	0	0	15,561	5,187	0	0	5,187	5,187	0	0	5,187	5,187	0	0	5,187
g. Other Direct		6,291	0	14,461	20,752	2,097	0	4,820	6,917	2,097	0	4,820	6,917	2,097	0	4,820	6,917
Total Direct Costs		78,357	35,007	14,461	127,825	26,119	11,669	4,820	42,608	26,119	11,669	4,820	42,608	26,119	11,669	4,820	42,608
h. Indirect Costs		14,430	10,002	0	24,432	4,810	3,334	0	8,144	4,810	3,334	0	8,144	4,810	3,334	0	8,144
Project Subtotal		92,787	45,009	14,461	152,257	30,929	15,003	4,820	50,752	30,929	15,003	4,820	50,752	30,929	15,003	4,820	50,752
Planning and Administration																	
Planning and Administration																	
a. Personnel																	
Project Coordinator		2,450	15,000	0	17,450	817	5,000	0	5,817	817	5,000	0	5,817	817	5,000	0	5,817
Michael		1,000	3,500	0	4,500	333	1,167	0	1,500	333	1,167	0	1,500	333	1,167	0	1,500
Jeremy		500	2,088	0	2,588	167	696	0	863	167	696	0	863	167	696	0	863
David		500	5,700	0	6,200	167	1,900	0	2,067	167	1,900	0	2,067	167	1,900	0	2,067
Total Personnel		4,450	26,238	0	30,738	1,483	8,763	0	10,246	1,483	8,763	0	10,246	1,483	8,763	0	10,246
b. Fringe Benefits		1,624	9,595	0	11,219	541	3,198	0	3,740	541	3,198	0	3,740	541	3,198	0	3,740
Total Direct Costs		6,074	35,883	0	41,957	2,025	11,961	0	13,986	2,025	11,961	0	13,986	2,025	11,961	0	13,986
h. Indirect Costs		1,736	10,252	0	11,988	579	3,417	0	3,996	579	3,417	0	3,996	579	3,417	0	3,996
Project Subtotal		7,810	46,135	0	53,945	2,603	15,378	0	17,982	2,603	15,378	0	17,982	2,603	15,378	0	17,982
TOTAL		399,999	640,060	222,406	1,262,465	130,730	197,975	74,135	402,840	130,730	197,975	74,135	402,840	130,730	197,975	74,135	402,840
Indirect Costs Total		73,886	141,916														

	HUD TL	TL	Other TL	Project TL	math check:
planning & admin 80,000 limit calc	79,980	177,699	0	41,957	257,659
research	74,177	113,549	59,081	246,807	246,807
outreach	325,822	526,511	163,325	1,015,658	1,015,658
	318,012	480,375	163,325	961,713	961,713
	392,189	593,925	222,406	1,208,520	1,208,520
outreach prop	0.80	0.80	0.80	0.80	2
research prop	0.20	0.20	0.20	0.20	1
plan & admin add back in research	1,562	9,227	0	10,789	10,789
plan & admin add back in outreach	6,248	36,908	0	43,156	43,155
research grand tl	75,739	122,776	59,081	257,596	257,596
outreach grand tl	324,260	517,284	163,325	1,004,869	1,004,869
II II	399,999	640,060	222,406	1,262,465	1,262,465

Verification of Match
for New Grants

U.S. Department of Housing
and Urban Development
Office of Policy Development and Research

OMB Approval No. 2528-0180
(exp. 99/99/9999)

Public reporting burden for this collection of information is estimated to average 5 hours per response, including the time for reviewing instructions, searching existing data sources, gathering and maintaining the data needed, and completing and reviewing the
collection of information. The information collected on this form is utilized to calculate and verify the amount of matching resources as
a percentage of total project costs. This collection of information is authorized by Public Law 100-242, section 501. This agency may
not collect this information, and you are not required to complete this form, unless it displays a currently valid OMB control number.
HUD has submitted a request for Office of Management and Budget (OMB) approval to collect this information. That approval is
pending.

Record of Match Commitments

List of matching sources		Check if commitment letter is included and activity is eligible for match
1.	State University	$640,060	[YES]
2.	City	$63,606	[YES]
3.	Housing	$45,000	[YES]
4.	Technical College	$43,000	[YES]
5.	County Government	$33,000	[YES]
6.	Partner	$30,000	[YES]
7.	Partner	$5,000	[YES]
8.	Community Recycling Center	$1,800	[YES]
9.	GEAR-UP	$1,000	[YES]

Page 1 of 3

Verification of Match (cont'd.)

CALCULATION OF THE MATCH

1. REQUIRED MATCH:

A. Research Total Project Costs::

75,739	+	181,857	=	257,596
(Grant request for Research)		(Match for Research)		(Research Total Project Costs)

Research match should be:

257,596	X	50%	=	128,798
(Research Total Project Costs)				

B. Outreach Total Project Costs::

324,260	+	680,609	=	1,004,869
(Grant request for Outreach)		(Match for Outreach)		(Outreach Total Project Costs)

Outreach match should be:

1,004,869	X	25%	=	251,217.25
(Outreach Total Project Costs)				(Required Research Match)

C. Required Total Match:

128,798	+	251,217.25	=	380,015.25
(Required Research Match-from 1.A.)		(Required Outreach Match-from 1.B.)		(Required Total Match)

2. ACTUAL MATCH FOR STATUTORY PURPOSES:

COUNT ONLY THOSE ITEMS WHICH ARE ELIGIBLE AND FOR WHICH THERE ARE COMMIT-MENT LETTERS, USING THE FORM HUD-30001. THAT FORM AND THE FIRST PART OF THIS WORKSHEET SHOULD CONFORM.

Research match provided: 181,857

Outreach match provided: 680.609

    Total match provided: 862,466

Match provided is more than match required:

    XXX   Yes   No

3. ACTUAL MATCH FOR FACTOR 4 PURPOSES:

Actual total match provided (from # 2 above):   862,466

Minus indirect match: 141,816

Actual total match for following calculations: 720,650

4. MATCH OVERAGE

$$\frac{\text{Total Actual Match (w/o indirect costs)(from 3)}}{\text{Total Required Match (from 1.C.)}} = \frac{720,650}{380,015.25} = 1.90$$

(As long as the number produced is more than 1, use only amount to the right of the decimal point to determine overage. If the number is less than 1, there is no match overage and you are not eligible for any points under this subfactor.)

5. MATCH FROM OUTSIDE SOURCES

$$\frac{\text{Total Match from Outside Sources}}{\text{Total Actual Match (w/o indirect costs) (from 3)}} = \frac{222,406}{720,650} = .31$$

Federal Register / Vol. 67, No. 58 / Tuesday, March 26, 2002 / Notices   **13937**

Community Outreach
Partnership Centers Program
Matching Requirements

U.S. Department of Housing
and Urban Development
Office of Policy Research
and Development

OMB Approval No. 2528-0180
(exp. 2/28/2003)

	Federal Share $	Match $	Total Cost $	Match as Percent of Total Cost
Research Activities: (list)				
Public Sector Capacity Study				
Economic Policy Study				
Housing Policy Study				
20% Planning and Administration				
Subtotal	75,739	181,857	257,596	20 %
Outreach Activities: (list)				
Leadership Training/Public Policy Seminars				
Historical Preservation				
GIS/GPS Training				
Entrepreneurial Development & Bus. Incubator				
Community History/Oral History Program				
Literacy/GED Training				
Fair Housing Training for Landlords/Tenants				
Solid Waste Education				
Pollution Monitoring Program				
Environmental Academy & Training Institute				
80% Planning & Administration				
Subtotal	324,260	680,609	1,004,869	80 %
Total	399,999	862,466	1,262,465	

Federal Register / Vol. 67, No. 58 / Tuesday, March 26, 2002 / Notices   13939

Community Outreach
Partnership Centers Program
**Breakdown of Outreach and
Research Activities**

**U.S. Department of Housing
and Urban Development**
Office of Policy Research
and Development

OMB Approval No. 2528-0180
(exp. 2/28/2003)

The information collection requirements contained in this notice of funding availability and application kit will be used to rate applications, determine eligibility, and establish grant amounts for the Community Outreach Partnership Centers (COPC) program.

Total public reporting burden for collection of this information is estimated to average 80 hours. This includes the time for reviewing instructions, searching existing data sources, gathering and maintaining the data needed, and completing and reviewing the collection of information.

The information submitted in response to the notice of funding availability for the COPC program and HSI-WSP program is subject to the disclosure requirements of the Department of Housing and Urban Development Reform Act of 1989 (Pub.L. 101-235, approved December 15, 1989, 42 U.S.C. 3545).

The agency may not conduct or sponsor, and a person is not required to respond to, a collection of information unless the collection displays a valid control number.

	Total Cost $	Percent of Total Project Cost
Total Research Activities	257,596	20 %
Total Outreach Activities	1,004,869	80 %
Total	1,262,465	

CHAPTER 5

The Grant Proposal Narrative

You have completed a search of available funding from foundations and government agencies. You have sketched out a program idea in a rough version—the one that you used to identify viable funding sources—and in a more polished version that served as the basis for your proposal budget. This program idea includes the specific obligations assumed by your organization and any partner organizations, and the relationships among them in the proposed program. You know approximately what you will spend money on, and you have documented the basis of those costs in your budget and budget justification. It certainly seems like the program planning and design process is winding down, yet there is a very large piece of the application narrative that remains unfinished—the proposal itself.

What should be included in the proposal narrative description? What should be left out? Where does one begin? The subject of this chapter is the proposal narrative—your opportunity to describe your proposed program and convince the funding source to which you are applying that your program is deserving of its investment. The chapter begins with a discussion of the general approach to completing a project/program narrative, suggests logical structures for developing unstructured narratives, and provides a discussion of each of the components that make up a typical program narrative structure. Various space-saving visual tools and strategies are discussed in the process, including tables, Gantt charts, time lines, and others.

Before I introduce the elements that make up a typical proposal narrative, it is a good idea to consider the general approach you should have in mind as you begin. The following section reviews important overarching considerations that should be observed as you prepare to write any grant proposal narrative.

GENERAL APPROACH TO PROGRAM NARRATIVES

Preliminary Considerations

The program narrative serves multiple purposes, among which is the need to communicate the plans you have for the program in question—to explain what you plan to do with the money. However, this is probably not the most important consideration for most proposal narratives. The funder is certainly interested in what you plan to do, but it first needs to know whether there is a real need for its involvement. Funders approach grant applications with a few general questions in mind. You should keep these questions in mind as well—and in doing so learn to

149

think like the person(s) reading the proposal. Generally speaking, a grant maker will ask "Why should I be involved? Is there a need or problem that should be addressed, and is it a need or problem that my organization is interested in abating?" So, your first task is to define the nature of the problem to be solved, envision what the world (or some smaller geographic area, organization, or group) would look like if you successfully implement the desired program, and then convey the problem, approach, and desired results effectively in writing.

Bardach (2005) explains the importance of properly defining a problem in conducting an effective policy analysis. The problem definition shapes each of the ensuing steps and affects the ultimate outcome. Problem definition is equally important in advocating for a preferred alternative, such as is the case in grant writing. A grant is a proposal to address a problem or need. The way you define the problem determines whether the funder will be interested, and you should draw upon your research to isolate a problem description that reflects the extent of the problem, conveys the need for action, and simultaneously matches the funder's stated interests. The description of the proposed program you provide will conform to this problem definition, and the expected outcomes must be directly related to it as well. In short, a solid problem definition will lead to a stronger grant proposal. By extension, a proposal that fails to make a clear connection between a problem, the program, and the results will not fare favorably in review.

Effective problem definition is described in more detail in the following section, but from a general perspective, consider the following examples of problem statements:

1. Lots of workers lost their jobs following a recent plant closure.
2. As a result of a manufacturing plant closure, more than 200 local residents have recently been laid off from jobs that paid wages greater than the community average.
3. A major textile manufacturing plant recently closed its doors in response to international competitive price pressures, leaving behind 250 relatively high-wage, but low-skilled laborers in a three-county area. Many having no postsecondary education, these newly unemployed workers lack the knowledge and skills necessary to compete with younger workers for scarce jobs in the local economy.

Each communicates the same general information, but the earlier examples leave out important details. The problem is clearly defined in the final example, and the funder will immediately appreciate what the program intends to do, and whether it wants to be involved.

Using problem statement (3), if the proposal continues by describing a program to develop a new industrial park, the funding agency might begin to wonder if the applicant truly understands the problem. The problem statement used suggests an adult education or retraining program. The same social or economic condition can be used to generate multiple problem definitions, all of which have merit. Consider this alternative:

1. A major textile manufacturing plant recently closed its doors in response to international competitive price pressures, leaving behind 250 relatively high-wage, but low-skilled laborers in a three-county area. A diverse service-based local economy provides numerous opportunities for entrepreneurial activities; however, the current credit crisis has caused trepidation among local lenders for high-risk business loans. There are no available microcredit sources for entrepreneurial activity in the area.

The same local economic condition is cited, but the problem is framed differently—to suit the applicant's desire to initiate a micro loan program, or possibly to suit a program or funding agency with a strong interest in providing micro credit.

The problem definition should guide your proposal, but for any given problem, you can usually frame its definition to fit your proposal or a particular funder. Entman (1993, p. 52) argues that "to frame is to select some aspects of a perceived reality and make them more salient ... in such a way as to promote a particular problem definition, causal interpretation, moral evaluation, and/or treatment recommendation for the item described." And Pralle (2006) indicates that multiple policy frames are able to exist side by side in public policy agenda setting, such as "health and environment" versus "agricultural and economic" in the case of pesticide policy. Sometimes frames compete, and sometimes they are reconcilable. The same agenda-setting lesson can be applied to grants because the intent is to put your problem on the official agenda (see Birkland 2005, p. 110-112) of the funding agency and simultaneously convince it to adopt your proposed solution. Weaver (2007) perceives two levels of agenda setting—the issue itself, and the attributes of the issue. From this perspective, we might consider the problem definition to apply to the second level of agenda setting (the issue's attributes). Few would argue that closure of a manufacturing plant is not a problem for a community and its residents. However, the specific attributes may provide ground for debate, and this is why careful problem definition is so important. Several frames could be developed to suit the attributes of this particular issue, ranging from a need for education to the need for better facilities to stimulate industrial recruitment, to entrepreneurial training. The larger need caused by the plant closure has many attributes, and many of them are worthy of treatment, so selecting one frame does not mean that the others aren't important; it means your program has a clear focus and is more likely to bring about concise results in the area of concern.

Once the funder has answered its first question—whether there is a genuine problem that fits its interests—it will ask other important questions. "Who will benefit from the program?" "Why is our money necessary or essential for this program?" "Is the proposed program a reasonable solution to the problem?" or "Is it the best solution to the problem?" And of course, "Does this organization have the skill and will to implement the proposed program?" Each of these questions deserves some thought or attention before you begin writing the proposal narrative.

As you prepare to describe a local problem, it is a good idea to determine who it affects, and then determine how your program directly or indirectly benefits those individuals, organizations, or groups. How does the problem affect these beneficiaries, and how does the proposed solution expect to benefit them? As a general rule, funders will view direct impacts on the beneficiaries more favorably than they will indirect impacts. So, to the extent possible, it is wise to map out all of the potential impacts and benefits and be prepared to describe those that are most significant; that is, those impacts that are most important to the program, and those that are thought to be of particular interest to the funder. In pursuing this step, you are developing the foundation of a program theory—the cause and effect relationships of your program that link the inputs and the problem to the outputs, outcomes, and the problem's reduction, resolution, or abatement. Program theory refers to the mechanism(s) that mediate between the delivery (and receipt) of the program and the emergence of the outcomes of interest (Weiss 1998, p. 57). In other words, how the program causes the results. Understanding the program theory is a good way to link the program to the problem and link the program outputs to the problem's expected resolution. Moreover, program theory highlights a number of key points around which the program's management and evaluation plans should be developed. These are points at which things occur, in a logical order, that produce measurable outputs. Let's consider program theory in more detail.

Program theory is an explanation of how the intervention or program causes the expected results. If there is no clear understanding of the theory behind a program, there is no compelling evidence for why it is expected to work. As Posavac and Carey (2003) indicate, "When there is no conceptual framework linking the interventions to the projected outcomes, it is hard to do an effective evaluation or improve on practice," and "program design is less effective without theory" (p. 61). Understanding how your program works highlights ways it improves on existing practice and provides a framework for evaluating its performance. This knowledge is essential to determining whether the program should be replicated in similar situations elsewhere. But most important for the task at hand, understanding how the pieces of your program fit together and function together will help you to provide a clear and concise written description that explains how the program will operate to bring about the desired results in light of the existing problem.

Program theory emphasizes the responses people have to program activities (Weiss 1998). It is concerned with the processes that take place between program activities. Closely related is the concept of implementation theory. Implementation theory explicitly considers what steps must be taken to bring about each intermediate result. To clarify, implementation theory concerns program activities—the things you do to bring about the desired mechanism of change. Program theory is the mechanism through which change occurs—it is a process that moves people (or the project) to the next stage. Posavac and Carey (2003, p. 61–62) suggest that a clear program theory is useful because it accomplishes the following:

- Assists planners, staff members, grant writers (such as yourself), and evaluators to understand how the program works
- Allows one to identify the intermediate results of the program, and not just the bottom line
- Helps one to know where to look when we conduct an evaluation

An example is in order to clarify the program theory concept. Program theory maps out a series of causal relationships between the program activities and participant responses. So, let's consider law enforcement activities as our focus. From time to time, state highway patrol officers embark on activities that differ from their typical patrol or response operating patterns. A common approach in recent years has been safety blitzes— a concentrated period of time where a law enforcement agency deploys its full resources, often in a targeted area. Let's consider the program theory behind such an approach. The program theory is a story that connects the pieces, and the implementation theory describes activities that bring about the desired responses. Following I present a relatively simple program theory for this type of program, with the implementation theory in parentheses:

Awareness of high-intensity police activity causes drivers to adjust their behavior (media announcement). Under normal patrol operations, many offenders are not caught and continue to offend (more officers present, coordinated approach). Visibility of police activities causes reductions in speed and increases in driver caution (highly visible, concentrated activities). Offenders cited for traffic safety violations fear the fines associated with a second offense and will be reluctant to reoffend (more traffic stops, no warnings). Slower speed and greater driver caution reduce accidents and fatalities.

Figure 5.1 presents the program theory graphically to demonstrate how the steps are logically related, and how the mechanisms of change bring about the desired results. The specific targets are drivers, and particularly unsafe drivers. The beneficiaries are all automobile passengers. Also not defined clearly in Figure 5.1 is that such programs may be more effective where highway traffic volume is very high. This may inform the location that is targeted, or

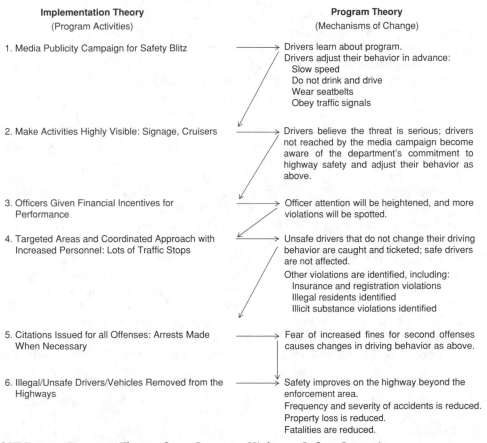

Implementation Theory (Program Activities)	**Program Theory** (Mechanisms of Change)

1. Media Publicity Campaign for Safety Blitz	Drivers learn about program.
	Drivers adjust their behavior in advance:
	  Slow speed
	  Do not drink and drive
	  Wear seatbelts
	  Obey traffic signals

2. Make Activities Highly Visible: Signage, Cruisers	Drivers believe the threat is serious; drivers not reached by the media campaign become aware of the department's commitment to highway safety and adjust their behavior as above.
3. Officers Given Financial Incentives for Performance	Officer attention will be heightened, and more violations will be spotted.

4. Targeted Areas and Coordinated Approach with Increased Personnel: Lots of Traffic Stops	Unsafe drivers that do not change their driving behavior are caught and ticketed; safe drivers are not affected.
	Other violations are identified, including:
	  Insurance and registration violations
	  Illegal residents identified
	  Illicit substance violations identified

5. Citations Issued for all Offenses: Arrests Made When Necessary	Fear of increased fines for second offenses causes changes in driving behavior as above.
6. Illegal/Unsafe Drivers/Vehicles Removed from the Highways	Safety improves on the highway beyond the enforcement area. Frequency and severity of accidents is reduced. Property loss is reduced. Fatalities are reduced.

FIGURE 5.1   Program Theory for a Common Highway Safety Campaign

Adapted from: Weiss 1998, p. 57.

it may also affect the time at which the effort is undertaken, such as a busy holiday travel weekend when drunk driving is expected to be particularly high.

When the program theory is well understood, it becomes very easy to explain it in the proposal narrative. Each of the pieces can be discussed in order, their relationship to each other can be discussed, and the intermediate effects of each step can be identified and explained. Each step forms the basis of an implementation plan—all that must be added is a fixed time element within which each activity will occur. In this case, it is relatively simultaneous for any targeted area, but if you include a map of the state's interstate highways, it might be possible to show how the enforcement pattern will improve safety statewide in a concerted regular effort. Also, each step provides the basis for evaluation—what we expect to observe if the program works, and how we can measure it. Program theory is essential to crafting an understandable and effective program narrative.

With a problem clearly defined, and the targets and beneficiaries identified, the funder will still wonder why it has been consulted: "Why is our money necessary or essential for this program?" Your narrative must provide a reasonable response to this question, even if it is not explicitly required by the program guidelines. Why isn't city revenue available? Why can't the program be paid for out of the police department's regular operating budget? The answers to these questions may be very simple, or very complex. Of course, any reallocation of existing resources results in adjustments to the current basket of services provided.

It may be enough to say that the state budget last year reduced the state police allocation by 5%, so an already strapped department can't afford the additional payroll expense to be incurred as a result of the proposed program. Of course, this argument should be made only if true. Or part of the problem definition might explain the issue at hand in relation to finances. For example, if we were considering a city police department rather than a state department, the local plant closure caused lower city tax revenues, forcing current year budget cuts, while unemployment has led to increased crime with no budget to fight it. It might also be the case that staff could be reallocated to perform the blitz, but that would leave other areas (or shifts) with lower levels of police protection and poor response time. And if a program is innovative, or a pilot program with unknown results, external funding provides an impetus to evaluate the proposal's effectiveness so that it can be built into future budgets to sustain its success. The key is that the foundation or other grant making agency will probably wonder why a problem of such importance has not been funded with existing revenues—it is up to you to make a compelling case for the involvement of the particular external funder you have identified.

Another general question of interest is whether the proposed program is a reasonable solution to the problem. A corollary question is whether it is the best possible solution to the problem under the given circumstances. Here again, program theory comes into play. The relationships between program activities and outputs and outcomes should be fairly convincing and easy to explain. **Figure 5.2** shows the relationship

FIGURE 5.2   Relationships Underlying Program Theory

between inputs, outputs, outcomes, and impact that drive the program theory discussed earlier. The crux of this overarching question is to determine whether the program theory you have proposed is the best possible alternative. How could you change it to improve upon the idea? Is there another approach altogether that would be more likely to bring about the desired response?

This question is not one that has to be addressed directly, but the answer should appear in the program narrative as you develop it. It is not necessary to state that your program is the best alternative, or even that you believe it is. But you should acknowledge why it is necessary, or why it is ideal for your unique circumstance. In other words, this program is ideal given the problem and the local context. It may be the case that your program is one piece of a larger strategy that combines several approaches. It would be acceptable to describe the larger mission, identify all of the approaches or programs to be used, and identify the important role that the selected piece contributes to that mission. In doing so, it is necessary to point out how the results are expected to differ should the program not be funded. So, to summarize, you must convince the funder that the program is appropriate, that it is ideally suited to the problem in its local context, and that absent the program the problem will continue or worsen. The guidelines may not specifically request this information, but a skilled grant writer will recognize that the funder is interested in this information and find ways to communicate it throughout the proposal.

The final general question to keep in mind before beginning your proposal is the funder's interest in your ability to carry out the proposed project as planned. Does this organization have the skill and will to implement the proposed program? This question addresses organizational capacity, which takes a number of forms. Financial capacity is important, in that it ensures that the organization is stable and will continue to operate during the funding period. Management capacity is important to ensure that the organization runs smoothly and soundly. Does the organization have a dedicated accounting staff? Does it have a grant management system to ensure funds are properly accounted for and dispersed? Does it produce audited annual financial statements in a timely fashion each year, and so on. There are many, many dimensions to organizational management capacity, and their relative importance will vary according to the particular program of interest, its size, and the organization's size relative to the proposed project. If your proposal involves purchasing laptop computers and using them in the field for mobile GED training, how will you ensure their proper care and transport? Do you have a dedicated information technology staff? Similarly, if your annual operating budget is $100,000, and you have applied for a $1 million grant, the funder will have concerns about your ability to execute the project successfully because it is on a much larger scale than your typical programs.

Staff capacity may be general, such as accounting, or technology staff as considered previously, but there may be call for very specific skills and abilities. In this case, the funding agency will be concerned with the staff members you propose to utilize in implementing those portions of the program. It is not at all uncommon for funders to request a management plan that identifies staff members responsible for particular activities along with information about their education, training, and experience. If you are evaluating the impact of the highway safety blitz, it may be necessary to have an individual with statistical and evaluation training to manage the data collection and analysis process. If you are providing literacy training, you should be using a person with skills directly related to such activities as well. In other words, a computer programmer may not be the best choice for your program evaluation, and an evaluation specialist may not be ideal for managing IT security. The funder will be interested in such details to ascertain how likely the plan is to succeed. Although no plan is ever guaranteed success, elements such as those discussed here raise red flags for reviewers and call into doubt the applicant's capacity and likelihood of success.

To review, we have discussed several broad questions that funding agencies are likely to consider as they review your proposal. They may not ask for specific information about any of them, but often they do. Even when that information is not directly requested, the concerns are real, and the funding agency will be interested in the extent to which your program will address the identified problem. You should approach the program narrative with these considerations in mind and find ways to respond to these concerns as you go. Sometimes it is best to include a section about the organization's capacity, including successful past grant programs, that discusses the management system. Sometimes these details are better provided in discussion in other areas of the proposal. In large part, it depends on the space limitations provided as well as the structure of the guidelines and required information. Is there a problem? Who will benefit from the program? Why is our money needed? Is the program appropriate/ideal for the situation? Can this applicant pull off what it proposes?

Programs rarely operate in isolation from their organizational environment, so it is best to begin any proposal with an introduction to the problem that includes information about the area and the organization—this communicates the operating environment in which the program will take place. In other words, context matters (Bardach 2004, p. 211). With any policy or program, there is a basic mechanism, a tool that will be used to bring about the desired result. Computer-based adult literacy training is such a tool. So is highway patrol and citation. A more complicated program might combine several policy tools in a unique manner. For example, individuals with need for literacy training might be identified and invited to attend a program orientation. From that point their literacy would be assessed and their life situation would be taken into consideration to assign them to one or more simultaneously operating programs that are directly suited to their needs. These might include basic reading comprehension, computer-based GED training, and financial literacy training, among others. Here the unique contribution is not the trainings, per se, but the triage feature that brings in numerous differently skilled individuals and links them to training best suited to their needs. In the case of the highway blitz mentioned earlier, the tool is not unique, but the concentrated, targeted police enforcement is. It is important that you have a clear idea of the mechanism you plan to utilize to bring about the desired impact on the identified problem.

Once you have a clear conceptualization of the core mechanism, it is necessary to consider what Bardach (2004) refers to as contingent features. That is, features of the program that will make the program more effective if present. These may be derived from the institutional, political, economic, or interpersonal context in which the program is operating (Bardach 2004, p. 211). In other words, the characteristics of the program's context will make it more or less viable. A proposed faith-based program in a community with no churches may be a great policy mechanism, except the context provides no supportive resources that would make it successful. Similarly, the use of signage, media campaigns, scheduling during heavy traffic holidays, and financial incentives for police officers are contingent features of the proposed program that are expected to add to its ultimate success, and therefore its ability to reduce the problem in question.

So, before you begin the narrative process, you will need to have a clear idea of what you intend to do, how you will do it, what features of your organization or community will make it more successful, what barriers you have to overcome, and how you can achieve the objective in the time frame of the grant and with the funds requested in the budget. With the program clearly defined in this fashion, you can begin the process of drafting a proposal narrative.

Effective Communication

Program narratives are diverse, and they serve the interests of the funding agency. This means that different funders will ask for different types of information in the proposal narrative. The information they seek has a purpose—to determine whether or not your proposed activity conforms to their values, purpose, and interests. In short, the best way to approach a proposal narrative is to first consider what the funder wants to know. The questions to which they ask you to respond will indicate the things they think are important, and the research you did during the search phase should give you a very good idea about the answers they expect to receive to their questions. In other words, it is best to think about the proposal as though you are a potential grant reviewer evaluating it. What things would the funder like to see? What things would alarm them? Once you master the art of seeing your own organization and program through the eyes of the funding agency, the process of writing the narrative will become quite simple.

Before going any further, it is necessary to point out that grant proposals are formal written documents, and they are intended to be read by one or more reviewers or evaluators. It is absolutely essential that spelling and grammar be correct, and that the document be free of errors in punctuation and form. Grant proposals are formal descriptions—technical writing—and they usually do not read like a conversation. As a general rule, proposals are written in third person, although there is no formal expectation that this be the case. The use of pronouns (I, we, she/he, they, and so forth) can lead to confusion regarding who is to do what. Even the most careful writer may inadvertently say "they" will do something without clearly indicating who "they" might be. For example, it is better to say, "The poverty rate in Jefferson County has ranged from 10% to 12% over the past 5 years" than to say "Our poverty rate has been as high as 12% during the past 5 years." Although the latter statement may be true, it is far less clear than the former statement; it is not even clear to which geographic area the statement applies. The usual rules of writing apply—if you are writing in third person, you should stick with it throughout the proposal. Because space limitations often constrain grant writers, it is essential to write as clearly and concisely as possible. This is the first rule of proposal writing.

Also, it is important that you write to be read—do not use overly technical jargon that may not be understood by the expected audience. If your proposal will be reviewed by peers that have working knowledge of the concepts, it may be acceptable to use technical language. If the reader is a trustee for a foundation or an agency bureaucrat, he or she may not have the expertise to interpret a technical proposal without explanation. Write in active voice and present the future as it will look once your organization has implemented the proposed program. Write positively. Avoid using conditional words such as *might*, *may*, *could*, and instead indicate that the program *will* achieve the desired results. Any subjectivity present in your language may provide the reader room for doubt; of course, you should avoid exaggeration, hyperbole, and promises that are not realistic. A superficial, or unrealistic, proposal looks as bad to a reviewer as a tentative proposal full of doubt and contingencies.

With the generalities out of the way, what sorts of things are funders looking for in a proposal narrative? Although the list could extend many pages, the key information most funders seek usually falls into the following categories: (1) information about the recipient organization, for description and eligibility determination, (2) information about the area in need of funding, (3) information about the clients to be served, (4) general information about the program or project to be delivered, (5) the specific program approach, including the interventions or tools to be used to bring about the desired results (and their timing), (6) the organization's management capacity, or likelihood of success, (7) information about the project staff, particularly pertaining to their experience and expertise, (8) anticipated outputs, outcomes, and impacts to be generated by the program, including a plan for evaluating program success, and (9) sustainability of the program beyond the period of grant funding. This list includes general items that funders often seek, but should not be taken as a list of issues to discuss in every program narrative.

Each request for proposals or program description will provide guidelines to which you must respond in drafting your proposal narrative. The key is not to include all relevant information, but rather to describe the program adequately and provide clear, concise, and specific responses to the questions identified in the RFP or guidelines. Foundations often make grants for which no published competition guidelines exist. In this case, it is a good idea to discuss your program and the funder's goals with a program officer. As you recall from earlier chapters, many foundations do not make "unsolicited awards"; that is, they fund only programs they preselect to receive funding. It may well be that your program could qualify for future funds, but you will have to first find your way onto the funder's radar. The funder may verbally communicate important points to address in your request that may not be provided in formal written guidelines. In other words, the second rule in composing the proposal narrative is to follow the rules provided by the funding agency. The third rule is to seek guidance when none is available in formal written guidelines or RFPs.

Following the rules is often more difficult than it sounds. Rules for the proposal narrative may take many forms. There may be (and usually are) rules concerning the number of pages allowed, the minimum typeface, preferred fonts, limits on margin size and spacing, and so forth. These issues seem mundane, and none of them are central to communicating information about the proposed program. Why do grant makers issue such challenging requirements? In short, because the funders have to read the proposals that are submitted. These rules exist because over time some ambitious grant seekers have found ways to put more information on a page, which increases the difficulty of reading the information.

If a program is truly competitive, then distributional equity cannot be achieved—there is never enough money to bring about the desired result for all potential beneficiaries. So, agencies, and particularly government agencies that must be concerned for equity in the funding decisions they make, have resorted to process equity measures to provide fair opportunities where fair outcomes cannot be guaranteed (Gormley & Balla 2008). The deadline is one such measure—each applicant has the same amount of time to complete and submit an application. Font size and line spacing are other examples. The smaller the font, the more information you can provide, which is unfair to another applicant less inclined to "cheat."

There is another reason to keep your writing well formatted with adequate white space on the page: it is easier for the reader. The more white space on the page, the less eye strain the reader will suffer, and the more likely the reader will be to read your proposal from start to finish with accurate comprehension (Wordsmith Associates 2008). This is achieved by writing shorter paragraphs with space between them, by keeping line spacing open, and keeping page margins relatively wide. Use a simple, clean font such as Times New Roman. Scripts and other fonts do not make your work appear more professional—they make it harder to read. If the guidelines specify requirements for these details, follow them. If the requirements are presented as minimums or maximums, then you may adjust your work to make it more readable as long as it still meets the rules.

One of the great challenges of writing a proposal narrative, whether it is to a foundation or a government agency, is space limitation. It should now be clear that these limitations are given in the interest of fairness and to facilitate proposal review and evaluation by the funding agency. But most grant seekers will quickly find it very difficult to adequately explain the proposed program in the limited space provided—especially detail-oriented individuals (see Chapter 3). Very intuitive writers may find it more difficult to fill the provided space because they think in broader strokes and leave key details out of the program description. Nonetheless, most grant seekers find it a challenge to balance detail with the space provided, and usually write more than can be submitted.

I recommend this approach. Write a thorough, clear, but still concise, narrative that conveys as fully as possible every detail of what you intend to do. Make sure this document is formatted according to the funder's stated requirements, of course, and then reduce the volume until it is within the page limit. You will find yourself rewording sentences, replacing verbiage with tables or charts that better communicate your points, and removing detail that is interesting but not essential to the reader's understanding of your proposed program. This process applies to both unstructured and structured narrative response requirements; the difference is that you may be writing a section under the write-and-reduce method, or you may be writing the entire narrative that way.

Other program rules apply to information that must be included in your narrative, but the format is rarely specified. Some foundations do provide very specific formats, which should be followed. The vast majority simply tell you what they want to know and leave it to you to provide the information. It is customary for RFPs to specify topics that should be addressed in the proposal narrative, and the grant writer should take this as a sign that those topics will form the basis of an evaluation tool to be used by the reader. There is a tendency among detail-oriented persons (Sensing individuals, from Chapter 3) to respond to each request without concern for the readability of the document. The narrative should be approached holistically. It should generate a cohesive picture of the proposed program and link that program to the documented need for it in the community, to the organization's unique capacity to combat the problem and the proposal's unique ability to do so.

The proposal should correspond in principle to the budget, to the evaluation plan, and most important, to the stated purpose and goals of the funder's program. In other words, the proposal narrative is not a question and answer exercise; rather it is an artistic combination of several pieces of information important to the funder that are presented in a readable and easily understandable format. So, as you begin to dissect RFPs and proposal guidelines, keep in mind that the narrative should read more like a story than an interview. However, returning to document formatting, it is very important to include clear section divisions and headings that reflect the content. You should make it as easy as possible for the funder to find the information it is interested in.

To introduce the general elements of a typical proposal narrative, I begin with the case of a grant opportunity with an unstructured application process—one that has no formal guidelines to follow.

Guidance for Unstructured Proposals

Many foundations provide limited guidance for applications, though they will frequently request information with a page limit, and they may pose particular questions of interest. It is very common, in fact, for foundations to filter potential grant seekers with letters of inquiry. A letter of inquiry is a gate-keeping technique that keeps the foundation from reading proposals it is not interested in funding, and that keeps applicants from spending inordinate amounts of time drafting proposals that have no interest to the foundation.

Letters of inquiry are usually limited to one or two pages, and they ask for very specific information, including a description of the applicant, the need to be met, and a general program description. Some may ask you to disclose how the program relates to the foundation's stated interests and how the foundation's resources are essential to the program. The exact format or content depends on the foundation, and you should seek information to determine the foundation's expectations before issuing your inquiry. In other words, you should treat the letter of inquiry like a true grant proposal. You should provide all of the information it requests, and you should provide it in the format, and with respect to the limitations, the foundation specifies. In some circumstances, it might be acceptable to include attachments, such as brochures or program descriptions that provide deeper information, should the funder desire to examine such information.

The funder will review your inquiry and determine whether your organization and proposed program are, by virtue of location, service provided, or values, of interest. If so, you will receive an invitation to submit a formal proposal. In this case, some foundations will provide structured guidelines that should be followed. Others will specify any constraints they expect, usually in the form of page limits and key information to include, and you may proceed with some variant of the unstructured proposal I discuss later.

The basic components of any proposal, whether structured or unstructured, are very similar. Different sources call them by different names, or weigh the relative importance of each differently, and so they modify the basic structure to best suit their needs. The following list itemizes the most common components of a proposal narrative, and it provides a sound model to follow in soliciting funding from an unstructured or open-ended inquiry:

1. Cover letter
2. Abstract/executive summary (usually one page)
3. Introduction (establish credibility as an applicant)
4. Need statement/problem definition (describe why you need the grant)
5. Objectives/goals (attempt to resolve aforementioned need): refine idea, tell exactly what you intend to do
6. Methods and procedures/implementation plan (logically tied to goals): methods you will use to achieve the objectives within the stated time frame
7. Evaluation plan
8. Continuation/sustainability plan: should include information on donors, tax revenue
9. Budget (tied to procedure)

Some of these components are not part of the proposal narrative in the proper sense, notably the budget and cover letter, but for some completely unstructured proposals, this is the full list of items to address, and the budget may be worked in at the end of the narrative. The budget is simply a part of the proposal. I consider each of these components in turn.

Cover Letter

The proposal cover letter, also referred to as a transmittal letter, is intended to communicate three things. First, the letter introduces your organization and sometimes documents your eligibility for the program. Second, it explains that the attached document is a complete grant application for a particular program. And finally, it allows you to express gratitude to the funding agency for considering your proposal and provide contact information regarding the funding decision. Cover letters should be very concise so that these three elements are not difficult to identify. Transmittal letters differ from letters of inquiry and should not be used to provide excessive information about your organization or proposed program or project. In general, they are not considered part of the application for federal awards, so information included in them may not make it to the reviewers, and when it does, it may not be considered during the application review.

The same principles apply to foundation funding, but foundations often have more open-ended and flexible application procedures. You may find that cover letters to a foundation provide an opportunity to include more information about the program. Because many foundations have unstructured funding, that is, they do not have formal program names, it is a good idea to provide a concise explanation of your program—what it will do, and for what type of activity the funds are requested—so that they can determine how to categorize it in their review process.

Again, whatever information is included, the three key pieces of information should stand out clearly. In most cases, a cover letter is only one page. Under no circumstance should it exceed two pages. **Figure 5.3** provides an example of a cover letter for a federal grant application to the Economic Development Administration. You will notice it is addressed to the Kentucky representative. For this particular program, all grant applications are "filtered" through the agency's state representative.

May 1, 2009

Mr. Bob Hunter
Economic Development Representative
U.S. Department of Commerce
Economic Development Administration
771 Corporate Drive, Suite 200
Lexington, KY 40503-5477

Dear Mr. Hunter:

The [Applicant Organization Name] is requesting funding through the United States Department of Commerce, Economic Development Administration to conduct a feasibility study for the establishment of a new tourist attraction in [Location]. These funds are being requested through the Local Technical Assistance Program, CFDA # 11.303.

Enclosed you will find all required documentation for the application process. Included in these materials are form SF-424, including the proposed project budget, a brief narrative constituted by responses to those questions required by the EDA, and a 7.5″ USGS topographical map of the area in which the proposed feasibility study will take place.

If you have any questions or concerns, please contact me at the following:
    [Address]
    [Telephone]
    [Fax]
    [E-mail]

This project holds the future of [Location] at its heart. We appreciate your assistance and kind review of this proposal as we seek to provide unique new development opportunities for the [Location] area.

Sincerely,

[Agency Executive Signature]
[Agency Executive Title]

FIGURE 5.3   Sample Cover Letter 1

Figure 5.4 provides a second example of a cover letter addressed directly to the federal agency, in this case the U.S. Department of Housing and Urban Development. Naturally, these letters would appear on official letterhead with actual signatures in the grant application packet.

The cover letter is an item that can be written at any time, given you already know what it needs to include. It is a good idea to write it up-front so that it does not cause any unnecessary delays in the application submission process. One important component that should be addressed at this stage is your project title. To make the proposal real, it should have a name, and creativity is encouraged. A descriptive title is preferred so that the name conveys the program purpose. The name can be referred to throughout the remainder of the proposal narrative, used in letters of support, and most applications request the project title on their application forms. The federal program name will often serve as the name for your project.

June 4, 2003

Processing and Control Unit
Office of Community Planning and Development
Department of Housing and Urban Development
451 Seventh Street SW
Room 7255
Attn: YouthBuild Program
Washington, DC 20410

Dear YouthBuild Program Officer:

Enclosed please find our application, one original and two copies, for the U.S. Department of Housing and Urban Development YouthBuild Program. The [Applicant's Division Name] is an interdisciplinary research unit of [Applicant Name], providing applied research and community development outreach programs to the Appalachian region. This proposed grant project results from partnership with organizations throughout our region, including the [Names of Key Partners], and others.

Our proposed project will serve [Name] County, including the City of [Name], with training, education, and on-site experience for high school dropouts aged 18–24. These participants will be provided training to aid them in completing their GED, while learning construction skills and gaining valuable on-the-job experience rehabilitating public housing units. Through this program, we will reduce poverty and unemployment while increasing educational attainment, employability, and the quality of housing in this market area.

If you have any questions or concerns, please contact me at the following:
    [Address]
    [Telephone]
    [Fax]
    [E-mail]

We appreciate your consideration of our YouthBuild application and we hope to include HUD in our intergovernmental partnership for redevelopment of distressed rural areas of the Appalachian region.

Best regards,

[Agency Official Signature]
[Agency Official's Title]

FIGURE 5.4   Sample Cover Letter 2

Abstract/Executive Summary

A grant's executive summary is a one-page document that precedes the program narrative. The executive summary is intended to describe the applicant, the problem or need to be addressed, the nature of the proposed project, and the general program approach. It is the first impression the funding agency reviewer will have of the proposed program, and it sets the tone as she reviews the detailed proposal. It is extremely important to emphasize the unique problem to be addressed, the unique features of the proposal, and the applicant's (or partnership's) unique abilities to implement the proposal.

Even when proposals are required to be double-spaced, the executive summary is often single spaced. Before assuming that is appropriate, it is still important to ensure that the guidelines do not apply formatting requirements to the executive summary as well. Naturally, it is essential that the executive summary be clear, concise, and easy to read and understand. Even when single-spaced, it is best to leave some open space on the page and to use headings, subheadings, or outlines to make information easier to process.

The executive summary, though the first thing the reviewer sees, is best left to be written after the proposal narrative itself is complete. This helps to ensure that the executive summary is indeed an accurate summary of the proposal, and not a general reflection of the program idea or approach. The goal is to ensure that the summary and the proposal narrative communicate the same information. After reading the executive summary, the proposal reviewer should be able to nod in agreement. He should understand exactly what problem is to be solved, how it will be solved (the key mechanism or tools to be applied), and how the applicant will successfully bring about the desired results. Reading the rest of the proposal narrative should add to the reviewer's understanding of the program, not confuse or confound it.

Introduction

The introduction, as its name implies, is the first section of the proposal narrative. It is an opportunity to introduce your organization and proposed program to the funding agency. You should tell who you are, establishing eligibility for the program in the process. It is appropriate to provide a brief history of the organization—when it was instituted, for what purpose, and how it has changed over time. Included here should be reference to any special organizational characteristics that affect eligibility, such as nonprofit status, status as a public or private institution of higher education, a tribal government, or a municipality or other government agency. Your operating authority and management should be clear—if a nonprofit organization, you might briefly describe the board of directors and the governance structure. You should communicate your mission, your vision, your key programs, and your general strategic approach. You should also introduce them to your service area (geographic) and to the specific target population (individuals, groups, or organizations) that you serve. In discussing the organization's target population, it is often beneficial to discuss their characteristics—distinguishing features that make them eligible for your services.

On some occasions, especially when the program in question involves specialized services or staff, it is appropriate to discuss those staff and service roles to provide an introduction to their experience or expertise. Grants to fund academic research are focused on a key researcher or a team of research investigators and their expertise in the field of interest. In cases such as these, the institution and its resources to support the proposed program will be discussed, including key project staff and their experience and expertise.

If there have been significant planning and preparation meetings that provide a foundation for the proposed project, they should be included in the introductory discussion as well. Advisory boards that were formed during the development process (Chapter 3) coordinated plans for the program. Studies that were conducted to determine the most salient problems should be mentioned. Each activity that shows the organization is capable and willing to tackle the problem, and that it understands the problem well, should be highlighted as space provides.

The introduction is generally very brief, though some programs provide structured guidelines for responding, including specific elements to include. In such cases, it is better to err on the side of completeness rather than brevity, so long as it does not overstep the allowable space usage. It is very helpful to create an introduction that provides basic information about the applicant organization, but as with most components of a grant proposal, it is wise to link the organization to the specific subject of the grant.

So, for example, a university application could discuss size, number of faculty, number of students, the type of programs offered, and so on. And this information is useful, but it would be better to focus on the organizational unit that will be doing the work. Likewise, it is preferred to discuss and describe the organization's work in the policy area under which the grant program falls. So, for a housing grant, you would discuss your work to provide housing, or work with residents to obtain housing, or a survey of housing quality you recently conducted. For a program that is intended to link university research capacity to community problems, you would focus on past outreach efforts in the community. **Figure 5.5** provides an example of just such an introduction that was drafted to be used for proposals with a community outreach focus. The boilerplate language used in the introduction section can often be modified slightly to make it reusable in future grant applications. Again, learning to recycle information is a good way to work smarter rather than harder.

Figure 5.6 provides an example used for a multiorganizational partnership led by the same organization. It focuses on the experience of the lead applicant, but it emphasizes the experience and contributions of key partners that provide expertise in areas central to the focus of the grant program where the applicant organization had particular weaknesses. The specific experience cited in this description is focused in the area of housing to match the focus of the proposal for which it was drafted. Also, note that this excerpt has subheadings that reflect particular areas of interest (Sections I-B and I-C are provided; I-A has been withheld from the example). This example was drawn from a federal grant program with a very specific set of response requirements in the introduction section. As the primary heading reflects, this introductory section is labeled "Applicant Capacity and Relevant Organizational Experience." This is the key difference between unstructured and structured proposal narrative guidelines—the material to be included is precisely described. So, although this still serves as the introduction, the information included is more concise than general, and it is presented in a format that fits the funder's requirements. What should be apparent is that there are specific areas of interest to the funder, which it requests be addressed in the narrative. Here the interest is on learning what abilities the applicant has to carry out the proposed program.

In the way of summary, then, the introduction provides a concise review of the organization and its history, mission, vision, strategy, and approach. It also provides a very short description of the program or project to be undertaken. While discussing general characteristics, a good introduction will relate the organization to the subject matter of the proposal at hand, providing examples of experience and work with similar programs and activities in the past. It sets the stage for the narrative to come. When the reviewer considers the overarching questions that were raised in the beginning of the chapter, including the organization's capacity to fulfill the project, the introduction should provide a coherent answer that directly relates to the proposed project.

Rating Factor One: Capacity of the Applicant and Relevant Organizational Experience

The Morehead State University (MSU) Institute for Regional Analysis and Public Policy (IRAPP) was established at MSU in 1998 as a Kentucky Program of Distinction to help meet Morehead State University's responsibilities for providing applied research and organized public service to meet the needs of the region. The overall goal of IRAPP is to integrate university resources (e.g., faculty specialization, student energy, and technical assistance) with regional resources (e.g., human capital, businesses, public agencies, and rich natural resources) to develop the region's many potentials. Specifically, academic programs, research initiatives, and service activities will connect MSU faculty and students in partnerships with citizens, educators, political leaders, and policymakers to develop action plans that promote the sustainable economic development of the region. Through basic and applied research, IRAPP focuses on problems facing communities in a changing society, works toward the development of services in response to the identified needs of rural communities, engages in program and policy evaluation, and serves as a resource for policymakers by providing information.

In fulfilling the broader mission of the university, the Institute for Regional Analysis and Public Policy is developing programs to enhance individual's and families' lives through interdisciplinary research and education at the community, state, national, and international levels. There is a strong emphasis with IRAPP on the social and behavioral sciences, and this emphasis includes applied research, education programs, and community and economic development activities. This initiative was created through collaborations between Morehead State University IRAPP and fellows from public and private, profit and nonprofit organizations.

IRAPP is located administratively within the Office of the Vice President for Academic Affairs at MSU, and is a university-wide research unit, on par with academic colleges of the University. The Dean of IRAPP is on the Deans Council and there are 30 faculty affiliated with IRAPP from 12 disciplines across the university. IRAPP has several high-quality students enrolled in its five selective academic programs, and 20 students work in IRAPP projects throughout the year. IRAPP facilitates collaborative work related to community and economic development by increasing attention to issues within the university and community at large. IRAPP sponsored nine faculty research grants last year to engage faculty with active research agendas across the university. IRAPP is governed by faculty from the university as well as an advisory board of individuals from both the private and public sectors of the community, state, and nation.

Several of IRAPP's initiatives and programs already under way feature the linkages of university research with community capacity building. The Atlas of Appalachia project develops an electronic atlas to be published in conjunction with the 2000 census. IRAPP is working with the University of Kentucky Press to delivery a web-based Kentucky Encyclopedia for use by individuals, organizations, and educators. And the IRAPP Center for Virtual Appalachia is a web-based research database and research clearinghouse featuring 5,000 files and more than 10,000 entries linking data, research, and information on all aspects of Appalachia to a centralized, Internet-based delivery vehicle.

FIGURE 5.5   Sample Language Used in a Proposal Introduction

Source: Courtesy of Morehead State University.

The CVA will be an interactive web-based resource for citizens to access comprehensive information about Appalachia and participate in education programs, civic projects, and policy advocacy. The CVA is an asynchronous learning platform that will serve as a catalyst for community-initiated responses to public policy needs, provision of education and research programs, and delivery of capacity-building technical assistance.

IRAPP is currently collaborating with 15 colleges and universities from across the broader Appalachian region in concert with the Appalachian Regional Commission to establish a consortium of Appalachian Research Centers and Institutes. IRAPP also participates in a regional planning and policy initiative led by the Kentucky Chamber of Commerce, Leadship Kentucky, Inc., and the Kentucky League of Cities. And IRAPP has built a broad partnership for delivery of regional telecommunications capacity with all Kentucky Area Development Districts, the University of Kentucky, East Kentucky Corporation, and the Center for Rural Development. This partnership establishes a community-based, rural telecommunications network that integrates education and technical assistance programming with comprehesive capacity building. The central focus of the project is development of the Center for Virtual Appalachia (CVA). This network would result in the linking and leveraging of resources for community development. IRAPP continues developing regional community and economic partnerships that improve the lives of citizens across our service region through research, education, and service.

The Institute for Regional Analysis and Public Policy's (IRAPP) two divisions (Academic Programs and Applied Research, Service, and Policy) integrate teaching, applied research, and public service activities to address issues, including economic development, that significantly affect eastern Kentucky, Appalachia, and rural America in general.

IRAPP's five bachelor's degrees (environmental science, geography, government, social work, and sociology) include a unifying core of six courses in Regional Analysis. Our two master's programs under development (biology and sociology) have an emphasis in Regional Analysis and Public Policy in addition to the core courses.

Examples of projects under development that exemplify national distinction:

- The Internet publication of **The Kentucky Encyclopedia**, produced under contract for the University Press of Kentucky, is currently being released. See more at http://www.moreheadstate.edu/news/05162001-05.html.

- **The Atlas of Appalachia**, by IRAPP with support from Western Kentucky University, the University of Kentucky, East Carolina University, and Marshall University, is scheduled for release on CD-ROM in 2002. This release date will allow for inclusion of selected 2000 census data with portions available on the World Wide Web.

- Collaboration with 13–15 colleges and universities and the Appalachian Regional Commission (ARC) to establish **Consortium of Appalachian Research Centers**.

FIGURE 5.5   (Continued)

- Collaboration with the MSU College of Science and Technology to establish the **Space Science Center**. The Office of Economic Development and Research Outreach will be created through this project as a joint program between Morehead's Science and Technology College and IRAPP. This effort will connect research and science to the region and provide the type of telecommunications infrastructure that makes eastern Kentucky competitive in the information age economy. The Office of Economic Development and Research Outreach will provide a mechanism to deliver the economic development potential of the science and research infrastructure of this project to the businesses and entrepreneurs throughout our region. IRAPP will deploy two weather stations, operate a weather database and archive, and deploy GPS base stations in the region and operate these and conduct a range of regional analysis research.

- Contract with Ky Housing Corporation to conduct 2001 Statewide Homeless Survey.

- Contract with State GIS Office and Cabinet for natural resources to map and model forest fires in Pike, Martin, and Johnson Counties.

- Partnership with four counties, business partners, and other educational entities on USDE Gear Up Project.

- Collaboration with Perry, Wayne, and Rowan Counties for submission of HUD-Youth Build Project (proposal denied but will be resubmitted).

- Collaboration with NASA, NOAA, CPE, State Government, the University of Kentucky, and Center for Rural Development on Space Science Center.

- Partnership with numerous ADDs on technology transfer, tourism development, and economic devlopment research and outreach.

- Collaboration with Appalachian universities and colleges to establish an **Appalachian Research Consortium**.

- Partnership with Hazard and Southeast Community Colleges to establish the **ARC Kentucky Appalachian Higher Education Network**.

- Partnership with Appalachian universities to offer collaborative course in fall 2001 with students on each campus developing projects related to Appalachia's sustainable economic future. Students will share ideas and develop projects with presentations to the **Appalachian Regional Commission** in November of 2001.

FIGURE 5.5   (Continued)

Need Statement/Problem Definition

As I indicated earlier, the problem statement provides the frame for the remainder of the proposal. It determines the background against which the reader views the proposed activities, and provides the baseline against which the proposal will be judged. The term *Need Statement* is often used interchangeably with *Problem Definition* or *Problem Statement*. As the name implies, the purpose of this section is to justify the funder's involvement in the program. Why should it be involved? Why is the program needed? Those central questions are the subject of this section.

I. APPLICANT CAPACITY AND RELEVANT ORGANIZATIONAL EXPERIENCE

I-B. ORGANIZATIONAL STRUCTURE: A board of regents governs Morehead State University; the president of the university executes this board's mandates and oversees the university's many departments and programs. MSU's annual operating budget exceeds $80 million. MSU's Division of Administration and Fiscal Services has developed policies and procedures that govern all facets of the university's operation including personnel management, budgetary oversight and fiscal management, contracting, physical plant maintenance, and information systems. The Vice President for Administration and Fiscal Services ensures that all university activities occur in accordance with the University's Strategic Plan, the Council for Post-secondary Education's Campus Master Plan (for capital planning), and other internal and external controls to maintain the institution's fiscal integrity and to provide taxpayer accountability. The university operates in compliance with federal and state policies, procedures, and regulations, and follows Generally Accepted Accounting Principles (GAAP) within the dictates of statute. MSU undergoes annual audits by Kentucky's Auditor of Public Accounts. In short, MSU maintains a state-of-the-art financial accounting system, supplemented by regulatory policies and procedures (viewable at http://www.morehead-st.edu).

For the purpose of the proposed program, IRAPP will act as the designated governing administrative unit of the university, and all management decisions will be made by IRAPP in accordance with existing university policies, procedures, and regulations. The dean of IRAPP will conduct general oversight and coordination of all program activities and will manage program personnel. IRAPP's Director of Research and Development will directly plan and implement major initial program components until a project coordinator can be hired, providing direct oversight for the duration of the program. The Project Coordinator will carry out day-to-day program activities and will manage staff and resources to ensure compliance with grant requirements and general university policies, acting as liaison between the partner institutions and IRAPP to ensure that advisory input is regularly assimilated. Partner institutions will form an advisory committee that will collaborate in participant recruitment, selection, and counseling, and to develop the master schedule for all program components.

I-C. RELEVANT EXPERIENCE: Experience relevant to this project might be characterized in terms of three major categories: education, housing, and outreach. Morehead State University's rich history of service extends back to 1887, when, as the Morehead Normal School, it first served students. The institution came under state control in 1922, and achieved university status in 1966. Education and outreach have been successfully executed throughout MSU's history; however, to reduce internal duplication of effort and provide a coordinated response to the unique needs of Appalachian Kentucky, the Institute for Regional Analysis and Public Policy (IRAPP) was established in 1998. A Kentucky Program of Distinction, IRAPP is a multidisciplinary unit of MSU that provides applied research and organized public service to meet the needs of eastern Kentucky and the greater Appalachian region. IRAPP works to more fully develop the region's potential through academic programs, research initiatives, and service activities that connect MSU faculty and students in partnerships with citizens, educators, political leaders, and policymakers to promote sustainable economic development of the region.

FIGURE 5.6   Introduction Section for a Housing-Related Grant Program
Source: Courtesy of Morehead State University.

IRAPP is located administratively within the Office of the Vice President for Academic Affairs at MSU, and is a university-wide research unit, on par with academic colleges of the university. The Dean of IRAPP is on the Deans Council and there are 30 faculty affiliated with IRAPP from 12 disciplines across the university.

In building expertise related to issues relevant to rural Kentucky, IRAPP has recruited faculty members who exhibit research specialization and interest in the field of housing. Moreover, IRAPP is currently conducting the Kentucky Housing Corporation's Statewide Homeless Survey and is in the process of establishing an Appalachian Housing Research Center. IRAPP regularly collaborates on projects with Morehead Housing and other local and regional housing partners. IRAPP brings expertise in traditional higher education as well as the field of housing research. Additionally, IRAPP has participated extensively in the Hazard, Kentucky, Youth-Build project, performing activities associated with instruction, recruitment, evaluation, etc. IRAPP has administered numerous federal grants (in excess of $10 million) since its inception in 1998, including a 2002 HUD Community Outreach Partnership Center (COPC) grant.

IRAPP exhibits the experience necessary (education, outreach, and housing) to conduct the proposed program and has developed strong partnerships to strengthen that experience. Two primary partners will fill this gap. Operating for more than 25 years, Rowan Technical College (RTC) is the region's top provider of vocational and technical education. RTC offers adult literacy and GED programs as well as a light construction curriculum that includes work-site preparation, framing, electrical installation/repair, tools and machinery operations, carpentry, and work safety. RTC will provide the construction curriculum component of this project and will contribute significantly to the GED literacy training component. The City of Morehead Housing Authority brings to this project construction experience and site access to allow participants to gain hands-on skills and experience in the community. The experience of these organizations is unparalleled in the community, and their combined participation will make the program a success.

FIGURE 5.6   (Continued)

One of the single greatest mistakes novice grant writers make (and I made my share as a novice as well) is to present need from a general perspective. Writers frequently present data on poverty, unemployment, income, and educational attainment. And these data can certainly demonstrate need for a program. However, it often seems that data are presented with no clear emphasis. This may be an artifact of accessibility and the writer's familiarity with certain types of data, or it may be because of a fundamental misunderstanding of the purpose behind a need section in the program narrative. The particular need dimensions identified previously are easy to understand, and the data are readily available for many geographic areas. The deeper issue is to understand what constitutes a good problem definition and to learn how to craft one. A good problem definition will succinctly get to the heart of the matter by identifying the exact concern the proposal seeks to address, diagnosing its cause, and conveying its importance to the individuals, groups, or communities affected. A proper frame sets the stage for the proposed solution you are about to unveil, so it is very important that the problem definition be focused, and not general.

What constitutes a problem? Identifying the problem is very similar to identifying strategic issues facing an organization in a typical strategic planning exercise (Bryson 2004). Except in the case of grant applications, we are looking outside the organization to the operating environment to identify issues that require our attention. I elaborated on the development of problem statements in the preceding sections of this chapter and do not reconsider that topic here except to indicate how to improve on them. As I indicated previously, the problem statement should be focused, not general. A good problem definition can usually be improved by thinking in quantities—is there too much or too little? Is the problem growing or contracting? By what magnitude? Bardach (2005) suggests thinking in terms of deficit and excess. For example, a simple problem definition might begin as the following: "There are too many illegal dumps in this county." But one illegal dump is too many, so the definition needs clarification. The following is an improvement: "The number of illegal roadside dumps in the county has increased to 500—an average rate of 10% per year over the past 5 years—leading to degradation of water quality." That definition is clear, and I now know where the proposal is heading. The definition could just as easily have ended "—causing a problem for public health" or "—leading to unsightly landscapes and detracting from tourist opportunities by naturalists and outdoorsmen." Either example is acceptable, but they point toward different program alternatives.

The next step is to document the problem; to justify the applicant's involvement in solving it. This task requires obtaining data, analyzing them, and providing references to the resources used. No, it is not sufficient to tell the funding agency that the problem exists. If that were the case, the best grant writers would be storytellers or repeat winners of the state liar's competition. Some data sources are more respectable than others. As a general rule, any government-collected and government-provided data are preferred to local data collected by the applicant organization. On the other hand, any data collected and published in a formal report can be used, and in every case the dataset or the published report should be attributed as the source in the application. You should be honest with the data you collect. It is unethical to use deceitful data—that is, data that do not truly represent the area. You should keep in mind that any data you use might be investigated by the reviewer for accuracy, so it is important to provide the source and to clearly explain the geographic area or subpopulation it represents.

Again, general data paint a general picture. Specific data document a specific problem—namely, the one developed in your problem statement. You should select and use measures that reflect the constructs directly stated in your problem definition. So, for literacy, you might use educational attainment as a reflective measure, but reading comprehension test scores would be better. Poverty is probably not a good measure, unless you can demonstrate the relationship between literacy, education attainment, and poverty, in which case you would have a clear case for including it. For public highway safety, income levels are fairly meaningless, unless you are documenting a lack of local funds. On the other hand, data that reflect traffic counts, the number of accidents, traffic violations and citations, or the dollar amounts of property loss are more useful. These data are adequate by themselves, but they are more meaningful when they are discussed as a proportion or percentage. So, the number of accidents per 100,000 highway miles driven provides a number that can be compared across areas of different sizes or with different highway types and qualities. Water quality can be measured by parts per million of key pollutants, but human response might be greater to an itemized list of local creeks and streams that are closed to recreation areas because of public health concerns related to water quality.

The key with data collection is to be fairly selective. You want to identify as many information sources as possible to include in your documentation, but you also face finite space limitations. It is best to select a number of variables, examine the measures, and utilize those that (1) best match your specific problem definition, and (2) show the greatest disparity or need relative to other places (and potential competing applications!). The statistics you use must match the problem as you have defined it. You must document the particular problem, not everything that is wrong with your community.

For some problems, such as the illegal dumps mentioned previously, a photograph of a representative roadside dump might be included to help the reader understand the nature and extent of the problem. Obviously, a picture takes up space on a page, and it should only be included if it is more valuable than the words that would fill its space. As a note, the problem/need section is the most common home for photographs, tables, charts, and graphs. As already stated, the value should be weighed carefully before using precious narrative space for these devices. But many times, photos can replace literally thousands of words, as the adage so aptly states. When used, these figures and tables must be produced in black and white to ensure that they are readable and understandable when duplicated on a standard copy machine. Multicolored lines in a graph can be very compelling, until the graph is photocopied in black and white for distribution to reviewers—then, they become meaningless and confusing.

Tables are useful to demonstrate levels of a problem in different geographic areas or during different years. With a table, you can easily identify the target area and several geographic comparison areas and present comparison data for several variables in a clear format. Tables save a great deal of space when used effectively. Charts and graphs, on the other hand, are better for demonstrating change over time—the trend of the problem. Naturally, it is more compelling to show a graph with a problem on the rise than to show one level or decreasing. In the latter cases, it may be best to focus on the absolute level of the problem rather than its trend. Following are examples of data comparisons for several geographic areas and times.

Table 5.1 presents geographic comparison data across a series of variables for several areas. Geographies are usually compared to state and national averages, and to city and county averages if they are smaller local areas as is the case here. **Figure 5.7** illustrates the use of a bar graph to compare the relative rurality of several geographic areas. **Table 5.2** compares change in employment by industrial sector in a single county over a series of recent years. **Table 5.3** shows how two pieces of information can be combined to tell a more compelling story. Here, the number of births is compared to the number of deaths, showing the absolute increase or decrease in each Alabama county's population. Population loss is then ranked by county for comparison.

Table 5.4 presents a unique analysis that compares the tax bases of several areas—counties and cities in two states (Kentucky and Alabama)—and examines the changes over the most recent 10-year period. **Figure 5.8** examines the change in average household sewer rates for clients of a large municipal sewer system over a period of several years. This graph shows a steep growth trend in rates over time, resulting from debt payments brought about in part by a significant federal consent decree in 1996. **Figure 5.9** shows the same county's total debt level associated with sewer revenue warrants and its change and composition over time.

TABLE 5.1   Table Comparing General Demographic Data

	Hayden, AL	Census Block Group[1]	West Blount County[2]	Alabama	United States
1990 Population	385	982	7,063	4,040,587	248,709,873
2000 Population	470	1,406	10,137	4,447,100	281,421,906
% Increase in population	81.9%	69.8%	69.7%	90.9%	88.4%
Median income 1999	$31,484	$36,719	$41,346	$34,135	$41,994
Median Age		34.5	35.8	35.8	35.3
Population over 16 in the workforce	194	629	4,741	1,900,089	128,279,228
Population over 16 work out of county		546	3,900	400,437	29,600,841
% Of population that work out of county		86.8%	82.3%	21.1%	23.1%
Population that work from home	4	4	114	39,303	4,184,223

[1]Census Block Group 2 is the Block Group in which Hayden is located.

[2]West Blount County is Census Tract 506, which encompasses most of the western section of Blount County including Hayden.

Adapted from: Hall and Handley 2007, p. 8.

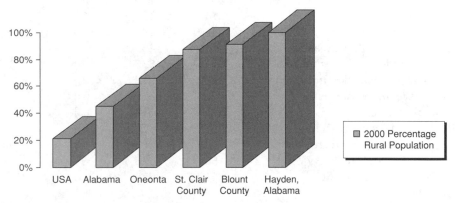

FIGURE 5.7   Bar Chart Showing Percentage Rural Population

Adapted from: Hall and Handley 2007, p. 15.

TABLE 5.2   Employment Change Over Time by Industrial Sector

Total Full-Time and Part-Time Employment by NAICS Industry
Blount County, AL
(Number of Jobs)

	2001	2003	2005	% Change (2001–2005)
Total employment	17,520	17,061	17,948	2.44%
Wage and salary employment	10,594	9,795	9,983	−5.77%
Proprietors employment	6,926	7,266	7,965	15.00%
Farm proprietors employment	1,351	1,310	1,275	−5.63%
Nonfarm proprietors employment	5,575	5,956	6,690	20.00%
Farm employment	1,506	1,466	1,416	−5.98%
Nonfarm employment	16,014	15,595	16,532	3.23%
Private employment	13,880	13,416	14,288	2.94%
Forestry, fishing, related activities, and other	(D)	(D)	(D)	—
Mining	(D)	(D)	(D)	—
Utilities	(D)	(D)	(D)	—
Construction	2,105	2,157	2,409	14.44%
Manufacturing	2,651	1,462	(D)	—
Wholesale trade	442	503	500	13.12%
Retail trade	2,199	2,301	2,154	−2.05%
Transportation and warehousing	(D)	(D)	(D)	—
Information	142	187	192	35.21%
Finance and insurance	460	495	506	10.00%
Real estate and rental and leasing	409	453	551	34.72%
Professional and technical services	545	536	638	17.06%
Management of companies and enterprises	(D)	(D)	(D)	—
Administrative and waste services	(D)	(D)	(D)	—
Educational services	(D)	(D)	(D)	—
Health care and social assistance	(D)	(D)	(D)	—
Arts, entertainment, and recreation	185	283	298	61.08%
Accommodation and food services	581	636	653	12.39%
Other services, except public administration	1,610	1,678	1,836	14.04%
Government and government enterprises	2,134	2,179	2,244	5.15%
Federal, civilian	99	100	98	−1.01%
Military	302	302	326	7.95%
State and local	1,733	1,777	1,820	5.02%
State government	160	164	163	1.88%
Local government	1,573	1,613	1,657	5.34%

Source: Bureau of Economic Analysis 2008.

TABLE 5.3   Population Replacement in Alabama Counties: Population Change Analysis 2000–2006 (by Rank)

Alabama	Births 2000–2006 375,808	Deaths 2000–2006 287,990	Population Loss/Gain Births Minus Deaths 87,818
Winston County	63	3,421	−3,358
Tallapoosa County	3,019	3,421	−402
Walker County	5,622	5,943	−321
Covington County	2,792	3,098	−306
Etowah County	7,891	8,175	−284
Fayette County	1,230	1,491	−261
Marion County	2,199	2,399	−200
Lamar County	1,058	1,231	−173
Chambers County	2,752	2,915	−163
Clay County	947	1,102	−155
Butler County	1,699	1,831	−132
Conecuh County	996	1,096	−100
Coosa County	724	820	−96
Macon County	1,568	1,646	−78
Geneva County	1,881	1,958	−77
Cherokee County	1,665	1,693	−28
Crenshaw County	1,094	1,097	−3
Colbert County	3,824	3,813	11
Henry County	1,278	1,262	16
Cleburne County	1,073	1,056	17
Randolph County	1,747	1,719	28
Choctaw County	1,128	1,067	61
Pickens County	1,709	1,636	73
Bullock County	968	856	112
Sumter County	1,128	1,005	123
Greene County	861	715	146
Hale County	1,445	1,288	157
Lauderdale County	5,989	5,810	179
Perry County	1,169	951	218
Jackson County	3,954	3,706	248
Washington County	1,357	1,105	252
Franklin County	2,632	2,373	259
Lowndes County	1,174	906	268
Bibb County	1,653	1,352	301
Monroe County	1,940	1,617	323
Marengo County	1,890	1,566	324
Escambia County	3,128	2,794	334
Barbour County	2,249	1,874	375

TABLE 5.3   (Continued)

Alabama	Births 2000–2006 375,808	Deaths 2000–2006 287,990	Population Loss/Gain Births Minus Deaths 87,818
Wilcox County	1,309	903	406
Lawrence County	2,535	2,117	418
Cullman County	6,024	5,551	473
Clarke County	2,311	1,763	548
Russell County	4,072	3,483	589
Pike County	2,530	1,930	600
Chilton County	3,410	2,773	637
Coffee County	3,531	2,866	665
Talladega County	6,427	5,606	821
Blount County	4,197	3,248	949
Dallas County	4,441	3,482	959
St. Clair County	5,329	4,238	1,091
Calhoun County	9,446	8,189	1,257
Autauga County	3,994	2,359	1,635
Limestone County	5,280	3,618	1,662
DeKalb County	6,061	4,237	1,824
Dale County	4,741	2,797	1,944
Elmore County	5,962	3,686	2,276
Baldwin County	11,615	9,294	2,321
Houston County	7,990	5,586	2,404
Marshall County	8,336	5,887	2,449
Morgan County	9,338	6,520	2,818
Lee County	8,845	4,908	3,937
Tuscaloosa County	13,789	9,349	4,440
Montgomery County	20,956	12,921	8,035
Madison County	22,785	14,258	8,527
Shelby County	15,463	6,165	9,298
Jefferson County	57,195	45,540	11,655
Mobile County	36,683	24,587	12,096

Source: Hall 2008.

Each of these examples is provided to convey a particular problem. Each graph or chart portrays a problem in a particular light. Some compare geographies, others compare time, and still others compare both. The key is to identify the graphical aid—whether chart, table, graph, or picture—that conveys the most information in the least space while effectively representing the problem you have identified. Geographic comparison contextualizes the problem; temporal comparison indicates the prevalence of the problem and its rate of change over time.

TABLE 5.4 Comparison of Local Fiscal Capacity, Selected Cities and Counties

Walker County Areas	1990	2000	1990 Base Calculation	1990 Base Calculation (2000 dollars)	2000 Base Calculation	Raw Comparison Results		Inflation-Adjusted Results	
						Total Income Change	% Change	Change in Real Total Income	% Change
Jasper City, AL									
# Households	5,360	5,728							
Median Household Income	22,476	33,044	120,471,360	147,610,693	189,276,032	68,804,672	57.11%	41,665,339	28.23% Raw
# Families in Poverty	455	393	110,244,780	135,080,308	176,289,740	66,044,960	59.91%	41,209,432	30.51% Poverty-Adjusted
Walker County, AL									
# Households	25,554	28,364							
Median Household Income	20,464	29,076	522,937,056	640,742,341	824,711,664	301,774,608	57.71%	183,969,323	28.71% Raw
# Families in Poverty	2,806	2,715	465,515,072	570,384,549	745,770,324	280,255,252	60.20%	175,385,775	30.75% Poverty-Adjusted
Alabama Total									
# Households	1,506,790	1,737,080							
Median Household Income	23,597	34,135	35,555,723,630	43,565,582,763	59,295,225,800	23,739,502,170	66.77%	15,729,643,037	36.11% Raw
# Families in Poverty	158,369	153,113	31,818,690,337	38,986,684,724	54,068,713,545	22,250,023,208	69.93%	15,082,028,821	38.69% Poverty-Adjusted

TABLE 5.4 (Continued)

Comparison Areas	1990	2000	1990 Base Calculation	1990 Base Calculation (2000 dollars)	2000 Base Calculation	Raw Comparison Results Total Income Change	% Change	Inflation-Adjusted Results Change in Real Total Income	% Change
Richmond City, KY									
# Households	7,199	10,801							
Median Household Income	15,588	25,533	112,218,012	137,498,062	275,781,933	163,563,921	145.76%	138,283,871	100.57% Raw
# Families in Poverty	1,023	922	96,271,488	117,959,165	252,240,507	155,969,019	162.01%	134,281,342	113.84% Poverty-Adjusted
Somerset City, KY									
# Households	4,237	4,792							
Median Household Income	16,810	22,362	71,223,970	87,269,037	107,158,704	35,934,734	50.45%	19,889,667	22.79% Raw
# Families in Poverty	520	468	62,482,770	76,558,652	96,693,288	34,210,518	54.75%	20,134,636	26.30% Poverty-Adjusted
Madison County, KY									
# Households	20,010	27,181							
Median Household Income	21,388	32,861	427,973,880	524,386,219	893,194,841	465,220,961	108.70%	368,808,622	70.33% Raw
# Families in Poverty	2,442	2,204	375,744,384	460,390,660	820,769,197	445,024,813	118.44%	360,378,537	78.28% Poverty-Adjusted
Pulaski County, KY									
# Households	18,895	22,674							
Median Household Income	18,198	27,370	343,851,210	421,312,712	620,587,380	276,736,170	80.48%	199,274,668	47.30% Raw
# Families in Poverty	2,775	2,429	293,351,760	359,436,937	554,105,650	260,753,890	88.89%	194,668,713	54.16% Poverty-Adjusted
Kentucky Total									
# Households	1,379,610	1,591,739							
Median Household Income	22,534	33,672	31,088,131,740	38,091,548,645	53,597,035,608	22,508,903,868	72.40%	15,505,486,963	40.71% Raw
# Families in Poverty	163,206	140,519	27,410,447,736	33,585,369,878	48,865,479,840	21,455,032,104	78.27%	15,280,109,962	45.50% Poverty-Adjusted

Source: Hall 2008, p. 32.

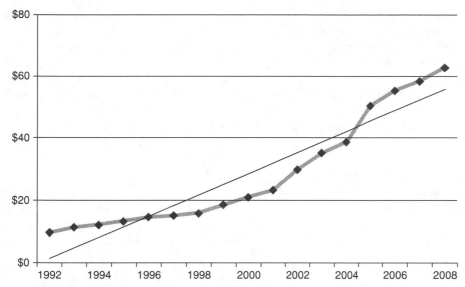

FIGURE 5.8   Household Sewer Bill Growth in Jefferson County, Alabama

Adapted from: Howell-Moroney and Hall 2008.

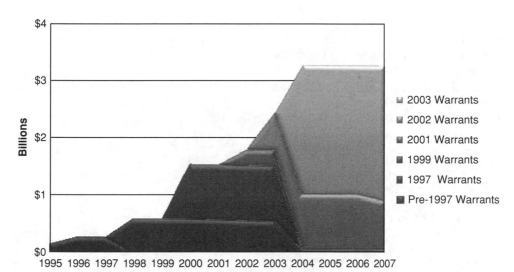

FIGURE 5.9   Composition of Jefferson County, Alabama Sewer Revenue Warrants

Adapted from: Howell-Moroney and Hall 2008.

Another approach to comparison is to use the average of contiguous geographic areas rather than listing them individually. This approach might be used when your county or service area has a significant problem, but one or more adjacent counties experience the same problem more severely. So, consider a hypothetical situation: Wayne County has an unemployment rate of 10% compared to Clinton County (12%), Pulaski County (6%), and McCreary County (8%). If you list Clinton County, it is clear that you are not addressing the most problematic area. If you average the surrounding counties (12 + 6 + 8 = 26; 26 / 3 = 8.7%), your local problem has the appearance of being worse (because 10% > 8.7%). You should learn to present need in the most favorable light for your local area.

Common Data Sources Used to Document Need

As you approach the need/problem section of your program narratives, you will become familiar with more and more datasets that may be appropriate for your focus area. Although the specific sources will depend on your substantive focus and the particular problem definition you develop, a number of common sources may prove beneficial additions to your toolkit:

U.S. Census Bureau (www.census.gov)
- General population info, government info
- Comparisons by sub-county areas, and so forth

Bureau of Economic Analysis (www.bea.gov)
- Economic development info
- County estimates of compensation by industry
- Per capita personal income information available by county
- BEARFACTS

Bureau of Labor Statistics (www.bls.gov)
- Employment and unemployment data
- Productivity data

Appalachian Regional Commission (www.arc.gov)
- Distressed counties

Mississippi Delta Regional Authority (www.dra.gov)
- Distressed counties

U.S. Department of Education (www.ed.gov)
- School data
- Education attainment
- Dropout rates

Department of Health and Human Services (www.hhs.gov)
- Temporary Assistance for Needy Families (TANF), Aid to Families with Dependent Children (AFDC) data
- Health data, concentration of illnesses
- Child support data
- Elderly population data

National Science Foundation (www.nsf.gov)
- High-tech data: Science and engineering
- Science and engineering degrees granted
- Research and development spending

Federal Bureau of Investigation (www.fbi.gov)
- Uniform Crime Reports

U.S. Environmental Protection Agency (www.epa.gov)
- Environmental statistics

U.S. Department of Agriculture (www.usda.gov)
- Grocery stores
- Health ratings
- Farm and commodity data
- Rurality (rural–urban continuum codes)
- Other agriculture statistics

It is good to use data from sources such as these because the information has been collected in a uniform fashion using the same methodology across areas, making it easily comparable. And of course, government data are available free of charge in most cases. Other economic data may be available from various sources. Oftentimes, such data project expected levels of key variables for future years. Two examples include these:

Dismal Scientist (www.dismal.com): International and national data
Woods & Poole Economics (www.woodsandpoole.com): Projections into the future

And at times, local data sources may prove to be beneficial, such as the State Data Center in your state; for example, the Alabama State Data Center (http://cber.cba.ua.edu/asdc.html). States also develop unique data sets by area of interest. An example is a website launched in 2008 to provide a one-stop resource for Texas economic development information (www.texasahead.org). Kentucky provides information pertaining to economic development and industrial recruitment at www.thinkkentucky.com. You may easily find numerous unique data sources available with a simple Internet search.

Objectives/Goals

You have completed the needs assessment, or problem definition, and are ready to move on to the program's goals and objectives. The goals and objectives section is your opportunity to focus on the future. Having clearly documented the problem to be addressed, your goals and objectives communicate what you plan to accomplish. Once again, this section of the proposal should logically connect the outcomes to be achieved to the problem as you defined it. Logic and order are important components of the objectives/goals section because the pieces need to fit together to tell the story. Think back to the earlier program theory section. Program theory identifies outputs that occur at each stage in the implementation process, so if you have a clear program theory, you should be able to identify the important outputs, outcomes, and impacts in the order in which they occur.

The key purpose behind this section is to communicate the ultimate goal(s) of the program, but for many social programs the expected results are esoteric and difficult to measure. This section must have a future perspective. It must describe the state of the problem that is expected to result from the program's successful implementation. The best applications are those that quantify the problem in the need section, and then provide a clear quantitative indication of the effect that is expected to result from the program. So, if the purpose is to reduce traffic fatalities on the state's interstate highways, the stated goal might be to reduce the number of fatalities by 10% over the same period during the preceding year. That may be the primary goal, but there are other significant outcomes that we expect to result from the proposed highway safety blitz activity. Loss of property should be reduced, and we might specify a similar percentage reduction to communicate our expectations. Injury accidents should be reduced. Insurance claims would, as a result, also decline. And of course, future accidents will be prevented by taking unsafe drivers or vehicles off the roadways. For each of these goals, except the latter, we can specify a clear percentage reduction (a relative measure) and an actual amount (an absolute measure) to communicate our goals and expectations. It is in fact impossible to know whether or not a future accident has been prevented, so rather than focusing on outcomes, in this case it is necessary to consider the outputs—citations that will be issued, arrests that will be made, and so on.

The goals I have discussed so far fall under the classification of substantive goals—goals tied directly to the problem. There are also process goals to be considered in many programs; that is, expectations about when important steps will be taken to bring about the proposed outcomes in the time specified by the proposal. So, for example, goals might include appointment of a new multiagency task force by a certain date, development of media announcements that attract drivers' attention, development of a coordinated enforcement plan to follow in implementing the blitz, and so forth. These process goals are somewhat mundane to describe, perhaps, but they are important to communicate the relationship between the proposed activities, their outputs, and the ultimate outcomes and impacts that are expected. I highlight the difference between substantive goals and process goals here to foreshadow their relationship to the program's evaluation plan. Program theory is essential to designing and describing a program and its goals, but it is also quite useful in developing a plan to evaluate the program's implementation and effects.

Posavac and Carey (2003, p. 53–55) describe three general types of goals: implementation goals, intermediate goals, and outcome goals. It is necessary for there to be some program activity before any outcomes can be achieved—these activities are implementation goals. For our example, the implementation goals are the process goals identified earlier. There may actually be a greater or lesser number of such goals, and the level of detail may vary. Generally, it is a good idea to filter the goals to be included in this section so that it doesn't read like a technical manual with instructions for how to implement the program. It should certainly reflect the outputs, outcomes, and impacts expected, and only the very important process or implementation goals. Intermediate goals are the things that will occur as a result of implementation, but that do not reflect the ultimate outcomes. So, if the implementation goals are startup activities, intermediate goals are generally the initial outputs that make up our substantive goals, such as traffic stops made, citations written, and arrests made. Each of these goals might be more specific with regard to particular categories (speeding, driving while intoxicated, insurance violations, seatbelt violations, and so forth). And naturally, outcome goals reflect the true change in the problem state. Figure 5.10 reveals the relationships among goal types, activities, and results.

In the example provided, there is really only one goal: public safety. Thus, the objectives are to reduce fatalities, injuries, and accidents. In some programs, there are multiple goals, a fact that adds some complexity to our understanding. Generally speaking, *goals* are broad areas within which we hope to make an impact, and *objectives* are specific, quantifiable

Implementation Goals ──────▶	Intermediate Goals ──────▶	Outcome Goals
(*Process Goals*)	(*Substantive Goals, Initial*)	(*Substantive Goals*)
Startup Activities	Outputs	Outcomes, Impacts
Task Force Established (date)	Traffic Stops (#)	Fatalities
Media Plan Completed (date)	Citations Written (#)	Injury Accidents
Enforcement Plan Completed (date)	Arrests Made (#)	Property Loss Accidents
Officers Trained (date)	(#s by Total, by Event, or Both)	"Public Safety"
Officers Scheduled (date)		
Support Staff Scheduled (date)		
Events Occur as Scheduled (dates)		

FIGURE 5.10   Relationship of Goal Types, Activities, and Program Results

measures that we will use to assess progress toward the goal. Whatever terminology you use, you should realize that there is a hierarchy of broad goals under which more specific intentions can be revealed. The level of detail you provide will depend on the space limitations of the proposal, the relative importance of the activity or outcome to the proposal, and your ability to use figures and tables to present more information in less space.

In presenting estimates of outputs and outcomes to be achieved, it is best to be clear about the absolute and relative levels of performance (or change in performance) expected. The goals section should clearly link process goals and substantive goals in a logical, hierarchical fashion. And most of all, the goals you set should be realistic and achievable by your organization within the time frame of the proposal. The program may have lasting or enduring effects, and these can be discussed as well. All in all, the goals section presents an image of what impact on the stated problem the funding agency should expect to observe if they make the grant award. This section requires you to think and write positively, but realistically. Oftentimes, it is beneficial to itemize the activities, outputs, and outcomes in a tabular format, such as in Figure 5.10, to save space and convey the relationships between goals and objectives at different levels.

Methods and Procedures/Implementation Plan

The implementation plan is focused less on the goals and objectives, and more on the steps that will be taken to bring them to fruition. It is your work plan, sometimes also called the *scope of work*. The process goals are really the targets of this explanatory section. Just like process goals led to substantive goals, one or more steps lead to each of the process goals. These steps are often overlapping and occur simultaneously. In short, then, the implementation plan becomes a description of what will be done, when, by whom, and for what purpose. You provide a detailed plan for how you will implement the proposed program. And upon award, this section will serve as the instruction manual for how to implement the project.

It is often beneficial to include a discussion of certain activities that will be completed prior to the project start date. Of course, grant funds cannot be used to pay for activities that occur in advance of the project start date. But, if activities and processes will be ongoing in the period between application and award date that will have a meaningful impact on the project's startup time or success, these activities should be mentioned.

The implementation plan begins with the award date and continues through the end of the proposed grant period. If the funding source is particularly interested in sustainability or continuation, it may be advisable to keep the implementation plan open-ended rather than closed at the last date of the project. For example, "Sessions will be held weekly for the duration of the project" is a closed-ended activity description. An open-ended alternative might read, "Weekly sessions will continue for each cohort of students for the prescribed 10-week period beginning January 1, 2009, July 1, 2009, January 1, 2010, and every 6 months thereafter." If funding for continuation is not available, the project will expire at the end of the award period, but you do not want to convey to the funder that you do not expect to sustain the program.

What should a work plan include? As noted previously, you should begin by thinking about key activities in the process that *must occur for the program to generate the desired results*. These activities should occur in a logical order, and you should be able to describe that order and the relationship of one step to the next. You will allocate staff to project activities, and then describe what they will do and when they will do it to ensure that the process goals are achieved. Some key tools that are useful in developing an implementation plan are time lines, activity lists or sequences, and management plans.

A project time line provides an overall picture of the activities that are scheduled to occur. If there are multiple overlapping activities, then overlapping time lines can be used. One particular tool that aids in prescribing the timing of numerous overlapping project activities is a Gantt chart. Figures can be compiled in a variety of ways to communicate effectively the program's planned course of action. The key idea to remember is that the tool should communicate your intended plans clearly. An interesting figure that is difficult to read is meaningless. And any figure that is provided must be labeled, referred to in the text, and discussed or explained. Otherwise, it simply fills up space.

Figure 5.11 presents a time line that arrays key project activities by the general area, the specific project, and over time. Because this time line was used for a 3-year project, the level of detail is relatively low. Information is provided in quarterly increments to show the relationships of activities, some recurring, and some not. This project utilized diverse staff, so in large part, the activities did not interfere with one another.

Table 5.5 presents a time line for a very short project—a feasibility study—in a chart format. By using Microsoft Excel, it is possible to present activities as rows and periods of time as columns; entering an *X* in the cell indicates that the activity takes place during that time. Another technique is to fill the cell with a dark color to reflect an activity taking place. This is the general style used in a Gantt chart. In this example, activities are broken down by weeks, indicated by each individual cell. Important process goals are identified in bold typeface while the key implementation steps fall under them in normal typeface.

When project activities are not overlapping and are relatively straightforward, the Gantt chart may require more space than its benefit provides. In these cases, a simple time line is more appropriate. **Figure 5.12** provides an example for a simple research project.

In addition to project time lines, management plans are useful tools that are sometimes included in the implementation plan section of program narratives. If the project is complex, it

B. Community Outreach Partnership Center Project Timeline

COMMUNITY ORGANIZING AND PLANNING

ID	Project Name	2002-4	2003-1	2003-2	2003-3	2003-4	2004-1	2004-2	2004-3	2004-4	2005-1	2005-2	2005-3	2005-4
1A	Training/Public Policy Seminars	Contact Leaders	…	Seminar 1	…	Seminar 2	…	Seminar 3	…	Seminar 4	…	Seminar 5	Compilation and Report Publication	Evaluation
1B	Historical Preservation	Obtain Area Maps	Consult GIS/GPS Technician	…	Delineate Districts	Recruit & Train Volunteers	Begin Data Collection	Data Collection and Entry	…	…	…	…	Compilation and Report Publication	…
1C	GIS/GPS Training	Contact Agencies & Officials	Schedule Training Sessions	…	Training Session 1	…	Training Session 2	Feedback Session	Training Session 3	…	Training Session 4	…	Participant Feedback Session	…
1D	Public Sector Capacity Study	Planning Session	Study Outline	Catalog Government Agencies	…	…	Data Collection	…	…	…	…	Data Analysis and Report Publication	…	…

ECONOMIC DEVELOPMENT AND NEIGHBORHOOD REVITALIZATION

ID	Project Name	2002-4	2003-1	2003-2	2003-3	2003-4	2004-1	2004-2	2004-3	2004-4	2005-1	2005-2	2005-3	2005-4
2A	Entrepreneurial Training	Institutional Mtg.	Recruitment	Informational Mtg.	Training Sessions	…	…	Feedback Session	Training Sessions (Cont.)	…	…	…	Outcome Assessment	…
2B	Economic Policy Study	Planning Session	Workload Distribution	Literature Review	Develop Methodology	Data Collection	…	…	…	…	…	Apply Methodology to City	…	Report Publication

EDUCATION

ID	Project Name	2002-4	2003-1	2003-2	2003-3	2003-4	2004-1	2004-2	2004-3	2004-4	2005-1	2005-2	2005-3	2005-4
3A	Community History/Oral History	Purchase Equipment	Recruitment	Train Volunteers	Outreach	Information Collection/Transcription	…	…	…	…	…	…	Materials Presented to Libraries	…
3B	Literacy/GED Supplement	Coordination Meeting	Recruitment/Marketing Sessions	…	…	…	…	…	Progress Evaluation	Recruitment/Marketing Sessions	…	Community Presentations	…	Evaluation

HOUSING

ID	Project Name	2002-4	2003-1	2003-2	2003-3	2003-4	2004-1	2004-2	2004-3	2004-4	2005-1	2005-2	2005-3	2005-4
4A	Fair Housing Seminars	Materials Compiled	Tenant Seminars	…	Landlord Seminars	…	Tenant Seminars	…	Landlord Seminars	…	Tenant Seminars	…	Landlord Seminars	…
4B	Housing Policy Study	Planning Session	Literature Review	…	…	Identify/Categorize Policies	…	…	Data Collection	…	City Case Study	…	Publication	…

ENVIRONMENT

ID	Project Name	2002-4	2003-1	2003-2	2003-3	2003-4	2004-1	2004-2	2004-3	2004-4	2005-1	2005-2	2005-3	2005-4
5A	Solid Waste Education	Discussants Scheduled	Materials Compiled	…	Sessions Held	…	…	Activities & Evaluation	…	…	…	…	Feedback	…
5B	Pollution Monitoring Program	School Materials Compiled & Distributed	School Visits & Teacher Training	…	First Year Activities	…	…	…	Second Year Activities	…	…	…	…	Evaluation
5C	Environmental Academy & Training Institute	Planning & Material Preparation	Training Sessions Held	Marketing	Seminar 1	Seminars 2–3 + Feedback Session	Seminars 4–5	Seminar 6	Seminar 1	Seminars 2–3	Seminars 4–5	Seminar 6	Feedback & Evaluation	…

FIGURE 5.11 Time Line of Key Project Activities by Quarter

Source: Courtesy of Morehead State University 2002.

185

TABLE 5.5   Weekly Time Line of Project Activities by Process Goals

	Study Months (and Weeks)												
	May	*June*				*July*				*August*			
Tasks	4	1	2	3	4	1	2	3	4	1	2	3	4
FEASIBILITY STUDY:													
ORG. STRUCTURE AND STARTUP													
Benchmarks and Models Identified	X												
Structure, Operation, Budget Info Collected	X	X											
PLANNING AND DEVELOPMENT													
Implementation Plan	X	X	X										
Market/Environmental Assessment													
Review Existing Literature			X	X	X	X							
Market Assessment			X	X	X	X							
County Environmental Assessment				X	X	X	X						
Business Plan													
Funding Sources Identified	X												
Phasing the Concept into Reality					X	X	X	X	X				
Plan for Recruiting/Maintaining Support					X	X	X	X	X				
Fundraising Plan					X	X	X	X	X				
Proposed Budget Projection						X	X	X	X	X			
FINAL ANALYSIS													
Final Analysis						X	X	X	X	X			
Compilation of Final Report											X	X	X
Results Dissemination												X	X

Adapted from: Hall and Handley 2007, p. 3.

might be advisable to provide a simple organizational chart that shows the relationships of various program actors. **Figure 5.13** shows a simple organizational chart representing the safety blitz example. Charts of this nature generally supply information about accountability relationships that exist between individuals, organizational units, or program partners, and thus show who has project authority to ensure that tasks are completed. It is common to find core staff and management identified by name within each division in grant applications because, again, the purpose is to communicate as much information as possible in as little space as is feasible.

Workplan

April 13, 2006	• UKCPR Small Grants Conference; submit project to UAB IRB
June 1, 2006	• Project start date
August 1, 2006	• Literature review complete
August 15, 2006	• Data collected; database manipulated into panel format
September 15, 2006	• Analysis complete
September 30, 2006	• Initial results presented at SECoPA 2006, Athens, GA
January 15, 2007	• Results and discussion written
February 15, 2007	• Draft manuscript completed and circulated for comment
May 31, 2007	• Project completion date; journal-length manuscript Submitted to UKCPR and to JPAM or JPART for review

FIGURE 5.12   Simple Project Time Line

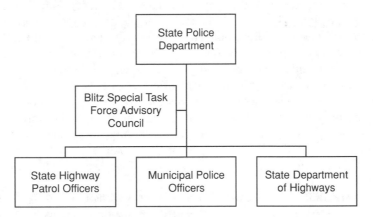

FIGURE 5.13   Organizational Chart Example

It is advisable to name key project personnel, their duties, and their responsibilities, in the scope of work, and there are two methods of doing so. You may provide information about program staff and their duties and responsibilities in a concise section of the narrative, either in written form or by generating a table that lists them. The alternative is to discuss key personnel as you describe the tasks to be performed. A combination of these methods is sometimes advisable—especially for particularly complex programs.

So, for example, your scope of work may provide a graph to reflect the overall management plan. **Figure 5.14** provides an example of the simplest version of such a list. More complicated versions might indicate specific activities for which staff are responsible, or the amount of time they are contributing to the project. Alternatively, you can simply note the name of the individual responsible for each activity as you list the activities. Such as: "Water quality samples will be drawn from each of the four key tributaries that feed the Rock Creek watershed once per week for the duration of the project (student volunteers supervised by Jane Smith). The water samples will be appropriately labeled and analyzed, with results posted to the project website within one day of collection (Susan Tucker)." The focus of the latter method is on the activity rather than the person, but it still demonstrates

Name	Title	Organization	Project Role
John Doe	Executive Director	Applicant	Program Director
Jane Smith	Research Scientist	Applicant	Field Work Manager
Susan Tucker	Research Scientist	Applicant	Lab Manager
Billy Johnson	Counselor	School System	Recruitment/Training Coordinator
Jill Wu	Marketing Director	XYZ Media	Media Coordinator

FIGURE 5.14　Organization Management Plan: Key Personnel and Responsibilities Example

that the applicant has a clear plan for implementing the activities discussed. Management plans convey organizational capacity and demonstrate the depth of program planning that has taken place in advance of the application.

These tools notwithstanding, there is still need for extensive narrative description of the activities to take place. Figure 5.15 provides a sample of a scope of work for a relatively simple grant-funded project with no application structure or requirements. This work plan corresponds to the project time line in Table 5.5. The scope of work for the entire project is presented in one page, plus the corresponding table, even though there was no established limit for the proposal. The intent is to provide sufficient explanation and clarity for the funder to understand the proposed activities. In this case, there is no reference to the program staff because the proposal was developed in consultation between the staff and the funding agency. A lengthier example is provided in the chapter appendix. This narrative was developed for a 2003 HUD YouthBuild application proposal. Although a structured proposal, it provides a sound example of the nature of the scope of work or implementation plan for a typical program narrative.

The implementation plan or scope of work details actions that are to be taken to bring about the results the program promises. It is tied directly to the goals and objectives, and therefore also to the problem definition. Activities that do not directly or indirectly lead to the outcomes of interest will be suspect and should not be detailed.

Another key linkage that should not be overlooked at this point is that between the work plan and the budget. There are two important errors to be avoided, and you should always check for both before submitting your proposal. First, the budget indicates the cost of salaries and wages, as well as supplies and equipment that are to be used in the program implementation. If the implementation plan does not describe the personnel listed in the budget, or if it indicates significantly less effort than is budgeted, a good reviewer will make note of the discrepancy and penalize the application. Likewise, if you list an expensive piece of equipment in the budget but fail to show its significance in the program implementation plan, the reviewer will wonder if it is really a necessary purchase. Remember—we wrote the budget first so that it could be used as the framework for the program narrative. It is important to check your work to make sure these contributions add up. So, if John Doe is slated to provide 25% effort to the project (per the budget), then the plan should indicate that he will spend 10 hours per week on project management duties.

The second consideration regards the timing of expenditures. If your budget is annual, but covers a 3-year period, then the time line of expenditures in the budget should correspond to the implementation time line. If equipment is budgeted in year 1, but the implementation

Scope of Work:
The research team will conduct an applied research project to fulfill the principal desires the Foundation has expressed. The research will include three primary foci, including feasibility, operational comparison, and start-up and funding.

First, a rudimentary feasibility study will be conducted to assess demand and need for an arts center in [Name] County in the I-65 corridor. An environmental assessment will take a closer look at logistics associated with the county demographics, proposed locations, and project costs associated with developing a Performing Arts Center. In building this analysis, competing and complementary organizations will be examined and compared. This market assessment will consist of an assessment of performing arts facilities in the area, within the state, and within other nationwide areas with similar demographics. The market assessment will also assess available attractions within the area to develop a needs assessment and a gap analysis as it relates to the Foundation and the proposed Performing Arts Center. The combined goal of these two efforts will be to determine the role such a center would play in a holistic amenities-based tourism strategy as well as its role in enhancing quality of life for the local community.

The report's **second component** will emphasize organizational structure and startup. This component will identify 10 community performing arts centers to be used as models for the Center. The result will be a composite of varied models from which project proponents can select. The emphasis will be on providing sound examples of each, including (1) standalone visual and performing arts centers, (2) visual and performing arts centers combined with community center/convention center operations, and (3) centers that serve as visual and performing arts centers while hosting office space for a hub of nonprofit and community organizations. The report will provide benchmark examples of organizational structure, operation, and budget for each model.

The plan's **third component** will assess planning and development issues. Drawing on need identified in the community (phase 1) and potential organizational structures (phase 2), the investigators will develop a recommended strategy with alternatives. Based on the recommended strategy, this section will include a proposed phased implementation plan to move from grassroots organizing to a center ready for use. It will assess community collaboration potential and will suggest a model that includes collaboration between the organization, other community organizations, and governments and elected officials. A business plan will be developed for guidance in implementing the proposed model. The business plan will include details associated with recruiting and maintaining support for the project, developing a fund-raising plan for the center, and providing a proposed budget and projected budget for the next 3–5 years. This component will also include a prioritized list of potential government and foundation funding sources, including detailed funding objectives and preferences for each funding source.

These deliverables will be provided to the Foundation in a final report (print and electronic format) with supporting documentation. The final report will produce an overall justification for the Center, as well as recommended alternative strategies. It will discuss anticipated problems and strengths to assist in the project development decision-making process. This professional report will be suitable for use in future planning efforts and as documentation for funding requests to support project development. The report will be presented during a Foundation meeting to interested community members. The written report will be completed by 31 August 2007.

FIGURE 5.15   Sample Scope of Work

plan refers to its purchase and use in year 2, the reviewer will once again develop concerns about the applicant's management ability. Consistency among the various elements of the proposal is necessary, and the lack thereof is a common mistake that will rarely be overlooked by a skilled reviewer. The implementation plan will suggest key points at which data should be collected or program results observed, so it shares a clear connection to the evaluation plan as well.

Evaluation Plan

What is the point in writing an evaluation plan? What is there to evaluate? This is a relevant question—and it leads us to ask what the funder means by evaluation. There are two general meanings conveyed by the term *evaluation* in grant proposals. The first is a simple process evaluation that assesses whether the project was implemented as planned and in a timely fashion. In this regard, even the most simple and straightforward programs require a basic evaluation plan to provide implementation information to include in periodic grant reports. The plan in this case communicates who will evaluate the program, what key items they will measure and how, and how the results will be reported and communicated to the agency and to the funding source. Key considerations include who will serve as the program evaluator and whether they are internal program staff or external contractual evaluators, key activities to monitor, key data to collect, and the timing of such activities.

In short, the assumption for this sort of evaluation is that the implementation plan be executed as written. Any variations from the plan would be noted, reported, and explained. In the evaluation literature, such evaluations are referred to as formative evaluations in that the information is fed back into program administration to correct problems or deficiencies. It is thus an integral component of program management in that it identifies the process that will be used to identify mistakes or shortcomings and correct them before they evolve into more significant problems for the program.

A more involved variety of program evaluation takes the program's success into consideration. This summative, or outcome, evaluation asks not only whether the program was implemented as planned, but whether it generated the expected outputs and outcomes and ultimately whether it had an effect on the problem of interest. Why include outcome evaluation in a program? Many grant programs are funded because they represent innovative ways to deliver services, and there is an interest on the part of program leaders and funding agency representatives in learning whether or not the program works, and how well. In the case of federal government agencies, outcome evaluations may be used to report results of grant making activities for credit claiming and accountability purposes. If programs are funded but are not affecting the problem in the manner expected, then the programs may need to be adjusted. An applicant that does not show some interest in the results to be obtained may appear disingenuous. **Figure 5.16** provides an example of a summative evaluation plan to be conducted internally.

If the proposal is to conduct research or to conduct a social experiment, then learning the effect of the program is the central purpose of the activity, and evaluation should be much more than an afterthought. Scientific and research proposals require a much higher degree of rigor in their methodology, and usually require the services of a competent evaluation specialist or a peer in the same field of research who is capable of evaluating the methodology utilized and the results obtained in an unbiased manner.

Program staff will be responsible for evaluation activities, including data collection, analysis, and reporting. Key outcome measures and expectations are detailed below.

This initial YouthBuild program will serve 15 participants. Four (4) new housing units for home-ownership will be constructed at the Habitat for Humanity property located at 69 College St. An 87% rate of GED or certificate completion is expected, with 13 completing the certification out of 15 enrolled in training. One hundred percent of participants (15 of 15) will either be placed in employment or enrolled in higher education within the first quarter after program completion. All participants will grow in literacy and numeracy as a result of this program from a sub-GED level to a GED level. Because this program will serve a population with very low literacy and numeracy levels initially, it is expected that the gains will be between 50% and 150% on an individual basis.

The key outcomes of this YouthBuild program are the following: educational advancement for at-risk population (education), occupational training and experience for at-risk population (employment), local housing improvements (housing), improved leadership abilities for young people (leadership), an improved sense of community and citizenship by a traditionally alienated group (citizenship), and self-sufficiency and entrepreneurial abilities (sufficiency). Key benchmarks for these outcomes are identified below.

Marketable Skills Dimension

Education   (1) 15 participants enrolled, (2) literacy/GED courses held, (3) students tested, (4) literacy levels exceed 50% improvement, (5) GEDs earned by 13/15 of the class (about 87%).

Employment   (1) 15 participants enrolled, (2) light construction courses offered, (3) students complete light construction curriculum satisfactorily, (4) on-site rehabilitation experience averages 20 hours/week, (5) consultations with area employers take place, (6) participants not enrolled in higher education are employed within one quarter of program completion.

Housing   (1) Improvements made to approximately 67 rental housing units in Wayne County.

Psychological Dimension

Leadership   (1) Leadership curriculum completed, (2) students develop examples of activities that demonstrate leadership.

Citizenship   Students meet with (1) government officials and (2) community leaders, (3) students are presented with opportunities for volunteer service, (4) students participate in one community service project prior to program completion.

Sufficiency   (1) Students take part in entrepreneurial training component, (2) basic financial skills training completed, (3) students learn self-employment requirements.

Additionally, average attendance and program attrition will be measured as quantifiable outcomes that demonstrate progress toward program goals.

FIGURE 5.16   Summative Evaluation Plan Example: Internally Conducted

Source: Courtesy of Morehead State University 2003.

Program staff members have the greatest level of program knowledge, and they are close to the program; however, they have an interest in showing the program in the most favorable light possible. In other words, they know the details better than anyone, but they can't be trusted to tell the true story about the program. For this reason, it is often advisable to consult with an independent external evaluator. Although they will have to spend more time becoming familiar with the project, they will be able to objectively assess whether the program is performing well and convey suggestions for improvement to program staff.

What should the evaluation plan look like? If you have a sound program theory, then you already know how various activities are linked together, and you understand the outcomes that are expected to result at each stage. This is the core of evaluation planning. Each node at which an activity takes place provides an opportunity to assess whether the activity occurred, whether it was timely, whether it was conducted as planned, and what results were obtained. Moreover, the implementation plan developed in the previous section provides a map of activities and steps and links them to the time line during which they should be conducted. Though similar to the audit function, an evaluation can take the additional step of determining whether funds were expended as intended, in the correct amounts, and at the correct times. The evaluator can perform some basic calculations to determine the final cost-benefit ratio for the program based on its outcomes.

Once again, you see that the evaluation plan is linked backward to earlier parts of the proposal, and consistency is essential. If the proposed evaluation plan considers elements that are not central to the problem, or that extend beyond the goals and objectives identified, then it will not represent a sound evaluation of the program's worth. The implementation plan documents the series of measures that should be evaluated during the course of a process evaluation. The goals and objectives give the key outcomes that should be measured in the course of a summative evaluation. Moreover, the relationship between implementation goals, intermediate goals (outputs), and outcome goals (outcomes/impacts) provides an opportunity to assess the linkages the program theory assumed. In other words, if we thought that traffic blitzes should improve highway safety, we can measure those outputs and outcomes and perform a relatively simple statistical analysis to determine the relationship of the program to the outcome of interest. Again, the more confidence demanded in the program's impact, the more rigorous the methodology must be. Experimental or quasi-experimental designs can be used to rule out plausible alternative explanations for the program results. But for these methods to be used, the program must be designed to include a control or comparison group and/or time period. And that means an evaluator should be consulted during program design, well before the grant application is written.

As a note, many evaluators (and university researchers in general) are willing and able to assist with program evaluation design in exchange for the right to perform the evaluation if and when the grant is funded. Customarily, these fees are included in the consulting category of the budget, and the evaluator is identified in this section of the proposal narrative. It is not necessary for an external evaluator to perform evaluations—especially if the program is very simple. The funder may not even require or desire an evaluation. When it does, program staff may be tasked to perform process evaluation necessary for reporting, whereas external evaluators are tasked with the final outcome evaluation to assess program impacts. A more sophisticated discussion of program evaluation is provided in Chapter 10.

Continuation/Sustainability Plan

Most grant making agencies, whether implicitly or explicitly, have a desire to make a difference. From Chapter 1 recall that foundations have largely abandoned expressive giving in favor of instrumental giving efforts. That is, they want to know that their funds will have a significant impact. They have learned to leverage their investments by requiring local match funds, as have government grant making agencies. There is a strong desire by many funders to know that their investment will be institutionalized—that it will live on beyond the project performance period. In this way, they view the grant award as seed money to assist with project startup, and they expect the recipient to sustain the program with its own revenues once the grant funding expires. The continuation/sustainability plan is usually a brief section that documents your plans for continuing the program when grant funding expires. As with other sections of the narrative, this is your opportunity to demonstrate commitment to the project, to show efforts to plan well in advance, and to convey your organization's capacity.

The single largest concern with sustaining any program is funding. It is customary to detail sources of funds you will pursue to provide continued program support. It is advisable to indicate that these fund-raising efforts will begin well in advance of the project completion date because waiting until funds expire would result in a service gap. As a general rule, foundations are not pleased to hear that you will seek continuation funding from other foundations or even government grants. A more appealing continuation plan is one that raises new revenues from individual or corporate donors, or one that begins to generate fees for services provided. This sustainability plan might call for providing the program for a fee but waiving expenses for low-income individuals. Or once the service has been demonstrated to be valuable, contracts from local governments could pay the expenses or fees for clients they refer to the program. Another alternative is to absorb the program staff salaries and expenses into the operating budget as a regular expense. It may be necessary to scale the program to fit organizational resources in some cases, but of course the funder would not be pleased to see its investment shrink. Each program is different, and what would be considered feasible as a continuation strategy will vary for each program as well. Creativity and thoughtfulness will often lead to plans and strategies that suggest strong management capacity and strong likelihood of sustainability.

Another technique that demonstrates likely sustainability or program continuation is a list of examples of past grant programs that have been sustained beyond the funding period and the methods used to sustain them. Evidence of past success is a strong indicator of future performance.

Budget

Considering the lengthy discussion of the budget in the previous chapter, it is not necessary to belabor its construction again here. Many unstructured funding opportunities will not have official forms or guidelines, so the budget is submitted as a part of the proposal narrative. When this is the case, it is usually attached, and any additional budget justification is appended following the budget document.

Guidance for Structured Proposals

The chapter thus far has provided several general suggestions for how to approach the proposal narrative and has addressed the key elements that are most commonly included in grant RFPs. For unstructured requests, the model presented earlier represents a boilerplate that can be adapted and adjusted to fit page limitations or the funder's expressed interests. In this final section, I provide a few tips for responding to RFPs and other formal guidelines that require specific responses to specific questions, or otherwise require a standard application format.

The single most important requirement when responding to a formal RFP is to read the requirements thoroughly in advance, usually multiple times. For very complicated guidelines, highlight key areas and make notes. Federal government RFPs are notorious for stringent guidelines and requirements, and they can produce a great deal of frustration for applicants writing under the pressure of the clock. Reading the rules up front will save lots of corrections, and the related frustration, near the end of the application process.

After you have read and thoroughly understand the program's rules and requirements, *follow them*. Do not deviate. Do not vary. The rules of the game are intended to ensure process equity, and the information requested is very likely the information that will be used to score the proposal. So, you may write a stellar narrative explaining how your program will serve participants, but if the requirement asks only for the number of participants that will be served, you will lose the points. Always follow the rules and guidelines to the letter.

It is customary for federal programs to document the criteria for grant awards in the Funding NOFA. These criteria usually have point values associated with them, and each criterion often lists issues that should be addressed. In preparing to respond to the RFP, I find it most helpful to copy and paste these criteria from the NOFA in the *Federal Register* directly into a word processing document. I then reformat the text to appear as an outline, retaining each section heading and subheading for which point values are provided. Under each heading, the selected pieces of information are converted into a bullet list—a checklist of sorts—that can be deleted one at a time as the information is added to that section of the proposal. The technique is thus not to write the proposal from scratch, and then try to make it fit the RFP; that strategy is painfully difficult and prone to failure. Rather, the approach is to respond to the scoring factors provided, tailoring your response to include the information—and only the information—the funding agency will use to determine the score for your proposal.

You should, of course, keep the lessons from the unstructured proposal in mind as you do this. The pieces of the proposal must still come together and tell a coherent story, and each section or component of the proposal narrative and the entire proposal must reconcile with the others. I find myself frequently rereading what I have written and comparing it to the RFP to ensure internal consistency and clear relationship to the award factors delineated.

What federal (and other) RFPs often fail to do is suggest how many pages you should use to respond to each of the award factors. Is there a general rule of thumb that should be followed? No section is more important than any other on its face, but knowledge of each

Paper applications will not be accepted from applicants that have not been granted a waiver. If an applicant is granted a waiver, the Office of University Partnerships (OUP) will provide instructions for submission. All applicants submitting applications in paper format must have received a waiver to the electronic application submission requirement and the application must be received by HUD on or before the application deadline date. All paper applications must be submitted on 8½–by-11-inch paper, double-spaced, on one side of the paper, with one-inch margins (for the top, bottom, left, and right sides of the document), and printed in standard Times New Roman 12-point font.

V. Application Review Information

A. Criteria

1. *Rating Factor 1: Capacity of the Applicant and Relevant Experience (25 Points).* This factor addresses the extent to which the applicant has the resources, experience, and capacity necessary to successfully complete the proposed project by the and of the grant performance period.

a. *Knowledge and Experience for First Time Applicants (25 Points). For Previously Funded Applicants (10 Points).* For the purpose of responding to this subfactor only, Previously Funded Applicants are any applicants that received funding in FY 2001 through FY 2007. If an applicant received a grant prior to these years they should respond to this factor as a First Time Applicant. This definition is relevant to this rating factor ONLY.

In rating this subfactor, HUD will consider how well an applicant clearly addresses the following:

(1) Identifies key project team members/staff and partners, their titles and names (e.g., project manager/coordinator—Sally Susan Smith, etc.) respective roles, and time each individual will allot to this project.

If key personnel have not been hired, identity the position title, description of duties and responsibilities, and qualifications to be considered in the selection of personnel, including subcontractors and consultants;

(2) Describes the knowledge and relevant experience of the proposed project team member/staff and partners (as outlined above) that will conduct the day-to-day project activities, consultants (including technical assistance providers), and contractors in planning and managing the type of project for which funding is being requested; and

(3) Explains the institution's experience and capacity to administer and monitor the type of project for which funding is being requested.

Applicant's staff and partners' (as outlined above) experience and the institution's capacity to do the work will be evaluated in terms or recent and relevant knowledge and skills to undertake the proposed eligible program activities. HUD will consider experience within the last five (5) years to be recent and experience pertaining to similar activities to be relevant.

b. *Past Performance (15 Points) for Previously Funded Grant Applicants Only.* This subfactor will evaluate how well an applicant has performed successfully under completed and/or open HUD HSIAG grants. Applicants must demonstrate this by addressing the following information for all previously completed and open HUD/HSIAG grants:

(1) A list of all HUD/HSIAG grants received between FY 2001 through FY 2007, including the dollar amount awarded and the amount expended and obligated as of the date the application is submitted;

(2) A list detailing the date the project(s) was completed; was it completed during the original three-year grant performance period; if not completed, why (including when it was or will be completed); if the project is still in progress, provide details on the project's current status;

(3) A description of the achieved results (outcomes) consistent with the approved project management plan. If not completed as proposed, explain why;

(4) A list comparing the amount of proposed leveraged funds and/or resources (outlined in the original application) to the amount that was actually leveraged as of the date the application is submitted; and

FIGURE 5.17   Hispanic-Serving Institutions Assisting Communities FY 2008 Award Criteria (Sample Section)

Source: Federal Register 2008.

(5) A detailed description of compliance with all reporting requirements, including timeliness of submission, whether reports were complete and addressed all information (both narrative and financial) as required by the grant agreement.

HUD will also review an applicant's past performance in managing funds, including but not limited to the ability to account for funding appropriately; timely use of funds received from HUD; meeting performance targets for completion of activities; timely submission of required progress reports; compliance with the program's terms and conditions; and receipt of promised leveraged resources. In evaluating past performance, HUD reserves the right to deduct up to ten (10) points from this rating score as a result of the information obtained from HUD's records (i.e., progress and financial reports, monitoring reports, Program Outcome Logic Model submissions, and amendments).

3. *Rating Factor 3: Need/Extent of the Problem (5 Points).*

a. Rating Factor 2. addresses the extent to which there is a need for funding the proposed project and an indication of the importance of meeting the need(s) in the target area. The need(s) described must be relevant to the activities for which funds are being requested. In addressing this factor, applicants should provide, at a minimum, the following and cite statistics and/or analyses contained in at least one or more current, sound, and reliable data sources:

(1) Describe the need(s); and

(2) Describe the importance of meeting the proposed needs.

b. In rating this factor, HUD will consider only current data that is specific to the area where the proposed project activities will be carried out. Sources for localized data can be found online at: *http://www.ffiec.gov.*

c. HUD will consider data collected within the last five (5) years to be current. However, applicants must utilize the most current version of the data source(s) that exists. To the extent that the targeted community's Five Year Consolidated Plan and Analysis of Impediments to Fair Housing Choice (A1) identify the level of the problem and the urgency in meeting the need, applicants should include references to these documents in the response to this factor.

Other reliable data sources include, but are not limited to, Census reports, law enforcement agency crime reports, Public Housing Agencies' Comprehensive Plans, community needs analyses such as those provided by the United Way, the applicant's institution, and other sound, reliable, and appropriate sources. Needs in terms of fulfilling court orders or consent decrees, settlements, conciliation agreements, and voluntary compliance agreements may also be addressed. (See the *Federal Register* for more.)

FIGURE 5.17   (Continued)

section's importance to the granting agency suggests an approach. The points available for a grant application can be discerned by totaling the available points for each criterion or subcriterion in the award factors. Out of simplicity, these usually total to 100 points, but it is wise to double-check the math to be sure. Once you know the total points available, you can determine the proportion or weight that each component bears in the total score. This information can then be used to determine the approximate proportion of the available page limit that should be allocated to each factor. If the goals and objectives section is valued at 10 points out of 100 total, it is worth 10% of the total points. If the page limit is 15 pages, then it should receive about 10% of the available space, or 1.5 pages.

This approach is never exact, and you will find that the use of graphics and tables makes it easy to provide some information without using all of the space allotted. In these cases, you are able to expound in other sections until the total space is used. In such a situation, I usually make certain that I am comfortable with each section's response, and if none have obvious weaknesses, I begin using the space in whichever section has the greatest point weighting. An example of the detailed federal award criteria is provided in **Figure 5.17**; you will see a heading

"*V. Application Review Information*"; this is where the scoring criteria begin. This excerpt comes from the *Federal Register* announcement (NOFA) for the FY2008 Hispanic Serving Institutions Assisting Communities Program requirements (*Federal Register* 2008, p. 27083).

CONCLUSION

This chapter has provided an overview of the approach to preparing to develop a proposal narrative, including learning to think like a funder, writing clearly, following rules, and so on. A boilerplate framework for proposals that do not have formal guidelines or requirements is presented, along with examples and tips for completing each section. The chapter concludes with an approach to follow in responding to RFPs that do have formal guidelines and requirements. With the proposal narrative completed, it is time to complete any required forms and prepare to submit the grant. Chapter 6 presents forms and other documentation that must be completed.

REFERENCES

Bardach, Eugene. 2004. Presidential Address—The extrapolation problem: How can we learn from the experience of others? *Journal of Policy Analysis and Management* 23(2): 205–220.

Bardach, Eugene. 2005. *A Practical Guide to Policy Analysis: The Eightfold Path to More Effective Problem Solving, 2nd Edition*. Washington, DC: CQ Press.

Birkland, Thomas A. 2005. *An Introduction to the Policy Process: Theories, Concepts, and Models of Public Policy Making, 2nd Edition*. Armonk, NY: M. E. Sharpe.

Bryson, John M. 2004. *Strategic Planning for Public and Nonprofit Organizations, 3rd Edition*. San Francisco: Jossey-Bass Publishers.

Bureau of Economic Analysis. 2008. Regional Economic Accounts. Accessed January 2, 2009. Available at: http://www.bea.gov/bea/regional/reis/action.cfm.

Entman, R. M. 1993. Framing: Toward clarification of a fractured paradigm. *Journal of Communication* 43(4): 51–58.

Federal Register 73(92), Monday, May 12, 2008.

Gormley, William T., Jr. and Steven J. Balla. 2008. *Bureaucracy and Democracy: Accountability and Performance, 2nd Edition*. Washington, DC: CQ Press.

Hall, Jeremy L. 2008. Feasibility study: Establishing a community-based arts center in Jasper, Alabama. Unpublished report.

Hall, Jeremy L. and Donna M. Handley. 2007. Economics of the Arts for Western Blount County. Unpublished report.

Howell-Moroney, Michael and Jeremy L. Hall. 2008. Waste in the sewer: The collapse of accountability and transparency in public finance in Jefferson County, Alabama. Unpublished manuscript.

Posavac, Emil J. and Raymond G. Carey. 2003. *Program Evaluation: Methods and Case Studies, 6th Edition*. Upper Saddle River, NJ: Prentice Hall.

Pralle, Sarah. 2006. The "mouse that roared:" Agenda setting in Canadian pesticides politics. *Policy Studies Journal* 34(2): 171–194.

Weaver, David H. 2007. Thoughts on agenda setting, framing, and priming. *Journal of Communication* 57(1): 142–147.

Weiss, Carol H. 1998. *Evaluation: Methods for Studying Programs and Policies, 2nd Edition*. Upper Saddle River, NJ: Prentice Hall.

Wordsmith Associates. 2008. Writing Tips. Accessed May 14, 2008. Available at: http://www.wordsmithassociates.com/writing_tips.htm.

APPENDIX: SAMPLE PROGRAM NARRATIVE

Source: Courtesy of Morehead State University.

III. Soundness of Approach

III-A-1. Workplan—Coordination of Activities

Our program partners include the _____ County Habitat for Humanity, _____ State University, _____ County Government, _____ Housing Authority, _____ County Schools, _____ County Adult Education Center, and others. These institutions will serve on an advisory committee, assist with participant recruitment and program marketing, assist with on-site instruction, and integrate existing GED programs to better serve participants in this YouthBuild program.

We will utilize a vast array of university and community resources. [Partner] can provide special needs counseling and mental health services through its Psychology Department and Social Work Department programs. [Partner] can also provide volunteer enrichment activities and mentoring activities to the YouthBuild participants to help them develop a broader understanding of the importance of education and job skills for a hopeful, fulfilling, and productive adult life. [Applicant] will connect participants with mentors in their field of interest to encourage, support, and advise and to provide career networking resources leading to permanent employment. Participants will be referred to social services in the areas of Food Stamps, health care, child care, and transportation to meet special needs. United Way provides healthcare and child care referrals and resources. Coordinating community efforts and resources, YouthBuild participants' special needs, concerns, and obstacles will be addressed in a manner that enables them to complete the program successfully.

III-A-2. Workplan—Self-Sufficiency

Program participants' accrued benefits from this program will be multifaceted. Participants will receive high school credentials, college credit courses in light construction (framing, electrical/plumbing, etc.), and on-the-job experience building new residential units in the community. These aspects provide participants with the ability to apply for and receive jobs in the community, while also giving them the background knowledge to leverage market or above-market wages for their labor. Income from the program in the form of payment for on-the-job training will provide participants with disposable income that will increase their housing choice, as well as housing choice for low-income residents of the community who will have a wider selection of housing from which to choose as a result of the construction component. Leadership training and policy awareness will acquaint participants with their rights, responsibilities, and choices to play a meaningful role in community life.

III-A-3. Workplan—Sustainability

This initial YouthBuild grant leverages tremendous support from various institutions and agencies in the community. This award will allow that support to be institutionalized and the partnerships solidified to allow the program to function on a continuing basis with reduced external support in the future.

III-B. Program Components

The YouthBuild program will embrace a series of components designed to fulfill four goals: (1) improved educational attainment and literacy for the at-risk population, (2) development of job skills and provision of hands-on work experience in the construction field for the aforementioned population, (3) provision of education and career counseling for program participants, and (4) new construction of much-needed low-income housing in the target community. Through the attainment of these primary goals, this project will also strengthen ties between existing community organizations and increase community volunteerism.

Outreach, Recruitment, and Selection will make up the initial project phase. [Applicant] will engage a broad range of partners in the community to recruit each cohort of participants. [Applicant] has worked with community leaders in _____ County to form an advisory board that will serve as the venue for local management, decision making, and oversight. [Applicant] will work closely with the advisory board to utilize its institutional capacity to recruit participants. [Applicant] faculty, the project coordinator, and program staff will conduct informational sessions at local venues for public information meetings and recruitment presentations. [Applicant] will create brochures and flyers to be distributed and displayed at the public school systems, _____ Department of Employment Services offices, city and county government facilities, chamber of commerce member businesses, the Employment Security Commission, Social Service waiting rooms, the waiting areas of local businesses, the public library, local churches and religious schools, Ministry Family Services offices, the YMCA, Boys and Girls Clubs, neighborhood stores, laundry mats, and homeless shelters. Case workers will promote the program at agencies such as social services and the housing authority to encourage potential participants to apply. Finally, [Applicant] will use school dropout lists from _____ County Schools and [Applicant]'s GED program to make personal contacts with eligible youth to inform them of the program and recruit those interested.

Special outreach efforts will target eligible young women and young women with dependent children. We will target Appalachia Work First and School to Work welfare recipients who fall into the 18- to 24-year-old age group and who are either members of welfare families or are recipients themselves with dependent children. For potential participants with dependents, we will provide referrals to child care assistance agencies such as social services, church day care services, local Family Resource Centers, and Head Start. The Department of Social Services has a transportation department for participants who need help getting to and from program activities. Family Services and [Applicant] can provide special assistance for non-English-speaking participants. The [Partner] Psychology Department and Social Work Department can provide special counseling help for participants with mental health needs. Pooling resources and using public partners as both program promoters and support service providers is an important recruiting component. Furthermore, demonstrating to potential participants that they will receive necessary support from public agencies to overcome obstacles will instill a sense of security and confidence, which is a fundamental recruiting tool.

With rigorous recruiting efforts, we will institute a selection system with well-defined criteria. Our selection system includes an application and screening process. Recruits will complete an application specifying their name, address, phone number (if applicable), age (must be 18 to 24 years old), family status, income (they must fall into the very low-income bracket), number of dependents (if any), level of educational attainment (must be drop-out), special needs (child care, transportation, housing, physical or mental health, etc.), and reasons they are interested in participating in the program.

The project coordinator will schedule interviews with eligible applicants to assess interest and commitment. [Applicant] will develop an informal contract outlining YouthBuild program requirements and goals that each applicant aspires to reach during and after the program. Selections will be made based on participant eligibility, interest, and personal commitment. Twenty applicants will be selected for the initial annual program cycle, though attrition is expected to reduce this number to 15 graduates. [Applicant] will create a ranked applicant backup list from which to readily select when attrition creates any early participant drops.

Educational and Job Training, Leadership Development, Support Services. Educational components of this YouthBuild project will be performed by the two higher education partners: [Applicant] and [Partner]. Cooperatively, these higher education partners provide a wide range of educational programming including (1) educational attainment with the provision of a GED certificate program; (2) job training through [Applicant]'s light construction curriculum, which includes training in the areas of work-site preparation, framing, electrical installation/repair, tools and machinery operations, carpentry, and work safety; (3) educational and job training support through adult literacy assessment and support, English as a Second Language (ESL), educational tutoring, as well as educational and career planning and counseling; (4) career development through life skills and leadership training; and upon completion of the YouthBuild program; (5) employment placement through [Applicant] and [Partner]; (6) specialized content academic course exposure through public policy, advocacy, and entrepreneurship programs as part of the Leadership Course; and (7) research support for utilization of advanced instructional and assessment methods, evaluation design, and data analysis through [Applicant].

Based upon examination assessment using the Test of Adult Basic Education (TABE), students will be placed in an adult literacy and GED completion program at [Applicant]. These basic skills courses at [Applicant] emphasize helping all individuals gain the competencies and skills they need to function effectively in society. It is assumed that participants in our program will have a baseline literacy level of at least seventh grade.

A Human Resources Development (HRD) course will be offered through [Applicant] to develop basic workplace skills that are key to employment readiness, including job readiness, interpersonal skills, group skills, motivation and goal setting, listening and oral communication skills, problem-solving skills, and assessment of career and employment goals. Residential Framing certificate courses will be offered as part of a Light Construction curriculum by [Applicant]. That overall curriculum includes work-site preparation, framing, electrical installation/repair, tools and machinery operations, carpentry, and work safety. The YouthBuild participants will be enrolled in the Residential Framing certificate program that includes Carpentry I, Carpentry II, Construction Safety, and Blueprint Reading/General Construction. The instructors will interview participants and conduct assessment and site assistance related to positive performance in the courses and completion of the certificate. [Partner] will also provide a Leadership, Citizenship, and Entrepreneurship Training curriculum.

[Applicant] will provide instructors for all GED, Adult Literacy, Leadership Training, HRD Training, and Residential Framing courses. [Applicant] will test and assess each applicant, and then develop a course of study applicable to each student's current skill level. [Applicant] will also provide academic tutoring and counseling support and English as a

Second Language instruction. [Applicant] will provide General Education Development (GED) courses through the Continuing Education division. For those students who wish to further skill development beyond the YouthBuild program, [Applicant] offers courses in carpentry, plumbing, welding, and wiring. [Partner] will provide instruction for the public policy, advocacy, entrepreneurial components of the Leadership Course, and academic counseling components. [Applicant] and [Partner] instructors will be utilized as academic counselors in the subject areas of interest to program participants.

Program participants will spend 50% of their time in on-site training and work activities, and 50% of their time in education, training, and other support activities. The scheduling plan is as follows for each of the program components: the academic components including the HRD course, the Adult Basic Skills (GED), and Residential Framing will be in two semesters over the course of the year. The Adult Basic Skills would be conducted throughout the yearlong program and is offered with great flexibility by [Applicant] to achieve maximum accommodation. Participants would, on average, spend 4 hours a day in on-site training and construction work, and 4 hours in academic education and training components and support services. The participants will be enrolled in the program 12 total months. Participants' time will be equally distributed between on-site construction work, and Education, Leadership, Counseling, and Support Services.

Education stipends will be paid to participants who maintain attendance and academic progress in the amount of $500 per participant ($15,000 TL). The stipend amount is in accord with rates of stipend to support students averaged between institutions and programs. The cost of tuition, fees, materials, and expenses related to the education, training, and work are covered by the program, allowing stipends to assist with living or non-program related costs.

[Applicant] and [Partner] will cooperatively develop a leadership training program to serve program participants. This program will integrate the most advanced research in the field of leadership training with the special needs of the demographic target population in our program. The participants will be involved in mentoring programs throughout the project, and these mentoring activities will be integrated into the curricular design. Additionally, the leadership program will complement the volunteerism objectives of the community partners and structured activities with the [Partner] Social Work Department and the other support services. The developed course will be offered during the second semester of the academic program, although a holistic approach to leadership development will undergird all program activities.

[Partner] will develop a seminar series to focus on public policy issues salient to the state, the Appalachian region, and _____ County. Participants will be given some basic academic tools for understanding the policy process and the American intergovernmental system of policy delivery. These tools will enable participants to address more effectively and understand more comprehensively the policy issues facing their state and community. Advocacy workshops will be held during the course of the project to provide participants with the knowledge to effectively affect government and improve their capabilities for representation of interests in the policy system. As a result of this advocacy workshop series, participants will understand how to contact their elected officials, how to address local issues of concern at local government meetings, and how to affect the agenda-setting process in public policy making. A business entrepreneurial seminar will help participants understand our economic system and the processes of developing and engaging business opportunities.

For youth with emotional and behavioral issues, the [Department] at [Partner] will provide counseling and support services through the [Partner] Psychology Department and Social Work Department. The [Partner] Psychology Department engages a network of public-academic and community partnerships focused on developing a community-based, family-centered, culturally competent, strength-based, collaborative system of care for children who have emotional and behavioral issues and their families. Faculty and students from Psychology and Social Work serve as coordinators of a comprehensive system of care and will regularly meet with the youth's support team.

The Educational Opportunity Center at [Applicant] as well as Counseling Centers at [Applicant] and [Partner] provide academic, career, and personal counseling services for current and prospective students and would provide these services to our participants. The staff consists of professionally trained, master's-degree-level counselors who have extensive experience in the field of student development. They are committed to helping people achieve their potential through education and personal growth. Students needing therapeutic personal counseling may be referred to outside agencies for additional help. In addition to individual counseling, workshops, educational planning services, and academic advising will be utilized.

Appalachian YouthBuild program participants will undertake valuable housing construction work during the on-site training component. As part of the strategic planning and redevelopment efforts in the targeted community, houses will be constructed to increase the affordable housing stock to meet the needs of the community's low- and moderate-income residents and families. Four worksites will allow youth to receive on-site training and build affordable housing in the community. In _____ County, the Habitat for Humanity is constructing four new housing units for homeownership at their [Address] property. The housing partner will ensure at least a five to one participant to supervisor ratio. Participants will engage in on-site training and construction work that applies and expands those skills learned as part of their academic course instruction. The Residential Framing certificate program will provide participants with carpentry skills, blueprint reading, and general construction skills to provide them a strong foundation as entry-level workers at these sites. Course instruction in construction safety, and the HRD training, will assist in developing safe and productive workers at the on-site training and construction locations.

Youth will be involved with hands-on work experience including the application of their carpentry skills and a tailored plan related to their interests and demonstrable skill levels. The on-site training and construction work will be tailored to individual interest and capacity as much as possible, such that the maximum employable skills are developed. The overall capabilities available through the [Applicant] construction curriculum provide for training in work-site preparation, framing, electrical installation and repair, tools and machinery operations, carpentry, and work safety, and [Applicant] works with businesses to tailor specific skills training. The overall partnership between the contractors and developers, the not-for-profit sector, and the higher education partners, ensures that participants will achieve the maximum skills development in this program.

YouthBuild participants will receive both quality construction training and exemplary supervision by professionals to accomplish the on-site work component. On-site supervisors are professionals from the contracting community with numerous years of experience and expertise in the field. For each project site, the on-site supervisor/trainer to participant ratio will be at least one to five. By incorporating a low ratio, trainees will receive one-on-one training, supervision, and support. One cohort of 20 initial participants will be admitted, with 15 expected to complete the program during the first year.

YouthBuild participants will receive wages set at $5.50 per hour during their on-site training and work experience. This is a fair amount because it is above minimum wage but below the market wage for construction workers. In addition to the hourly on-site construction work wage, participants will receive a stipend when participating in the required educational activities. We expect the offering of a stable income, along with valuable educational and training opportunities, to be an adequate work-related incentive package.

III-C. Strategy for Job Placement

The Project Coordinator will utilize the strong working relationships with the Educational Opportunity Center at [Applicant] and [Partner]'s Career Center to provide career counseling and mentoring services. Their staff will provide resume-writing skills, job seeking skills, and human resource development to assist our YouthBuild participants with career planning and development while in our program, with employment placement upon completion, and with ongoing assistance into the future beyond the period of the program. Each participant will write their own resume, and program graduates will attend a career day with prospective employers. [Applicant] and [Partner] will provide academic counseling including career development planning related to continued training and postsecondary education. Through these positive and flexible exposures to learning, participants will also be encouraged to explore further educational options that complement their personal and career goals.

Participants will meet representatives from area colleges and universities when the group visits [Applicant] for a College Day Orientation organized in cooperation with the [Applicant] Admissions Office. [Partner] hosts a yearly Spring Career Day that helps visitors learn the different educational requirements to be successful in a particular field. After visiting College Day at [Applicant] and Career Day at [Partner], participants will take part in a career and education goal-setting exercise. From this exercise, the YouthBuild project coordinator will work with participants one on one to ensure that each person gets the direction needed to continue his/her work toward educational and career goals. YouthBuild graduates who indicate they want to continue their education at the 2-year or 4-year level will have the opportunity to learn about financial aid, scholarships, and grants for education. The YouthBuild project coordinator will coordinate a financing education workshop to introduce participants to a variety of funding sources.

YouthBuild participants will receive entrepreneurial education during the 12-month program. Entrepreneurs in the construction field and construction support fields such as masonry, sheet rocking, painting, and maintenance will be invited to classes to talk with participants about personal experiences and success. Individuals that set goals of owning their own business will have the opportunity to visit the Southern _____ Small Business Development Center to talk with an entrepreneurial counselor. [Partner] will conduct a business entrepreneurial seminar as a part of the Leadership Course.

III-D. Expected Outcomes

There will be several areas of measured objectives, including recruitment, attendance, retention, education attainment, job placement, college placement, leadership, volunteerism, and new home units constructed. Our proposed program's resultant outcomes include (Recruitment) developing an outreach system that results in a factor of five times the needed applicant pool and three times the qualification threshold; (Attendance) the attendance percentage across all activities will average at least 90%; (Retention) 75% of participants will remain in the program for the full year; (GED achievement) 87% of participants will obtain their GEDs and 100% will successfully complete at least three examination stages as part of their GED program; (Job Placement) 100% of participants will be employed in good wage jobs within 1 year of completion of the program or will be enrolled in higher education; (Housing Units) 100% of the four housing units in the program will be completed; (College Placement) 40% of participants will continue postsecondary education within 2 years of program completion; (Leadership) 50% of participants will engage in public advocacy or demonstrable community leadership activities within 1 year of program completion; (Volunteerism) 50% of participants will continue community volunteerism at least 1 year beyond program completion.

CHAPTER 6

Miscellaneous Forms and Documentation

Following the pattern set out by the preceding chapters, you (or your grant writing team) should have a list of viable funding opportunities, and you should have been able to select at least one request for proposals or foundation program to which you intend to apply. You should have considered the composition of the grants team, both internally and externally, individually and organizationally, and should have developed a program idea. From Chapters 4 and 5, you should now have developed that solid program idea into a convincing program narrative and supporting budget that demonstrate need, convey the idea and proposed implementation plan, and show how the organization or team has the necessary capacity to fulfill the proposed endeavor. With all of these components in place, there is one final component to consider prior to submitting your grant application—and a grant writer must attend to these miscellaneous details because they may have the ability to make or break a grant proposal. Applications require more than the narrative and a budget; all federal grant applications require submission of a series of standard forms, and many federal and state agencies also require their own specialized forms. Foundations are less apt to require an application form, but many do. It goes without saying that it would be a terrible shame for an excellent application to go unfunded because a required form was not submitted or was completed incorrectly. The attention to detail required throughout the application process is of particular importance when it comes to forms.

Many would-be grant writers offer only a passing glance when examining application forms that require detailed, specific information. In fact, many writers opt to leave the forms as the last step in grant writing because they seem so self-explanatory and simple. They just have to be filled out, right? Unfortunately, completing forms can be more complicated. For this reason, I suggest reviewing forms more thoroughly and gathering all of the requisite data well in advance of the submission date. Some data will not be available until the program narrative and budget are finalized, so completing the forms must wait until the time of submission, hence this chapter's placement in the book following budget and narrative components. However, finding the information the forms require may pose a challenge and should be an early priority. So, what kind of information do these forms ask for? What is their purpose?

Forms gather pertinent information about the applicant and its location, the project and its location, the amount of funding requested, the amount of match to be provided, the program applied to, and importantly, the signature of an organization official who is authorized to enter into agreements with funding sources. The standard, or government-wide, forms are used to collect standard information for reporting and to ensure that sufficient information is available to determine the applicant's—and the project's—eligibility. They also force applicants to structure their budget information to fit a consistent and uniform format that enables ready comparison of projects, evaluation of cash flow needs, and other concerns the granting agency might have. Finally, in the case of federal grants, forms provide assurances that the applicant has not engaged in any activities that would legally disqualify them (disbarment), that any lobbying efforts on behalf of the project are disclosed, and that the applicant agrees to the commitments made in the proposal, should it be funded.

In past years, it was useful to begin a chapter such as this with a discussion of distinct grant application forms and where to find them. Today, that discussion is less relevant. When submitting grant applications through Grants.gov, the act of selecting a funding opportunity to which you wish to apply causes the system to propagate the forms necessary for application to that program automatically. Also relegated to history are the days of maintaining a working typewriter and an ample supply of correction fluid in the office to complete, and correct, photocopies of standard forms. Technology has finally caught up, and the Grants.gov system not only allows, but requires completion of the forms electronically. It is also more user-friendly with the addition of pull-down menus and with automatic completion of program name and number information. In short, Grants.gov saves many hassles and it eliminates the possibility of mistakes that are common on forms filled out by users who may not understand that certain sections of the form call for precategorized information.

But on the off chance you identify a program that permits submission through some other means, Grants.gov also provides the repository of all active and archived federal forms. The forms repository is located at http://www.grants.gov/agencies/aforms _repository_information.jsp, and the listing of active form categories is available at https:// apply.grants.gov/FormsMenu?source=agency.

The following sections of this chapter examine forms and their required content, organized by grant type, beginning with government-wide federal forms, continuing with a brief discussion of specialized federal agency forms, and then concluding with a discussion of foundation and other grant application forms.

GOVERNMENT-WIDE FEDERAL GRANT APPLICATION FORMS

Federal grant applications require a set of common forms that add consistency to the process and that create familiarity for those individuals who work with federal grants, whether agency employees or applicants. The core set of federal grant forms that are common to all federal grant applications is referred to as standard, or government-wide, forms. They are readily identifiable by their labeling system, which begins with the letters *SF*, which stand for standard form. This group of mandatory forms includes the following:

SF-424	Application for Federal Assistance
SF-424A	Budget Information for Non-Construction Programs
SF-424B	Assurances for Non-Construction Programs
SF-424C	Budget Information for Construction Programs
SF-424D	Assurances for Construction Programs

As you may have gathered, SF-424 is the universal form, which traditionally serves as a cover sheet for federal grant proposals. The remaining four forms comprise two separate categories—construction and non-construction—with SF-424A and SF-424B being mandatory for non-construction programs whereas SF-424C and SF-424D are mandatory for construction programs. These forms, as well as the instructions for completing SF-424, appear in the appendix to this chapter for your reference. Although you probably won't ever have to seek these forms out individually, it is valuable to know in advance what information they expect you to provide and in what format. To facilitate that process, I review each of these government-wide forms in turn.

As mentioned earlier, federal grant applications share a common cover form (SF-424) that communicates essential information to the agency, including the applicant's eligibility, the amount requested, and the general purpose of the project. To save frustration, it is best to be prepared with the correct information the form calls for prior to attempting to complete it and submit it through the Grants.gov portal. What information does SF-424 call for? I consider each section of the form in sequential order, and you should refer to the instructions provided in the chapter appendix for additional clarification.

1. *Type of Submission.* This section of the form contains three options: Preapplication, Application, and Changed/Corrected Application. Most submissions will fall into the Application category because only select discretionary grant programs require submission through a formal preapplication process. The Preapplication category is selected in those instances when this is the case. Preapplications are used as a screening mechanism by some programs, so two application phases are required to obtain grant funding. A preapplication may be optional as simply a tool for the agency to estimate its workload, but in most cases a preapplication is a requirement with a separate and earlier deadline than the actual application deadline. The final category, Changed/Corrected Application, should be self-explanatory. As the SF-424 instructions note, this category may be used prior to the closing date for an application if you need to make changes or correct errors, but may be used after the application closing date only when the agency requests a correction be made.

2. *Type of Application.* Applications take three forms, including New Applications, Continuations, and Revisions to existing awards. The term *New Application* may be misleading, particularly if you heed my advice in Chapter 3 to rework material from unsuccessful applications and resubmit it to recurring program competitions in subsequent years. Generally speaking, any first-time application for funding is a new application. If I submitted an application in 2007 that was not funded, and then rewrote the proposal and resubmitted it in 2008, it is still a new application. If my organization is administering an award through a particular federal program for a local project and I submit an application for a second project in another local neighborhood, it is still considered a new application.

As the name implies, Continuations are extensions of the project through an additional budget period—usually a year—beyond the projected completion date for your project. These extensions have no effect on the project budget or the federal commitment except to extend the period over which funds are drawn. Revisions are changes that affect the federal government's obligation or contingent liability (contingent liability may be affected by changing the project duration). There are five categories that may be selected individually or in combination: A. Increase Award, B. Decrease Award, C. Increase Duration, D. Decrease Duration, and E. Other. Naturally, neither the duration nor the amount can simultaneously be increased and decreased, so the combination of letters must be logical. If the reason for the Revision is E. *Other*, then the reason must be specified in the space provided. It should be apparent from this description that all new applications fall under the new category; the Continuation and Revision distinctions are tools of grant management more than grant application, although the revisions must be submitted through the same formal process in some cases.

3. *Date Received.* This field on the SF-424 should be left blank because it is to be completed by the federal agency.

4. *Applicant Identifier.* If the federal agency has assigned the applicant a specific identifier, it should be entered in this space. Otherwise, it should be left blank.

5a. *Federal Entity Identifier.* This space is reserved for the federal entity identifier number assigned to the organization by the relevant federal agency. If no such number has been assigned, it should be left blank.

5b. *Federal Award Identifier.* Upon being awarded a grant, the award will be assigned a unique federal award identifier number specific to that grant. So, for new applications—those that were listed as "New" in field 2—this space should be left blank. For continuations and revisions, the unique award identifier should be included.

6. *Date Received by State.* If the application is reviewed by the state, the appropriate state agency will complete this field for its purposes. It should be left blank on your application form.

7. *State Application Identifier.* If the state reviews proposals (this occurs with programs covered by E.O. 12372), the application will be assigned a unique state identifier number as well. You should also leave this field blank in submitting your application.

8. *Applicant Information.* A series of fields is required to disclose the applicant's complete contact information:

a. Legal Name refers to the official legal name of the organization as it appears on its incorporation paperwork or as it is listed in the Central Contractor Registry.

b. Employer/Taxpayer Identification Number (EIN/TIN) is the applicant's unique nine-digit identification number provided by the Internal Revenue Service. It should be entered in the standard organizational format xx-xxxxxxx; for international applicants, the number 44-4444444 should be used.

c. Organizational DUNS is yet another unique identifier assigned to your organization by Dun and Bradstreet; DUNS stands for the Data Universal Numbering System. For those readers who may have been reading this explanation of standard federal grant forms, wondering what is so difficult about obtaining this standard information, the DUNS number may be the first time-consuming barrier. The reality is that few people who do not write grants on a regular basis would have any reason to be familiar with their organization's EIN, DUNS, or federal identifier. If a DUNS number has not previously been assigned to your organization, one may be obtained by contacting Dun and Bradstreet at the following link: https://eupdate.dnb.com/requestoptions.asp?cm_re=HomepageB*Resources*DUNSNumberLink.

d. Address is a self-explanatory field, though you should exercise caution to ensure that the information you provide is complete. Also, you should note that the address field requires not only the standard postal delivery information, but other information including the organization's county and country.

e. Organizational Unit refers to a specific division, department, and unit of your organization that will be responsible for carrying out the grant activities. The specific data will depend on the internal structure of your organization. Some examples include the Department of Planning and Policy, the Department of Streets and Transportation, the Major Crime Task Force, or other similar distinctions that represent the division that is responsible for the grant application and proposed activities. This will assist federal program officers in appropriately directing questions about your application to the most knowledgeable individuals.

f. The Name and Contact Information of Person to Be Contacted on Matters Involving This Application field requires the applicant to designate one person who should be consulted if questions arise or if the agency needs to communicate with a responsible person either about the application itself or during the term of the grant agreement. This person is usually a project director or his or her direct supervisor. Some medium- and large-sized organizations may have internal policies that require the same liaison contact to be listed on every grant application, regardless of who wrote the grant or who will implement the project. Centralizing federal affairs operations has the advantage of ensuring a consistent organizational response, and prevents decentralized contacts throughout the organization from accidentally allowing federal requests to fall through the cracks. For small organizations, this point is often moot because the same person is required to play all three roles.

9. *Type of Applicant.* This field allows the applicant to identify up to three organization types that best characterize the applicant organization. The form instructions clearly indicate that the applicant should make these selections in accordance with agency requirements—a hint that some agencies may ask for fewer than three applicant types. The possible types from which to choose are listed in **Figure 6.1**. It is rare that an organization would not fit into at least one of the named categories, but if that is the case, it should be designated by the letter *X* and described.

10. *Name of Federal Agency.* Enter the proper name of the federal agency to which the application for grant funding is being made. Do not use abbreviations. When using the electronic version of the forms made available through Grants.gov, this field self-populates with the appropriate agency name.

11. *Catalog of Federal Domestic Assistance Number and Title.* As with the federal agency name, these two fields also self-populate when using Grants.gov. For alternative submissions, the 5-digit grant program number and the official title listed in the CFDA (www.cfda.gov) for the program should be listed.

12. *Funding Opportunity Number/Title.* This is the official funding number and program title associated with the Grants.gov funding opportunity announcement. Although the number is unique, the opportunity title will be very similar or identical to the CFDA program title. As was the case in previous fields, this field also self-populates when the form is completed using Grants.gov.

13. *Competition Identification Number/Title.* Yet another means of distinguishing the program and competition to which your submission applies is the competition number and title. If a number and title apply, as indicated in the funding opportunity announcement, they should be entered here. These fields also self-populate in a Grants.gov submission.

A. State Government

B. County Government

C. City or Township Government

D. Special District Government

E. Regional Organization

F. U.S. Territory or Possession

G. Independent School District

H. Public/State Controlled Institution of Higher Education

I. Indian/Native American Tribal Government (Federally Recognized)

J. Indian/Native American Tribal Government (Other than Federally Recognized)

K. Indian/Native American Tribally Designated Organization

L. Public/Indian Housing Authority

M. Nonprofit with 501(c)3 IRS Status (Other than Institution of Higher Education)

N. Nonprofit without 501(c)3 Status (Other than Institution of Higher Education)

O. Private Institution of Higher Education

P. Individual

Q. For-Profit Organization (Other than Small Business)

R. Small Business

S. Hispanic-Serving Institution

T. Historically Black Colleges and Universities (HBCUs)

U. Tribally Controlled Colleges and Universities (TCCUs)

V. Alaska Native and Native Hawaiian Serving Institutions

W. Non-Domestic (non-U.S.) Entity

X. Other (specify)

FIGURE 6.1   Standard Applicant Type Categories Used on SF-424
Source: SF-424.

14. *Areas Affected by the Project.* This field is open-ended, meaning that all affected areas should be listed in the provided space or on the continuation page. It is important to include geographic areas at an appropriate level of aggregation. So, if a program serves a few cities or counties within a state, or specific cities and counties across states, the city or county names and state names should be included (for example, Casey County, Kentucky; Russell County, Kentucky; Limestone County, Alabama; Hayden, Alabama; Guntersville, Alabama). Alternatively, if a program serves an entire state, or benefits a population broadly scattered across a state or portions thereof, the state name should be listed

(Alabama, Kentucky, California, Texas). Care should be taken to ensure that all affected areas are included.

15. *Descriptive Title of Applicant's Project.* This field is intended to serve as a concise abstract of the project, describing what it does. For this reason, the field is large enough to accommodate approximately one sentence. At the organizational level, programs funded by grants often assume the name of the federal program for local organizational purposes. Rather than "YouthBuild" or "Community Development Work Study Program," which are names of federal programs that might be used internally by the applicant organization, this field should communicate something about the project to federal agency representatives. For example, a descriptive title might read: "Rowan County Youth Development Training Project: A Program to Stimulate Interest in Applied Construction Trades among Low-/Moderate-Income or Minority High School Dropouts in Rural Rowan County, KY, through Commercial Apprenticeships and GED Training." This hypothetical title explains the goal of the grant program, explains its target area and its target population, and provides some clues about the mechanisms that will be used to realize the stated objectives. This is not a title that would be used commonly among project members, but it is important to provide as much description as possible for agency purposes on SF-424. It can take a while to craft a well-written descriptive title that explains the project approach in the space allotted on the federal form.

16. *Congressional District.* (a) In this field, enter the state and U.S. congressional district number in which the applicant is located. If the organization has multiple offices in more than one district, use the one where the entity is legally incorporated, that is, the organization's headquarters. The appropriate format is the two-letter state abbreviation followed by a hyphen and a 3-digit code corresponding to the district number. So, Tennessee's 3rd congressional district would be listed as TN-003, Texas's 11th district would be listed as TX-011, and so on. (b) This second congressional district field applies not to the applicant, but to the location(s) of the project to be carried out. If the project covers portions of a state or states, the affected congressional districts should be listed. If the project covers an entire state or states, then it is not necessary to list all of the district numbers; rather, the affected areas can be abbreviated as XX-all. So "WA-all; CA-012; OR-003" in this field means that the project covers or affects all U.S. congressional districts in the state of Washington as well as Oregon's 3rd and California's 12th congressional districts. If the proposed project falls outside the United States, the code 00-000 should be entered. If you do not know your congressional district or the area in which your project is located, you can determine it by consulting the state maps available from the following website: http://www.nationalatlas.gov/printable/congress.html. Keep in mind that congressional districts shift as a result of reapportionment every 10 years following the decennial census. Ensure that you are consulting a directory for the appropriate year.

17. *Proposed Project Start and End Dates.* Although the project dates specified in the program narrative may be discussed or described in terms of project months (I prefer to use calendar months because most programs are affected by seasonal cycles or organizational calendars in some important way), the dates provided on the SF-424 must be calendar dates. Most federal funding is made available through competitions the year preceding the beginning of a new federal fiscal year. That is, budgets and appropriations inform agencies

that they will have program funding available upon the start of the new fiscal year. The federal fiscal calendar runs from October 1 through September 30. Most grants that seek to correspond to the fiscal year and begin as soon as possible will assume a start date of October 1. So, a 36-month project might have a start date of 10/01/2009 and an end date of 09/30/2012. It is, above all, important to ensure that the dates you select correspond with the program narrative and the implementation plan described therein.

18. *Estimated Funding.* The common version of the SF-424 requires the applicant to provide estimates of the total funding to be contributed by the federal agency and by the applicant (own-source match) and by other sources (in-kind or cash match). The categories are Federal, Applicant, State, Local, Other, Program Income, and Total, which is the sum of the previous categories. This paints a ready picture of the total program costs, the federal share, and the match commitment from the applicant and other sources. Some older versions of SF-424 eliminate the categories and list only federal share and the combined total match funds from all sources. Care should be taken to ensure that the total project costs and the funding contributions in each category correspond to the program budget developed and included in other forms.

19. *Is Application Subject to Review by State Under Executive Order 12372 Process?* The program description, the CFDA, and *Federal Register* announcements will indicate whether or not a given program is covered by the intergovernmental review executive order. If review is required, then the box corresponding to the response "a. This application was made available to the state under the Executive Order 12372 process for review on _____" should be checked and the date the application was provided to the State Single Point of Contact (SPOC) should be indicated in the appropriate field. The discretion left to the states by E.O. 12372 means that they may choose to review some federal programs covered by the order and not others. If the program is covered by the Executive Order, but is not eligible for review by the state SPOC, field b should be selected. If the program description indicates that the program is not covered by E.O. 12372, then field c should be selected.

20. *Is the Applicant Delinquent on Any Federal Debt?* Most applicants will select the "no" response to this question. Any organization that is delinquent on federal debt will have a situation unique to their setting; consequently, they should check the "yes" box and provide an adequate explanation of the delinquency in the provided field that continues at the end of the SF-424 form.

21. *Certifications and Assurances.* The "I Agree" box must be checked to indicate the authorized representative's agreement with the provisions included in, or referenced by, the assurance clause. The authorized representative's name, title, and contact information must then be provided. In this electronic age, signatures are handled electronically upon submission, and the submission date is propagated by the system upon submitting the form. The authorized representative, it should be pointed out, is not the grant writer or other manager. It is the person who has legal authority to enter into binding contractual agreements on behalf of the applicant organization. For most organizations this is the executive director or president. In very large public bureaucracies, a designated official other than the highest administrator may be charged with authorizing grant agreements.

All of these components, if taken individually, seem relatively mundane and tame, but the time associated with collectively assembling all of this data and incorporating it into the form can be extensive and should not be postponed until the last possible moment before submitting the federal grant application. Following SF-424, budget forms and assurances must be completed for projects, with SF-424A and B being required for non-construction projects and SF-424C and D being required for construction projects. I turn next to SF-424B and D—the assurances—because they are simplest, and I end the discussion of government-wide forms with SF-424A and C, the budget forms.

SF-424B and D are simple—they require the organization name and the title of the certifying official to be entered in the appropriate fields; the signature and date are propagated upon submission through Grants.gov. The assurance statements represent 18 conditions of award to which the applicant agrees upon submitting an application for non-construction programs, and 19 conditions for construction programs. These conditions range from following Presidential Executive Orders to complying with the Flood Disaster Protection Act and nondiscrimination laws. This form directly states the conditions that were discussed in abstract terms in Chapters 1 and 2. Moreover, the applicant certifies that it has the necessary capacity to carry out the activities and will do so within the stated time frame.

The conditions of award are significant and should be weighed before generating a federal grant application. Some organizations have been unwilling to follow federal grant conditions. For example, in the past some states have declined federal transportation funds to avoid adopting seat belt laws and raising the legal drinking age. The specific conditions differ between non-construction and construction programs, with the latter including provisions that are more specific to projects of a construction nature such as compliance with the Davis–Bacon Act (which regulates labor standards), for example. The discussion of government-wide forms concludes with a discussion of SF-424A and SF-424C, the budget summary forms for non-construction and construction projects, respectively.

Budget forms disclose not only the cash needs for the project by federal agency and program, but also by expenditure object category and by timing. SF-424A is the appropriate budget form to use for non-construction grant projects, and it will probably be the form with which most grant writers will become most familiar. The form includes information about project costs by quarter in the first year, and annually for subsequent project years. This cash flow information aids the federal agency in evaluating effective planning and in preparing for necessary cash flow demands it will face during the fiscal year. A budget form that is given proper attention will match all budget information provided in the proposal, but more important, it will match the implementation plan for the grant by demonstrating how cash flow will be logically phased to correspond to key project activities. Budget information from this form must also correspond to the total budget and match information provided in item 18 of SF-424.

Completing form SF-424A for the first time can be confusing and frustrating, but the form is very logical, and once you have learned how the sections fit together, it is quite straightforward. I discuss the components of the form by section because that is the way it is organized. Section A is the Budget Summary Section, which consists of five rows and seven columns. For most grant applications, only two rows will be utilized—row 1 and row 5. Four separate rows are provided in this section for complex projects with components that are simultaneously proposed to be funded by different federal grant programs, and the fifth row is a summation of estimated funds across all of the programs (rows 1–4) summed by column. The seven columns include: (a) the grant program function or activity, (b) the CFDA number of the federal program, estimated unobligated funds from (c) federal and

(d) non-federal sources, and the requested new or revised budget for the project from (e) federal and (f) non-federal sources as well as (g), the sum of columns (e) and (f) by row. For new grants, columns (c) and (d) will not be used. These columns would be used for application submissions requesting a continuance or revision, not a new request. Once you understand this, Section A becomes simple to complete.

Let us assume a hypothetical budget scenario for an application to the U.S. Department of Housing and Urban Development's Community Outreach Partnership Center Program, with a grant request of $400,000. In row 1, column (a), you would type "COPC," which is the common abbreviation for the program name. Continuing across the row, in column (b) you would type "14.511," which is the program's CFDA number. Because this is a new grant application, columns (c) and (d) are skipped. The new application budget request is $400,000, and we assume our organization has compiled 150% of that amount for match, or $600,000. So, in column (e) you would type "400,000" and in column (f) you would enter "600,000" for a total amount in column (g) of "1,000,000." Because we are assuming a simple application, we would then transfer the same entries from columns (e), (f), and (g) to their same column location in row 5, "Totals." If this were a complex application, each of the entries in rows 1 through 4 would be added to attain the appropriate sums for row 5, and cell 5(g) would indicate the total budget for the complete project including all of its components. If you are completing the PureEdge version of the form using Grants.gov, the information you enter that should remain consistent throughout the form will be entered automatically for you, and the form also automatically computes totals across cells and rows as well. This feature both reduces errors and makes errors easy to spot. **Table 6.1** presents this section of the form with our hypothetical information.

Section B, Budget Categories, forces the applicant to ensure that its budget categories comply with the standard object codes in grant budgeting: Personnel, Fringe Benefits, Travel, Equipment, Supplies, Contractual, Construction, Other, and Indirect Costs. In this section, the specific federal budget requests across each of the object class categories listed earlier are the information of interest; they are listed in row 6(a–k) on the form. The column numbers in this section correspond to the row numbers in the previous one. The first step in completing this section is to transfer the grant program label from the rows in Section A to the column headings in Section B, row 6. So, in cell 6(1), "COPC" should be entered. For our simple grant application example, only rows 1 and 5 were used in Section A, so only columns 1 and 5 are used in this section. Because this section is asking for information about only the federal grant funds, the total amount entered in cell 6(k)(1) must be equal to the amount entered in cell 5(e) in the previous section of the form. Again, because this is a simple application with only one federal program, the values entered in the cells in column (1) can be transferred to column (5), which represents the total federal funds requested for each object class category, their subtotals, and total. As with the previous section, if there were multiple programs, they would be entered in columns (2) through (4) and summed to find the values for column (5). Row 7 incorporates anticipated program income. Some programs may involve user fees or other charges that result in program income for each of the program activities. If program income is expected, it should be budgeted and included in the appropriate cells on this form. An example of this form using the hypothetical contents discussed is provided in **Table 6.2**.

TABLE 6.1 SF-424A, Section A Example

OMB Approval No. 4040-0006
Expiration Date 04-30-2008

BUDGET INFORMATION–Non-Construction Programs

SECTION A–BUDGET SUMMARY

Grant Program Function or Activity (a)	Catalog of Federal Domestic Assistance Number (b)	Estimated Unobligated Funds		New or Revised Budget		
		Federal (c)	Non-Federal (d)	Federal (e)	Non-Federal (f)	Total (g)
1. COPC	14.511	$	$	$ 400,000.00	$ 600,000.00	$ 1,000,000.00
2.						0.00
3.						0.00
4.						0.00
5. Totals		$	$	$	$	$

Source: SF-424A

215

TABLE 6.2 SF-424A, Section B Example

SECTION B–BUDGET CATEGORIES

6. Object Class Categories	(1) COPC	Grant Program, Function, or Activity			Total
		(2)	(3)	(4)	(5)
a. Personnel	$ 220,000.00	$	$	$	$ 220,000.00
b. Fringe Benefits	44,000.00				44,000.00
c. Travel	6,000.00				6,000.00
d. Equipment	0.00				0.00
e. Supplies	4,500.00				4,500.00
f. Contractual	25,000.00				25,000.00
g. Construction	0.00				0.00
h. Other	0.00				0.00
i. Total Direct Charges (sum of 6a–6h)	299,500.00				$ 299,500.00
j. Indirect Charges	100,500.00				$ 108,500.00
k. TOTALS (sum of 6i and 6j)	$ 400,000.00	$ 0.00	$ 0.00	$ 0.00	$ 400,000.00
7. Program Income	$ 0.00	$	$	$	$ 0.00

Source: SF-424A

Section C forces the applicant to disclose, again, for each program component set out in Section A, the amount of match funds or resources that will be made available for that activity by the fund source. Rows 8 through 11 correspond, as before, to the programs listed in Section A, column (a), rows 1–4. Cell 8(a) should receive the entry "COPC" as the program name, with cell 8(b) receiving the amount of match funds the applicant organization is contributing to the proposed project. Cell 8(c) receives the amount of match contribution pledged by the state or state agencies, and cell 8(d) constitutes the match received from all other sources. Cell 8(e) is totaled by row, and represents the total of all non-federal monies pledged to the project. The cautious reader will note that the total in this cell must correspond to the total in cell 5(f) in Section A. Because our example is simple, rows 9 through 11 are left blank and row 12 should be identical to row 8. This, again, is only the case in simple projects. Complex projects with multiple programs listed would be totaled by column to complete row 12. And, as has been the case in each section thus far, using the form in Grants.gov adds simplicity because it calculates all of the totals by row and column automatically.

Another potential source of confusion regards situations when the applicant is a state agency or instrumentality. The three columns in this section, applicant, state, and other, are mutually exclusive of one another. So, if the applicant is a state agency, the match it is contributing from agency funds is listed as applicant match, and any match funds from other state agencies would be listed under the state column heading. Monies should never be duplicated between columns because this will lead to mathematical inconsistencies among the sections of the form. **Table 6.3** provides our hypothetical example, assuming that the applicant organization provides $400,000 in match, state agencies provide $25,000, and other sources are responsible for $175,000 of the budgeted match funding for the project. These totals sum to $600,000, equal to the amount in Section A, cell 5(f).

Section D calls for the applicant to forecast its cash needs by quarter for each of four quarters in the project year, and for both federal and non-federal funding commitments. As with all budget figures, the numbers entered here should be derived from the budget and program narrative and should be a legitimate estimation of cash needs. Entering the quarterly estimates in the Grants.gov form results in automatic calculation of the first-year totals presented in the first column, "Total for 1st Year." Section E requires annual cash flow information for federal funds only, and this time by funding program. The program title is entered to correspond with those listed in Section A, and the amount entered in cell 16(b) should match the total amount in the first column of row 13 in Section D. Because this is a 3-year project, the estimates for cells 16(b) through 16(d) should sum to the total federal grant request amount in cell 1(e). For complex grants, the total across row 16 should correspond to cell 1(e), the row 17 total should correspond to cell 2(e), row 18 totals should sum to cell 3(e), and the total across row 19 would correspond to cell 4(e). Row 20 calls for the total annual federal cash flow estimate across all federal programs involved in the request. So, the sum of the four cells in row 20 must add to the total in cell 5(e) from Section A. **Table 6.4** presents our hypothetical estimate for consideration and comparison.

The final element of the SF-424A is Section F, cells 21 and 22. This row asks the applicant to ascertain the portion of total grant project costs that are direct and indirect across

TABLE 6.3   SF-424A, Section C Example

SECTION C–NON-FEDERAL RESOURCES

(a) Grant Program	(b) Applicant	(c) State	(d) Other Sources	(e) TOTALS
8. COPC	$ 400,000.00	$ 25,000.00	$ 175,000.00	$ 600,000.00
9.				
10.				
11.				
12. TOTAL (sum of lines 8–11)	$ 400,000.00	$ 25,000.00	$ 175,000.00	$ 600,000.00

Source: SF-424A

TABLE 6.4 SF-424A, Sections D and E Example

SECTION D—FORECASTED CASH NEEDS

	Total for 1st Year	1st Quarter	2nd Quarter	3rd Quarter	4th Quarter
13. Federal	$ 100,000.00	$ 15,000.00	$ 25,000.00	$ 30,000.00	$ 30,000.00
14. Non-Federal	$ 125,000.00	0.00	40,000.00	40,000.00	45,000.00
15. TOTAL (sum of lines 13 and 14)	$ 225,000.00	$ 15,000.00	$ 65,000.00	$ 70,000.00	$ 75,000.00

SECTION E—BUDGET ESTIMATES OF FEDERAL FUNDS NEEDED FOR BALANCE OF THE PROJECT

	FUTURE FUNDING PERIODS (Years)			
(a) Grant Program	(b) First	(c) Second	(d) Third	(e) Fourth
16. COPC	$ 100,000.00	$ 150,000.00	$ 150,000.00	$ 0.00
17.				
18.				
19.				
20. TOTAL (sum of lines 16–19)	$ 100,000.00	$ 150,000.00	$ 150,000.00	$ 0.00

Source: SF-424A

both the federal and the non-federal match categories. This is not computed automatically because it requires information to which only the applicant is privy. The information should be readily available in your detailed program budget because it was already used to calculate the match amounts in earlier sections. As with all other data in this form, the two cells should sum to an amount equal to that found in cell 5(g)—the total amount of the project cost from all sources and programs. Direct charges (the same as direct costs) are all direct costs from each of the contributing sources. The federal direct charge amount is presented in cell 6(i)(1) ($299,500).

The amount of matching funds that are direct, versus indirect, will depend on each contributor's indirect cost rate. The applicant's contribution to the project is $400,000, and it has an indirect cost rate of 33.6% of total direct costs; this was used to calculate the amount in cell 6(j)(1) for federal indirect costs ($100,500), so the same rate applies to the organization's own fund contributions. This means that the detailed proposal budget had to break down the components of the match amount into specific categories (just like federal funds were in Section B of the form). Each organization contributing funds to the project may have indirect costs that are or are not listed as match. If they are listed as match, they will appear in the appropriate place in the detailed program budget. If they do not appear in match commitment letters, they cannot be imputed because indirect costs are calculated on the basis of a negotiated federal agreement and must be explicitly stated by the match source. To avoid confusion in our example, I assume that all of the partners had an equal indirect cost rate of 33.6%, and thus the $600,000 in match funds consisted of $398,400 in direct costs and $201,600 in indirect costs. So, federal direct charges of $299,500 plus match direct charges of $398,400 equal total direct charges of $697,500. Federal indirect charges were $101,500 and match indirect charges were $201,600, for total indirect charges of $302,100. Total indirect charges ($302,100) plus total direct charges ($697,900) sum to $1,000,000—the total project cost found in cell 5(g), as expected. Table 6.5 presents an example of this section of the form.

Although the categories of expenditures are different for form SF-424C, the budget form for construction projects, the principles are similar, and thus do not require such a sophisticated explanation or an example as was provided with SF-424A. Form SF-424C appears in this chapter's appendix. The next section considers the second group of forms—agency-specific forms.

AGENCY-SPECIFIC FORMS

In addition to the required government-wide forms that accompany each federal grant application, many agencies require additional forms. It is not possible to provide a complete list of such forms for each agency and program here, but it is valuable to point out their existence. You should now have developed a very strong feel for detail and carefully reading calls or requests for grant proposals and other agency guidelines. The information contained in these documents was shown to be essential for developing the budget and narrative, and it is equally important for identifying any forms that must be completed and submitted along with the application. In other words, grant writers must learn to pay attention to detail and in so doing ensure that they highlight all requirements for

TABLE 6.5 SF–424A, Section F Example

SECTION F—OTHER BUDGET INFORMATION	
21. Direct Charges: $697,900.00	22. Indirect Charges: $302,100.00

Source: SF-424A

how to develop a proposal, what not to include, and in this case, what additional information to include.

Examples of agency-specific forms include SF-LLL, the form that standardizes disclosure of lobbying activities—which is required for some agency programs. The National Science Foundation utilizes its own agency-specific cover page (both of these forms are included in the chapter appendix as examples). The U.S. Department of Education form ED-SF-424 collects additional information about the applicant that is not included in the basic standard form. Other agencies have similar specific required forms that must be located, understood, completed, and submitted with your grant application. A listing of required and optional forms in the SF-424 family is provided in **Table 6.6**; a similar listing of miscellaneous forms is provided in **Table 6.7**.

In addition to required forms, many agencies also provide optional forms that may be completed at the grant writer's discretion. Although not required, these forms are used as survey instruments to help agencies collect information about their applicants or about applicants' perceptions of the agency. So, they may, in fact, be in the grant writer's best interest to complete, though they do not directly affect the application itself. A grant writer must be able to differentiate required forms, whether government-wide or agency-specific, from optional forms.

APPLICATION FORMS FOR OTHER FUNDING SOURCES

Non-governmental grants, whether foundation grants or corporate grants, and state grants may require application forms to be submitted with the grant proposal. Forms are like surveys in that they are used to collect information about the applying organization and some summary information about the request. Many funding sources are able to tell very quickly by glancing at an application cover page whether or not the program is within their funding scope. Many foundations utilize an application form that provides space in which to respond to specific questions. When this is the case, the space provided should be considered the maximum allowable, and the responses should be tailored to concisely fit within that framework. In this case, the form also serves as the narrative. It is also common for some questions to indicate that it is appropriate to utilize more space when needed, in which case your application becomes the form with attached narrative components. Other application forms provide a hybrid of questions to be answered on the form and others to be answered in narrative format, resulting in the same set of narrative attachments to the form.

When applying to a particular foundation or agency, it is always a good idea to make sure that they do not have a formal application packet or an application form that must be included with a grant application. Sometimes this means contacting the agency or foundation program officer to inquire about application procedures. In essence, it is always best—if not required—to provide the agency with a grant application that meets the requirements it has established and in the format it requests. Forms are an important part of the application process and they should not be overlooked.

TABLE 6.6   Listing of Agency-Specific Forms Related to the SF-424 Family

Form Type	Form Name	OMB Control Number
Agency Specific	ANA Application Information	0970-0261
Agency Specific	Attachments	Not Available
Agency Specific	Budget Narrative Attachment Form	Not Available
Agency Specific	CD511 Form	
Agency Specific	CIS Budget	1103-0027
Agency Specific	COPS Application Attachment	1103-0098
Agency Specific	COPS Budget	1103-0097
Agency Specific	CSREES Application Modification	0524-0039
Agency Specific	CSREES NRI Proposal Type Form	0524-0039
Agency Specific	CSREES Supplemental Information	0524-0039
Agency Specific	Certification of Compliance	1103-0027
Agency Specific	DOE SEP Narrative Information Worksheet	1910-5126
Agency Specific	DOI Project Details	1029-0059
Agency Specific	DOL Budget Information Form LMI Base Programs	1220-0079
Agency Specific	DOL Budget Information Form LMIAAMC	1220-0079
Agency Specific	Dept of Education Budget Information for Non-Construction Programs (ED-524)	1890-0004
Agency Specific	Dept of Education Combined Assurances (ED-80-0013)	
Agency Specific	Dept of Education Supplemental Information for SP-424	Not Available
Agency Specific	Disclosure of Lobbying Activities (SF-LLL)	0348-0046
Agency Specific	ED Abstract Form	
Agency Specific	ED Certification Debarment (ED-80-0014)	
Agency Specific	ED FIPSE Budget Summary	
Agency Specific	ED FIPSE Consortium Partners Identification Form	
Agency Specific	ED FIPSE Project Title	
Agency Specific	ED GEPA427 Form	1890-0007
Agency Specific	EPA 4700-4	2090-0014
Agency Specific	EPA Key Contacts Form 5700-54	4040-0003
Agency Specific	Faith Based EEO Survey	1890-0014
Agency Specific	Grants.gov Lobbying Form	Not Available

TABLE 6.6   (Continued)

Form Type	Form Name	OMB Control Number
Agency Specific	HHS Checklist Form PHS-5161	0920-0428
Agency Specific	HUD Applicant Recipient Disclosure Report	2510-0011
Agency Specific	HUD Comment Suggestions Form	
Agency Specific	HUD Community Initiative Form	
Agency Specific	HUD Detailed Budget Form	2501-0017
Agency Specific	HUD Facsimile Transmittal	2525-0118
Agency Specific	HUD Fiscal Year Activity Report	2502-0261
Agency Specific	HUD Lead Factor 3	2539-0015
Agency Specific	HUD Opportunity Program	2577-0229
Agency Specific	HUD ROSS	2577-0229
Agency Specific	HUD Race Ethnic Form	2535-0113
Agency Specific	HUD Verification of Match	2528-0180
Agency Specific	Head Start Attachments	0970-0207
Agency Specific	Head Start Budget Form	0970-0207
Agency Specific	Head Start Program Approach	0970-0207
Agency Specific	NARA NEH Budget	3136-0134
Agency Specific	NARA Project Staff File Attachment	
Agency Specific	NARA Project Summary Attachment	
Agency Specific	NARA Subvention Form	Not Available
Agency Specific	NEA Organization & Project Profile	3135-0112
Agency Specific	NEA Supplemental Information	3135-0112
Agency Specific	NEH Budget	3136-0134
Agency Specific	NEH Coverpage Supplemental	3136-0134
Agency Specific	Objective Work Plan	0980-0204
Agency Specific	Other Attachments Form	Not Available
Agency Specific	Project Abstract Summary	0980-0204
Agency Specific	Project Narrative Attachment Form	Not Available
Agency Specific	Protection of Human Subjects	0990-0263
Agency Specific	SSA Additional Assurances Certifications	Not Available
Agency Specific	SSA SF424 Section G	

Source: Grants.gov 2007.

TABLE 6.7 Listing of Miscellaneous Agency-Specific Forms

Type	Form Name	OMB Number
Agency Specific	ANA Application Information	0970-0261
Agency Specific	CSREES Application Modification	0524-0039
Agency Specific	CSREES NRI Proposal Type Form	0524-0039
Agency Specific	CSREES Supplemental Information	0524-0039
Agency Specific	DOE SEP Narrative Information Worksheet	1910-5126
Agency Specific	DOI Project Details	1029-0059
Agency Specific	Dept of Education Supplemental Information for SF-424	Not Available
Agency Specific	Dept of Education Supplemental Information for SF-424	Not Available
Agency Specific	ED Abstract Form	
Agency Specific	ED Abstract Form	
Agency Specific	ED FIPSE Project Title	
Agency Specific	EPA 4700-4	2090-0014
Agency Specific	EPA 4700-4	2090-0014
Agency Specific	HHS Checklist Form PHS-5161	0920-0428
Agency Specific	HHS Checklist Form PHS-5161	0920-0428
Agency Specific	HHS Checklist Form PHS-5161	0920-0428
Agency Specific	HUD Applicant-Recipient Disclosure Report	2510-0011
Agency Specific	HUD Applicant-Recipient Disclosure Report	2510-0011
Agency Specific	HUD Comment Suggestions Form	
Agency Specific	HUD Comment Suggestions Form	
Agency Specific	HUD Opportunity Program	2577-0229
Agency Specific	HUD Opportunity Program	2577-0229
Agency Specific	HUD Verification of Match	2528-0180
Agency Specific	HUD Verification of Match	2528-0180
Agency Specific	Head Start Program Approach	0970-0207
Agency Specific	NASA—Other Project Informaion	
Agency Specific	NASA—Principal Investigator and Authorized Representative Supplemental Data Sheet	2700-0085

TABLE 6.7   (Continued)

Type	Form Name	OMB Number
Agency Specific	NEA Organization & Project Profile	3135-0112
Agency Specific	NEA Supplemental	3135-0112
Agency Specific	NEA Supplemental Information	3135-0112
Agency Specific	NSF Application Checklist	3145-0058
Agency Specific	NSF Deviation Authorization	3145-0058
Agency Specific	NSF FastLane System Registration	3145-0058
Agency Specific	NSF Suggested Reviewers	3145-0058
Agency Specific	Objective Work Plan	0980-0204
Agency Specific	Objective Work Plan	0980-0204
Agency Specific	Organization Project Profile	3135-0112
Agency Specific	Other Attachments Form	Not Available
Agency Specific	PHS 398 Checklist	0925-0001
Agency Specific	PHS 398 Research Plan	0925-0001
Agency Specific	Project Abstract Summary	0980-0204
Agency Specific	Project Abstract Summary	
Agency Specific	Protection of Human Subjects	0990-0263
Agency Specific	Protection of Human Subjects	0990-0263
Agency Specific	SBIR/STTR_Information	0925-0001

Source: Grants.gov 2007.

CONCLUSION

This chapter, though somewhat technical, is intended to familiarize the reader with forms, their purpose, and the essentiality of ensuring their inclusion and accuracy in accordance with program requirements set out by the funding source. Agencies conceive of information in categories and in varying levels of importance. They then design forms and application materials that enable them to collect the necessary information in a systematic and consistent manner that increases their ease in locating information that they deem relevant to their decision process. This facilitates ready comparison of proposals on a number of criteria, including amount requested, location, geographic breadth, and so on. Forms reduce the time it takes for agencies to come to funding determinations, and they are also used to certify agreement with certain conditions of award. It is the grant writer's responsibility to read program requirements and RFPs with a detailed eye toward all requirements, of which the required forms are one essential component.

REFERENCES

Grants.gov. 2007. Apply for Grants. Accessed January 2, 2009. Available at: http://apply.grants.gov/apply/Form
    Links?family=7.

APPENDIX

The following pages present forms you may encounter in the grant application process.

APPLICATION FOR FEDERAL ASSISTANCE SF-424 - MANDATORY

* 1.a. Type of Submission:

☐ Application

☐ Plan

☐ Funding Request

☐ Other

* Other (specify)

* 1.b. Frequency:

☐ Annual

☐ Quarterly

☐ Other

* Other (specify)

* 1.d. Version:

☐ Initial   ☐ Resubmission   ☐ Revision   ☐ Update

* 2. Date Received:
Completed by Grants.gov upon submission.

STATE USE ONLY:

3. Applicant Identifier:

5. Date Received by State:

4a. Federal Entity Identifier:

6. State Application Identifier:

4b. Federal Award Identifier:

1.c. Consolidated Application/Plan/Funding Request?

Yes ☐   No ☐

7. Applicant Information:

* a. Legal Name:

* b. Employer/Taxpayer Identification Number (EIN/TIN):

* c. Organizational DUNS:

d. Address:

* Street 1:

Street 2:

* City:

County:

* State:

Province:

* Country:

* Zip/Postal Code:

e. Organizational Unit:

Department Name:

Division Name:

f. Name and contact information of person to be contacted on matters involving this submission:

Prefix:

* First Name:

Middle Name:

* Last Name:

Suffix:

Title:

Organizational Affiliation:

* Telephone Number:

Fax Number:

* Email:

APPLICATION FOR FEDERAL ASSISTANCE SF-424 - MANDATORY (continued)

* 8.a. Type of Applicant:

* Other (specify):

b. Additional Description:

* 9. Name of Federal Agency:

10. Catalog of Federal Domestic Assistance Number:

CFDA Title:

11. Areas Affected by Funding:

12. Congressional Districts of:

* a. Applicant: b. Program/Project:

Attach an additional list of Program/Project Congressional Districts if needed.

13. Funding Period:

a. Start Date: b. End Date:

14. Estimated Funding:

* a. Federal ($):   b. Match ($):

* 15. Is Submission Subject to Review by State Under Executive Order 12372 Process?

☐ a. This submission was made available to the State under the Executive Order 12372 Process for review on:

☐ b. Program is subject to E.O. 12372 but has not been selected by State for review.

☐ c. Program is not covered by E.O. 12372.

APPLICATION FOR FEDERAL ASSISTANCE SF-424 - MANDATORY (continued)

* 16. Is The Applicant Delinquent On Any Federal Debt?

Yes ☐   No ☐

17. By signing this application, I certify (1) to the statements contained in the list of certifications** and (2) that the statements herein are true, complete and accurate to the best of my knowledge. I also provide the required assurances** and agree to comply with any resulting terms if I accept an award. I am aware that any false, fictitious, or fraudulent statements or claims may subject me to criminal, civil, or administrative penalties. (U.S. Code, Title 218, Section 1001)

** I Agree ☐

** This list of certifications and assurances, or an Internet site where you may obtain this list, is contained in the announcement or agency specific instructions.

Authorized Representative:

Prefix:	* First Name:

Middle Name:

* Last Name:

Suffix:	* Title:

Organizational Affiliation:

* Telephone Number:

* Fax Number:

* Email:

* Signature of Authorized Representative:

Completed by Grants.gov upon submission.

* Date Signed:

Completed by Grants.gov upon submission.

Attach supporting documents as specified in agency instructions.

APPLICATION FOR FEDERAL ASSISTANCE SF-424 - MANDATORY (continued)

* Consolidated Application/Plan/Funding Request Explanation:

APPLICATION FOR FEDERAL ASSISTANCE SF-424 - MANDATORY (continued)

* Applicant Federal Debt Delinquency Explanation:

INSTRUCTIONS FOR THE SF-424

Public reporting burden for this collection of information is estimated to average 60 minutes per response, including time for reviewing instructions, searching existing data sources, gathering and maintaining the data needed, and completing and reviewing the collection of information. Send comments regarding the burden estimate or any other aspect of this collection of information, including suggestions for reducing this burden, to the Office of Management and Budget, Paperwork Reduction Project (0348-0043), Washington, DC 20503.

PLEASE DO NOT RETURN YOUR COMPLETED FORM TO THE OFFICE OF MANAGEMENT AND BUDGET. SEND IT TO THE ADDRESS PROVIDED BY THE SPONSORING AGENCY.

This is a standard form (including the continuation sheet) required for use as a cover sheet for submission of preapplications and applications and related information under discretionary programs. Some of the items are required and some are optional at the discretion of the applicant or the Federal agency (agency). Required items are identified with an asterisk on the form and are specified in the instructions below. In addition to the instructions provided below, applicants must consult agency instructions to determine specific requirements.

Item	Entry:	Item	Entry:
1.	**Type of Submission:** (Required): Select one type of submission in accordance with agency instructions • Preapplication • Application • Changed/Corrected Application – If requested by the agency, check if this submission is to change or correct a previously submitted application. Unless requested by the agency, applicants may not use this to submit changes after the closing date.	10.	**Name Of Federal Agency:** (Required) Enter the name of the Federal agency from which assistance is being requested with this application.
		11.	**Catalog Of Federal Domestic Assistance Number/Title:** Enter the Catalog of Federal Domestic Assistance number and title of the program under which assistance is requested, as found in the program announcement, if applicable.
2.	**Type of Application:** (Required) Select one type of application in accordance with agency instructions. • New – An application that is being submitted to an agency for the first time. • Continuation – An extension for an additional funding/budget period for a project with a projected completion date. This can include renewals. • Revision – Any change in the Federal Government's financial obligation or contingent liability from an existing obligation. If a revision, enter the appropriate letter(s). More than one may be selected. If "Other" is selected, please specify in text box provided. A. Increase Award B. Decrease Award C. Increase Duration D. Decrease Duration E. Other (specify)	12.	**Funding Opportunity Number/Title:** (Required) Enter the Funding Opportunity Number and title of the opportunity under which assistance is requested, as found in the program announcement.
		13.	**Competition Identification Number/Title:** Enter the Competition Identification Number and title of the competition under which assistance is requested, if applicable.
		14.	**Areas Affected By Project:** List the areas or entities using the categories (e.g., cities, counties, states, etc.) specified in agency instructions. Use the continuation sheet to enter additional areas, if needed.
3.	**Date Received:** Leave this field blank. This date will be assigned by the Federal agency.	15.	**Descriptive Title of Applicant's Project:** (Required) Enter a brief descriptive title of the project. If appropriate, attach a map showing project location (e.g., construction or real property projects). For preapplications, attach a summary description of the project.
4.	**Applicant Identifier:** Enter the entity identifier assigned buy the Federal agency, if any, or the applicant's control number if applicable.		
5.a.	**Federal Entity Identifier:** Enter the number assigned to your organization by the Federal Agency, if any.	16.	**Congressional Districts Of:** (Required) 16a. Enter the applicant's Congressional District, and 16b. Enter all District(s) affected by the program or project. Enter in the format: 2 characters State Abbreviation – 3 characters District Number, e.g., CA-005 for California 5th district, CA-012 for California 12th district, NC-103 for North Carolina's 103rd district. • If all congressional districts in a state are affected, enter "all" for the district number, e.g., MD-all for all congressional districts in Maryland. • If nationwide, i.e. all districts within all states are affected, enter US-all. • If the program/project is outside the US, enter 00-000.
5.b.	**Federal Award Identifier:** For new applications leave blank. For a continuation or revision to an existing award, enter the previously assigned Federal award identifier number. If a changed/corrected application, enter the Federal Identifier in accordance with agency instructions.		
6.	**Date Received by State:** Leave this field blank. This date will be assigned by the State, if applicable.		
7.	**State Application Identifier:** Leave this field blank. This identifier will be assigned by the State, if applicable.		
8.	**Applicant Information:** Enter the following in accordance with agency instructions:		
	a. Legal Name: (Required): Enter the legal name of applicant that will undertake the assistance activity. This is that the organization has registered with the Central Contractor Registry. Information on registering with CCR may be obtained by visiting the Grants.gov website.	17.	**Proposed Project Start and End Dates:** (Required) Enter the proposed start date and end date of the project.
	b. Employer/Taxpayer Number (EIN/TIN): (Required): Enter the Employer or Taxpayer Identification Number (EIN or TIN) as assigned by the Internal Revenue Service. If your organization is not in the US, enter 44-4444444.	18.	**Estimated Funding:** (Required) Enter the amount requested or to be contributed during the first funding/budget period by each contributor. Value of in-kind contributions should be included on appropriate lines, as applicable. If the action will result in a dollar change to an existing award, indicate only the amount of the change. For decreases, enclose the amounts in parentheses.

c. Organizational DUNS: (Required) Enter the organization's DUNS or DUNS+4 number received from Dun and Bradstreet. Information on obtaining a DUNS number may be obtained by visiting the Grants.gov website.	**19.** **Is Application Subject to Review by State Under Executive Order 12372 Process?** Applicants should contact the State Single Point of Contact (SPOC) for Federal Executive Order 12372 to determine whether the application is subject to the State intergovernmental review process. Select the appropriate box. If "a." is selected, enter the date the application was submitted to the State.
d. Address: Enter the complete address as follows: Street address (Line 1 required), City (Required), County, State (Required, if country is US), Province, Country (Required), Zip/Postal Code (Required, if country is US).	**20.** **Is the Applicant Delinquent on any Federal Debt?** (Required) Select the appropriate box. This question applies to the applicant organization, not the person who signs as the authorized representative. Categories of debt include delinquent audit disallowances, loans and taxes. If yes, include an explanation on the continuation sheet.
e. Organizational Unit: Enter the name of the primary organizational unit (and department or division, (if applicable) that will undertake the assistance activity, if applicable. **f. Name and contact information of person to be contacted on matters involving this application:** (required), organizational affiliation (if affiliated with an organization other **on**: Enter the name (First and last name than the applicant organization), telephone number (Required), fax number, and email address (Required) of the person to contact on matters related to this application.	**21.** **Authorized Representative**: (Required) To be signed and dated by the authorized representative of the applicant organization. Enter the name (First and last name required) title (Required), telephone number (Required), fax number, and email address (Required) of the person authorized to sign for the applicant. A copy of the governing body's authorization for you to sign this application as the official representative must be on file in the applicant's office. (Certain Federal agencies may require that this authorization be submitted as part of the application.)

9.	**Type of Applicant**: (Required) Select up to three applicant type(s) in accordance with agency instructions.	

A. State Government	M. Non-profit
B. County Government	N. Non-profit
C. City or Township Government	O. Private Institution of Higher Education
D. Special District Government	P. Individual
E. Regional Organization	Q. For-Profit Organization (Other than Small Business)
F. U.S. Territory or Possession	
G. Independent School District	R. Small Business
H. Public/State Controlled Institution of Higher Education	S. Hispanic-Serving Institution
I. Indian/Native American Tribal Government (Federally Recognized)	T. Historically Black Colleges and Universities (HBCUs)
J. Indian/Native American Tribal Government (Other than Federally Recognized)	U. Tribally Controlled Colleges and Universities (TCCUs)
K. Indian/Native American Tribally Designated Organization	V. Alaska Native and Native Hawaiian Serving Institutions
L. Public/Indian Housing Authority	W. Non-Domestic (Non-US) Entity
	X. Other (specify)

SF-424A

BUDGET INFORMATION - Non-Construction Programs

SECTION A - BUDGET SUMMARY

Grant Program Function or Activity (a)	Catalog of Federal Domestic Assistance Number (b)	Estimated Unobligated Funds		New or Revised Budget		
		Federal (c)	Non-Federal (d)	Federal (e)	Non-Federal (f)	Total (g)
1.		$	$	$	$	$
2.						
3.						
4.						
5. Totals		$	$	$	$	$

SECTION B - BUDGET CATEGORIES

6. Object Class Categories	GRANT PROGRAM, FUNCTION OR ACTIVITY				Total
	(1)	(2)	(3)	(4)	(5)
a. Personnel	$	$	$	$	$
b. Fringe Benefits					
c. Travel					
d. Equipment					
e. Supplies					
f. Contractual					
g. Construction					
h. Other					
i. Total Direct Charges (sum of 6a–6h)					$
j. Indirect Charges					$
k. TOTALS (sum of 6i and 6j)	$	$	$	$	$
7. Program Income	$	$	$	$	$

SF-424A (continued)

SECTION C - NON-FEDERAL RESOURCES				
(a) Grant Program	(b) Applicant	(c) State	(d) Other Sources	(e) TOTALS
8.	$	$	$	$
9.				
10.				
11.				
12. TOTAL (sum of lines 8–11)	$	$	$	$

SECTION D - FORECASTED CASH NEEDS					
	Total for 1st Year	1st Quarter	2nd Quarter	3rd Quarter	4th Quarter
13. Federal	$	$	$	$	$
14. Non-Federal	$				
15. TOTAL (sum of lines 13 and 14)	$	$	$	$	$

SECTION E - BUDGET ESTIMATES OF FEDERAL FUNDS NEEDED FOR BALANCE OF THE PROJECT				
(a) Grant Program	FUTURE FUNDING PERIODS (Years)			
	(b) First	(c) Second	(d) Third	(e) Fourth
16.	$	$	$	$
17.				
18.				
19.				
20. TOTAL (sum of lines 16–19)	$	$	$	$

SECTION F - OTHER BUDGET INFORMATION	
21. Direct Charges:	22. Indirect Charges:
23. Remarks:	

SF–424B

ASSURANCES - NON-CONSTRUCTION PROGRAMS

NOTE: Certain of these assurances may not be applicable to your project or program. If you have questions, please contact the awarding agency. Further, certain Federal awarding agencies may require applicants to certify to additional assurances. If such is the case, you will be notified.

As the duly authorized representative of the applicant, I certify that the applicant:

1. Has the legal authority to apply for Federal assistance and the institutional, managerial and financial capability (including funds sufficient to pay the non-Federal share of project cost) to ensure proper planning, management and completion of the project described in this application.

2. Will give the awarding agency, the Comptroller General of the United States and, if appropriate, the State, through any authorized representative, access to and the right to examine all records, books, papers, or documents related to the award; and will establish a proper accounting system in accordance with generally accepted accounting standards or agency directives.

3. Will establish safeguards to prohibit employees from using their positions for a purpose that constitutes or presents the appearance of personal or organizational conflict of interest, or personal gain.

4. Will initiate and complete the work within the applicable time frame after receipt of approval of the awarding agency.

5. Will comply with the Intergovernmental Personnel Act of 1970 (42 U.S.C. §§ 4728–4763) relating to prescribed standards for merit systems for programs funded under one of the 19 statutes or regulations specified in Appendix A of OPM's Standards for a Merit System of Personnel Administration (5 C.F.R. 900, Subpart F).

6. Will comply with all Federal statutes relating to nondiscrimination. These include but are not limited to: (a) Title VI of the Civil Rights Act of 1964 (P.L. 88–352) which prohibits discrimination on the basis of race, color or national origin; (b) Title IX of the Education Amendments of 1972, as amended (20 U.S.C. §§ 1681–1683, and 1685–1686), which prohibits discrimination on the basis of sex; (c) Section 504 of the Rehabilitation

Act of 1973, as amended (29 U.S.C. § 794), which prohibits discrimination on the basis of handicaps; (d) the Age Discrimination Act of 1975, as amended (42 U.S.C. §§ 6101–6107), which prohibits discrimination on the basis of age; (e) the Drug Abuse Office and Treatment Act of 1972 (P.L. 92–255), as amended, relating to nondiscrimination on the basis of drug abuse; (f) the Comprehensive Alcohol Abuse and Alcoholism Prevention, Treatment and Rehabilitation Act of 1970 (P.L. 91–616), as amended, relating to nondiscrimination on the basis of alcohol abuse or alcoholism; (g) §§ 523 and 527 of the Public Health Service Act of 1912 (42 U.S.C. §§ 290 dd-3 and 290 ee-3), as amended, relating to confidentiality of alcohol and drug abuse patient records; (h) Title VIII of the Civil Rights Act of 1968 (42 U.S.C. §§ 3601 et seq.), as amended, relating to nondiscrimination in the sale, rental or financing of housing; (i) any other nondiscrimination provisions in the specific statute(s) under which application for Federal assistance is being made; and, (j) the requirements of any other nondiscrimination statute(s) which may apply to the application.

7. Will comply, or has already complied, with the requirements of Titles II and III of the Uniform Relocation Assistance and Real Property Acquisition Policies Act of 1970 (P.L. 91–646) which provide for fair and equitable treatment of persons displaced or whose property is acquired as a result of Federal or federally-assisted programs. These requirements apply to all interests in real property acquired for project purposes regardless of Federal participation in purchases.

8. Will comply, as applicable, with provisions of the Hatch Act (5 U.S.C. §§ 1501–1508 and 7324–7328) which limit the political activities of employees whose principal employment activities are funded in whole or in part with Federal funds.

SF-424B (continued)

9. Will comply, as applicable, with the provisions of the Davis-Bacon Act (40 U.S.C. §§ 276a to 276a–7), the Copeland Act (40 U.S.C. § 276c and 18 U.S.C. § 874), and the Contract Work Hours and Safety Standards Act (40 U.S.C. §§ 327-333), regarding labor standards for federally-assisted construction subagreements.

10. Will comply, if applicable, with flood insurance purchase requirements of Section 102(a) of the Flood Disaster Protection Act of 1973 (P.L. 93–234) which requires recipients in a special flood hazard area to participate in the program and to purchase flood insurance if the total cost of insurable construction and acquisition is $ 10,000 or more.

11. Will comply with environmental standards which may be prescribed pursuant to the following: (a) institution of environmental quality control measures under the National Environmental Policy Act of 1969 (P.L. 91–190) and Executive Order (EO) 11514; (b) notification of violating facilities pursuant to EO 11738; (c) protection of wetlands pursuant to EO 11990; (d) evaluation of flood hazards in floodplains in accordance with EO 11988; (e) assurance of project consistency with the approved State management program developed under the Coastal Zone Management Act of 1972 (16 U.S.C. §§ 1451 et seq.); (f) conformity of Federal actions to State (Clean Air) Implementation Plans under Section 176(c) of the Clean Air Act of 1955, as amended (42 U.S.C. §§ 7401 et seq.); (g) protection of underground sources of drinking water under the Safe Drinking Water Act of 1974, as amended (P.L. 93–523); and, (h) protection of endangered species under the Endangered Species Act of 1973, as amended (P.L. 93–205).

12. Will comply with the Wild and Scenic Rivers Act of 1968 (16 U.S.C. §§ 1271 et seq.) related to protecting components or potential components of the national wild and scenic rivers system.

13. Will assist the awarding agency in assuring compliance with Section 106 of the National Historic Preservation Act of 1966, as amended (16 U.S.C. § 470), EO 11593 (identification and protection of historic properties), and the Archaeological and Historic Preservation Act of 1974 (16 U.S.C. §§ 469a-1 et seq.).

14. Will comply with P.L. 93–348 regarding the protection of human subjects involved in research, development, and related activities supported by this award of assistance.

15. Will comply with the Laboratory Animal Welfare Act of 1966 (P.L. 89–544, as amended, 7 U.S.C. §§ 2131 et seq.) pertaining to the care, handling, and treatment of warm blooded animals held for research, teaching, or other activities supported by this award of assistance.

16. Will comply with the Lead-Based Paint Poisoning Prevention Act (42 U.S.C. §§ 4801 et seq.) which prohibits the use of lead-based paint in construction or rehabilitation of residence structures.

17. Will cause to be performed the required financial and compliance audits in accordance with the Single Audit Act Amendments of 1996 and OMB Circular No. A-133, "Audits of States, Local Governments, and Non-Profit Organizations."

18. Will comply with all applicable requirements of all other Federal laws, executive orders, regulations, and policies governing this program.

* Signature of Authorized Certifying Official Completed on submission to Grants.gov.	* Title
* Applicant Organization	* Date Submitted Completed on submission to Grants.gov.

SF–424C

Budget Information—Construction Programs

Note: Certain Federal assistance programs require additional computations to arrive at the Federal share of project costs eligible for participation. If such is the case you will be notified.

Cost Classification	a. Total Cost	b. Costs Not Allowable for Participation	c. Total Allowable Costs (Column a–b)
1. Administrative and legal expenses	$ .00	$ .00	$ .00
2. Land, structures, rights-of-way, appraisals, etc.	$ .00	$ .00	$ .00
3. Relocation expenses and payments	$ .00	$ .00	$ .00
4. Architectural and engineering fees	$ .00	$ .00	$ .00
5. Other architectural and engineering fees	$ .00	$ .00	$ .00
6. Project inspection fees	$ .00	$ .00	$ .00
7. Site work	$ .00	$ .00	$ .00
8. Demolition and removal	$ .00	$ .00	$ .00
9. Construction	$ .00	$ .00	$ .00
10. Equipment	$ .00	$ .00	$ .00
11. Miscellaneous	$ .00	$ .00	$ .00
12. **Subtotal**	$ .00	$ .00	$ .00
13. Contingencies (Sum of lines 1–11)	$ .00	$ .00	$ .00
14. **Subtotal**	$ .00	$ .00	$ .00
15. Project (program) income	$ .00	$ .00	$ .00
16. **Total Project Costs** (Subtract #15 from #14)	$ .00	$ .00	$ .00

Federal Funding

17. Federal assistance requested, calculate as follows: Enter eligible costs from line 16c _____ Multiply x _____ %
(Consult Federal agency for Federal percentage share).
Enter the resulting Federal share. .... $ .00

SF-424C (continued)

Public reporting burden for this collection of information is estimated to average 3 hours per response, including the time for reviewing instructions, searching existing data sources, gathering and maintaining the data needed, and completing and reviewing the collection of information. Send comments regarding this burden estimate or any other aspect of this collection of information, including suggestions for reducing this burden to the Office of Management and Budget, Paperwork Reduction Project (0348–0041), Washington, D.C. 20503. Please do not return your completed form to the Office of Management and Budget; send it to the address provided by the sponsoring agency .

This sheet is to be used for the following types of applications: (1) "New" (means a new [previously unfunded] assistance award); (2) "Continuation" (means funding in a succeeding budget period which stemmed from a prior agreement to fund); and (3) "Revised" (means any changes in the Federal government's financial obligations or contingent liability from an existing obligation). If there is no change in the award amount there is no need to complete this form. Certain Federal agencies may require only an explanatory letter to effect minor (no cost) changes. If you have questions please contact the Federal agency.

Column a.— If this is an application for a "New" project, enter the total estimated cost of each of the items listed on lines 1 through 16 (as applicable) under " **Cost Classifications**."

If this application entails a change to an existing award, enter the eligible amounts **approved under the previous award** for the items under "**Cost Classification**."

Column b.—If this is an application for a "New" project, enter that portion of the cost of each item in Column a. which is **not** allowable for Federal assistance. Contact the Federal agency for assistance in determining the allowability of specific costs.

If this application entails a change to an existing award, enter the adjustment [+ or (–)] to the previously approved costs (from column a.) reflected in this application.

Column c.—This is the net of lines 1 through 16 in columns "a." and "b.". "

Line 1—Enter estimated amounts needed to cover administrative expenses. Do not include costs which are related to the normal functions of government. Allowable legal costs are generally only those associated with the purchase of land which is allowable for Federal participation and certain services in support of construction of the project.

Line 2—Enter estimated site and right(s)-of-way acquisition costs (this includes purchase, lease, and/or easements).

Line 3—Enter estimated costs related to relocation advisory assistance, replacement housing, relocation payments to displaced persons and businesses, etc.

Line 4—Enter estimated basic engineering fees related to construction (this includes start-up services and preparation of project performance work plan).

Line 5—Enter estimated engineering costs, such as surveys, tests, soil borings, etc.

Line 6—Enter estimated engineering inspection costs.

Line 7—Enter estimated costs of site preparation and restoration which are not included in the basic construction contract.

Line 9—Enter estimated cost of the construction contract.

Line 10—Enter estimated cost of office, shop, laboratory, safety equipment, etc. to be used at the facility, if such costs are not included in the construction contract.

Line 11—Enter estimated miscellaneous costs.

Line 12—Total of items 1 through 11.

Line 13—Enter estimated contingency costs. (Consult the Federal agency for the percentage of the estimated construction cost to use.)

Line 14—Enter the total of lines 12 and 13.

Line 15—Enter estimated program income to be earned during the grant period, e.g., salvaged materials, etc.

Line 16—Subtract line 15 from line 14.

Item 17—This block is for the computation of the Federal share. Multiply the total allowable project costs from line 16, column "c." by the Federal percentage share (this may be up to 100 percent; consult Federal agency for Federal percentage share) and enter the product on line 17.

SF–424D

ASSURANCES - CONSTRUCTION PROGRAMS

Public reporting burden for this collection of information is estimated to average 15 minutes per response, including time for reviewing instructions, searching existing data sources, gathering and maintaining the data needed, and completing and reviewing the collection of information. Send comments regarding the burden estimate or any other aspect of this collection of information, including suggestions for reducing this burden, to the Office of Management and Budget, Paperwork Reduction Project (0348–0042), Washington, DC 20503.

Please do not return your completed form to the Office of Management and Budget. Send it to the address provided by the sponsoring agency.

Note: Certain of these assurances may not be applicable to your project or program. If you have questions, please contact the Awarding Agency. Further, certain Federal assistance awarding agencies may require applicants to certify to additional assurances. If such is the case, you will be notified.

As the duly authorized representative of the applicant:, I certify that the applicant:

1. Has the legal authority to apply for Federal assistance, and the institutional, managerial and financial capability (including funds sufficient to pay the non-Federal share of project costs) to ensure proper planning, management and completion of project described in this application.

2. Will give the awarding agency, the Comptroller General of the United States and, if appropriate, the State, the right to examine all records, books, papers, or documents related to the assistance; and will establish a proper accounting system in accordance with generally accepted accounting standards or agency directives.

3. Will not dispose of, modify the use of, or change the terms of the real property title or other interest in the site and facilities without permission and instructions from the awarding agency. Will record the Federal awarding agency directives and will include a covenant in the title of real property acquired in whole or in part with Federal assistance funds to assure non-discrimination during the useful life of the project.

4. Will comply with the requirements of the assistance awarding agency with regard to the drafting, review and approval of construction plans and specifications.

5. Will provide and maintain competent and adequate engineering supervision at the construction site to ensure that the complete work conforms with the approved plans and specifications and will furnish progressive reports and such other information as may be required by the assistance awarding agency or State.

6. Will initiate and complete the work within the applicable time frame after receipt of approval of the awarding agency.

7. Will establish safeguards to prohibit employees from using their positions for a purpose that constitutes or presents the appearance of personal or organizational conflict of interest, or personal gain.

8. Will comply with the Intergovernmental Personnel Act of 1970 (42 U.S.C. §§ 4728–4763) relating to prescribed standards of merit systems for programs funded under one of the 19 statutes or regulations specified in Appendix A of OPM's Standards for a Merit System of Personnel Administration (5 C.F.R. 900, Subpart F).

9. Will comply with the Lead-Based Paint Poisoning Prevention Act (42 U.S.C. §§ 4801 et seq.) which prohibits the use of lead-based pain in construction or rehabilitation of residence structures.

10. Will comply with all Federal statutes relating to nondiscrimination. These include but are not limited to: (a) Title VI of the Civil Rights Act of 1964 (P.L. 88–352) which prohibits discrimination on the basis of race, color or national origin; (b) Title IX of the Education Amendments of 1972, as amended (20 U.S.C. §§1681–1683, and 1685–1686), which prohibits discrimination on the basis of sex; (c) Section 504 of the Rehabilitation Act of 1973, as amended (29) U.S.C.§ 794), which prohibits discrimination on the basis ofhandicaps; (d) the Age Discrimination Act of 1975, as amended (42 U.S.C. §§ 6101–6107), which prohibits discrimination on the basis of age; (e) the Drug Abuse Office and Treatment Act of 1972 (P.L. 92–255), as amended relating to nondiscrimination on the basis of drug abuse; (f) the Comprehensive Alcohol Abuse and Alcoholism Prevention, Treatment and Rehabilitation Act of 1970 (P.L. 91–616), as amended, relating to nondiscrimination on the basis of alcohol abuse or alcoholism; (g) §§ 523 and 527 of the Public Health Service Act of 1912 (42 U.S.C. §§ 290 dd-3 and 290 ee 3), as amended, relating to confidentiality of alcohol and drug abuse patient records, (h) Title VIII of the Civil Rights Act of 1968 (42 U.S.C. §§ 3601 et seq.), as amended, relating to nondiscrimination in the sale, rental or financing of housing; (i) any other nondiscrimination provisions in the specific statue(s) under which application for Federal assistance is being made; and (j) the requirements of any other nondiscrimination statue(s) which may apply to the application.

SF-424D (continued)

11. Will comply, or has already complied, with the requirements of Titles II and III of the Uniform Relocation Assistance and Real Property Acquisition Policies Act of 1970 (P.L. 91–646) which provide for fair and equitable treatment of persons displaced or whose property is acquired as a result of Federal and federally-assisted programs. These requirements apply to all interests in real property acquired for project purposes regardless of Federal participation in purchases.

12. Will comply with the provisions of the Hatch Act (5 U.S.C. §§ 1501–1508 and 7324–7328) which limit the political activities of employees whose principal employment activities are funded in whole or in part with Federal funds.

13. Will comply, as applicable, with the provisions of the Davis-Bacon Act (40 U.S.C. §§ 276a to 276a-7), the Copeland Act (40 U.S.C. § 276c and 18 U.S.C. § 874), and the Contract Work Hours and Safety Standards Act (40 U.S.C. §§ 327–333) regarding labor standards for federally-assisted construction subagreements.

14. Will comply with flood insurance purchase requirements of Section 102(a) of the Flood Disaster Protection Act of 1973 (P.L. 93–234) which requires recipients in a special flood hazard area to participate in the program and to purchase flood insurance if the total cost of insurable construction and acquisition is $10,000 or more.

15. Will comply with environmental standards which may be prescribed pursuant to the following: (a) institution of environmental quality control measures under the

National Environmental Policy Act of 1969 (P.L. 91–190) and Executive Order (EO) 11514; (b) notification of violating facilities pursuant to EO 11738; (c) protection of wetlands pursuant to EO 11990; (d) evaluation of flood hazards in floodplains in accordance with EO 11988; (e) assurance of project consistency with the approved State management program developed under the Coastal Zone Management Act of 1972 (16 U.S.C. §§ 1451 et seq.); (f) conformity of Federal actions to State (Clean Air) implementation Plans under Section 176(c) of the Clean Air Act of 1955, as amended (42 U.S.C. §§ 7401 et seq.); (g) protection of underground sources of drinking water under the Safe Drinking Water Act of 1974, as amended (P.L. 93–523); and, (h) protection of endangered species under the Endangered Species Act of 1973, as amended (P.L. 93–205).

16. Will comply with the Wild and Scenic Rivers Act of 1968 (16 U.S.C. §§ 1271 et seq.) related to protecting components or potential components of the national wild and scenic rivers system.

17. Will assist the awarding agency in assuring compliance with Section 106 of the National Historic Preservation Act of 1966, as amended (16 U.S.C. § 470), EO 11593 (identification and protection of historic properties), and the Archaeological and Historic Preservation Act of 1974 (16 U.S.C. §§ 469a-1 et seq).

18. Will cause to be performed the required financial and compliance audits in accordance with the Single Audit Act Amendments of 1996 and OMB Circular No. A-133, "Audits of States, Local Governments, and Non-Profit Organizations."

19. Will comply with all applicable requirements of all other Federal laws, executive orders, regulations, and policies governing this program.

* Signature of Authorized Certifying Official	* Title
Completed on submission to Grants.gov.	
* Applicant Organization	* Date Submitted
	Completed on submission to Grants.gov.

SF–LLL
_____

DISCLOSURE OF LOBBYING ACTIVITIES

Complete this form to disclose lobbying activities pursuant to 31 U.S.C.1352

| Review Public Burden Disclosure Statement |

1. * Type of Federal Action:	**2. * Status of Federal Action:**	**3. * Report Type:**
☐ a. Contract	☐ a. Bid/Offer/Application	☐ a. Initial Filing
☐ b. Grant	☐ b. Initial Award	☐ b. Material Change
☐ c. Cooperative Agreement	☐ c. Post-Award	
☐ d. Loan		
☐ e. Loan Guarantee		
☐ f. Loan Insurance		

4. Name and Address of Reporting Entity:

☐ Prime ☐ SubAwardee

* Name

* Street 1   Street 2

* City   State   Zip

Congressional District, if known:

5. If Reporting Entity in No.4 is SubAwardee, Enter Name and Address of Prime:

6. * Federal Department/Agency:

7. * Federal Program Name/Description:

CFDA Number, *if applicable:*

8. Federal Action Number, *if known:*

9. Award Amount (*if known*):

$

10. a. Name and Address of Lobbying Registrant:

Prefix   * First Name   Middle Name

* Last Name   Suffix

* Street 1   Street 2

* City   State   Zip

b. Individual Performing Services   (including address if different from No. 10a)

Prefix   * First Name   Middle Name

* Last Name   Suffix

* Street 1   Street 2

* City   State   Zip

11.

Information requested through this form is authorized by title 31 U.S.C. section 1352. This disclosure of lobbying activities is a material representation of fact upon which reliance was placed by the tier above when the transaction was made or entered into. This disclosure is required pursuant to 31 U.S.C. 1352. This information will be reported to the Congress semi-annually and will be available for public inspection. Any person who fails to file the required disclosure shall be subject to a civil penalty of not less than $10,000 and not more than $100,000 for each such failure.

* Signature: Completed on submission to Grants.gov.

*Name: Prefix   * First Name   Middle Name

* Last Name   Suffix

Title:

Telephone No.:

Date: Completed on submission to Grants.gov.

Federal Use Only:

National Science Foundation
Grant Application Cover Page

Please complete the following NSF forms in conjunction with the relevant Research and Related forms. If you are an organization or individual and you are not registered with NSF FastLane, please complete the Organization and Individual Registration Form in this package.

1. Funding Opportunity Number
*Funding Opportunity Number: [   ]   Opportunity closing date: [   ]

2. NSF Unit Consideration
Go to **https://www.fastlane.nsf.gov/pgmannounce.jsp** and follow the instructions to find the Division and Program information for this funding opportunity.

*Division Code: [   ]   Division Name: [   ]
*Program Code: [   ]   Program Name: [   ]

3. Principal Investigator (PI) Information
*Degree Type: [   ]   *Degree Year: [   ]

[ ]   Check here if you are currently serving (or have previously served) as a PI, co-PI or Program Director (PD) on any Federally funded project.

4. Co-Principal Investigator (co-PI) Information

NSF applications can identify a maximum of four co-Principal Investigators. Please enter below the co-PI information exactly as entered on the Research and Related Senior/Key Person form.

co-PI 1
Prefix: [   ]   *First Name: [   ]   Middle Name: [   ]   *Last Name: [   ]   Suffix: [   ]
*Degree Type: [   ]   *Degree Year: [   ]

co-PI 2
Prefix: [   ]   *First Name: [   ]   Middle Name: [   ]   *Last Name: [   ]   Suffix: [   ]
*Degree Type: [   ]   *Degree Year: [   ]

co-PI 3
Prefix: [   ]   *First Name: [   ]   Middle Name: [   ]   *Last Name: [   ]   Suffix: [   ]
*Degree Type: [   ]   *Degree Year: [   ]

co-PI 4
Prefix: [   ]   *First Name: [   ]   Middle Name: [   ]   *Last Name: [   ]   Suffix: [   ]
*Degree Type: [   ]   *Degree Year: [   ]

5. Other Information

Check Appropriate Box (es) if this proposal includes any of the items listed below.

[ ] Beginning Investigator (Grant Proposal Guide (GPG), Chapter I.A)   [ ] Disclosure of Lobbying Activities (GPG, Chapter II.C.1.e)

[ ] Small Grants for Exploratory Research (GPG, Chapter II.D.1)   [ ] Historic Places (GPG, Chapter II.C.2.j)

[ ] Accomplishment-Based Renewal (GPG, Chapter V.B.2)   [ ] High Resolution Graphics/Other Graphics Where Exact Color Representation Is Required For Proper Interpretation (GPG, Chapter I.G.1)

6. Additional Single-Copy Documents   Attach PDF Files

CHAPTER 7

Submitting Your Grant

The search for funding opportunities is discussed at length in Chapter 2, and grant seekers learned to review program descriptions and RFPs to ascertain information of use at various stages in the grant writing and submission processes. Budget requirements—allowable costs, anticipated award amounts, and match requirements—figure into our program budgets in Chapter 4. Program requirements and rating factors presented in the *Federal Register* notices provide a framework for our narrative descriptions in Chapter 5. Requirements for forms that are required to be submitted with the application packet are discussed in Chapter 6. This chapter focuses on developing an effective plan for coordinating, compiling, and submitting the completed grant application in accordance with the agency requirements given in RFPs and program requirements. As with other components, funding agencies and foundations specify instructions for submitting grant proposals, and attention to detail in this area will be rewarded. Whereas there are hundreds of wrong ways to go about submitting a grant, there is usually only one correct way. Of course the exception proves the rule: the National Science Foundation, for example, accommodates applications submitted through its own FastLane system as well as the Grants.gov system. For most agencies and programs, there will be only one correct method of submitting your completed grant.

In devising a system to ensure timely and complete submission of your grant application in accordance with agency requirements and deadlines, it is essential to have a plan in place. There are several questions that should be addressed prior to proceeding. Many small organizations lack systems and rules to govern grant-related activities. On the other hand, there are numerous large, hierarchical organizations that do have formal systems, rules, and regulations governing grant submission. It is important to realize into which category your organization falls because the responsibility of submitting the completed grant application may be assumed to accrue to the grant writer, or the grant writer may be explicitly prohibited from submitting an application. Universities and other large organizations often have a separate office with staff specializing in grant submission and other related activities. These individuals not only have roles and responsibilities that will affect your submission, but they also present additional red tape. Red tape (Bozeman 2000) is not all bad. Much like grant conditions serve an ultimate public purpose, despite the frustrations they cause, red tape may also serve an ultimate organizational purpose. In the university setting (and there is no universally compatible model), numerous offices may require time to review your proposal before it can be officially submitted. For example, the proposal may be reviewed for conflicts of interest, it may be reviewed to ensure the protection of human subjects, and of course, grants officers may read through your proposal for technical errors in need of repair. Each of these steps serves a valuable purpose.

Centralized grant offices provide additional functions in the form of internal coordination and specialization. An organization as large as a university or a city (some have tens of thousands of employees) may submit grants daily to various agencies. Repetition of familiar tasks ensures accuracy and minimizes technical errors during the submission process. Another significant role these offices play is reduction or elimination of duplicate proposals. Many programs limit each organization to only one application in a given competition, so the centralized office prohibits inadvertent duplicate submissions by two unrelated persons or organizational divisions.

Which organization are you, and how does it affect you? The burden of responsibility is always on the grant writer or team to ensure timely completion of the application materials. The difference is that if you are required to submit the grant application yourself, you must plan accordingly and allow sufficient time to do so without error. If, on the other hand, you rely on a specialized individual to submit grants on your behalf, your burden is in the form of an earlier deadline imposed by that individual to allow him or her time to process it according to internal agency policy and procedures. You also bear the burden of coordinating with that person to arrive at a deadline and to transfer all materials in the appropriate format. So, whatever the case, there is responsibility attached, and experienced grant writers learn to anticipate and fulfill such requirements, however they may be structured within their organizations.

If the burden is on you, you must take several additional steps to prepare for the submission process. Chief among them is identifying the submission method. If you are submitting to a foundation with no firm deadlines, this is not important. But if you are trying to ensure that the proposal is received in time for a quarterly board meeting, then you should be aware of your submission options and use them to plan accordingly.

Most grants submitted in paper format—though it is becoming a feature of the past—are dispatched via overnight courier because they guarantee on-time delivery and they provide proof of delivery and delivery time that can be used to substantiate any misunderstandings between the submitter and the receiver. If you are using Grants.gov to submit, then you should allow ample time for problems to occur. Electronic submission, though quick and efficient, is also unreliable. If all applicants waited until the last moment before a deadline to submit their application, the increased traffic may consume bandwidth or server capacity and lead to a short, but very costly delay. Never wait until the last possible moment to submit your grant. If you do, it is best to plan your electronic submission to occur the evening prior to the due date or the morning of the due date at the latest to allow for any unforeseen errors. This provides time to both reattempt your submission and to inform agency staff of the problem.

In no business or endeavor is Murphy's Law more relevant than that of grant writing and submission. If you are making the required number of copies, the copier will jam and run out of toner on the same day. You will arrive at the courier drop box only to find that it has been relocated. Leading up to an electronic submission, your computer will freeze or even delete the files you intend to submit. In short, if it can go wrong, it most likely will. Or, the more cynical version of that law holds that the worst possible thing that can happen will happen, and at the worst possible time. For those superstitious readers, it may be considered bad luck or even a bad omen. It is probably just a function of the hurried nature of a grant completion under pressure from an impending deadline. Perhaps it is the time-sensitive nature of the entire venture, or perhaps it is the limited capacity of the human mind to readily attend to and integrate every detail. Whatever the case, it is an immutable fact that if it can go wrong, it will. Reality is that all contingencies can't be planned for, so a grant submission schedule requires some degree of flexibility. Because deadlines hold hard and fast, any flexibility to be attained must be facilitated by planning to complete the grant sooner than it is due. My recommendation is that you use planning to prevent falling victim to your own weaknesses and faults, especially the cognitive bias of overconfidence (Bazerman 2006). Everyone procrastinates sometimes, but limiting the extent to which that is possible will save great frustration.

If you are using Grants.gov for the first time, you should additionally be aware that you must first register with the system—a process that may take several days. You should tend to these concerns well in advance of the application deadline. In fact, it is best to set these steps into motion prior to developing the proposal. Experience has taught that precious last moments are usually devoted to correcting and improving proposals, leaving no time or patience to simultaneously struggle with the submission portal and related technical issues. As noted in Chapter 6, even after all of the program narrative information and budget are complete, there are still forms to complete and upload. There is just no time available to become frustrated by the submission system.

REVERSE PLANNING AND ORGANIZATION

So, how should one plan for submission? As noted, the calendar must be developed through reverse planning beginning with the final moment the agency or foundation will receive your proposal for consideration. It is very logical to plan backward in this fashion. We do it every day in our jobs and in our classes, seeing that papers are done on time and that projects are complete before their deadlines. To arrive at work on time, we calculate the amount of time it will take to get there, allowing for trouble, to determine the latest possible time of departure. The same principle applies, and it should feel very familiar to do so. However, unlike such personal tasks, when working as a grant team our planning must allow for coordination among various actors working together to compile assorted components of the proposal. Table 7.1 contains, in reverse logical order, a series of components that might be scheduled to ensure timely submission.

Developing a time line and a work plan like this one takes very little time. What can only be learned from experience is estimating how much time should be set aside for each of the component stages in the proposal development and submission process. Some proposals are longer than others, some are more complicated, and some involve broader partnerships. Even the most experienced grant writer will underestimate the time certain steps take, and as already noted, no one can plan for all possible contingencies. That is why it is a good idea to build in sufficient flexibility to allow some give-and-take when the pieces do not come together at the precise moment you anticipated that they would. Implementation always differs from the best-laid plans.

TABLE 7.1   Example of a Presubmission Workplan and Time Line

Example Date	*Activity*
6/15/2007	Agency Deadline
6/13/2007	Faux Deadline
6/13/2007	Electronic Submission
6/12/2007	[Submission via overnight courier]
6/11/2007	Signatures
6/4/2007	Institutional Routing Deadline
6/1/2007	Cover Letter Composed
6/1/2007	Forms Completed
6/1/2007	Proposal Finalized
5/31/2007	Proposal Components Integrated
5/30/2007	Proposal Components Collected from Team Members
5/7/2007	Budget Completed
5/7/2007	Letters of Support Received
4/30/2007	Application Components Assigned to Team Members
4/30/2007	Proposed Program and Partners Agreed
4/16/2007	Forms Reviewed and Relevant Information Obtained
4/6/2007	Registration with Grants.gov Completed
4/2/2007	Application Packet Downloaded
4/2/2007	Download PureEdge Viewer Software from Grants.gov
4/2/2007	Registration with Grants.gov Initiated
4/2/2007	Funding Opportunity Identified

With a work plan in place, there is one simple rule that applies to each and every grant submission you will ever attempt: pay attention to the guidelines and follow the funder's rules for formatting, compiling, copying, and delivering, to the letter. RFPs and grant proposal guidelines are detailed for a reason—the details matter to the funder. The better you are able to make your proposal fit those guidelines, the better chance your application has of being reviewed and funded.

Many funders will not consider proposals that fail to meet their submission requirements, including even something as simple as the correct number of copies submitted. Is any component of your proposal prohibited from being included? If so, it should be cut. Is there any required item you have neglected to include? If so, it should be included. Does the funder require printed materials to appear only in black and white? If so, your color copies should be replaced. If they do not specify, each of your copies should appear as the original in full color to portray your application in the best possible light with each of its potential readers. Should the materials be stapled? Or should they be bound with clips? Or perhaps the funder prefers to receive them loose. It is incumbent upon the grant writer or responsible team member to follow these rules.

One characteristic of submission guidelines that should never be overlooked is the time and date due. Most readers will have already ascertained these data's importance in the discussion of reverse planning. However, many will overlook the fact that times may mean different things to different people. Does the time refer to the funder's time zone, the applicant's, or a specific time zone? Grants.gov allows most programs to be submitted by 5:00 P.M. on the deadline date according to the submitter's local time, for example. This is one detail that should certainly be noticed, and if the requirements are not clear, it would be wise to inquire of the program officer.

The rules and guidelines provided usually do not affect the content of the proposal in any meaningful way, but your organization's response to them makes an impression on the funder. Of course, the first impression is the most important. This process tells them how conscientious your organization is in attending to detail and how much effort you put into the tasks you perform. Many funders have a specific address to which grant proposals should be addressed, or have different addresses for use depending on the method you utilize to convey the packet. You should make sure you have addressed your completed packet to the correct location according to the funder's preferences and the means of delivery selected. The list and discussion of such details could easily extend many pages, but this brief list should readily demonstrate the sort of details to which you must attend during the submission process and the essential nature of following the rules provided without the slightest deviation.

Following are a few basic rules to follow in preparing a grant for submission:

1. Begin early.
2. Know the rules. Follow the rules. Do not deviate from the rules.
3. Plan ahead with a calendar; set firm deadlines.
4. Plan to submit early; allow flexibility for problems.
5. Submit only using the method prescribed by the funder.
6. Given a choice, overnight couriers offer speed, a more precise guarantee of on-time delivery, and superior tracking options.
7. Know your own organization's rules and structure before beginning.
8. Be sure to maintain copies of complete application materials on file.
9. Always seek delivery confirmation.
10. Be prepared to take the blame for anything that goes wrong, strive to prevent things from going wrong, and document your efforts in doing so.

Following these rules will help you to maintain your sanity during the crunch that grant applications can create. Although I have limited my discussion so far to the idea that grant applications are singular occurrences, bounded by finite constraints defined by the writer's preferences, the process is rarely so neat and simple. Professional grant seekers work simultaneously on multiple projects and require superior organizational skills and self-motivation to manage their time and responsibilities effectively. Rather than one simple calendar that might be used by a grant seeker in a small organization to pursue one grant, grants teams in grant offices usually find it advisable to compile one master calendar for the group that includes all of the application projects simultaneously being developed. Planning ahead, negotiating roles, and allowing flexibility for pieces that are late make the process a little smoother and help to reduce conflict and frustration. Working as a team means that tempers have to be kept in check under even the most strenuous pressure.

Having a process and following the rules are the two essential components to preparing a grant submission. Foundations may accept applications via mail or electronically. Some may have formal submission requirements while others are more informal. The breadth of foundations and their application procedures is far too broad to attend to in this chapter, or in any book, and doing so would only lead back to that which I have already stated: a grant writer must follow the rules set out by the funder for submission.

Government grants are much more standardized as a result of the Grants.gov system implementation, so a discussion of that system is warranted. Within only a few years of its inauguration, Grants.gov has experienced rapid growth and processes an ever-increasing number of federal grant applications on behalf of the agencies it serves. Grants.gov went online for the first time in October 2003 (Grants.gov 2007d). It has grown from 17 agencies and 1,140 submissions in its first year, to 26 agencies with more than 90,000 submissions in 2006, and 101,281 grant submissions received in the first 8 months of fiscal year 2007 (Grants.gov 2007d). The 26 federal agencies participating in Grants.gov are listed in **Table 7.2**. Seekers of federal funds must become familiar with this system.

TABLE 7.2   Twenty-Six Federal Agencies' Grant Opportunities Available via Grants.gov

Agency for International Development
Corporation for National and Community Service
Department of Agriculture
Department of Commerce
Department of Defense
Department of Education
Department of Energy
Department of Health and Human Services
Department of Homeland Security
Department of Housing and Urban Development
Department of the Interior
Department of Justice
Department of Labor
Department of State
Department of Transportation
Department of the Treasury
Department of Veterans Affairs
Environmental Protection Agency
Institute of Museum and Library Services
National Aeronautics and Space Administration
National Archives and Records Administration
National Endowment for the Arts
National Endowment for the Humanities
National Science Foundation
Small Business Administration
Social Security Administration

Adapted from: Grants.gov 2007a.

USING GRANTS.GOV

Before exploring the intricacies of Grants.gov and its submission process, permit me a moment of nostalgic reflection on the days prior to the advent of electronic submission. In the old days, before Grants.gov, federal grants had to be submitted in paper form, often with multiple copies. Electronic systems came about for a number of reasons. First of all, paper delivery takes time, whereas electronic submission is virtually instantaneous. Electronic submission is costless to the submitter, whereas paper submissions required postage or courier fees. Paper takes up tremendous amounts of space while digital submissions take up less space than the head of a pin, more or less. Paper is heavy but data are light. And, perhaps one of the more important aspects of the shift, packages shipped in the mail and via courier can be used to transmit hazardous materials, such as anthrax, that cannot be transmitted electronically. A program officer for the Appalachian Regional Commission once joked with me that my agency's application had been received, and that it was "nice and crispy" from the irradiation process to which it had been subjected. So, electronic submission eliminates the need to irradiate mailed grant applications prior to passing them on to the program officers. An added benefit is that it is possible to back up data in electronic format much more easily and with greater accuracy than data provided on paper.

The submission of federal grant applications in the days of print submission included careful organization of each piece of the application (cover letter, SF-424, SF-424A, SF-424B, Executive Summary, Narrative, Budget, Budget Narrative, Miscellaneous Forms, Letters of Support, and Appendices of other related information) into one massive packet, stamping the original copy with page numbers using a mechanical numbering machine, and then standing over the application packet as it fed into a photocopier piece by piece to ensure that it did not contain errors. These copies were then stamped with self-inking stamps as "original," "copy" (as many as needed), and "file," and then inspected once again for errors before being frantically driven to the courier receiving location with the latest open office hours.

Electronic submission eliminates all of the time associated with these activities because no duplication has to occur. No hurried driving is necessary. The packet is organized automatically by the system. Submitting your proposal through Grants.gov is as easy as falling down a set of stairs. In Chapter 2, I advocated beginning the search for federal funding elsewhere because Grants.gov doesn't provide the comprehensive picture of available federal funds that can be found in the Catalog of Federal Domestic Assistance. When it comes to submitting the grant application, however, Grants.gov performs its task quite well—as it should because it is now the only means of submitting grants for most federal agencies.

Anyone can use Grants.gov to search, review, and even download funding opportunities, but to actually submit a grant application requires registration. Most readers new to grant seeking would come to Grants.gov after identifying an available federal funding announcement and then reading about its detailed requirements in the *Federal Register*, which indicates the availability of the application packet there and the requirement that the grant be submitted through the Grants.gov portal. After searching the funding opportunities section of the website, the grant seeker locates the desired program application packet. To access the program guidelines through Grants.gov a user can click the Full Announcement link on any individual program announcement page. To download the application packet, however, it is first necessary to download the PureEdge Viewer software that displays the application material and manages form completion and submission. The software can be installed free of charge by browsing to this link: http://www.grants.gov/PEViewer/ICSViewer602_grants.exe. Grants.gov is currently in the process of eliminating PureEdge documents in favor of more common file formats.

Once the PureEdge Viewer software is installed, clicking the How to Apply link on any program announcement page will take you to the application download page. Clicking the Download link under the heading Instructions and Application then opens a new window for the program application packet. This window offers the option of entering your e-mail address to be informed of any changes that may be made to the program announcement of interest prior to its closing date. In Grants.gov, *closing date* refers to the program deadline, which is the point at which the portal closes and refuses to accept program applications. Anyone who has worked with federal government grants knows all too well that program announcements are frequently altered, and it is fairly common for deadlines to be extended as well. It would be very wise to permit the system to notify you of any changes if you intend to submit an application.

Other than the e-mail option, this window offers you two options for download: the application instructions and the application package. Clicking the instructions link opens the program application instructions. Clicking the application package link automatically starts the software and loads the desired application packet interface, allowing you to complete forms and upload and save components of your application. This process can be completed offline and saved for submission through the Grants.gov portal when complete.

Before proceeding with the application process, however, it is wise first to register with Grants.gov as an organization and as an authorized organization representative (AOR; whether this is you or some other organizational representative), and then seek authorization as an AOR by your organization. These three steps must occur prior to being able to submit a grant application through the portal. Why should you start so early? If you're not already registered, there are several pieces of information that can add to the basic delay of registering. To register the organization with Grants.gov, you must secure the following items (Grants.gov 2007c):

1. *DUNS number.* As you discovered in Chapter 6, the DUNS number is required on the SF-424. If you do not have a number, it can be obtained by visiting http://fedgov .dnb.com/webform and requesting one. This is complete the day it is requested.
2. *Central Contractor Registry (CCR) registration.* This step requires an authorizing official to register the organization as a federal contractor by visiting http://www.ccr.gov. This step may take 2 days to complete.
3. *ORC credentials.* Operational Research Consultants (ORC) provides credentials (username and password) for Grants.gov users. To register, you must have the DUNS number and be registered as a federal contractor. To obtain credentials for your organization, visit http://apply.grants.gov/OrcRegister. This process is completed the day of the request.
4. *Grants.gov registration.* Using the ORC credentials, you must register with Grants.gov by entering the provided username and password on the login page https://apply .grants.gov/ApplicantLoginGetID. This takes approximately 1 day.

5. *EPOC Response.* The Grants.gov system protects applicant organizations from individuals submitting grants on their behalf by establishing contact with the authorized e-business point of contact. This person is notified by e-mail when Grants.gov registration is complete, and he or she must log on to Grants.gov and designate you as an authorized organizational representative (AOR). This will enable you to submit grant applications through the portal. It is possible to designate multiple AORs for the same organization. This process takes an additional 1 to 2 days to complete.

You should be able to see how complicated this process can be for first-time applicant users. The good news is that upon completing the registration process, it never has to be repeated, so for subsequent grant applications you will need only your username and password. You will also want to ensure that your AOR status continues in force because an authorized organizational representative can make changes to the designated AORs within the organization.

Grants.gov offers a specific set of instructions for preparing and submitting your grant application in four steps. The details of each step are presented in Figures 7.1 through 7.4. These steps include downloading the application package (**Figure 7.1**), completing the application package (**Figure 7.2**), submitting the application package (**Figure 7.3**), and tracking the status of your application (**Figure 7.4**). The system is, as noted previously, quite user-friendly. It prevents errors of oversight, it checks spelling, and it allows you to submit an application only when all of the required pieces are complete. For first-time users, the online narrated tutorial presented in Figure 7.2 may be a very useful place to start familiarizing yourself with the system.

In the way of final thoughts and suggestions, as the deadline for your program approaches, you should visit Grants.gov to check for important alert messages regarding system downtime for maintenance or holidays that might affect your submission plans.

Step 1: Download a Grant Application Package. (https://apply.grants.gov/forms_apps_idx.html)

- Downloading a grant application package allows you to complete it offline and route it through your organization for review before submitting.

- You will need the Funding Opportunity Number (FON) and/or CFDA number of the desired grant. (http://www.grants.gov/applicants/find_grant_opportunities.jsp)

- To view the downloaded application package, you will need to install the PureEdge Viewer (Windows EXE File) (http://www.grants.gov/PEViewer/ICSViewer602_grants.exe). There are basic system requirements for using the PureEdge Viewer. If you are a non-Windows user, please refer to the support page (http://www.grants.gov/resources/download_software.jsp).

FIGURE 7.1   Steps Required to Download a Grant Application Package from Grants.gov
Adapted from: Grants.gov 2007b.

Step 2: Complete the Grant Application Package.

- Now that you have finished step 1, complete the grant application offline.

- Instructions on how to open and use the forms in the package are on the application package cover sheet. You will also have access to agency application instructions, which will include what is required for your submission.

- Save changes to your application as you go. Grants.gov does *not* automatically save changes.

- The package cannot be submitted until all required fields have been completed.

- View a narrated tutorial on how to complete a grant application package (http://www.grants.gov/images/Application_Package.swf).

- If you are having problems completing the package, view the Frequently Asked Questions page (http://www.grants.gov/help/applicant_faqs.jsp).

FIGURE 7.2   Steps Required to Complete a Grant Application Package from Grants.gov
Adapted from: Grants.gov 2007b.

Step 3: Submit the Completed Grant Application Package.

- Click the Submit button located at the top of the application package cover page. It will not be live until you have:
  - Completed all required forms
  - Attached all required documents
  - Saved your application package

- If the Submit button is active and you are still unable to submit the application, make sure that your computer meets the system requirements (http://www.grants.gov/applicants/system_requirement.html) and you have the latest version of the PureEdge Viewer (http://www.grants.gov/PEViewer/ICSViewer602_grants.exe).

- Review the summary to confirm the application will be submitted to the correct program. Click Yes if this information is correct.

- If you are not already connected to the Internet, you will be directed to do so and will need to log in to Grants.gov using your username and password.

- After you have clicked the Sign and Submit button on the summary page, your application package will automatically be uploaded to Grants.gov.

- A confirmation screen will appear once the upload is complete. A Grants.gov tracking number will be provided at the bottom of this screen, as well as the submission's official date and time. Record the tracking number so that you may refer to it should you need to contact Grants.gov for support (http://www.grants.gov/contactus/contactus.jsp).

- If you are using a dial-up modem, it may take several minutes for the application to upload and be submitted. A high-speed Internet connection or DSL connection will process the application much faster.

FIGURE 7.3   Steps Required to Submit a Grant Application Through Grants.gov
Adapted from: Grants.gov 2007b.

Step 4: Track the Status of a Submitted Grant Application Package.

- Once your application has been submitted, you can check the status on the Track Your Application page (http://www.grants.gov/applicants/track_your_application.jsp). You can identify your application by CFDA number, Funding Opportunity Number, Competition ID, and/or Grants.gov tracking number.

FIGURE 7.4   Tracking the Status of a Grant Application Through Grants.gov
Adapted from: Grants.gov 2007b.

ALTERNATIVE SUBMISSION SCHEMES

Not all agencies or programs are alike, and consequently, many of them utilize a variation on the traditional application process. Agency requirements differ. Some discretionary programs may be filtered through a formal preapplication process whereas others are left to open competition. Two common categories of differences are of note: preapplications and notifications of intent to apply. A mandatory preapplication simply means that there are two stages to the application process, and that a preapplication must be submitted prior to an initial deadline and the final application must be completed and submitted by a second, later deadline. Preapplications typically mean that the full application stage is open only to preapplicants who are invited to submit full applications. This technique is used to weed out less appropriate applicants and is a courtesy to applicants for very large programs that require extensive data collection and lengthy narratives in that they are not subjected to an arduous application process for a competition in which they are not likely to prevail. Preapplications may be required to be sent first to a local or state office of the federal agency before a full application is forwarded to the national program office to allow feedback and initial eligibility assessment.

The *notice of intent to apply* may be mandatory or optional. In either case, it is intended to assist the agency's planning efforts by estimating how many applications it can expect to receive. This requirement may serve a second, and very important, purpose because it limits competition to applicants that demonstrate that they have been aware of the program for a particular length of time, allowing adequate time for proposal preparation.

NOTIFICATION OF THE STATE SINGLE POINT OF CONTACT

The final consideration to keep in mind regarding federal grant proposal submissions is the *state single point of contact* (SPOC) designated under Executive Order 12372 that was introduced in Chapter 1 (see Figure 1.4). Four questions must be clarified in figuring out whether you should send a copy of your proposal to your state for review:

1. Does the grant program to which I am applying require intergovernmental (EO 12372) review?
2. Does my state participate? Does my state have a designated SPOC?

3. Has my state SPOC designated the program to which I am applying as eligible for review?

4. What are my state's rules and guidelines for submission?

It makes no sense to submit a copy of your application if it is not necessary. Question 1 can be answered by reviewing the program announcements in the *Federal Register*; it will provide information about whether the grant program requires review. If it does not, then this consideration is moot. Question 2 can be answered by reviewing the current list of participating state SPOCs (**Figure 7.5**). If your state is not on the list, this consideration is moot.

ARKANSAS	**CALIFORNIA**
Tracy L. Copeland	Grants Coordination
Manager, State Clearinghouse	State Clearinghouse
Office of Intergovernmental Services	Office of Planning and Research
Department of Finance and Admin.	P.O. Box 3044, Room 222
1515 W. 7th Street, Room 412	Sacramento, CA 95812-3044
Little Rock, AR 72203	Telephone: (916) 445-0613
Telephone: (501) 682-1074	Fax: (916) 323-3018
Fax: (501) 682-5206	state.clearinghouse@opr.ca.gov
tracy.copeland@dfa.state.ar.us	
DELAWARE	**DISTRICT OF COLUMBIA**
Jennifer L. Carlson	Marlene Jefferson
Associate Fiscal and Policy Analyst	DC Government Office of Partnerships
Office of Management and Budget	and Grants Development
Budget Development, Planning and	441 4th Street, NW
Administration	Washington, DC 20001
Haslet Armory, Third Floor	Telephone: (202) 727-6518
122 William Penn Street	Fax: (202) 727-1652
Dover, DE 19901	marlene.jefferson@dc.gov
Telephone: (302) 739-4206	
Fax: (302) 739-5661	
jennifer.carlson@state.de.us	
FLORIDA	**GEORGIA**
Lauren P. Milligan	Barbara Jackson
Florida State Clearinghouse	Georgia State Clearinghouse
Florida Department of Environmental Protection	270 Washington Street, SW, 8th Floor
3900 Commonwealth Boulevard	Atlanta, GA 30334
Mail Station 47	Telephone: (404) 656-3855
Tallahassee, FL 32399-3000	Fax: (404) 656-7916
Telephone: (850) 245-2161	gach@mail.opb.state.ga.us
Fax: (850) 245-2190	
lauren.milligan@dep.state.fl.us	

FIGURE 7.5   List of States Participating in EO 12372 Intergovernmental Review and SPOCs

Source: U.S. Government 2008.

ILLINOIS	IOWA
Roukaya McCaffrey Department of Commerce and Economic Opportunities 620 East Adams, 6th Floor Springfield, IL 62701 Telephone: (217) 524-0188 Fax: (217) 558-0473 roukaya_mccaffrey@illinoisbiz.biz	Kathy Mabie Iowa Department of Management State Capitol Building Room G12 1007 E Grand Avenue Des Moines, IA 50319 Telephone: (515) 281-8834 Fax: (515) 242-5897 kathy.mabie@iowa.gov
KENTUCKY	MAINE
Ron Cook The Governor's Office for Local Development 1024 Capital Center Drive, Suite 340 Frankfort, KY 40601 Telephone: (502) 573-2382 / (800) 346-5606 Fax: (502) 573-2512 ron.cook@ky.gov	Joyce Benson State Planning Office 184 State Street 38 State House Station Augusta, ME 04333 Telephone: (207) 287-3261 (direct) (207) 287-1461 Fax: (207) 287-6489 joyce.benson@state.me.us
MARYLAND	MICHIGAN
Linda C. Janey, JD Director, Maryland State Clearinghouse For Intergovernmental Assistance 301 West Preston Street, Room 1104 Baltimore, MD 21201-2305 Telephone: (410) 767-4490 Fax: (410) 767-4480 ljaney@mdp.state.md.us	William Parkus Southeast Michigan Council of Governments 535 Griswold, Suite 300 Detroit, MI 48226 Telephone: (313) 961-4266 Fax: (313) 961-4869 parkus@semcog.org
MISSISSIPPI	MISSOURI
Janet Riddell Clearinghouse Officer Department of Finance and Administration 1301 Woolfolk Building, Suite E 501 North West Street Jackson, MS 39201 Telephone: (601) 359-6762 Fax: (601) 359-6758 jriddell@dfa.state.ms.us	Sara VanderFeltz Federal Assistance Clearinghouse Office of Administration Commissioner's Office Capitol Building, Room 125 Jefferson City, MO 65102 Telephone: (573) 751-0337 Fax: (573) 751-1212 sara.vanderfeltz@oa.mo.gov

FIGURE 7.5   (Continued)

NEVADA	**NEW HAMPSHIRE**
Zofia Targosz Department of Administration Nevada State Clearinghouse Coordinator/SPOC 209 E. Musser Street, Room 200 Carson City, NV 89701 Telephone: (775) 684-0209 Fax: (775) 684-0260 clearinghouse@budget.state.nv.us	Jack Ruderman Acting Director, New Hampshire Office of Energy and Planning Attn: Intergovernmental Review Process James P. Taylor 57 Regional Drive Concord, NH 03301-8519 Telephone: (603) 271-2155 Fax: (603) 271-2615 irp@nh.gov
NEW YORK	**NORTH DAKOTA**
Linda Shkreli Office of Public Security Homeland Security Grants Coordination 633 3rd Avenue New York, NY 10017 Telephone: (212) 867-1289 Fax: (212) 867-1725	Jim Boyd ND Department of Commerce 1600 East Century Avenue, Suite 2 P.O. Box 2057 Bismarck, ND 58502-2057 Telephone: (701) 328-2676 Fax: (701) 328-2308 jboyd@state.nd.us
RHODE ISLAND	**SOUTH CAROLINA**
Joyce Karger Department of Administration One Capitol Hill Providence, RI 02908-5870 Telephone: (401) 222-6181 Fax: (401) 222-2083 jkarger@doa.state.ri.us	Jean Ricard Office of State Budget 1201 Main Street, Suite 870 Columbia, SC 29201 Telephone: (803) 734-1314 Fax: (803) 734-0645 jricard@budget.sc.gov
TEXAS	**UTAH**
Denise S. Francis Director, State Grants Team Governor's Office of Budget and Planning P.O. Box 12428 Austin, TX 78711 Telephone: (512) 305-9415 Fax: (512) 936-2681 grants@governor.state.tx.us	Sophia DiCaro Utah State Clearinghouse Governor's Office of Planning and Budget Utah State Capitol Complex Suite E210, PO Box 142210 Salt Lake City, UT 84114-2210 Telephone: (801) 538-1027 Fax: (801) 538-1547 sdicaro@utah.gov

FIGURE 7.5   (Continued)

WEST VIRGINIA	WISCONSIN
Bobby Lewis, Director Community Development Division West Virginia Development Office Building #6, Room 553 Charleston, WV 25305 Telephone: (304) 558-4010 Fax: (304) 558-3248 rlewis@wvdo.org	Division of Intergovernmental Relations Wisconsin Department of Administration 101 East Wilson Street, 10th Floor P.O. Box 8944 Madison, WI 53708 Telephone: (608) 266-7043 Fax: (608) 267-6917 spoc@doa.state.wi.us
AMERICAN SAMOA	**GUAM**
Pat M.Galea'i Federal Grants/Programs Coordinator Office of Federal Programs Office of the Governor Department of Commerce American Samoa Government Pago Pago, American Samoa 96799 Telephone: (684) 633-5155 Fax: (684) 633-4195 pmgaleai@samoatelco.com	Director Bureau of Budget and Management Research Office of the Governor P.O. Box 2950 Agana, Guam 96910 Telephone: 011-671-472-2285 Fax: 011-472-2825 jer@ns.gov.gu
NORTH MARIANA ISLANDS	**PUERTO RICO**
Ms. Jacoba T. Seman Federal Programs Coordinator Office of Management and Budget Office of the Governor Saipan, MP 96950 Telephone: (670) 664-2289 Fax: (670) 664-2272 omb.jseman@saipan.com	Jose Caballero/Mayra Silva Puerto Rico Planning Board Federal Proposals Review Office Minillas Government Center P.O. Box 41119 San Juan, Puerto Rico 00940-1119 Telephone: (787) 723-6190 Fax: (787) 722-6783
VIRGIN ISLANDS	
Ira Mills Director, Office of Management and Budget 41 Norre Gade Emancipation Garden Station, Second Floor Saint Thomas, Virgin Islands 00802 Telephone: (340) 774-0750 Fax: (340) 776-0069 lrmills@usvi.org	

FIGURE 7.5   (Continued)

(Please note that the list does change from time to time, and you should consult the Office of Management and Budget's website for current information.) Questions 3 and 4 require you to contact your SPOC (if your state has one) to learn which programs they review and how you should submit your application to them for the intergovernmental review process. About half of the states currently participate in the intergovernmental review process.

CONCLUSION

This chapter has presented a review of the key considerations that affect not only submitting grant applications, but the process of organizing and planning in advance to confront the deadlines and obstacles that present themselves as you proceed. This chapter concludes the second section of the book focused on developing and submitting grant applications to viable funding sources for your program. The key requirement of any grant submission is simply to follow the rules, detailed though they may be.

REFERENCES

Bazerman, Max J. 2006. *Judgment in Managerial Decision Making, 6th Edition.* Hoboken, NJ: John Wiley & Sons, Inc.

Bozeman, Barry. 2000. *Bureaucracy and Red Tape.* Upper Saddle River, NJ: Prentice Hall.

Grants.gov. 2007a. Agencies that Provide Grants. Accessed May 18, 2007. Available at: http://www.grants.gov/aboutgrants/agencies_that_provide_grants.jsp.

Grants.gov. 2007b. Apply for Grants. Accessed May 18, 2007. Available at: http://www.grants.gov/applicants/apply_for_grants.jsp.

Grants.gov. 2007c. Get Registered. Accessed May 18, 2007. Available at: http://www.grants.gov/applicants/get_registered.jsp.

Grants.gov. 2007d. Technical Alerts. Grants.gov surpasses 100,000 submissions! Accessed May 18, 2007. Available at: http://www.grants.gov/aboutgrants/technical_alerts.jsp.

U.S. Government, Office of Management and Budget. 2008. Intergovernmental Review (SPOC List). Accessed January 2, 2009. Available at: http://www.whitehouse.gov/omb/grants/spoc.html.

CHAPTER 8

The Decision Process and Beyond

You have submitted your grant. You followed instructions to the letter, compiled a narrative and application packet that fits the funder's interests, clearly demonstrates need, and makes a compelling argument why your organization deserves to be awarded funding for the proposed project. You also followed instructions perfectly in submitting the grant to the correct location, in the proper format, and prior to the proposal deadline. This is cause to celebrate, and you should take a deep breath and bask in the reward this moment brings. Your work is not yet complete, however, and it is advisable to be aware of what happens next so that you can plan accordingly. It is also a good idea to reflect on the process you have just completed and evaluate those things that went well and those that went poorly. Among the questions you should ask yourself in evaluating the results of the grant proposal process are the following:

- What would I do differently if I had to do this again?
- What deadlines did I fail to meet in my proposal development and submission process? How can I prevent it from happening next time?
- Which components of the grant were hardest to compile? Why?
- Which parts of the finished product am I pleased with?
- Which parts of the finished product am I displeased with? How could I improve them?
- Did I encounter any trouble with my external partners? Did any of them fail to live up to their part of the agreement developed at the beginning of the process? Should I rethink any of these partnerships in the future?
- Did all of the grant team members perform their responsibilities properly and in a timely manner? Does anyone deserve reprimand or accolades?

These questions reframe your thoughts away from the proposal itself and back to your organization and its management. Remember, grant seeking is an organizational activity—it is a means to an end. Evaluating the process and its success will set you on footing to make changes in the next iteration of the process. In so doing, you will streamline the application process and improve your organization's performance. And in the grants business, performance means a combination of quality, quantity, and efficiency.

So, do celebrate, perhaps as a team, and take advantage of the opportunity to jointly debrief team members. Their experiences and your perceptions probably vary somewhat, so soliciting their feedback will only lead to more informed changes in the process. So, what happens next? The proposal is off to the agency or foundation, and you are left wondering when a decision will be made. These can be very anxious days, weeks, and months, so it is best to inform yourself about when to worry before engaging yourself full-time with preoccupation regarding your proposal's status. Almost all funding sources will provide you with key information about the decision process in the proposal guidelines or request for proposals. You will be most interested to know how long the decision process will take, that is, when announcements will be made, and how applicants will be notified. Funders provide this information in part because frequent inquiries from applicants can be time consuming and distracting for their staff as well.

TIMING

So, how long does it take to review a grant and make a funding decision? You must keep in mind the funder's goal in making grants—it wants to maximize the public value to be created. This being the case, proposals are evaluated on the basis of not only their content, but their competition. A funding decision is not made on each application, per se, but on the application in relation to all of the other proposals in the pool. This being the case, it is most common (almost universal) for all awards to be announced at the same time, when the proposal evaluation process is complete for all proposals in the application pool.

Most proposals will be evaluated, and funding decisions returned, within 3 months (90 days). This allows plenty of time to complete the decision process, but it also fits the funding calendar. Foundations often make awards on a quarterly cycle, so decisions should be expected before the next cycle's proposal deadline, as the staff should then be engaged by a new set of proposals. Federal agency programs are usually awarded on an annual cycle. The nature of the federal budget process is such that program announcements must precede application deadlines, which must precede evaluation and award decisions. For a great number of programs, these activities are completed in time to permit new projects' start dates to coincide with the beginning of the federal fiscal year on October 1.

Federal agencies will usually post award decision dates in the RFP or program guidelines information. These decision dates, as noted, allow time from the application submission deadline to process, review, score, and rank proposals. That being said, the number of applications received may affect not only your application's success, but also the amount of time it takes for the agency to complete the review. Because this reality always exists, you should treat the decision date as a guideline, not an immutable fact. Funding opportunity announcements usually use somewhat equivocal language to communicate this inconsistency. For example, the Federal Highway Administration's Work Zone Safety Grants program announcement indicates that "FHWA anticipates making awards on or about August 01, 2006" (Grants.gov 2006, p. 16). Sometimes agencies fail to provide an estimate, such as the U.S. Department of Agriculture Cooperative State Research, Education, and Extension Service's Community Food Projects Competitive Grants Program (U.S. Department of Agriculture 2007). We discussed the use of letters of intent in Chapter 6; this program requires a letter of intent to be submitted prior to the formal application. Although the Community Food Projects program does not estimate a funding decision date, it does indicate the date by which determinations will be made on which applicants submitting letters of intent will be informed of their status regarding permission to submit a full proposal (U.S. Department of Agriculture 2007).

Foundations also utilize estimated award decision dates. The Brain Aneurysm Foundation Research Grant Program Application and Guidelines states, "Awards will be determined by August 2007" (Brain Aneurism Foundation 2006, p. 7). The Usibelli Foundation—of Usibelli Coal Mine—estimates award decision dates on the basis of each quarterly submission date—with a very rapid turnaround. The decisions are made following quarterly meeting of the foundation's Allocations Committee, so proposals submitted prior to March 1 will be decided by March 31, those submitted by June 1 will be decided by June 30, and so on (Usibelli Coal Mine 2007). The Ford Foundation estimates that the process leading up to grant approval is usually complete within 3 months (Ford Foundation 2008).

METHOD OF NOTIFICATION

How is notification made regarding your grant proposal? Although this varies across funders, it is sufficient to say that the official determination regarding your grant award will come in writing. Your first notification should be an acknowledgment of receipt. Sometimes the agency will give this notice via e-mail. For example, the Community Foods Program mentioned earlier uses e-mail to notify applicants submitting letters of intent whether they are invited to submit a full application (U.S. Department of Agriculture 2007). This means it is important not only to ensure accuracy of e-mail addresses used in the application materials, but also to consider whose e-mail should be included. The same is true of other contact information. Written notice sent via mail is still fairly common, though some funders are opting for the use of e-mail more regularly.

Sometimes agencies make funding announcements in the form of news releases to media outlets and through their websites. Although you will still receive official notification regarding your application, you may sometimes receive the awaited answer more quickly if you study an agency's website to determine where and when they make funding announcements. It will not be a surprise when you receive the official letter, but it can decrease your anticipated peace of mind. A responsible grant manager or grant writer always keeps a close watch for funding announcements and appears to have greater command of their responsibilities when they learn the outcome prior to the agency receiving official notification of award or a decision against award.

In my experience, announcements are often coordinated with local congressional offices to allow elected officials to claim credit for federal funding that flows into their district, even when it is competitively awarded without political influence. Are awardees treated differently from non-awardees? Almost always, the award recipients are notified in advance and rejected applications are notified somewhat later. Whether this is an administrative procedure designed to provide awardees the greatest lead time for preparation or whether it is designed to help agencies ensure that they do not send rejection letters to organizations that might be eligible if funds were made available (as a result of award negotiations or last-minute decisions to turn down funding) remains speculation.

Establishing a solid relationship with agency program officers may also speed time to knowledge of your application's funding decision. From time to time, program officers will telephone awardees to inform them that an award letter is in the mail or that it will be in the mail soon. Because the official award comes with endorsement of the award letter by an authorized government official, such telephone announcements should be treated as tentative, no matter how reliable their source.

Telephone announcements are fairly rare, but telephone inquiries are more common. What can you learn by phoning the program officer? First of all, it would be inconsiderate to telephone any funder to inquire about the status of award decisions prior to the estimated date the funder provided in the RFP or program guidelines and information statements. You should never harass a funder with such requests because they are likely to point you to the RFP to find the anticipated award date anyway, a spiteful suggestion to indicate you should have read the RFP more carefully in the first place. Of course, if the funder has not provided an estimated announcement date, it is always appropriate to inquire once as to when award notices should be expected. Because most decisions will take in excess of a month by even the most industrious reviews, you may wish to postpone your inquiry for 30 days from the application date. On the one hand, it would be nice to know, but on the other, the longer you wait, the closer the agency will be to making its decisions, and therefore the more accurate their estimate will be. It is acceptable to make inquiry of agencies at any point after the anticipated date they provide, whether in the original RFP or in response to a clarification request. No one enjoys being antagonized, so it is best to spread your inquiries out over time, with each subsequent inquiry following the date provided by the agency representative at your most recent request.

One question you should never ask is whether your organization's particular grant has been approved or rejected. Again, if you have a very solid working relationship with a program officer, he or she may give you a hint over the phone, but the officer is usually not permitted to discuss awards prior to the final award decisions and approval of his or her superiors. You should only inquire about award status in aggregate, not with regard to your organization's application specifically. As noted before, a telephone notification would be considered non-binding anyway, so agency personnel prefer to simply say, "I cannot discuss the specifics of any award decision," or some variation thereof.

So, you have reevaluated your application process, you have devised a plan for following up with agency or foundation staff to keep track of the decision process, and you know about when and how to expect your notice to arrive. As you begin to work on the next grant application in your queue, you may begin to wonder, "What takes them so long, anyway?" The reality is that most federal programs receive no fewer than 50 applications—one from each state is a minimal expectation. The Ford Foundation receives 40,000 applications per year for which only 2,500 will receive affirmations of award (Ford Foundation 2008). The number of proposals necessitates these lengthy review processes because reading takes time. The next section presents the most typical methods and processes used to review grant applications.

INSIDE THE AGENCY: HOW DECISIONS ARE MADE

As discussed in Chapter 6, agencies sometimes establish barriers to application to prevent receiving applications to review from applicants that are not eligible or for projects and amounts that are not feasible or that do not match the funder's goals and mission. Letters of intent and preapplications are techniques commonly used to reduce the number of applications that are subjected to technical review, which is the most time-consuming component of the review process. The Community Food Projects program (2007) is a good example of a program mandating letter of intent as a gateway to full proposal eligibility.

Agencies also utilize other means of avoiding a tenuous, detailed review of lengthy proposals, including a preliminary, or threshold, review. One example is HUD's Historically Black Colleges and Universities (HBCU) program. The *Federal Register* notice states, "Two types of reviews will be conducted: a) A threshold review to determine an applicant's basic eligibility; and b) A technical review for all applications that pass the threshold review to rate and rank the application" (U.S. Department of Housing and Urban Development 2007, p. 11474). This seems an appropriate point at which to once again reiterate the importance associated with detail. An application could be disqualified during the threshold review because it is not appropriately formatted, it contains forbidden appendices, the applicant lacks eligibility, or any number of other inconsistencies with the requirements established in the program funding announcement. So, once past the threshold review, attention to the rating factors and scoring criteria become the focus of review, as discussed in Chapter 5.

It is a complicated endeavor to write a grant that responds effectively to numerous evaluation criteria and assorted program goals and limitations. It is equally difficult to read and score applications with an eye toward their effectiveness in doing so. Technical review is complicated, and it is time consuming. More important, it is essential that the process be carried out in as uniform a manner as possible to ensure equity in funding decisions. Whereas foundations are private organizations that have no legal requirement to offer an explanation for their decisions with respect to a particular funding decision, the federal government does.

The federal government has a legal/constitutional requirement to ensure transparency in funding decisions provided through the Freedom of Information Act and through the fact that transparency is a core democratic constitutional value. "Belief in the openness of government to regular inspection is so firmly ingrained in our collective consciousness that transparency has innate value" (Koppell 2005, p. 96). Why have we come to place such a high value on transparency? Perhaps because the "growth in the size of the bureaucracy and the development of immensely technical and complex fields of specialization have placed tremendous powers in the hands of public officials" (O'Brien, Clarke, & Kamieniecki 1984, p. 339). Powerful parties in government require checks on their actions.

Piotrowski and Rosenbloom (2002) contend that transparency policies make the administration "comport better with U.S. democratic-constitutional values" (p. 645). "In democratic-constitutional theory, the question is not simply whether government does the right thing most of the time. A central issue . . . is how to prevent it from doing the wrong thing some of the time—or ever" (p. 648). What determines whether an action is wrong? How is it that we should not trust public officials to execute their duties honestly and rightly? The founding fathers struggled with such difficult questions but had the foresight to understand that government must come with restrictions to prevent it from overstepping its intended bounds. Writing in the *Federalist* 51, James Madison (1788) observed:

If men were angels, no government would be necessary. If angels were to govern men, neither external nor internal controls on government would be necessary. In framing a government which is to be administered by men over men, the great difficulty lies in this: you must first enable the government to control the governed; and in the next place oblige it to control itself. A dependence on the people is, no doubt, the primary control on the government; but experience has taught mankind the necessity of auxiliary precautions.

In Madison's words we find recognition of a stark reality—a government by the people is fallible, so precautions must be taken.

Transparency is a core democratic value; however, its value comes not from its existence but from the results it brings to bear. Transparency fosters accountability, holding public officials and administrators responsible for their actions. We rely on transparency to examine the inner workings of an agency and to assess its performance. What makes an organization transparent? According to Koppell (2005), the "critical question for evaluating organizational accountability along the transparency dimension is straightforward: Did the organization reveal the facts of its performance?" (p. 96). If we can observe the organization's outputs, and the process by which they were derived, then we can make valid assessments about its effort and overall performance. To hold an agency accountable for its actions, one must be able to observe those actions. *Accountability* conjures images of effective and responsible government when used in such general terms, and indeed that may be the result. The reality is a much clumsier term with varied and often misunderstood interpretations. What is accountability?

The essence of the problem is that, agreeing on the necessity of accountability, there is little agreement on which particular accountability mechanisms should receive priority (Roberts 2002). Different parties can—and do—press for accountability for such diverse concerns as finances, performance, and fairness (O'Connell 2005). Most notable among these pressures are the oft divergent foci of achieving core organizational tasks and providing the due process and transparency necessary to ensure a properly functioning democratic government. O'Brien, Clarke, and Kamieniecki (1984) emphasize the new era ushered in by the advancement of transparency policy: "Expertise and economy were the values emphasized in the past. Today, however, these must be tempered by more democratic norms, i.e., greater public involvement and a more open decision-making process" (p. 339).

How does this discussion of transparency and accountability relate to the federal grants enterprise? In short, the process must be conducted in such a way that it commands the confidence of applicants, and the public at large, in funding award decisions. This means that, through transparency policies, the process used to determine awards is available to the public so that the public has the ability to hold the agency accountable by analyzing the process used and voicing its opinion to the agency's political principals. As discussed in Chapter 1, the grants enterprise may be alternatively focused on equal distribution (substantive equity) or a fair method of allocation (distributional or process equity). Indeed, many grants are targeted with an explicit purpose that precludes substantive equity. Therefore, granting agencies rely on process equity to ensure that their decisions are able to stand the muster of public scrutiny.

The first consideration followed to help ensure equity is that grants be evaluated on a common basis. This is derived from the funding agency's outright statement of evaluation criteria and their weights in making award decisions. Second, it is accomplished by making the reviewer(s)' comments available to the applicant following the review. Many agencies automatically send the comments to the applicant, but some do so only upon request. Grant writers should always request and review agency comments on their applications. Agency comment provides the most accurate feedback in explaining why your application was not funded, and it provides direct guidance to you in understanding how the agency reviewed your proposal, what they looked for, and at what level of detail. The third mechanism agencies use to establish fairness is the use of outside experts, or peers, of the applicant. Expert reviewers are "individuals selected from among those recognized as uniquely qualified by training and experience in their respective fields to give expert advice on the merit of grant applications in such fields who evaluate eligible proposals submitted ... in their respective area(s) of expertise" (U.S. Department of Agriculture 2007, p. 33).

Peer review means that the agency selects individuals representing organizations like those applying, and in particular representatives of previous and current awardees who understand the program and its purposes and requirements better than anyone outside the program officers themselves. Hence, the scrutiny comes from program experts, and the blame falls on them rather than on program officials for the quality of the review. This does not alleviate government officials from responsibility, however. They are the ones responsible for selecting reviewers, so they are to blame for some of the result, even if they do not perform the technical review themselves. This leads to the fourth accountability mechanism utilized: team review.

To balance equity and efficiency, it is desirable to have both consistency and speed. To guarantee equity, the same person would have to read and score all of the applications because human reckoning can be held to absolute consistency only when it is confined to the mind of a single individual. To guarantee efficiency, each proposal would be reviewed by a different reviewer so as to speed up the scoring time and decision process. The resulting reality is a compromise position. Most agency programs utilize a team of reviewers—usually three—to evaluate each proposal. This triples the amount of reading and scoring required, but it allows for potential positive and negative biases to average out, leading to a final score reflective of the actual proposal quality, not of the reviewer's upset stomach or disdain for certain applicants. With the idea of an average in mind, our efficiency desires once again come to the fore, and as the number of proposals increases, the number of review teams increases. Although not able to provide perfectly identical reviews across teams, such teams of three or four individuals giving an average score makes a compelling case to justify a proposal's score. In other words, "Eddy, Betty, Sue, and Hugh gave an average score of 90.35" is more compelling than "Doug rated your proposal at 68." But reviewers are not perfect, and they do bring biases to the table, leading to a fifth mechanism to ensure accountability: conflict of interest requirements.

Bias is intolerable, and its effects are mitigated by a team review, but conflict of interest requirements further help to reduce its effect. Of course, it could be argued that the single reviewer's personal bias would lead to favorable decisions and unfavorable decisions that go beyond the quality of the proposal by itself. As a graduate of the University of Kentucky, I tend to view the school—and its basketball team—in a favorable light, so I am biased toward the school. I will avoid naming any particular basketball rivals, but suffice it to say I am biased against them, ceteris paribus. Agencies create strict rules governing conflict of interest that allow—and usually actually require—reviewers to disclose conflicts and recuse themselves from reviews of applications from the conflicting organizations. Examples of conflicts arise when you attended an institution of higher education, worked for the organization as an employee, serve as an evaluator in a consulting capacity for their grant programs, or have a financial interest in the organization or its programs. It would not be fair for a conflict to negatively—or positively—affect a proposal funding decision. Of course, if there is only one review team and one reviewer elects to recuse herself, then using multiple review teams provides a mechanism for swapping applications on which a given team has a conflict with those of another.

The sixth mechanism ensuring accountability is confidentiality. Keeping the identity of the specific reviewers confidential protects the reviewer from potential retribution, without which the remainder of the process would not function. It also eliminates the potential for applicants to attempt to influence any reviewer to score their proposal favorably, knowing that there would be no enforcement mechanism on such a bribe.

A final characteristic that can be used to ensure a fair review process is the procedural requirements to guarantee that each reviewer's score on a given team/proposal is within a point range. In other words, two reviewers evaluating a section of a grant proposal at 9 points out of 10, with a third team member evaluating the same proposal at 2 points out of 10, is a red flag. It indicates either that one reviewer's bias is being shown, that that reviewer caught a significant problem missed by the other two, and/or that some of the reviewers are less attentive to detail than others are. Forcing these three reviewers to discuss the difference in their scores provides an opportunity to bring such inconsistencies to light, to discuss the rationale, and to come to a common understanding of the proposal and the funding requirements prior to proceeding.

The merits of expert peer review notwithstanding, agencies do not always recruit reviewers from outside their ranks, instead opting to evaluate proposals in-house. Of course, this adds to the time requirement and burden on those staff members, and it exposes them to questions and claims of bias. To a varying extent, they may use some of the features of the peer review process to add merit to the argument that their decisions are defensible on process equity arguments. The reality is that such agencies may be reluctant to hand off their political power—their hard-won and hard-kept political power—to external reviewers with little or no interest in the political pressure or management concerns that face the agency on a day-to-day basis. The ability to determine funding decisions is a closely guarded bureaucratic power in many circles.

HUD's Office of University Partnerships operates an exemplary model of a federal peer review grant evaluation system. The review is conducted on site in Washington, DC, and panels of three reviewers collaboratively review and score each proposal. The overview of the OUP peer review process is presented in **Figure 8.1**.

FOUNDATION DECISIONS

If governments epitomize transparency, accountability, and equitable decision processes, foundations are their antithesis. Foundations are far more secretive about their decision

GENERAL INSTRUCTIONS

The role of a peer reviewer is to evaluate proposals to determine the degree to which they respond to the Factors for Award published in the Notice of Funding Availability (NOFA). Three people who make up a peer review panel will review each application. Each reviewer will evaluate all applications independently. The evaluation of proposals should be based on the analysis of the information provided in relation to the criteria contained under each "Factor for Award." This document provides *guidance* under each factor to assist the reviewer in scoring an application. Explanations and a range of scores are provided that define what constitutes a high, medium, or low score. In reviewing an application, please be aware that the information presented may not fall neatly into the designated category. However, it is imperative that a reviewer makes every attempt to find the information in the application. Points are to be assigned to each evaluation factor as indicated on the review form. It is critical that the applicant receives written comments that have substance and that summarize the application's major strengths and weaknesses. All comments *must be* written in complete sentences; however, comments may be presented in a bullet format. The comments must also support the numerical scores assigned to each factor. Although each panel member does not have to score each factor the same, the group must discuss variances in scores. **BE CONCISE AND SPECIFIC! If the applicant addresses the factor, state it, include page references, and move on.**

LEAD REVIEWER

During the review of applications, one panel member will serve as the lead reviewer for each application. As the lead reviewer, this individual is responsible for thoroughly reviewing the applications he or she is assigned and presenting comments and scores to the other reviewers for a thorough discussion. The lead reviewer is also responsible for providing consolidated typed comments and scores for each factor on behalf of all the reviewers.

After each reviewer has read and scored an application independently, the panel will meet as a group. During the initial meeting on each application, the lead reviewer will be responsible for making an oral presentation of his or her evaluation of the application to the other two panel members. After this presentation, the panel as a group will discuss in detail the individual strengths and weaknesses of the application, taking into account all three panel members' comments and scores. At the conclusion of the discussion, the lead reviewer is then responsible for creating the integrated documents that include his or her comments and all applicable comments made by the other two reviewers (duplicate comments should only be included once) and entering their scores for each factor into the *Summary Comment Sheet* document (*one write-up*). The panel must meet again once all comments have been integrated. Each reviewer must carefully review and verify that all *applicable comments* have been included in the revised document and the scores assigned are accurate and consistent with the strengths and weaknesses noted before they sign off on and submit it to an OUP staff person for review. Please make sure that comments from all reviewers are included. It is important that the voice of each reviewer is incorporated in the document. Once this occurs, the lead reviewer will give the panel leader all four comment sheets (the revised *Summary Comment Sheet*, the lead reviewer's *Individual Review Comment Sheet*, and the two other reviewer's comment sheets) for submission to a Danya staff member in the workroom.

FIGURE 8.1   Overview of the OUP Peer Review Process

Source: U.S. Department of Housing and Urban Development 2006.

The assigned OUP staff member will review all documents, make sure comments have been incorporated, review the scores given by each reviewer, and mark up the *Summary Comment Sheet* as needed, with comments, questions, and other required edits and return it to the panel leader (all markups will be written directly on the document and page tabs will be placed on the pages that need to be addressed). The panel leader will share all issues with the panel for further discussion and necessary revisions that the lead reviewer might need to include. The results of this discussion and the feedback from the OUP staff person will be incorporated in the lead reviewer's final draft. The first time the document is resubmitted, please submit the combined document and the individual comments of each reviewer so the OUP staff person can verify that all required information has been incorporated. The three panel members must agree upon necessary changes and sign off on the final review sheet indicating approval of all changes.

Each peer reviewer will serve as the lead reviewer on at least two applications to be reviewed by their three-person panel. All reviewers will know in advance who will be the lead reviewer for each grant application.

OTHER REVIEWERS

The other two individuals on the panel will be responsible for independently reading, reviewing, and scoring each application based on the criteria set forth in this document and the NOFA. Using the *Individual Reviewer Comment Sheet* provided, the other two individuals will type their comments under the appropriate factor, determine the score, and place the score on the first page of the review sheet under the appropriate factor. (Individuals should be sure to tally their scores and double-check their math.) Upon completion, the reviewer will sign the scoring sheet and be prepared to discuss the application with the other panel members.

Each reviewer's applicable comments and scores will be incorporated into the lead reviewer's comments for an application to produce one written set of comments acceptable to all three reviewers. Although an individual may not act as a lead reviewer on an application, each reviewer must carefully review and score each factor because all scores will be averaged to determine a final score.

PANEL LEADER

One member of each panel will serve as the panel leader for the duration of the review process. As the panel leader, this individual is responsible for setting the pace for the review, organizing team panel meetings, facilitating panel discussions, and resolving any issues and discrepancies that might arise. The panel leader is also responsible for submitting *all* documents to the OUP staff.

During the review process, panel leaders will be required to attend a brief meeting to discuss their team's progress, challenges, and any other concerns that might occur. The time and date of this meeting will be posted in the workroom.

FIGURE 8.1   (Continued)

processes than government funding sources are. They have traditionally veiled themselves in secrecy as private organizations operating outside the purview of the public eye. Fleishman (2007) identifies a number of common sins exhibited by foundations and their staffs, including arrogance, discourtesy, inaccessibility, arbitrariness, failure to communicate, and foundation ADD (attention deficit disorder), and attributes them to one underlying cause—the lack of accountability (p. 152–153).

As with government operations, accountability is never truly attainable without transparency; as private organizations, foundations have no requirements to be transparent in their dealings, except those provided in provisions of the IRS code that enable them to operate. Foundations may never reveal more about your proposal's fate than that it doesn't fit with the foundation's current funding priorities or that the foundation lacks sufficient funds to support all worthwhile projects. The process foundations use to make awards is also an internal process that is rarely disclosed. However, from time to time a foundation illuminates its process with a brief description.

For example, in its online grant inquiry process, the Ford Foundation offers an explanation of how it treats proposals it receives (Ford Foundation 2008). The foundation first determines whether the initial inquiry matches its areas of interest. If so, the inquiry is numbered and a confirmation letter is sent to the applicant organization. Each numbered inquiry is then reviewed by the relevant program officer to determine whether a full proposal is warranted. If so, the program officer will contact the applicant to help shape a full proposal. This initial process consumes about 6 weeks on average. The review process is much more involved: "If the proposal is being considered for a grant, the approval process—which includes meetings, site visits, grant negotiations, administrative and legal review and presentation of the grant for approval—is generally completed within three months but can take longer depending on the complexity of the project" (Ford Foundation 2008).

MANAGEMENT UNDER UNCERTAINTY

With an understanding of the purposes and processes of review, the applicant can better anticipate what to expect in a funding decision, whether affirmative or negative, and can better anticipate when to expect the decision. Following applications in queue is part of the management process. But these can be very trying times. Program personnel and agency administrators face pressure to do something because they are accountable to various stakeholders themselves—board members, elected officials, constituents, and so on.

During this waiting period, the applicant will face important concerns about what to do. What if the grant is awarded? Shouldn't the organization be preparing to implement the project? What if the grant is rejected? What then will become of the plans for the program? And what steps can be taken to alleviate the damage caused by another program delay? These are relevant questions, and the answers always depend on the unique situation.

As a general rule of thumb, it is never a good idea to assume requested funding will be received. Extending commitments on behalf of the organization, such as hiring new employees, recruiting participants, and other similar steps, would not be prudent. These actions have real ramifications for people and for other organizations. Hiring a new employee to be funded with 50% grant funding does not commit the organization to sustain that employment, but laying off a new hire is a sure way to dampen enthusiasm for the work and can cause damage to the organization's reputation. Keeping them on staff at half pay in absence of grant funding is obviously an insulting alternative. It is best to wait until funding is received before taking any step that would commit the organization to providing something of value with anticipated grant funds.

Of course, there are things that can and should be done. First, grant writers know there is a certain probability associated with awards and rejections. The first possibility is to apply for additional funding from other sources during the interim period to minimize future program delays in the event of rejection. If multiple awards are ultimately approved, then the program budget can be adapted to accommodate the additional funding, or one grant may be declined. Of course, money offered is seldom declined because applicants find creative ways to incorporate the funds into their operations under the guise of the program of interest. Naturally, it is illegal and unethical to indicate to a funder that grant money is used for one purpose while actually using it for another. But this dilemma often can be circumvented by identifying tasks and objects of expenditure that are directly related to the purpose for which the money was given. Another alternative, depending on the funder's preferences and limitations, is to request a delay in the start date for the project. This approach enables the applicant to expend funds from one source before beginning to use funds from the second or subsequent sources. This approach generally matches the organizational scale and the program needs much more closely than attempting to expend twice as much as is needed at one time. It has the added benefit of providing for longer program sustainability. In the case of federal awards, negotiating a delay in the project start date in concert with a no-cost extension would provide some relief. In the case of foundations, a request to defer the project start date would provide the flexibility needed. So, continuing the funding search is a logical step during the inevitable waiting period.

A second alternative is to monitor the operating environment for changes that would necessitate program adjustments or adaptations should funding be received. Hall (2007) suggests that organizations too often fail to monitor their environments adequately, leading them to persist with various strategies that may no longer be appropriate, or ideal, for the result they were intended to produce. Important changes to the organization's operating environment should be catalogued and retained to be used in a scope of work adjustment during the award negotiation/contract stage, should the funding result be positive. Again, it is usually better to negotiate changes up front if possible rather than performing an amendment later in the award period.

Third, it is reasonable to begin putting things in place that will facilitate rapid and successful implementation if award notice is received. This stops short of committing the organization to obligations that might have to be canceled if funds are not awarded. But drafting a position description for new staff to be hired and similar activities might speed the process. Keep in mind that activities occurring before the project start date are almost universally ineligible for grant reimbursement. So, if you intend to contribute staff time as match, or request reimbursement for certain activities, they should await receipt of the award. Contacting partner organizations and other project participants is one activity that will pay dividends in the end. Keep all partners and contributors up to speed on the status of the decision process, and be prepared to notify them as soon as notification is received, whether positive or negative. They will want to share in the celebration when notice is provided because they have made commitments and investments to the proposed program as well.

Although it is tempting to sit on one's hands and wait, that strategy is extreme. Some provisions can be made, and some steps can be taken to provide for the program's (or organization's) success during the grant evaluation period. In the following section, I consider the general approach organizations should take once notice is received.

BEYOND THE DECISION: NEXT STEPS

In the daily mail (or increasingly, e-mail) you find correspondence from the agency or foundation to which you applied. Inside awaits the answer you have been so anxiously awaiting. Chances are that the contents will not be the news for which you had hoped. Most programs receive far more applications than they have available resources to fund, so the odds are stacked against you from the beginning. Most notices are letters of rejection. Much of this text has concentrated on learning to tailor proposals to a particular funding source and learning to write effective grant proposals. These approaches will increase your odds of funding success because effective grant proposals are more likely to be funded. But one shouldn't lose sight of the larger organizational picture. Grants are one approach to realizing your organization's goals—they are rarely the only approach.

The rejection should be treated as a measure of progress rather than defeat. It is very tempting to discard the letter of rejection and move on. But a wise grant writer learns from his or her mistakes. You should always read and evaluate the comments you received. If you did not receive comments, the first thing you should do is ask the agency for them. Some agencies will have detailed evaluation comments, others will be more general in nature. Regardless of the quality of the comments, you should learn as much from them as possible. These comments often reveal more about the funding program's goals, and the agency's funding culture than you were able to obtain from the RFP or program description.

Why learn more about the program that just rejected your proposal? Back to Chapter 2, the search: what we learn about a funding agency determines whether our organization or program is a good fit for it. It helps us decide what to send it or not send it for consideration in the future. It also helps us shape our application to better fit the agency's goals on the next application cycle. And that is the real purpose for studying comments—to prepare for reapplication in the future.

Comments may reveal something of the funding agency, its preferences, and priorities, but they also reveal important information about your proposal. What are the weaknesses of your program approach? What parts of the proposal are not clear? This type of comment is useful not only for resubmission to the same agency in the future, but also for submission to an alternative funding source. Of course, your proposal should be retailored to suit the funding agency, but your program description may have weaknesses identified by the proposal reviewers. Government grants are more likely to provide sound, detailed comments than are foundations because of the accountability expectations. But even little information is better than none.

It should go without saying that you must be sure to read your own proposal after receiving the comments to figure out how to either change your proposed program or change your description of it to make it clearer to a reviewer. In other words, it is sometimes the proposed program that is at fault, and at other times it is the way you describe it. What a shame it would be to discard a completely acceptable project just because one or two reviewers didn't understand your description of it. Make the necessary changes, resubmit the work to the same funder in the next cycle if appropriate, or find a new potential funding source and reframe the proposal to match. Persevere. Many federal programs are extremely competitive, and it takes up to three or four cycles to perfect an application to the point that it is fundable relative to the competition.

Sometimes the correspondence includes more favorable news. Unlike rejection, the award notice is cause for celebration. There are three basic approaches to an award. First, the funder may mail you a check for all or part of the requested funds, which is more common with expressive giving than instrumental giving. If the purpose is to provide assistance, mailing the check saves the funder the expense of additional postage. This is a good day for a grant writer. More commonly, there are strings attached to grant awards, and notice is a formality to let you know that you will soon have paperwork to review and sign. In the second award approach, the federal agency or foundation may accept your grant as written, incorporate it as an appendix to a standard award contract, and mail your organization's authorized signatory agent a letter or contract to sign. The third approach is to negotiate changes in the proposed amount, activities, or approach that was described in your proposal, and then issue an award letter. Naturally, if you identified necessary changes during the interim period, now is the time to incorporate them into an amended scope of work. The grant is never official until it is signed, as is the case for any binding contract.

Who makes the award on behalf of the funding agency depends on the funder, and sometimes on the size of the award amount. In the case of foundations, grants of small amounts may be issued at the discretion of program officers whereas larger grant requests require approval by the full board. Federal funding recommendations are made by agency staff and program officers, but it is the designated agency agreement officer who has the power to commit the government to grant funds. A signed letter from that person indicates that the award is accepted and work may begin. The award date and the project start date do not have to be identical; it is usually the case that a proposed program would have a delayed start date from the award date, but this could be negotiated during the award process if necessary.

What is important to remember is that an award notice sets into action all of the necessary implementation steps that had been on hold. Commitments could now be made without fear of personal harm to stakeholders, although it is still advisable to wait until the formal contract is signed. Startup is a stressful time. The implementation plan is now set into action, and the program is afoot. A good implementation and management plan in the grant proposal will aid this process tremendously. If things have changed from the time of submittal, you should be aware of them and have contingency plans ready to substitute for the original plan. Sometimes an elaborate implementation plan was derived during the application process for which there was insufficient space in the program narrative. The proposal narrative provides the information for which the grant recipient will be accountable, but the more detailed version will probably aid in the implementation process. Meeting with key program staff and partners to organize for action is usually a necessary step.

An often overlooked step with affirmative notices is reviewing the enclosed comments. Award notices tend to make grant writers overly confident in their abilities, and there is a common tendency to ignore comments on successful proposals. Nonetheless, they may still reveal weaknesses in your program design. They may provide insight into the agency for future funding needs, and they may provide advice that would assist your writing style or proposal organization for future efforts. Overconfidence can lead to failure in any organization; we must strive to learn and adapt at every opportunity, keeping those strategies that are successful and abandoning those that are not (Audia, Locke, & Smith 2000; Hall 2007).

CONCLUSION

The decision process takes time, but it is usually in the funder's best interest to ensure that the process is as speedy as possible. In the case of government funding, speed is balanced with a concern for process equity and the accountability imposed on agency actions through transparency provisions such as freedom of information laws. What is essential to the grant writer is that the process is understood so that impatience awaiting a decision can be attenuated with an explanation for the necessity of the time such decisions take. Knowing how an agency reviews grants is a tremendous advantage to the application process because your approach is less blind than it would be otherwise. Agency technocrats may review a proposal very differently from how an expert from a university or a peer practitioner in the field might. Knowing each of these groups and knowing which of them will have the opportunity to sink their claws into your application tells you something of the way it should be formatted and framed and the level of sophistication that is acceptable in your program narrative.

When agency decision processes call for reviewers from peer institutions, it is a wise decision to step forward and volunteer as a peer reviewer. There is no money to be made reviewing grants—in fact, many reviews are conducted via e-mail and mail with provisions for teleconference when necessary. These reviews often include a stipend to make the effort worthwhile, but more often than not they have no financial benefit to the reviewer. Some reviews occur on-site at the agency office or at least at a central location in Washington, DC, with the logistical support needed to sustain a large group of reviewers around the clock. Whatever their shape or form, grant reviews give you the opportunity to read other completed proposals, learn the program and the process of evaluation that applications undergo, and meet other practitioners in the field who may provide network opportunities whose ultimate value cannot be ascertained.

The decision process provides your greatest opportunity for success in the next round of the grant competition, either through your direct participation in the review or through a careful consideration of the comments obtained from the agency with your rejection letter. Whatever the case, the agency decision process determines what opportunities and outputs are available for your benefit, and it is incumbent on you to be informed about that process if you expect to maximize the benefits it affords. Studying the agency and its process opens doors to success that you might not have considered from the vantage point of a unidimensional grant writer looking inward to the application rather than outward to the institutional network in which decisions are made.

Take advantage of the time between submittal and award to prepare and plan, or to seek contingency funding. And when the award letter arrives, make the most of it. Read the comments and learn from them to save time and increase success in future endeavors. When awards come, be sure to celebrate, and begin as promptly as possible following the proposed implementation plan. When the notice bears news of rejection, reassess priorities to determine whether the program is still warranted, consider alternative funding sources, and always consider non-grant alternatives to organizational problem solving.

REFERENCES

Audia, P., E. Locke, and K. Smith. 2000. The paradox of success: An archival study of strategic persistence following radical environmental change. *Academy of Management Journal* 43(5): 837–853.

Brain Aneurysm Foundation. 2006. Research Grant Program Application and Guidelines. Accessed May 20, 2007. Available at: http://www.bafound.org/involved/researchgrant-app.pdf.

Fleishman, Joel L. 2007. *The Foundation: A Great American Secret.* New York: Public Affairs.

Ford Foundation. 2008. How We Make Grants. Accessed August 20, 2008. Available at: http://www.fordfound.org/grants/inquiry/usa/2/en.

Grants.gov. 2006. Federal Grant Opportunity: Work Zone Safety Grants, Amendment No. 1. Accessed May 20, 2007. Available at: http://apply.grants.gov/opportunities/instructions/oppDTFH61-06-RA-00010-cidDTFH61-06-RA-00010-instructions.pdf.

Hall, Jeremy L. 2007. Implications of success and persistence for public sector performance. *Public Organization Review* 7(3): 281–297.

Koppell, Jonathan G. S. 2005. Pathologies of accountability: ICANN and the challenge of "multiple accountabilities disorder." *Public Administration Review* 65(1): 94–108.

Madison, James. 1788. The structure of the government must furnish the proper checks and balances between the different departments. *Federalist* 51. Accessed December 26, 2006. Available at: http://www.constitution.org/fed/federa51.htm.

O'Brien, Robert M., Michael Clarke, and Sheldon Kamieniecki. 1984. Open and closed systems of decision making: The case of toxic waste management. *Public Administration Review* 44(4): 334–340.

O'Connell, Lenahan. 2005. Program accountability as an emergent property: The role of stakeholders in a program's field. *Public Administration Review* 65(1): 85–93.

Piotrowski, Suzanne J. and David H. Rosenbloom. 2002. Non-mission-based values in results-oriented public management: The case of freedom of information. *Public Administration Review* 62(6): 643–657.

Roberts, Nancy C. 2002. Keeping public officials accountable through dialogue: Resolving the accountability paradox. *Public Administration Review* 62(6): 658–669.

U.S. Department of Agriculture. 2007. Community Food Projects Competitive Grants Program: FY 2007 Request for Applications. Accessed May 21, 2007. Available at: http://www.csrees.usda.gov/funding/rfas/pdfs/07_community_food.pdf.

U.S. Department of Housing and Urban Development. 2006. *Hispanic-Serving Institutions Assisting Communities: FY 06 Peer Reviewer Evaluation Guide.* Washington, DC: HUD Office of University Partnerships.

U.S. Department of Housing and Urban Development. 2007, March 13. Historically Black Colleges and Universities (HBCUs) Program. *Federal Register* 72(48): 11467–11476.

Usibelli Coal Mine. 2007. Usibelli Foundation. Accessed May 20, 2007. Available at: http://www.usibelli.com/foundation.html.

CHAPTER 9

Basics of Grant Management

If you are fortunate, the selection process found in your favor and you have received notice from the program officer or some other agency source that your application has been selected for award. The process of application has officially ended, and the process of grant management has begun. Who is responsible for managing the grant now that we know it will be awarded? The answer to that question varies from organization to organization, and the answer is often that no single individual bears complete responsibility for the grant's administration and management. For many organizations, grant management will not even be considered until the notice of award is received.

Failure to plan for this event may leave the grant writer or the project director with de facto responsibility. In fact, in smaller organizations, the project director (the person listed in the grant application and perhaps on SF-424 for the relevant contact information) was the grant writer, and that person had fully anticipated bearing responsibility for the grant's implementation and management. Organizations seeking funding for the first time may fail to make such considerations, having no formal plan for the administrative requirements associated with grant funding. Very large organizations that receive and administer vast numbers of grants have dedicated offices that specialize in and manage the organization's day-to-day interaction with federal agencies through requests and reports for a wide range of funded programs. For example, most universities have both an office of grant administration and an office of grant accounting, with the former specializing in bringing money into the institution, and the latter specializing in managing grants once received.

It is recommended that an organization develop a basic understanding of the process and requirements associated with grant management, and then develop a plan for carrying out those activities once the grant is awarded. The purpose of this chapter is to provide a synopsis of the requirements that you will encounter, or about which you should be aware, as you implement your funded program or activity. The focus of this chapter is based on federal grants management because it is the more stringent form of funding to manage and because it is the most systematized. This is not to say that foundation funding is easier to manage, for it is not, nor should it be. However, the lessons drawn from federal grant management can easily be transferred to the foundation setting.

The first thing to keep in mind as you embark on your grant management adventure is that rigidity and flexibility work together quite comfortably. Although you may feel that you have written the perfect grant proposal, you may immediately find yourself engaged with award managers and program officers in a negotiation over the final details of your project or proposal. For example, the Federal Highway Administration (FHWA) indicates,

"Before the actual award, FHWA will enter into negotiations concerning such items as program components, staffing and funding levels, and administrative systems. If the negotiations do not result in an acceptable submittal, the FHWA reserves the right to terminate the negotiation and decline to fund the applicant" (Grants.gov 2006, p. 16). So, the federal government may appear to be quite rigid, but you will find agencies to be both responsive and flexible when there is call for doing so. Likewise, your program will never be implemented precisely as you planned it—things happen during implementation that delay progress, that alter plans for administration, or that affect costs. The reality is that it is virtually impossible to carry out your project in a manner consistent with that proposed in the program narrative.

So, although the program is flexible, and the government program officials are open to some flexibility, the grant management system itself is overtly rigid, with forms, deadlines, rules, and procedures, including bureaucratic staff charged with the responsibility of overseeing the grants management process. For your program to flex in the necessary ways, the components of this rigid process must be understood.

A key initial lesson in grant management is that no activities or costs should be incurred on the project until the official start date of the project. The award date is the date indicated on the endorsed award letter committing the government funding for your proposal. The project start date is that same day or some future date at which both parties agree for the project to officially begin. You cannot begin activities or capture costs to be reimbursed or counted as match until the official start date of the proposal.

Your first opportunity to exercise effective grant management skills will be the negotiation leading up to the award letter. Even if the agency is willing to sign an official award letter without changes, you may wish to renegotiate the start date of your program to coincide with a concrete organizational calendar that is bound to differ from the abstract ideal proposed in the application for funding. It is always important to discuss such changes with agency program staff to determine their preferences regarding such initial changes versus postponing alterations until after the official award is made. It may also be the case that budgets need to be adjusted to account for periodic salary increases or changes to fringe benefit rates that occurred during the interim between application and award.

Generally speaking, changes initiated by the grantee must occur within the maximum award amount specified by the agency, so any increase must be met with equal decreases in other categories. Choosing an award date should be based on your organizational reality. If all of the required components are in place, or if the organization is strapped for cash, it may be advisable to move the start date as close as possible. If staff turnover has resulted in a key vacancy, it may be advisable to seek postponement of the start date until the organization has had time to recuperate and prepare to effectively administer the program. Some agencies will be less flexible with the start date than others are, so if the award date is assumed to be the start date, you must accept reality. But reality is kind in this regard too, for project time lines are also less rigid than they may first appear.

Negotiating the initial agreement may impose a number of concerns. If a federal agency is negotiating with you to establish the terms of your grant award, it is a good sign that your program and their objectives match. Of course, this very activity will represent a deviation from your proposal—a proposal that you submitted with full knowledge of the relevant conditions and expectations. Agency changes may be relatively minor, but they may also lead to undesirable changes to the program expectations. Although it would seem a terrible thing to lose a federal grant award, if the conditions imposed exceed the organization's willingness to accept them, then that should be made known in the negotiation process. As in any negotiation, you do not wish to be overpowered by the second party. But in this case, the second party has a substantial cash award to use as incentive in the negotiation process. Although your proposal may have been better, there is probably one next on the list that they would welcome if you decline. So, the reality is that federal changes will be welcomed, and conditions will be accepted in exchange for the desired funds in most cases. As stated in Chapters 1 and 2, the key is to know the conditions and your organization's willingness to accept them as a tradeoff for funding, and then to operate within the scope of that willingness.

With an award letter in place, the management system changes from one of negotiation to one of subjection to rules and regulations. Chief among considerations upon which the grants management process is built is accountability. Whereas transparency was identified as an important mechanism of accountability in Chapter 8, accountability in this sense is somewhat different. It is not so much accountability to the people at large that grant management strives to ensure as it is accountability to performance and to political superiors. If the federal government issued grant awards and then stepped away, there would not be an incentive for recipients to abide by the conditions to which they agreed; neither would there be an incentive to use funds in a manner consistent with federal objectives. So, the federal grants management system seeks to ensure this accountability from their grantees to secure favor with the political principals who oversee them. Political principals are incented to monitor agencies and grantees because they are, ultimately, accountable to their constituents in the electorate.

"Accountability is good—there is little disagreement on this point.... And yet while everyone agrees on its desirability, the meaning of accountability remains elusive" (Koppell 2005, p. 94). Koppell's (2005) key concern with accountability is that the scholarly literature has failed to achieve a uniform understanding as to what the term means; it refers to bureaucratic control in some contexts and transparency in others. He adds: "Relying on a single word to convey disparate conceptual understandings masks disagreement over a core issue of political science. The perpetuation of fuzziness regarding this important term is a failing of our discipline" (Koppell 2005, p. 94). And, "Lack of conceptual clarity presents more than a rhetorical problem. The many meanings of accountability suggested by the varied use of the word are not consistent with each other: that is, organizations cannot be accountable in all of the senses implied by this single word" (Koppell 2005, p. 95). That being said, there is widespread agreement on the purpose and the methods of accountability utilized in grants management.

All formal government systems have their basis in law, whether legislative or administrative, and grants management is true to form. For example, consider the U.S. Department of Transportation's Uniform Administrative Requirements for Grants and Agreements with Institutions of Higher Education, Hospitals, and Other Nonprofit Organizations (49 CFR Part 19). This lengthy law lays out, for transportation agencies, a set of uniform guidelines and requirements to follow in administration of federal grant awards, including preaward, postaward, and after-the-award requirements. In addition to standardizing the process, the law also prohibits the imposition of additional requirements on awardees. Subparts C and D of this law are included as Appendix 1 at the end of this chapter for reference. In addition, agencies are required to follow the guidelines developed in Office of Management and Budget (OMB) Circulars.

The primary function of laws like 49 CFR Part 19 is to ensure that funds are expended on their intended purposes and only on allowable costs. Thus, they often reference a core set of federal grant management documents known as Office of Management and Budget (OMB) Circulars. The OMB Circulars are guides that establish cost standards for different classifications of organizations. The allowable costs and cost standards that apply to your organization will depend on your organization's type. **Figure** 9.1 presents the most frequently referenced OMB Circulars. These publications are seldom updated and serve as the basis for agency decisions and determinations regarding allowable grant activities and costs. These standards add consistency and certainty to organization decisions, enhancing stability during the grant implementation period.

PERFORMANCE MANAGEMENT SYSTEMS

To maintain accountability standards, grant recipients are expected to implement systems to monitor grant activities and progress. To manage the project effectively, it is necessary to institute performance management systems that ensure that necessary data are collected on a timely basis. For example, persons spending time on grant activities must document that they were engaged in grant-related activities for a certain number of hours or an estimated percentage of their time. Collecting timesheets and related documentation on a regular basis enables regular reporting of grant-related effort, and thus reduces the difficulty required to recall the amount of time invested. Furthermore, regular reporting of this information enables responsible managers to alter staff responsibilities to ensure compliance with grant expectations.

Other important performance management system components include procurement and purchasing systems. These systems generate a paper trail for all expenditures, from a purchase order to an encumbrance to the purchase of and payment for required goods and services. Accounting systems must be set up to ensure that grant funds are not comingled with organization funds, further enhancing accountability in the system.

OMB Circular A-21	Cost Principles for Educational Institutions (Relocated to 2 CFR, Part 220)
OMB Circular A-87	Cost Principles for State, Local, and Indian Tribal Governments (Relocated to 2 CFR, Part 225)
OMB Circular A-102	Grants and Cooperative Agreements with State and Local Governments
OMB Circular A-110	Uniform Administrative Requirements for Grants and Other Agreements with Institutions of Higher Education, Hospitals, and Other Nonprofit Organizations (Relocated to 2 CFR, Part 215)
OMB Circular A-122	Cost Principles for Nonprofit Organizations (Relocated to 2 CFR, Part 230)
OMB Circular A-133	Audits of States, Local Governments, and Nonprofit Organizations

FIGURE 9.1   Commonly Referenced OMB Circulars by Organization Type
Source: Office of Management and Budget 1999.

The performance management system must extend beyond the organization's boundaries when other partner organizations are participating in the project as a collaborative. If they are recipients of contracts or subgrants from the federal award, they must be held to the same high standards as the recipient/prime organization. This is ensured contractually, but it must also be ensured from a performance standpoint. This is all to say that what your partners are doing must also be monitored and documented, and the information should also be fed into the system. The most important aspect of this process is to ensure that matching funds, usually of an in-kind nature, that are dedicated to the project are properly documented.

Much like internal employees are asked to document their time, partner organizations can be asked to document their efforts toward the project, distinguishing between grant-funded activities and match-funded activities. This is not a simple task. Collaborations often break down because organizations are reluctant to share autonomy and power (Agranoff 2006). Administrative requirements imposed from another organization may be viewed in this light—as threats to organizational power and autonomy. Collaborative decisions are more effective because they take multiple perspectives into account, but they are less efficient because assimilation of such diverse perspectives into conclusions takes time (Kiefer & Montjoy 2006). Furthermore, networks have collaborative costs as well as collaborative benefits, with the most common cost being the relinquishment of agency turf, authority, and resources (Agranoff 2006)—a high price to pay for many public agencies steeped in a tradition emphasizing competition for resources across vertical boundaries (Kettl 2006).

When all of its components are integrated, a high-quality performance management system makes information readily accessible, uniform, and easy to utilize in grant reporting—the component of grant management that most closely seeks to ensure accountability to the intended purpose stated in the grant award.

REPORTING

The usefulness of the performance management system is demonstrated on a quarterly, semiannual, or annual basis (depending on the program) when it is called upon to produce the evidence necessary to be included in official progress reports to the funding agency. There are two types of reports, and in most organizations the two functions are carried out separately and by different individuals. However, the purpose of reporting is to convey to agency managers and program staff that implementation is progressing, and that the organization knows what it is doing. The two types of reports that must be submitted are a financial report and a technical report. The financial report is filed using federal form SF-269, the Financial Status Report, in concert with SF-272, the Federal Cash Transactions Report. These forms cover the financial side of the reporting burden and document fund flows and project financial status. These forms are provided in Appendix 2 of this chapter for review.

The technical report is a narrative description that comes not from an organization accountant, but from the person directing the project implementation on the ground—the project director. This is a regular progress report that communicates activities that have taken place and their timeliness according to the plan presented in the application program narrative. The report offers an explanation for those components that are on time, those that are not, and how their status affects overall program implementation. The funding agency will view the reports together, so it is advisable for the project director to develop these periodic reports in conjunction with the financial reports, or after they are complete. It should be apparent why money was drawn down from the federal government agency, and in what amount, by comparing the reports side by side. So, if funds are being used more slowly than projected (and you will recall from Chapter 6 that you made cash flow projections on SF-424B), the report should note this trend and proffer an explanation. If funds are being used more quickly than anticipated, that trend should be noted and explained. The agency is concerned by rapid draw-downs because the project's sustainability depends on the availability of funding, and if the grant funds are used in the first 12 months, the project's success may be suspect for the remaining 24 months, assuming a 36-month project time line.

Coordination between the reports is important for another key reason—internal consistency. If the financial reports show no funds being drawn down but the technical report suggests significant project activity according to plan, the agency will note the discrepancy and endeavor to discover the cause. In all likelihood, one of the reports is incorrect, suggesting possible fraud, but certain management limitations. One possible explanation is that the performance is not being adequately tracked by the system that captures financial expenses. For example, if timesheets and effort reports are not submitted, the expenses would not be billed to the grant and no funds drawn down in spite of otherwise conscientious effort by program managers toward implementation. Inconsistency should be avoided at all costs, and sound performance management systems lend themselves to consistent information collection and reporting.

You should be mindful of the reporting requirements associated with your award and abide by them. Reports are generally due 30 days after the closing date of a federal budget quarter. Because the federal year begins on October 1, the closing dates for the year are Q1, December 31; Q2, March 31; Q3, June 30; and Q4, September 30, with reports due 30 days thereafter for each respective quarter. You may not be required to submit reports so frequently if your project time line is short or if the grant amount is small.

You should learn and comprehend the specific requirements you face, and then assimilate the requirements into your performance management system to be sure that information is collected and reported on a timely basis in order to ensure on-time submittal to the funding agency. You must be very careful to submit reports on time. If reports are submitted late, the organization will be considered delinquent and will jeopardize continued funding until reporting requirements are complete. And this means submitting late reports for each quarter or period that was missed, not just submitting one cumulative report covering the period. It is expected that funding will be frozen when this happens, but in some cases the grant may even be terminated.

So, reports take two forms—technical and financial—that should be developed in concert to paint a clear picture of the organization's project activities and their relationship to the federal funding used. They should be complete, accurate, and timely to ensure the organization's good standing with the federal agency. Moreover, complete and timely reports will prevent other problems that might taint the outcome of an annual audit.

RECORD RETENTION

A good performance management system will generate lots of documentation, including reports, data, and other documents to demonstrate the efforts undertaken in implementing the government grant project. These documents should not be discarded without first consulting record retention requirements. Many large organizations, cognizant of the space and maintenance requirements presented by large amounts of print documents, establish schedules to govern the disposal of important records after their useful life has expired. Federal grant requirements impose restrictions on organizations to retain certain documents, particularly financial documents, related to a grant project.

OMB Circular A-110 sets the standard at 3 years from the date that the final expenditure report is submitted to the agency, provided no audit or litigation has been opened (Office of Management and Budget 1999). At the point an audit or any litigation is opened tied to a particular award, records must be retained indefinitely until all claims have been resolved and final action taken. Although Circular A-110 sets the time frame for record retention at 3 years, that should not be assumed. For example, many student loan programs have 5-year retention schedules. To determine how long records should be retained, you should consult your notice of award, the OMB Circular governing awards to your institution, and any organizational schedules that your institution might have in place. You should always keep records for the longest period required by internal or external policy to be in compliance. Each organization should maintain a schedule that documents when each collection of records is to be expunged, and the records should be disposed of as soon as possible after that date to protect the organization from any future litigation or complaint.

AMENDMENTS

It is very common for unforeseen changes to occur. Sometimes things go better than anticipated, and sometimes worse, but the fact remains that things happen and your best laid plans will be altered against your will or as a result of your own ingenuity in identifying a better approach. Agencies are open to accepting changes to your program approach. Scope of work changes, as they are commonly known, are facilitated through scope of work amendments. Although at the street level we sometimes make changes in approach immediately, they should technically await the agency's formal approval of a formal request to amend the project's scope of work as described in the program narrative.

Either as a result of scope of work changes or as a result of inaccuracies in cost estimates and price changes, budget amendments are also frequently necessary. Budget amendments consist of requesting a transfer from one functional category to another (such as travel to salaries) and offering a justification for why the transfer is necessary. It may be that a suitable candidate for a grant-funded position could not be hired at the budgeted rate, or the staff person may be needed for a greater percentage of time than initially budgeted. These changes are common, and their approval is usually only a technicality, though the request and approval process is intended to ensure that the change will not alter the program's purpose or its intended or expected outcomes (except to improve them over the status quo without the amendment).

PURCHASING

Purchases made with federal funds must be in accordance with federal purchasing guidelines. This means that large purchases must undergo a competitive bid and award process. 41 U.S.C. 403(11) sets the threshold for small purchases and sole-source procurement at $25,000, indicating that purchases in excess of that amount must be put to bid through a competitive process. While the federal purchasing standards must be followed, they do not supersede state or local regulations that may apply to your organization. As a general rule, you should follow the more stringent set of requirements. So if you represent a state agency and state law requires projects over $5,000 to be bid, the federal law does not exempt you from the state requirement. You should seek bids for all projects in excess of $5,000 to fulfill both state and federal expectations.

WHERE THE MONEY COMES FROM

To obtain federal funds awarded through your grant, forms have to be filed requesting fund advances or reimbursements for costs incurred. Form SF-270 is a Request for Advance or Reimbursement, and SF-271 is an Outlay Report and Request for Reimbursement for Construction Programs. These forms are also presented in Appendix 2 of this chapter for reference.

AUDITS

Accepting federal grant funds means accepting audit provisions if certain conditions are met. **Figure 9.2** presents an overview of federal government audit requirements. Organizations that receive more than $500,000 in a given fiscal year are required to undergo a federal audit each year. Additional information can be obtained by visiting the Federal Audit Clearinghouse home page (http://harvester.census.gov/sac). Audits ensure that systems are in place to track and manage federal awards in compliance with all cost and recordkeeping standards. They are the strictest form of accountability, and a bad audit indicates that an organization has failed to maintain the high standards imposed on federal grant recipients. Problems are indicated by remarks on the audit and must be corrected to maintain eligibility for continued federal funding. A half million dollars seems like a generous threshold for mandatory audit, and to a small organization, it may be. The threshold prevents imposing strict requirements on organizations managing small amounts of federal funds or even occasional large sums, focusing attention rather on those organizations (such as universities and state government agencies) that receive awards in the tens to hundreds of millions of dollars each year.

By federal law (Title 31 U.S.C. Chapter 75), non-federal entities that expend $300,000 ($500,000 for fiscal periods ending after December 31, 2003) or more in federal awards annually are required to have audits conducted in accordance with Office of Management and Budget (OMB) Circular A-133 (revised June 27, 2003). The Circular, which applies to audits of states, local governments, and nonprofit organizations, provides detailed definitions and audit requirements, and requires "completed audit packages" to be submitted to the Federal Audit Clearinghouse (Clearinghouse). Completed audit packages must consist of:

(1) A "reporting package" as specified in the Circular (and which includes the audit report).

(2) A completed Form SF-SAC, "Data Collection Form for Reporting on Audits of States, Local Governments and Nonprofit Organizations." This form is based on information in the reporting package. It is signed by both the auditor and auditee, and used by the Clearinghouse as the basis for developing and maintaining the government-wide audit database (database).

(3) The Circular prescribes unified reporting requirements for states, local governments, and nonprofit entities, and mandates the use of the SF-SAC. The Circular applies to any covered non-federal entity with respect to its fiscal years which begin after June 30, 1996; for most entities this means initial submissions under the revised Circular covered fiscal years ending June 30, 1997 or later.

Approximately 40,000 audits are filed annually. The Clearinghouse retains copies of Form SF-SAC and the reporting packages for a period of at least 3 years.

Purposes

The purposes of the Clearinghouse are administrative. It acts as an agent for OMB and its primary purposes are to:

(1) Establish and maintain a government-wide database of single audit results and related federal award information

(2) Serve as the federal repository of single audit reports

(3) Distribute single audit reports to federal agencies

FIGURE 9.2   Overview of Audit Requirements for Federal Grant Recipients
Source: Federal Audit Clearinghouse 2008.

NO-COST EXTENSION

Grants are usually allowed an extension of the time period for performance, provided there is no additional cost incurred by the federal government for that change. A 1-year no-cost extension is usually available, and they are commonly approved by federal agencies when

The database consists of information about audits of federal awards as required by the Circular. Such information is available to the public. However, persons who seek to use the database are strongly urged to (1) understand the selective content of the database and (2) clarify questions about database information with (as appropriate) the federal oversight or cognizant agency or the Clearinghouse.

This database contains only a limited amount of data from the complete Circular reporting package. As such, any final analysis about a particular non-federal entity should be based upon the information in the full reporting required under the Single Audit Act Amendments of 1996 (including auditor's reports), rather than just the summary information from the data collection form.

Content

The database consists of information reported to the Clearinghouse on Form SF-SAC.

Form SF-SAC is submitted to the Clearinghouse by non-federal entities audited under the Circular. In general, Form SF-SAC and the database provide five kinds of information:

(1) General Information (Part I). This includes affected fiscal and audit period, type of audit, Employer Identification Number (EIN), Data Universal Numbering System number (DUNS) and federal cognizant or oversight agency.

(2) Auditee Information (Part I, Item 6). This includes basic information about the non-federal entity being audited such as address, phone number, contact name, and the auditee's certification of completeness and accuracy of the information provided on the SF-SAC.

(3) Auditor Information (Part I, Item 7). This includes basic information about the auditor and the auditor statement.

(4) Financial Statement of Audit Information (Part II). This includes information on type of financial statement and financial statement audit results.

(5) Federal Program Information (Part III). This includes information about the A-133 audit results, federal awards administered by the non-federal entity, and an identification of federal agencies required to receive audit reporting packages.

FIGURE 9.2   (Continued)

requested, provided sufficient justification exists to warrant the change. For example, it is common to argue that start-up delays postponed implementation by the target date. Following September 11, 2001, many awarded grant programs argued that the attacks and the economic ramifications significantly altered their plans and approach, causing an unpreventable delay. If you have been awarded a large grant and are finding it difficult within a small organization's budget to expend the resources in a timely manner (and this does happen!), a no-cost extension may be a viable option to consider. As with any amendment, extension requests must be formally made to the agency and approved before treating them as a given. If the extension is not approved, you will forfeit any remaining federal funds not expended by the project end date. For this reason, it is important to keep a close handle on project performance in order to anticipate necessary changes in time to seek approval from the funding agency prior to the project end date.

GRANT CLOSING/FINAL REPORT

Upon completion of the grant, either at the date it is scheduled to end or the date at which any negotiated extensions expire, a final report of expenditures and activities must be compiled and submitted. This report covers all activities and focuses on the program's success and failures. It is an evaluation, of sorts, of what was accomplished and how it aligns with the expectations laid out in the program narrative submitted with the application. Recent federal government focus has been placed on monitoring agency outcome performance, which includes the performance of agency-funded grant projects. Grant projects are under increased scrutiny regarding their outcomes; federal agency programs are evaluated by the PART system administered by the Office of Management and Budget. Lax performance standards (mostly resulting from the breadth of the program and difficulty establishing uniform measures) were significant enough to threaten the existence of the Community Development Block Grant program (CDBG) in 2005 when President George W. Bush recommended that it be collapsed into a new block grant program in the Department of Commerce (Handley 2008).

Usually the due date for final reports is longer than the time frame for periodic (quarterly) reports, but you should ensure clarity with the agency's expectations through award documentation or by asking the program officer. Although it may be tempting to ignore these reports, having drawn down all of the budgeted federal grant award, doing so would constitute a big mistake. Reports are required, and they must be complete to prevent the organization from being labeled delinquent. This means you will have to make restitution for the delinquent reports prior to receiving new federal funds. Like quarterly reports, and perhaps more so, the final report must be compiled and submitted on a timely basis.

CONCLUSION

This chapter has examined the most common elements of the federal grant management system including negotiating the award, reporting, amendments, no-cost extensions, audits, and budget and scope of work amendments. Though seemingly daunting, the tasks are made simple by a well-prepared and well-implemented organizational performance management system and familiarity with the expectations that come with each of your awards.

The chapter focused on federal grant management requirements because they are the most systematic and intense, but they also reflect the common grant management expectations that exist with foundation and other non-government grants. By learning the rules and expectations you face and developing a strong internal (and external, in the case of collaborative projects) management system, you can process grant management documents and requests with ease and confidence. It is worth noting that sound performance alongside timely and complete reports builds a foundation of trust that agencies may come to value and respect when the opportunity comes to apply for future awards. Delinquent, incomplete, or late reports are a sure way to ensure that the stream of external funding for your organization dries up; as you fail to meet the funding agency's expectations, you will face award terminations and possibly legal action in addition to a sour reputation among funding agencies. Manage grants with the same care and attention you afford the application process and success will follow.

REFERENCES

Agranoff, Robert. 2006. Inside collaborative networks: Ten lessons for public managers. *Public Administration Review* 66(6 supplement): 56–65.

Federal Audit Clearinghouse. 2008. Single Audit Disclaimer Information. Accessed January 8, 2009. Available at: http://harvester.census.gov/sac/dissem/disclaim.html.

Grants.gov. 2006, May 4. Federal Grant Opportunity: Work Zone Safety Grants, Amendment No. 1. Accessed May 20, 2007. Available at: http://apply.grants.gov/opportunities/instructions/oppDTFH61-06-RA-00010-cid -DTFH61-06-RA-00010-instructions.pdf.

Handley, Donna M. 2008. Community development and the U.S. intergovernmental grant system: Symposium introduction. *Journal of Public Budgeting, Accounting and Financial Management* 20(1): 38–45.

Kettl, Donald F. 2006. Managing boundaries in American administration: The collaboration imperative. *Public Administration Review* 66(6 supplement): 10–19.

Kiefer, John J. and Robert S. Montjoy. 2006. Incrementalism before the storm: Network performance for the evacuation of New Orleans. *Public Administration Review* 66(6 supplement): 122–130.

Koppell, Jonathan G. S. 2005. Pathologies of accountability: ICANN and the challenge of "multiple accountabilities disorder." *Public Administration Review* 65(1): 94–108.

U.S. Government, Office of Management and Budget. 1999. Circular A-110. Accessed May 22, 2007. Available at: http://www.whitehouse.gov/omb/circulars/a110/a110.html

APPENDIX 1

This appendix contains an exemplary set of grant management requirements governing the U.S. Deptartment of Transportation and its constituent agencies. This information is reproduced verbatim and was retrieved in this form on May 21, 2007 from http://www.dot.gov/ost/m60/grant/49cfr19.htm.

Title 49 Transportation
49 CFR Part 19—Uniform Administrative Requirements for Grants and Agreements with Institutions of Higher Education, Hospitals, and Other Nonprofit Organizations

SUBPART C Post-Award Requirements

Financial and Program Management
Sec. 19.20 Purpose of financial and program management.
Sections 19.21 through 19.28 prescribe standards for financial management systems, methods for making payments and rules for: satisfying cost sharing and matching requirements, accounting for program income, budget revision approvals, making audits, determining allowability of cost, and establishing fund availability.

Sec. 19.21 Standards for financial management systems.
   a. Federal awarding agencies shall require recipients to relate financial data to performance data and develop unit cost information whenever practical.
   b. Recipients' financial management systems shall provide for the following.
      1. Accurate, current and complete disclosure of the financial results of each federally sponsored project or program in accordance with the reporting requirements set forth in Sec. 19.52. If a Federal awarding agency requires reporting on an accrual basis from a recipient that maintains its records on other than an accrual basis, the recipient shall not be required to establish an accrual accounting system. These recipients may develop such accrual data for its reports on the basis of an analysis of the documentation on hand.
      2. Records that identify adequately the source and application of funds for federally sponsored activities. These records shall contain information pertaining to Federal awards, authorizations, obligations, unobligated balances, assets, outlays, income and interest.
      3. Effective control over and accountability for all funds, property, and other assets. Recipients shall adequately safeguard all such assets and assure they are used solely for authorized purposes.
      4. Comparison of outlays with budget amounts for each award. Whenever appropriate, financial information should be related to performance and unit cost data.
      5. Written procedures to minimize the time elapsing between the transfer of funds to the recipient from the U.S. Treasury and the issuance or redemption of checks, warrants or payments by other means for program purposes by the recipient. To the extent that the provisions of the Cash Management Improvement Act (CMIA) (Pub. L. 101-453) govern, payment methods of State agencies, instrumentalities, and fiscal agents shall be consistent with CMIA Treasury-State Agreements or the CMIA default procedures codified at 31 CFR part 205, "Withdrawal of Cash from the Treasury for Advances under Federal Grant and Other Programs."
      6. Written procedures for determining the reasonableness, allocability, and allowability of costs in accordance with the provisions of the applicable Federal cost principles and the terms and conditions of the award.
      7. Accounting records including cost accounting records that are supported by source documentation.

c. Where the Federal Government guarantees or insures the repayment of money borrowed by the recipient, the Federal awarding agency, at its discretion, may require adequate bonding and insurance if the bonding and insurance requirements of the recipient are not deemed adequate to protect the interest of the Federal Government.

d. The Federal awarding agency may require adequate fidelity bond coverage where the recipient lacks sufficient coverage to protect the Federal Government's interest.

e. Where bonds are required in the situations described above, the bonds shall be obtained from companies holding certificates of authority as acceptable sureties, as prescribed in 31 CFR part 223, "Surety Companies Doing Business with the United States."

Sec. 19.22 Payment.

a. Payment methods shall minimize the time elapsing between the transfer of funds from the United States Treasury and the issuance or redemption of checks, warrants, or payment by other means by the recipients. Payment methods of State agencies or instrumentalities shall be consistent with Treasury-State CMIA agreements or default procedures codified at 31 CFR part 205.

   1. Recipients are to be paid in advance, provided they maintain or demonstrate the willingness to maintain:
       i. Written procedures that minimize the time elapsing between the transfer of funds and disbursement by the recipient, and
       ii. Financial management systems that meet the standards for fund control and accountability as established in section Sec. 19.21.
   2. Cash advances to a recipient organization shall be limited to the minimum amounts needed and be timed to be in accordance with the actual, immediate cash requirements of the recipient organization in carrying out the purpose of the approved program or project. The timing and amount of cash advances shall be as close as is administratively feasible to the actual disbursements by the recipient organization for direct program or project costs and the proportionate share of any allowable indirect costs.

b. Whenever possible, advances shall be consolidated to cover anticipated cash needs for all awards made by the Federal awarding agency to the recipient.

   1. Advance payment mechanisms include, but are not limited to, Treasury check and electronic funds transfer.
   2. Advance payment mechanisms are subject to 31 CFR part 205.
   3. Recipients shall be authorized to submit requests for advances and reimbursements at least monthly when electronic fund transfers are not used.

c. Requests for Treasury check advance payment shall be submitted on SF-270, "Request for Advance or Reimbursement," or other forms as may be authorized by OMB. This form is not to be used when Treasury check advance payments are made to the recipient automatically through the use of a predetermined payment schedule or if precluded by special Federal awarding agency instructions for electronic funds transfer.

d. Reimbursement is the preferred method when the requirements in paragraph (b) cannot be met. Federal awarding agencies may also use this method on any construction agreement, or if the major portion of the construction project is accomplished through private market financing or Federal loans, and the Federal assistance constitutes a minor portion of the project.

1. When the reimbursement method is used, the Federal awarding agency shall make payment within 30 days after receipt of the billing, unless the billing is improper.
2. Recipients shall be authorized to submit request for reimbursement at least monthly when electronic funds transfers are not used.

e. If a recipient cannot meet the criteria for advance payments and the Federal awarding agency has determined that reimbursement is not feasible because the recipient lacks sufficient working capital, the Federal awarding agency may provide cash on a working capital advance basis. Under this procedure, the Federal awarding agency shall advance cash to the recipient to cover its estimated disbursement needs for an initial period generally geared to the awardee's disbursing cycle. Thereafter, the Federal awarding agency shall reimburse the recipient for its actual cash disbursements. The working capital advance method of payment shall not be used for recipients unwilling or unable to provide timely advances to their subrecipient to meet the subrecipient's actual cash disbursements.

f. To the extent available, recipients shall disburse funds available from repayments to and interest earned on a revolving fund, program income, rebates, refunds, contract settlements, audit recoveries, and interest earned on such funds before requesting additional cash payments.

g. Unless otherwise required by statute, Federal awarding agencies shall not withhold payments for proper charges made by recipients at any time during the project period unless the conditions in paragraphs (h)(1) or (2) of this section apply.

1. A recipient has failed to comply with the project objectives, the terms, and conditions of the award, or Federal reporting requirements.
2. The recipient or subrecipient is delinquent in a debt to the United States as defined in OMB Circular A-129, "Managing Federal Credit Programs." Under such conditions, the Federal awarding agency may, upon reasonable notice, inform the recipient that payments shall not be made for obligations incurred after a specified date until the conditions are corrected or the indebtedness to the Federal Government is liquidated.

h. Standards governing the use of banks and other institutions as depositories of funds advanced under awards are as follows.

1. Except for situations described in paragraph (i)(2) of this section, Federal awarding agencies shall not require separate depository accounts for funds provided to a recipient or establish any eligibility requirements for depositories for funds provided to a recipient. However, recipients must be able to account for the receipt, obligation and expenditure of funds.
2. Advances of Federal funds shall be deposited and maintained in insured accounts whenever possible.

i. Consistent with the national goal of expanding the opportunities for women-owned and minority-owned business enterprises, recipients shall be encouraged to use women-owned and minority-owned banks (a bank which is owned at least 50 percent by women or minority group members).

j. Recipients shall maintain advances of Federal funds in interest bearing accounts, unless the conditions in paragraphs (k)(1), (2) or (3) of this section apply.

1. The recipient receives less than $120,000 in Federal awards per year.

2. The best reasonably available interest bearing account would not be expected to earn interest in excess of $250 per year on Federal cash balances.

3. The depository would require an average or minimum balance so high that it would not be feasible within the expected Federal and non-Federal cash resources.

k. For those entities where CMIA and its implementing regulations do not apply, interest earned on Federal advances deposited in interest bearing accounts shall be remitted annually to Department of Health and Human Services, Payment Management System, P.O. Box 6021, Rockville, MD 20852. Interest amounts up to $250 per year may be retained by the recipient for administrative expense. In keeping with Electric Funds Transfer rules, (31 CFR part 206), interest should be remitted to the HHS Payment Management System through an electric medium such as the FED-WIRE Deposit system. Recipients which do not have this capability should use a check. State universities and hospitals shall comply with CMIA, as it pertains to interest. If an entity subject to CMIA uses its own funds to pay pre-award costs for discretionary awards without prior written approval from the Federal awarding agency, it waives its right to recover the interest under CMIA.

l. Except as noted elsewhere in this part, only the following forms shall be authorized for the recipients in requesting advances and reimbursements. Federal agencies shall not require more than an original and two copies of these forms.

1. SF-270, Request for Advance or Reimbursement. Each Federal awarding agency shall adopt the SF-270 as a standard form for all nonconstruction programs when electronic funds transfer or predetermined advance methods are not used. Federal awarding agencies, however, have the option of using this form for construction programs in lieu of the SF-271, "Outlay Report and Request for Reimbursement for Construction Programs."

2. SF-271, Outlay Report and Request for Reimbursement for Construction Programs. Each Federal awarding agency shall adopt the SF-271 as the standard form to be used for requesting reimbursement for construction programs. However, a Federal awarding agency may substitute the SF-270 when the Federal awarding agency determines that it provides adequate information to meet Federal needs.

Sec. 19.23 Cost sharing or matching.

a. All contributions, including cash and third party in-kind, shall be accepted as part of the recipient's cost sharing or matching when such contributions meet all of the following criteria.

1. Are verifiable from the recipient's records.

2. Are not included as contributions for any other federally assisted project or program.

3. Are necessary and reasonable for proper and efficient accomplishment of project or program objectives.

4. Are allowable under the applicable cost principles.

  5. Are not paid by the Federal Government under another award, except where authorized by Federal statute to be used for cost sharing or matching.
  6. Are provided for in the approved budget when required by the Federal awarding agency.
  7. Conform to other provisions of this part, as applicable.
  b. Unrecovered indirect costs may be included as part of cost sharing or matching only with the prior approval of the Federal awarding agency.
  c. Values for recipient contributions of services and property shall be established in accordance with the applicable cost principles. If a Federal awarding agency authorizes recipients to donate buildings or land for construction/facilities acquisition projects or long-term use, the value of the donated property for cost sharing or matching shall be the lesser of (1) or (2).
     1. The certified value of the remaining life of the property recorded in the recipient's accounting records at the time of donation.
     2. The current fair market value. However, when there is sufficient justification, the Federal awarding agency may approve the use of the current fair market value of the donated property, even if it exceeds the certified value at the time of donation to the project.
  d. Volunteer services furnished by professional and technical personnel, consultants, and other skilled and unskilled labor may be counted as cost sharing or matching if the service is an integral and necessary part of an approved project or program. Rates for volunteer services shall be consistent with those paid for similar work in the recipient's organization. In those instances in which the required skills are not found in the recipient organization, rates shall be consistent with those paid for similar work in the labor market in which the recipient competes for the kind of services involved. In either case, paid fringe benefits that are reasonable, allowable, and allocable may be included in the valuation.
  e. When an employer other than the recipient furnishes the services of an employee, these services shall be valued at the employee's regular rate of pay (plus an amount of fringe benefits that are reasonable, allowable, and allocable, but exclusive of overhead costs), provided these services are in the same skill for which the employee is normally paid.
  f. Donated supplies may include such items as expendable equipment, office supplies, laboratory supplies or workshop and classroom supplies. Value assessed to donated supplies included in the cost sharing or matching share shall be reasonable and shall not exceed the fair market value of the property at the time of the donation.
  g. The method used for determining cost sharing or matching for donated equipment, buildings and land for which title passes to the recipient may differ according to the purpose of the award, if the conditions in paragraphs (g)(1) or (2) of this section apply.
     1. If the purpose of the award is to assist the recipient in the acquisition of equipment, buildings, or land, the total value of the donated property may be claimed as cost sharing or matching.
     2. If the purpose of the award is to support activities that require the use of equipment, buildings, or land, normally only depreciation or use charges for equipment

and buildings may be made. However, the full value of equipment or other capital assets and fair rental charges for land may be allowed, provided that the Federal awarding agency has approved the charges.

h. The value of donated property shall be determined in accordance with the usual accounting policies of the recipient, with the following qualifications.

   1. The value of donated land and buildings shall not exceed its fair market value at the time of donation to the recipient as established by an independent appraiser (e.g., certified real property appraiser or General Services Administration representative) and certified by a responsible official of the recipient.

   2. The value of donated equipment shall not exceed the fair market value of equipment of the same age and condition at the time of donation.

   3. The value of donated space shall not exceed the fair rental value of comparable space as established by an independent appraisal of comparable space and facilities in a privately-owned building in the same locality.

   4. The value of loaned equipment shall not exceed its fair rental value.

   5. The following requirements pertain to the recipient's supporting records for in-kind contributions from third parties.

      i. Volunteer services shall be documented and, to the extent feasible, supported by the same methods used by the recipient for its own employees.

      ii. The basis for determining the valuation for personal service, material, equipment, buildings and land shall be documented.

i. Section 18(e) of the Federal Transit Act, as amended, (49 U.S.C. app. 1614(e)) provides that the Federal share for operating assistance shall not exceed 50 percent of the net cost. At least 50 percent of the remainder (the local share) must be derived from sources other than Federal funds or revenues of the system; and up to half of the local share may be derived from other Federal funds. For purposes of determining local share for Section 18 operating assistance, the term "Federal funds or revenues" does not include funds received pursuant to a service agreement with a State or local service agency or a private social service organization. Nonregulatory guidance is contained in FTA Circular 9040.1B, Section 18 Program Guidance and Grant Application Instructions, Chapter III, Section 7.

Sec. 19.24 Program income.

a. Federal awarding agencies shall apply the standards set forth in this section in requiring recipient organizations to account for program income related to projects financed in whole or in part with Federal funds.

b. Except as provided in paragraph (h) of this section, program income earned during the project period shall be retained by the recipient and, in accordance with Federal awarding agency regulations or the terms and conditions of the award, shall be used in one or more of the ways listed in the following.

   1. Added to funds committed to the project by the Federal awarding agency and recipient and used to further eligible project or program objectives.

   2. Used to finance the non-Federal share of the project or program.

   3. Deducted from the total project or program allowable cost in determining the net allowable costs on which the Federal share of costs is based.

c. When an agency authorizes the disposition of program income as described in paragraphs (b)(1) or (b)(2) of this section, program income in excess of any limits stipulated shall be used in accordance with paragraph (b)(3) of this section.

d. In the event that the Federal awarding agency does not specify in its regulations or the terms and conditions of the award how program income is to be used, paragraph (b)(3) of this section shall apply automatically to all projects or programs except research. For awards that support research, paragraph (b)(1) of this section shall apply automatically unless the awarding agency indicates in the terms and conditions another alternative on the award or the recipient is subject to special award conditions, as indicated in Sec. 19.14.

e. Unless Federal awarding agency regulations or the terms and conditions of the award provide otherwise, recipients shall have no obligation to the Federal Government regarding program income earned after the end of the project period.

f. If authorized by Federal awarding agency regulations or the terms and conditions of the award, costs incident to the generation of program income may be deducted from gross income to determine program income, provided these costs have not been charged to the award.

g. Proceeds from the sale of property shall be handled in accordance with the requirements of the Property Standards (See Sec. 19.30 through 19.37).

h. Unless Federal awarding agency regulations or the terms and condition of the award provide otherwise, recipients shall have no obligation to the Federal Government with respect to program income earned from license fees and royalties for copyrighted material, patents, patent applications, trademarks, and inventions produced under an award. However, Patent and Trademark Amendments (35 U.S.C. 18) apply to inventions made under an experimental, developmental, or research award.

i. Section 4(a) of the Federal Transit Act, as amended, (49 U.S.C. app. 1603(a)) allows FTA recipients to retain program income for allowable capital or operating expenses, but program income may not be used to refund or reduce the local share of a grant. The Section 16 and 18 programs, however, operate differently. Under the special authority to set appropriate terms and conditions for the Section 16 (b)(2) program, program income in the form of contract service revenue may be used as local share without a proportionate reduction in the Federal share. Similarly, Section 18 allows the use of program income in the form of contract service revenue as local share without requiring a proportionate reduction in the Federal share. Grantees must account for program income in their accounting systems, which are subject to audit. The accounting system must be capable of identifying program income and the purpose for which it was used. Nonregulatory guidance is contained in FTA Notice N 5.5005.1, Guidance on Program Income and Sales Proceeds.

Sec. 19.25 Revision of budget and program plans.

a. The budget plan is the financial expression of the project or program as approved during the award process. It may include either the Federal and non-Federal share, or only the Federal share, depending upon Federal awarding agency requirements. It shall be related to performance for program evaluation purposes whenever appropriate.

b. Recipients are required to report deviations from budget and program plans, and request prior approvals for budget and program plan revisions, in accordance with this section.

c. For nonconstruction awards, recipients shall request prior approvals from Federal awarding agencies for one or more of the following program or budget related reasons.

    1. Change in the scope or the objective of the project or program (even if there is no associated budget revision requiring prior written approval).

    2. Change in a key person specified in the application or award document.

    3. The absence for more than three months, or a 25 percent reduction in time devoted to the project, by the approved project director or principal investigator.

    4. The need for additional Federal funding.

    5. The transfer of amounts budgeted for indirect costs to absorb increases in direct costs, or vice versa, if approval is required by the Federal awarding agency.

    6. The inclusion, unless waived by the Federal awarding agency, of costs that require prior approval in accordance with OMB Circular A-21, "Cost Principles for Institutions of Higher Education," OMB Circular A-122, "Cost Principles for Nonprofit Organizations," or 45 CFR part 74 Appendix E, "Principles for Determining Costs Applicable to Research and Development under Grants and Contracts with Hospitals," or 48 CFR part 31, "Contract Cost Principles and Procedures," as applicable.

    7. The transfer of funds allotted for training allowances (direct payment to trainees) to other categories of expense.

    8. Unless described in the application and funded in the approved awards, the sub-award, transfer or contracting out of any work under an award. This provision does not apply to the purchase of supplies, material, equipment, or general support services.

d. No other prior approval requirements for specific items may be imposed unless a deviation has been approved by OMB.

e. Except for requirements listed in paragraphs (c)(1) and (c)(4) of this section, Federal awarding agencies are authorized, at their option, to waive cost-related and administrative prior written approvals required by this part and OMB Circulars A-21 and A-122. Such waivers may include authorizing recipients to do any one or more of the following.

    1. Incur pre-award costs 90 calendar days prior to award or more than 90 calendar days with the prior approval of the Federal awarding agency. All pre-award costs are incurred at the recipient's risk (i.e., the Federal awarding agency is under no obligation to reimburse such costs if for any reason the recipient does not receive an award or if the award is less than anticipated and inadequate to cover such costs).

    2. Initiate a one-time extension of the expiration date of the award of up to 12 months unless one or more of the following conditions apply. For one-time extensions, the recipient must notify the Federal awarding agency in writing with the supporting reasons and revised expiration date at least 10 days before

the expiration date specified in the award. This one-time extension may not be exercised merely for the purpose of using unobligated balances.

    i. The terms and conditions of award prohibit the extension.

    ii. The extension requires additional Federal funds.

    iii. The extension involves any change in the approved objectives or scope of the project.

3. Carry forward unobligated balances to subsequent funding periods.
4. For awards that support research, unless the Federal awarding agency provides otherwise in the award or in the agency's regulations, the prior approval requirements described in paragraph (e) of this section are automatically waived (i.e., recipients need not obtain such prior approvals) unless one of the conditions included in paragraph (e)(2) of this section applies.

f. The Federal awarding agency may, at its option, restrict the transfer of funds among direct cost categories or programs, functions, and activities for awards in which the Federal share of the project exceeds $100,000 and the cumulative amount of such transfers exceeds or is expected to exceed 10 percent of the total budget as last approved by the Federal awarding agency. No Federal awarding agency shall permit a transfer that would cause any Federal appropriation or part thereof to be used for purposes other than those consistent with the original intent of the appropriation.

g. All other changes to nonconstruction budgets, except for the changes described in paragraph (j) of this section, do not require prior approval.

h. For construction awards, recipients shall request prior written approval promptly from Federal awarding agencies for budget revisions whenever the conditions in paragraphs (h) (1), (2) or (3) of this section apply.

1. The revision results from changes in the scope or the objective of the project or program.
2. The need arises for additional Federal funds to complete the project.
3. A revision is desired which involves specific costs for which prior written approval requirements may be imposed consistent with applicable OMB cost principles listed in Sec. 19.27.

i. No other prior approval requirements for specific items may be imposed unless a deviation has been approved by OMB.

j. When a Federal awarding agency makes an award that provides support for both construction and nonconstruction work, the Federal awarding agency may require the recipient to request prior approval from the Federal awarding agency before making any fund or budget transfers between the two types of work supported.

k. For both construction and nonconstruction awards, Federal awarding agencies shall require recipients to notify the Federal awarding agency in writing promptly whenever the amount of Federal authorized funds is expected to exceed the needs of the recipient for the project period by more than $5000 or five percent of the Federal award, whichever is greater. This notification shall not be required if an application for additional funding is submitted for a continuation award.

l. When requesting approval for budget revisions, recipients shall use the budget forms that were used in the application unless the Federal awarding agency indicates a letter of request suffices.

m. Within 30 calendar days from the date of receipt of the request for budget revisions, Federal awarding agencies shall review the request and notify the recipient whether the budget revisions have been approved. If the revision is still under consideration at the end of 30 calendar days, the Federal awarding agency shall inform the recipient in writing of the date when the recipient may expect the decision.

Sec. 19.26 Non-Federal audits.

a. Recipients and subrecipients that are institutions of higher education or other non-profit organizations (including hospitals) shall be subject to the audit requirements contained in the Single Audit Act Amendments of 1996 (31 U.S.C. 7501-7507) and revised OMB Circular A-133, "Audits of States, Local Governments, and Nonprofit Organizations."

b. State and local governments shall be subject to the audit requirements contained in the Single Audit Act Amendments of 1996 (31 U.S.C. 7501-7507) and revised OMB Circular A-133, "Audits of States, Local Governments, and Nonprofit Organizations."

c. For profit hospitals not covered by the audit provisions of revised OMB Circular A-133 shall be subject to the audit requirements of the Federal awarding agencies.

d. Commercial organizations shall be subject to the audit requirements of the Federal awarding agency or the prime recipient as incorporated into the award document. [amended at 62 FR 45939 and 45947, August 29, 1997]

Sec. 19.27 Allowable costs.

For each kind of recipient, there is a set of Federal principles for determining allowable costs. Allowability of costs shall be determined in accordance with the cost principles applicable to the entity incurring the costs. Thus, allowability of costs incurred by State, local or federally recognized Indian tribal governments is determined in accordance with the provisions of OMB Circular A-87, "Cost Principles for State and Local Governments." The allowability of costs incurred by nonprofit organizations is determined in accordance with the provisions of OMB Circular A-122, "Cost Principles for Non-Profit Organizations." The allowability of costs incurred by institutions of higher education is determined in accordance with the provisions of OMB Circular A-21, "Cost Principles for Educational Institutions." The allowability of costs incurred by hospitals is determined in accordance with the provisions of Appendix E of 45 CFR part 74, "Principles for Determining Costs Applicable to Research and Development Under Grants and Contracts with Hospitals." The allowability of costs incurred by commercial organizations and those nonprofit organizations listed in Attachment C to Circular A-122 is determined in accordance with the provisions of the Federal Acquisition Regulation (FAR) at 48 CFR part 31.

Sec. 19.28 Period of availability of funds.

Where a funding period is specified, a recipient may charge to the grant only allowable costs resulting from obligations incurred during the funding period and any pre-award costs authorized by the Federal awarding agency.

Property Standards
Sec. 19.30 Purpose of property standards.

a. Sections 19.31 through 19.37 set forth uniform standards governing management and disposition of property furnished by the Federal Government whose cost was charged to a project supported by a Federal award. Federal awarding agencies shall require recipients to observe these standards under awards and shall not impose additional requirements, unless specifically required by Federal statute. The recipient may use its own property management standards and procedures provided it observes the provisions of Sec. 19.31 through 19.37.

b. Transfer of capital assets. Section 12(k) of the Federal Transit Act, as amended, (49 U.S.C. app. 1608(k)) allows the transfer without compensation of real property (including land) and equipment acquired under the Act for another public purpose under certain conditions. Procedures to allow these transfers have not been issued.

Sec. 19.31 Insurance coverage.

Recipients shall, at a minimum, provide the equivalent insurance coverage for real property and equipment acquired with Federal funds as provided to property owned by the recipient. Federally owned property need not be insured unless required by the terms and conditions of the award.

Sec. 19.32 Real property.

Each Federal awarding agency shall prescribe requirements for recipients concerning the use and disposition of real property acquired in whole or in part under awards. Unless otherwise provided by statute, such requirements, at a minimum, shall contain the following.

a. Title to real property shall vest in the recipient subject to the condition that the recipient shall use the real property for the authorized purpose of the project as long as it is needed and shall not encumber the property without approval of the Federal awarding agency.

b. The recipient shall obtain written approval by the Federal awarding agency for the use of real property in other federally sponsored projects when the recipient determines that the property is no longer needed for the purpose of the original project. Use in other project shall be limited to those under federally sponsored projects (i.e., awards) or programs that have purposes consistent with those authorized for support by the Department of Transportation.

c. When the real property is no longer needed as provided in paragraphs (a) and (b) of this section, the recipient shall request disposition instructions from the Federal awarding agency or its successor Federal awarding agency. The Federal awarding agency shall observe one or more of the following disposition instructions.

   1. The recipient may be permitted to retain title without further obligation to the Federal Government after it compensates the Federal Government for that percentage of the current fair market value of the property attributable to the Federal participation in the project.

   2. The recipient may be directed to sell the property under guidelines provided by the Federal awarding agency and pay the Federal Government for that percentage of the current fair market value of the property attributable to the Federal participation in the project (after deducting actual and reasonable selling and fix-up expenses, if any, from the sales proceeds). When the recipient is authorized or

required to sell the property, proper sales procedures shall be established that provide for competition to the extent practicable and result in the highest possible return.

3. The recipient may be directed to transfer title to the property to the Federal Government or to an eligible third party provided that, in such cases, the recipient shall be entitled to compensation for its attributable percentage of the current fair market value of the property.

Sec. 19.33 Federally owned and exempt property.

a. Federally owned property.

1. Title to federally owned property remains vested in the Federal Government. Recipients shall submit annually an inventory listing of federally owned property in their custody to the Federal awarding agency. Upon completion of the award or when the property is no longer needed, the recipient shall report the property to the Federal awarding agency for further Federal agency utilization.

2. If the Federal awarding agency has no further need for the property, it shall be declared excess and reported to the General Services Administration, unless the Federal awarding agency has statutory authority to dispose of the property by alternative methods (e.g., the authority provided by the Federal Technology Transfer Act (15 U.S.C. 3710(I)) to donate research equipment to educational and nonprofit organizations in accordance with E.O. 12821, "Improving Mathematics and Science Education in Support of the National Education Goals.") Appropriate instructions shall be issued to the recipient by the Federal awarding agency.

b. Exempt property. When statutory authority exists, the Federal awarding agency has the option to vest title to property acquired with Federal funds in the recipient without further obligation to the Federal Government and under conditions the Federal awarding agency considers appropriate. Such property is "exempt property." Should a Federal awarding agency not establish conditions, title to exempt property upon acquisition shall vest in the recipient without further obligation to the Federal Government.

Sec. 19.34 Equipment.

a. Title to equipment acquired by a recipient with Federal funds shall vest in the recipient, subject to conditions of this section.

b. The recipient shall not use equipment acquired with Federal funds to provide services to non-Federal outside organizations for a fee that is less than private companies charge for equivalent services, unless specifically authorized by Federal statute, for as long as the Federal Government retains an interest in the equipment.

c. The recipient shall use the equipment in the project or program for which it was acquired as long as needed, whether or not the project or program continues to be supported by Federal funds and shall not encumber the property without approval of the Federal awarding agency. When no longer needed for the original project or program, the recipient shall use the equipment in connection with its other federally sponsored activities, in the following order of priority:

1. Activities sponsored by the Federal awarding agency which funded the original project, then

2. Activities sponsored by other Federal awarding agencies.

d. During the time that equipment is used on the project or program for which it was acquired, the recipient shall make it available for use on other projects or programs if such other use will not interfere with the work on the project or program for which the equipment was originally acquired. First preference for such other use shall be given to other projects or programs sponsored by the Federal awarding agency that financed the equipment; second preference shall be given to projects or programs sponsored by other Federal awarding agencies. If the equipment is owned by the Federal Government, use on other activities not sponsored by the Federal Government shall be permissible if authorized by the Federal awarding agency. User charges shall be treated as program income.

e. When acquiring replacement equipment, the recipient may use the equipment to be replaced as trade-in or sell the equipment and use the proceeds to offset the costs of the replacement equipment subject to the approval of the Federal awarding agency.

f. The recipient's property management standards for equipment acquired with Federal funds and federally owned equipment shall include all of the following.

    1. Equipment records shall be maintained accurately and shall include the following information.

        i. A description of the equipment.

        ii. Manufacturer's serial number, model number, Federal stock number, national stock number, or other identification number.

        iii. Source of the equipment, including the award number.

        iv. Whether title vests in the recipient or the Federal Government.

        v. Acquisition date (or date received, if the equipment was furnished by the Federal Government) and cost.

        vi. Information from which one can calculate the percentage of Federal participation in the cost of the equipment (not applicable to equipment furnished by the Federal Government).

        vii. Location and condition of the equipment and the date the information was reported.

        viii. Unit acquisition cost.

        ix. Ultimate disposition data, including date of disposal and sales price or the method used to determine current fair market value where a recipient compensates the Federal awarding agency for its share.

    2. Equipment owned by the Federal Government shall be identified to indicate Federal ownership.

    3. A physical inventory of equipment shall be taken and the results reconciled with the equipment records at least once every two years. Any differences between quantities determined by the physical inspection and those shown in the accounting records shall be investigated to determine the causes of the difference. The recipient shall, in connection with the inventory, verify the existence, current utilization, and continued need for the equipment.

    4. A control system shall be in effect to insure adequate safeguards to prevent loss, damage, or theft of the equipment. Any loss, damage, or theft of equipment shall be investigated and fully documented; if the equipment was owned by the Federal Government, the recipient shall promptly notify the Federal awarding agency.

5. Adequate maintenance procedures shall be implemented to keep the equipment in good condition.

6. Where the recipient is authorized or required to sell the equipment, proper sales procedures shall be established which provide for competition to the extent practicable and result in the highest possible return.

g. When the recipient no longer needs the equipment, the equipment may be used for other activities in accordance with the following standards. For equipment with a current per unit fair market value of $5,000 or more, the recipient may retain the equipment for other uses provided that compensation is made to the original Federal awarding agency or its successor. The amount of compensation shall be computed by applying the percentage of Federal participation in the cost of the original project or program to the current fair market value of the equipment. If the recipient has no need for the equipment, the recipient shall request disposition instructions from the Federal awarding agency. The Federal awarding agency shall determine whether the equipment can be used to meet the agency's requirements. If no requirement exists within that agency, the availability of the equipment shall be reported to the General Services Administration by the Federal awarding agency to determine whether a requirement for the equipment exists in other Federal agencies. The Federal awarding agency shall issue instructions to the recipient no later than 120 calendar days after the recipient's request and the following procedures shall govern.

1. If so instructed or if disposition instructions are not issued within 120 calendar days after the recipient's request, the recipient shall sell the equipment and reimburse the Federal awarding agency an amount computed by applying to the sales proceeds the percentage of Federal participation in the cost of the original project or program. However, the recipient shall be permitted to deduct and retain from the Federal share $500 or ten percent of the proceeds, whichever is less, for the recipient's selling and handling expenses.

2. If the recipient is instructed to ship the equipment elsewhere, the recipient shall be reimbursed by the Federal Government by an amount which is computed by applying the percentage of the recipient's participation in the cost of the original project or program to the current fair market value of the equipment, plus any reasonable shipping or interim storage costs incurred.

3. If the recipient is instructed to otherwise dispose of the equipment, the recipient shall be reimbursed by the Federal awarding agency for such costs incurred in its disposition.

4. The Federal awarding agency may reserve the right to transfer the title to the Federal Government or to a third party named by the Federal Government when such third party is otherwise eligible under existing statutes. Such transfer shall be subject to the following standards.

   i. The equipment shall be appropriately identified in the award or otherwise made known to the recipient in writing.

   ii. The Federal awarding agency shall issue disposition instructions within 120 calendar days after receipt of a final inventory. The final inventory shall list all equipment acquired with grant funds and federally owned equipment. If the Federal awarding agency fails to issue disposition instructions within the 120 calendar day period, the recipient shall apply the standards of this section, as appropriate.

    iii. When the Federal awarding agency exercises its right to take title, the equipment shall be subject to the provisions for federally owned equipment.

Sec. 19.35 Supplies and other expendable property.

a. Title to supplies and other expendable property shall vest in the recipient upon acquisition. If there is a residual inventory of unused supplies exceeding $5000 in total aggregate value upon termination or completion of the project or program and the supplies are not needed for any other federally sponsored project or program, the recipient shall retain the supplies for use on non-Federal sponsored activities or sell them, but shall, in either case, compensate the Federal Government for its share. The amount of compensation shall be computed in the same manner as for equipment.

b. The recipient shall not use supplies acquired with Federal funds to provide services to non-Federal outside organizations for a fee that is less than private companies charge for equivalent services, unless specifically authorized by Federal statute as long as the Federal Government retains an interest in the supplies.

Sec. 19.36 Intangible property.

a. The recipient may copyright any work that is subject to copyright and was developed, or for which ownership was purchased, under an award. The Federal awarding agency(ies) reserve a royalty-free, nonexclusive and irrevocable right to reproduce, publish, or otherwise use the work for Federal purposes, and to authorize others to do so.

b. Recipients are subject to applicable regulations governing patents and inventions, including government-wide regulations issued by the Department of Commerce at 37 CFR part 401, "Rights to Inventions Made by Nonprofit Organizations and Small Business Firms Under Government Grants, Contracts and Cooperative Agreements."

c. The Federal Government has the right to:

    1. Obtain, reproduce, publish, or otherwise use the data first produced under an award; and

    2. Authorize others to receive, reproduce, publish, or otherwise use such data for Federal purposes.

d. (1) In addition, in response to a Freedom of Information Act (FOIA) request for research data relating to published research findings produced under an award that were used by the Federal Government in developing an agency action that has the force and effect of law, the Federal awarding agency shall request, and the recipient shall provide, within a reasonable time, the research data so that they can be made available to the public through the procedures established under the FOIA. If the Federal awarding agency obtains the research data solely in response to a FOIA request, the agency may charge the requester a reasonable fee equaling the full incremental cost of obtaining the research data. This fee should reflect costs incurred by the agency, the recipient, and applicable subrecipients. This fee is in addition to any fees the agency may assess under the FOIA (5 U.S.C. 552(a)(4)(A)).

    2. The following definitions apply for purposes of this paragraph (d):

        i. Research data is defined as the recorded factual material commonly accepted in the scientific community as necessary to validate research findings, but not any of the following: preliminary analyses, drafts of scientific papers, plans for future research, peer reviews, or communications with colleagues. This "recorded" material excludes physical objects (e.g., laboratory samples). Research data also do not include:

A. Trade secrets, commercial information, materials necessary to be held confidential by a researcher until they are published, or similar information which is protected under law; and

B. Personnel and medical information and similar information the disclosure of which would constitute a clearly unwarranted invasion of personal privacy, such as information that could be used to identify a particular person in a research study.

ii. Published is defined as either when:

A. Research findings are published in a peer-reviewed scientific or technical journal; or

B. A Federal agency publicly and officially cites the research findings in support of an agency action that has the force and effect of law.

iii. Used by the Federal Government in developing an agency action that has the force and effect of law is defined as when an agency publicly and officially cites the research findings in support of an agency action that has the force and effect of law.

e. Title to intangible property and debt instruments acquired under an award or subaward vests upon acquisition in the recipient. The recipient shall use that property for the originally authorized purpose, and the recipient shall not encumber the property without approval of the Federal awarding agency. When no longer needed for the originally authorized purpose, disposition of the intangible property shall occur in accordance with the provisions of paragraph Sec. 19.34(g).

Sec. 19.37 Property trust relationship.

Real property, equipment, intangible property, and debt instruments that are acquired or improved with Federal funds shall be held in trust by the recipient as trustee for the beneficiaries of the project or program under which the property was acquired or improved. Agencies may require recipients to record liens or other appropriate notices of record to indicate that personal or real property has been acquired or improved with Federal funds and that use and disposition conditions apply to the property.

Procurement Standards

Sec. 19.40 Purpose of procurement standards.

Sections 19.41 through 19.48 set forth standards for use by recipients in establishing procedures for the procurement of supplies and other expendable property, equipment, real property, and other services with Federal funds. These standards are furnished to ensure that such materials and services are obtained in an effective manner and in compliance with the provisions of applicable Federal statutes and executive orders. No additional procurement standards or requirements shall be imposed by the Federal awarding agencies upon recipients, unless specifically required by Federal statute or executive order or approved by OMB.

Sec. 19.41 Recipient responsibilities.

The standards contained in this section do not relieve the recipient of the contractual responsibilities arising under its contract(s). The recipient is the responsible authority, without recourse to the Federal awarding agency, regarding the settlement and satisfaction of all contractual and administrative issues arising out of procurements entered into in support of an award or other agreement. This includes disputes, claims, protests of award, source evaluation, or other matters of a contractual nature. Matters concerning violation of statute are to be referred to such Federal, State or local authority as may have proper jurisdiction.

Sec. 19.42 Codes of conduct.

The recipient shall maintain written standards of conduct governing the performance of its employees engaged in the award and administration of contracts. No employee, officer, or agent shall participate in the selection, award, or administration of a contract supported by Federal funds if a real or apparent conflict of interest would be involved. Such a conflict would arise when the employee, officer, or agent, any member of his or her immediate family, his or her partner, or an organization which employs or is about to employ any of the parties indicated herein, has a financial or other interest in the firm selected for an award. The officers, employees, and agents of the recipient shall neither solicit nor accept gratuities, favors, or anything of monetary value from contractors, or parties to subagreements. However, recipients may set standards for situations in which the financial interest is not substantial or the gift is an unsolicited item of nominal value. The standards of conduct shall provide for disciplinary actions to be applied for violations of such standards by officers, employees, or agents of the recipient.

Sec. 19.43 Competition.

All procurement transactions shall be conducted in a manner to provide, to the maximum extent practical, open, and free competition. The recipient shall be alert to organizational conflicts of interest as well as noncompetitive practices among contractors that may restrict or eliminate competition or otherwise restrain trade. In order to ensure objective contractor performance and eliminate unfair competitive advantage, contractors that develop or draft specifications, requirements, statements of work, invitations for bids, and/or requests for proposals shall be excluded from competing for such procurements. Awards shall be made to the bidder or offeror whose bid or offer is responsive to the solicitation and is most advantageous to the recipient, price, quality and other factors considered. Solicitations shall clearly set forth all requirements that the bidder or offeror shall fulfill in order for the bid or offer to be evaluated by the recipient. Any and all bids or offers may be rejected when it is in the recipient's interest to do so.

Sec. 19.44 Procurement procedures.

a. All recipients shall establish written procurement procedures. These procedures shall provide for, at a minimum, that the conditions in paragraphs (a)(1), (2) and (3) of this section apply.

1. Recipients avoid purchasing unnecessary items.
2. Where appropriate, an analysis is made of lease and purchase alternatives to determine which would be the most economical and practical procurement for the Federal Government.

3. Solicitations for goods and services provide for all of the following.
    i. A clear and accurate description of the technical requirements for the material, product or service to be procured. In competitive procurements, such a description shall not contain features, which unduly restrict competition.
    ii. Requirements which the bidder must fulfill and all other factors to be used in evaluating bids or proposals.
    iii. A description, whenever practicable, of technical requirements in terms of functions to be performed or performance required, including the range of acceptable characteristics or minimum acceptable standards.
    iv. The specific features of "brand name or equal" descriptions that bidders are required to meet when such items are included in the solicitation.
    v. The acceptance, to the extent practicable and economically feasible, of products and services dimensioned in the metric system of measurement.
    vi. Preference, to the extent practicable and economically feasible, for products and services that conserve natural resources and protect the environment and are energy efficient.
b. Positive efforts shall be made by recipients to utilize small businesses, minority-owned firms, and women's business enterprises, whenever possible. Recipients of Federal awards shall take all of the following steps to further this goal.
    1. Ensure that small businesses, minority-owned firms, and women's business enterprises are used to the fullest extent practicable.
    2. Make information on forthcoming opportunities available and arrange time-frames for purchases and contracts to encourage and facilitate participation by small businesses, minority-owned firms, and women's business enterprises.
    3. Consider in the contract process whether firms competing for larger contracts intend to subcontract with small businesses, minority-owned firms, and women's business enterprises.
    4. Encourage contracting with consortiums of small businesses, minority-owned firms and women's business enterprises when a contract is too large for one of these firms to handle individually.
    5. Use the services and assistance, as appropriate, of such organizations as the Small Business Administration and the Department of Commerce's Minority Business Development Agency in the solicitation and utilization of small businesses, minority-owned firms, and women's business enterprises.
c. The type of procuring instruments used (e.g., fixed price contracts, cost reimbursable contracts, purchase orders, and incentive contracts) shall be determined by the recipient but shall be appropriate for the particular procurement and for promoting the best interest of the program or project involved. The "cost-plus-a-percentage-of-cost" or "percentage of construction cost" methods of contracting shall not be used.
d. Contracts shall be made only with responsible contractors who possess the potential ability to perform successfully under the terms and conditions of the proposed procurement. Consideration shall be given to such matters as contractor integrity, record of past performance, financial and technical resources or accessibility to other necessary resources. In certain circumstances, contracts with certain parties

are restricted by 49 CFR part 29, the implementation of E.O.'s 12549 and 12689, "Debarment and Suspension."

e. Recipients shall, on request, make available for the Federal awarding agency, pre-award review and procurement documents, such as request for proposals or invitations for bids, independent cost estimates, etc., when any of the following conditions apply.

1. A recipient's procurement procedures or operation fails to comply with the procurement standards in this part.
2. The procurement is expected to exceed the small purchase threshold fixed at 41 U.S.C. 403(11) (currently $25,000) and is to be awarded without competition or only one bid or offer is received in response to a solicitation.
3. The procurement, which is expected to exceed the small purchase threshold, specifies a "brand name" product.
4. The proposed award over the small purchase threshold is to be awarded to other than the apparent low bidder under a sealed bid procurement.
5. A proposed contract modification changes the scope of a contract or increases the contract amount by more than the amount of the small purchase threshold.

f. Additional procurement procedures.

1. Section 165 of the STAA of 1982, as amended; Section 337 of the Surface Transportation and Uniform Relocation Assistance Act (STURAA) of 1987, 49 U.S.C. 1601, Section 1048 of the Intermodal Surface Transportation Efficiency Act of 1991, and Section 9129 of the Aviation Safety and Capacity Expansion Act of 1990, 49 U.S.C. app. 2226, impose Buy America requirements on the procurement of foreign products and materials by all recipients of FHWA, FTA, and Federal Aviation Administration (FAA) funds. Procedures are contained in 4 CFR part 660, Buy America Requirements and part 661, Buy America Requirements—STAA of 1982. In addition, for FTA recipients, non-regulatory guidance is contained in FTA Circular 4220.1B, Third Party Contracting Guidelines, Chapter I, Section 11. Non-regulatory guidance for FAA programs is contained in FAA Order 5100.38A and special conditions in grant awards.
2. Section 511(a)(16) of the Airport and Airway Improvement Act of 1982, 49 U.S.C. app. 2210, requires FAA recipients and subrecipients to extend the use of qualifications-based (e.g., architectural and engineering services) contract selection procedures to certain other related areas and to award such contracts in the same manner as Federal contracts for architectural and engineering services are negotiated under Title IX of the 1949 Federal Property and Administrative Services Act, or equivalent airport sponsor qualifications based requirements. Non-regulatory guidance for FAA programs is contained in FAA Order 5100.38A and special conditions in grant awards.
3. Section 3(a)(2)(C) of the Federal Transit Act, as amended, (49 U.S.C. app. 1602(a)(2)(C)) prohibits the use of grant or loan funds to support procurements utilizing exclusionary or discriminatory specifications. Nonregulatory guidance is contained in FTA Circular 4220.1B, Third Party Contracting Guidelines, Chapter I, Section 15 and Attachment A.

4. Section 1241(b)(1) of 46 U.S.C. and 46 CFR part 381, Cargo Preference–U.S. Flag Vessels impose cargo preference requirements on the shipment of foreign made goods for FTA recipients. Nonregulatory guidance is contained in FTA Circular 4220.1B, Third Party Contracting Guidelines, Chapter I, Section 10.

Sec. 19.45 Cost and price analysis.

Some form of cost or price analysis shall be made and documented in the procurement files in connection with every procurement action. Price analysis may be accomplished in various ways, including the comparison of price quotations submitted, market prices and similar indicia, together with discounts. Cost analysis is the review and evaluation of each element of cost to determine reasonableness, allocability, and allowability.

Sec. 19.46 Procurement records.

Procurement records and files for purchases in excess of the small purchase threshold shall include the following at a minimum:

a. Basis for contractor selection,
b. Justification for lack of competition when competitive bids or offers are not obtained, and
c. Basis for award cost or price.

Sec. 19.47 Contract administration.

A system for contract administration shall be maintained to ensure contractor conformance with the terms, conditions and specifications of the contract and to ensure adequate and timely follow up of all purchases. Recipients shall evaluate contractor performance and document, as appropriate, whether contractors have met the terms, conditions, and specifications of the contract.

Sec. 19.48 Contract provisions.

The recipient shall include, in addition to provisions to define a sound and complete agreement, the following provisions in all contracts. The following provisions shall also be applied to subcontracts.

a. Contracts in excess of the small purchase threshold shall contain contractual provisions or conditions that allow for administrative, contractual, or legal remedies in instances in which a contractor violates or breaches the contract terms, and provide for such remedial actions as may be appropriate.

b. All contracts in excess of the small purchase threshold shall contain suitable provisions for termination by the recipient, including the manner by which termination shall be effected and the basis for settlement. In addition, such contracts shall describe conditions under which the contract may be terminated for default as well as conditions where the contract may be terminated because of circumstances beyond the control of the contractor.

c. Except as otherwise required by statute, an award that requires the contracting (or subcontracting) for construction or facility improvements shall provide for the recipient to follow its own requirements relating to bid guarantees, performance bonds, and payment bonds unless the construction contract or subcontract exceeds $100,000. For those contracts or subcontracts exceeding $100,000, the Federal awarding agency may accept the bonding policy and requirements of the recipient, provided the Federal awarding agency has made a determination that the Federal

Government's interest is adequately protected. If such a determination has not been made, the minimum requirements shall be as follows.

1. A bid guarantee from each bidder equivalent to five percent of the bid price. The "bid guarantee" shall consist of a firm commitment such as a bid bond, certified check, or other negotiable instrument accompanying a bid as assurance that the bidder shall, upon acceptance of his bid, execute such contractual documents as may be required within the time specified.

2. A performance bond on the part of the contractor for 100 percent of the contract price. A "performance bond" is one executed in connection with a contract to secure fulfillment of all the contractor's obligations under such contract.

3. A payment bond on the part of the contractor for 100 percent of the contract price. A "payment bond" is one executed in connection with a contract to assure payment as required by statute of all persons supplying labor and material in the execution of the work provided for in the contract.

4. Where bonds are required in the situations described herein, the bonds shall be obtained from companies holding certificates of authority as acceptable sureties pursuant to 31 CFR part 223, "Surety Companies Doing Business with the United States."

d. All negotiated contracts (except those for less than the small purchase threshold) awarded by recipients shall include a provision to the effect that the recipient, the Federal awarding agency, the Comptroller General of the United States, or any of their duly authorized representatives, shall have access to any books, documents, papers and records of the contractor which are directly pertinent to a specific program for the purpose of making audits, examinations, excerpts and transcriptions.

e. All contracts, including small purchases, awarded by recipients and their contractors shall contain the procurement provisions of Appendix A to this part, as applicable.

Reports and Records

Sec. 19.50 Purpose of reports and records.

Sections 19.51 through 19.53 set forth the procedures for monitoring and reporting on the recipient's financial and program performance and the necessary standard reporting forms. They also set forth record retention requirements.

Sec. 19.51 Monitoring and reporting program performance.

a. Recipients are responsible for managing and monitoring each project, program, subaward, function or activity supported by the award. Recipients shall monitor subawards to ensure subrecipients have met the audit requirements as delineated in Sec. 19.26.

b. The Federal awarding agency shall prescribe the frequency with which the performance reports shall be submitted. Except as provided in Sec. 19.51(f), performance reports shall not be required more frequently than quarterly or, less frequently than annually. Annual reports shall be due 90 calendar days after the grant year; quarterly or semi-annual reports shall be due 30 days after the reporting period. The Federal awarding agency may require annual reports before the anniversary dates of multiple year awards in lieu of these requirements. The final performance reports are due 90 calendar days after the expiration or termination of the award.

    c. If inappropriate, a final technical or performance report shall not be required after completion of the project.

    d. When required, performance reports shall generally contain, for each award, brief information on each of the following.

      1. A comparison of actual accomplishments with the goals and objectives established for the period, the findings of the investigator, or both. Whenever appropriate and the output of programs or projects can be readily quantified, such quantitative data should be related to cost data for computation of unit costs.

      2. Reasons why established goals were not met, if appropriate.

      3. Other pertinent information including, when appropriate, analysis and explanation of cost overruns or high unit costs.

    e. Recipients shall not be required to submit more than the original and two copies of performance reports.

    f. Recipients shall immediately notify the Federal awarding agency of developments that have a significant impact on the award-supported activities. Also, notification shall be given in the case of problems, delays, or adverse conditions which materially impair the ability to meet the objectives of the award. This notification shall include a statement of the action taken or contemplated, and any assistance needed to resolve the situation.

    g. Federal awarding agencies may make site visits, as needed.

    h. Federal awarding agencies shall comply with clearance requirements of 5 CFR part 1320 when requesting performance data from recipients.

Sec. 19.52 Financial reporting.

    a. The following forms or such other forms as may be approved by OMB are authorized for obtaining financial information from recipients.

      1. SF-269 or SF-269A, Financial Status Report.

         i. Each Federal awarding agency shall require recipients to use the SF-269 or SF-269A to report the status of funds for all nonconstruction projects or programs. A Federal awarding agency may, however, have the option of not requiring the SF-269 or SF-269A when the SF-270, Request for Advance or Reimbursement, or SF-272, Report of Federal Cash Transactions, is determined to provide adequate information to meet its needs, except that a final SF-269 or SF-269A shall be required at the completion of the project when the SF-270 is used only for advances.

        ii. The Federal awarding agency shall prescribe whether the report shall be on a cash or accrual basis. If the Federal awarding agency requires accrual information and the recipient's accounting records are not normally kept on the accrual basis, the recipient shall not be required to convert its accounting system, but shall develop such accrual information through best estimates based on an analysis of the documentation on hand.

        iii. The Federal awarding agency shall determine the frequency of the Financial Status Report for each project or program, considering the size and complexity of the particular project or program. However, the report shall not be required more frequently than quarterly or less frequently than annually. A final report shall be required at the completion of the agreement.

    iv. The Federal awarding agency shall require recipients to submit the SF-269 or SF-269A (an original and no more than two copies) no later than 30 days after the end of each specified reporting period for quarterly and semi-annual reports, and 90 calendar days for annual and final reports. Extensions of reporting due dates may be approved by the Federal awarding agency upon request of the recipient.

2. SF-272, Report of Federal Cash Transactions.

    i. When funds are advanced to recipients the Federal awarding agency shall require each recipient to submit the SF-272 and, when necessary, its continuation sheet, SF-272a. The Federal awarding agency shall use this report to monitor cash advanced to recipients and to obtain disbursement information for each agreement with the recipients.

    ii. Federal awarding agencies may require forecasts of Federal cash requirements in the "Remarks" section of the report.

    iii. When practical and deemed necessary, Federal awarding agencies may require recipients to report in the "Remarks" section the amount of cash advances received in excess of three days. Recipients shall provide short narrative explanations of actions taken to reduce the excess balances.

    iv. Recipients shall be required to submit not more than the original and two copies of the SF-272 15 calendar days following the end of each quarter. The Federal awarding agencies may require a monthly report from those recipients receiving advances totaling $1 million or more per year.

    v. Federal awarding agencies may waive the requirement for submission of the SF-272 for any one of the following reasons:

        A. When monthly advances do not exceed $25,000 per recipient, provided that such advances are monitored through other forms contained in this section;

        B. If, in the Federal awarding agency's opinion, the recipient's accounting controls are adequate to minimize excessive Federal advances; or,

        C. When the electronic payment mechanisms provide adequate data.

b. When the Federal awarding agency needs additional information or more frequent reports, the following shall be observed.

1. When additional information is needed to comply with legislative requirements, Federal awarding agencies shall issue instructions to require recipients to submit such information under the "Remarks" section of the reports.

2. When a Federal awarding agency determines that a recipient's accounting system does not meet the standards in Sec. 19.21, additional pertinent information to further monitor awards may be obtained upon written notice to the recipient until such time as the system is brought up to standard. The Federal awarding agency, in obtaining this information, shall comply with report clearance requirements of 5 CFR part 1320.

    3. Federal awarding agencies are encouraged to shade out any line item on any report if not necessary.

    4. Federal awarding agencies may accept the identical information from the recipients in machine readable format or computer printouts or electronic outputs in lieu of prescribed formats.

    5. Federal awarding agencies may provide computer or electronic outputs to recipients when such expedites or contributes to the accuracy of reporting.

Sec. 19.53 Retention and access requirements for records.

   a. This section sets forth requirements for record retention and access to records for awards to recipients. Federal awarding agencies shall not impose any other record retention or access requirements upon recipients.

   b. Financial records, supporting documents, statistical records, and all other records pertinent to an award shall be retained for a period of three years from the date of submission of the final expenditure report or, for awards that are renewed quarterly or annually, from the date of the submission of the quarterly or annual financial report, as authorized by the Federal awarding agency. The only exceptions are the following.

    1. If any litigation, claim, or audit is started before the expiration of the 3-year period, the records shall be retained until all litigation, claims or audit findings involving the records have been resolved and final action taken.

    2. Records for real property and equipment acquired with Federal funds shall be retained for 3 years after final disposition.

    3. When records are transferred to or maintained by the Federal awarding agency, the 3-year retention requirement is not applicable to the recipient.

    4. Indirect cost rate proposals, cost allocations plans, etc. as specified in paragraph Sec. 19.53(g).

   c. Copies of original records may be substituted for the original records if authorized by the Federal awarding agency.

   d. The Federal awarding agency shall request transfer of certain records to its custody from recipients when it determines that the records possess long term retention value. However, in order to avoid duplicate recordkeeping, a Federal awarding agency may make arrangements for recipients to retain any records that are continuously needed for joint use.

   e. The Federal awarding agency, the Inspector General, Comptroller General of the United States, or any of their duly authorized representatives, have the right of timely and unrestricted access to any books, documents, papers, or other records of recipients that are pertinent to the awards, in order to make audits, examinations, excerpts, transcripts and copies of such documents. This right also includes timely and reasonable access to a recipient's personnel for the purpose of interview and discussion related to such documents. The rights of access in this paragraph are not limited to the required retention period, but shall last as long as records are retained.

   f. Unless required by statute, no Federal awarding agency shall place restrictions on recipients that limit public access to the records of recipients that are pertinent to an award, except when the Federal awarding agency can demonstrate that such records shall be kept confidential and would have been exempted from disclosure pursuant to the Freedom of Information Act (5 U.S.C. 552) if the records had belonged to the Federal awarding agency.

g. Indirect cost rate proposals, cost allocations plans, etc. Paragraphs (g)(1) and (g)(2) of this section apply to the following types of documents, and their supporting records: indirect cost rate computations or proposals, cost allocation plans, and any similar accounting computations of the rate at which a particular group of costs is chargeable (such as computer usage chargeback rates or composite fringe benefit rates).

1. If submitted for negotiation. If the recipient submits to the Federal awarding agency or the subrecipient submits to the recipient the proposal, plan, or other computation to form the basis for negotiation of the rate, then the 3-year retention period for its supporting records starts on the date of such submission.

2. If not submitted for negotiation. If the recipient is not required to submit to the Federal awarding agency or the subrecipient is not required to submit to the recipient the proposal, plan, or other computation for negotiation purposes, then the 3-year retention period for the proposal, plan, or other computation and its supporting records starts at the end of the fiscal year (or other accounting period) covered by the proposal, plan, or other computation.

Termination and Enforcement

Sec. 19.60 Purpose of termination and enforcement.

Sections 19.61 and 19.62 set forth uniform suspension, termination and enforcement procedures.

Sec. 19.61 Termination.

a. Awards may be terminated in whole or in part only if the conditions in paragraphs (a)(1), (2) or (3) of this section apply.

1. By the Federal awarding agency, if a recipient materially fails to comply with the terms and conditions of an award.

2. By the Federal awarding agency with the consent of the recipient, in which case the two parties shall agree upon the termination conditions, including the effective date and, in the case of partial termination, the portion to be terminated.

3. By the recipient upon sending to the Federal awarding agency written notification setting forth the reasons for such termination, the effective date, and, in the case of partial termination, the portion to be terminated. However, if the Federal awarding agency determines in the case of partial termination that the reduced or modified portion of the grant will not accomplish the purposes for which the grant was made, it may terminate the grant in its entirety under either paragraphs (a)(1) or (2) of this section.

b. If costs are allowed under an award, the responsibilities of the recipient referred to in Sec. 19.71(a), including those for property management as applicable, shall be considered in the termination of the award, and provision shall be made for continuing responsibilities of the recipient after termination, as appropriate.

Sec. 19.62 Enforcement.

a. Remedies for noncompliance. If a recipient materially fails to comply with the terms and conditions of an award, whether stated in a Federal statute, regulation, assurance, application, or notice of award, the Federal awarding agency may, in addition to imposing any of the special conditions outlined in Sec. 19.14, take one or more of the following actions, as appropriate in the circumstances.

1. Temporarily withhold cash payments pending correction of the deficiency by the recipient or more severe enforcement action by the Federal awarding agency.
2. Disallow (that is, deny both use of funds and any applicable matching credit for) all or part of the cost of the activity or action not in compliance.
3. Wholly or partly suspend or terminate the current award.
4. Withhold further awards for the project or program.
5. Take other remedies that may be legally available.

b. Hearings and appeals. In taking an enforcement action, the awarding agency shall provide the recipient an opportunity for hearing, appeal, or other administrative proceeding to which the recipient is entitled under any statute or regulation applicable to the action involved.

c. Effects of suspension and termination. Costs of a recipient resulting from obligations incurred by the recipient during a suspension or after termination of an award are not allowable unless the awarding agency expressly authorizes them in the notice of suspension or termination or subsequently. Other recipient costs during suspension or after termination which are necessary and not reasonably avoidable are allowable if the conditions in paragraphs (c)(1) or (2) of this section apply.

1. The costs result from obligations which were properly incurred by the recipient before the effective date of suspension or termination, are not in anticipation of it, and in the case of a termination, are noncancellable.
2. The costs would be allowable if the award were not suspended or expired normally at the end of the funding period in which the termination takes effect.

d. Relationship to debarment and suspension. The enforcement remedies identified in this section, including suspension and termination, do not preclude a recipient from being subject to debarment and suspension under E.O.s 12549 and 12689 and 49 CFR part 29 (see Sec. 19.13).

SUBPART D After-the-Award Requirements

Sec. 19.70 Purpose.
Sections 19.71 through 19.73 contain closeout procedures and other procedures for subsequent disallowances and adjustments.

Sec. 19.71 Closeout procedures.
a. Recipients shall submit, within 90 calendar days after the date of completion of the award, all financial, performance, and other reports as required by the terms and conditions of the award. The Federal awarding agency may approve extensions when requested by the recipient.

b. Unless the Federal awarding agency authorizes an extension, a recipient shall liquidate all obligations incurred under the award not later than 90 calendar days after the funding period or the date of completion as specified in the terms and conditions of the award or in agency implementing instructions.

   c. The Federal awarding agency shall make prompt payments to a recipient for allowable reimbursable costs under the award being closed out.

   d. The recipient shall promptly refund any balances of unobligated cash that the Federal awarding agency has advanced or paid and that is not authorized to be retained by the recipient for use in other projects. OMB Circular A-129 governs unreturned amounts that become delinquent debts.

   e. When authorized by the terms and conditions of the award, the Federal awarding agency shall make a settlement for any upward or downward adjustments to the Federal share of costs after closeout reports are received.

   f. The recipient shall account for any real and personal property acquired with Federal funds or received from the Federal Government in accordance with Sec. 19.31 through 19.37.

   g. In the event a final audit has not been performed prior to the closeout of an award, the Federal awarding agency shall retain the right to recover an appropriate amount after fully considering the recommendations on disallowed costs resulting from the final audit.

Sec. 19.72 Subsequent adjustments and continuing responsibilities.

   a. The closeout of an award does not affect any of the following.

     1. The right of the Federal awarding agency to disallow costs and recover funds on the basis of a later audit or other review.

     2. The obligation of the recipient to return any funds due as a result of later refunds, corrections, or other transactions.

     3. Audit requirements in Sec. 19.26.

     4. Property management requirements in Sec. 19.31 through 19.37.

     5. Records retention as required in Sec. 19.53.

   b. After closeout of an award, a relationship created under an award may be modified or ended in whole or in part with the consent of the Federal awarding agency and the recipient, provided the responsibilities of the recipient referred to in Sec. 19.73(a), including those for property management as applicable, are considered and provisions made for continuing responsibilities of the recipient, as appropriate.

Sec. 19.73 Collection of amounts due.

   a. Any funds paid to a recipient in excess of the amount to which the recipient is finally determined to be entitled under the terms and conditions of the award constitute a debt to the Federal Government. If not paid within a reasonable period after the demand for payment, the Federal awarding agency may reduce the debt by the provisions of paragraphs (a) (1), (2) or (3) of this section.

     1. Making an administrative offset against other requests for reimbursements.

     2. Withholding advance payments otherwise due to the recipient.

     3. Taking other action permitted by statute.

   b. Except as otherwise provided by law, the Federal awarding agency shall charge interest on an overdue debt in accordance with 4 CFR chapter II, "Federal Claims Collection Standards."

Appendix A to Part 19 Contract Provisions

All contracts, awarded by a recipient including small purchases, shall contain the following provisions as applicable:

1. Equal Employment Opportunity—All contracts shall contain a provision requiring compliance with E.O. 11246, "Equal Employment Opportunity," as amended by E.O. 11375, "Amending Executive Order 11246 Relating to Equal Employment Opportunity," and as supplemented by regulations at 41 CFR part 60, "Office of Federal Contract Compliance Programs, Equal Employment Opportunity, Department of Labor."

2. Copeland "Anti-Kickback" Act (18 U.S.C. 874 and 40 U.S.C. 276c)—All contracts and subgrants in excess of $2,000 for construction or repair awarded by recipients and subrecipients shall include a provision for compliance with the Copeland "Anti-Kickback" Act (18 U.S.C. 874), as supplemented by Department of Labor regulations (29 CFR part 3, "Contractors and Subcontractors on Public Building or Public Work Financed in Whole or in part by Loans or Grants from the United States"). The Act provides that each contractor or subrecipient shall be prohibited from inducing, by any means, any person employed in the construction, completion, or repair of public work, to give up any part of the compensation to which he is otherwise entitled. The recipient shall report all suspected or reported violations to the Federal awarding agency.

3. Davis-Bacon Act, as amended (40 U.S.C. 276a to a-7)—When required by Federal program legislation, all construction contracts awarded by the recipients and subrecipients of more than $2000 shall include a provision for compliance with the Davis-Bacon Act (40 U.S.C. 276a to a-7) and as supplemented by Department of Labor regulations (29 CFR part 5, "Labor Standards Provisions Applicable to Contracts Governing Federally Financed and Assisted Construction"). Under this Act, contractors shall be required to pay wages to laborers and mechanics at a rate not less than the minimum wages specified in a wage determination made by the Secretary of Labor. In addition, contractors shall be required to pay wages not less than once a week. The recipient shall place a copy of the current prevailing wage determination issued by the Department of Labor in each solicitation and the award of a contract shall be conditioned upon the acceptance of the wage determination. The recipient shall report all suspected or reported violations to the Federal awarding agency.

4. Contract Work Hours and Safety Standards Act (40 U.S.C. 327-333)—Where applicable, all contracts awarded by recipients in excess of $2,000 for construction contracts and in excess of $2,500 for other contracts that involve the employment of mechanics or laborers shall include a provision for compliance with Sections 102 and 107 of the Contract Work Hours and Safety Standards Act (40 U.S.C. 327-333), as supplemented by Department of Labor regulations (29 CFR part 5). Under Section 102 of the Act, each contractor shall be required to compute the wages of every mechanic and laborer on the basis of a standard work week of 40 hours. Work in excess of the standard work week is permissible provided that the worker

is compensated at a rate of not less than $1^1/_2$ times the basic rate of pay for all hours worked in excess of 40 hours in the work week. Section 107 of the Act is applicable to construction work and provides that no laborer or mechanic shall be required to work in surroundings or under working conditions which are unsanitary, hazardous or dangerous. These requirements do not apply to the purchases of supplies or materials or articles ordinarily available on the open market, or contracts for transportation or transmission of intelligence.

5. Rights to Inventions Made Under a Contract or Agreement—Contracts or agreements for the performance of experimental, developmental, or research work shall provide for the rights of the Federal Government and the recipient in any resulting invention in accordance with 37 CFR part 401, "Rights to Inventions Made by Nonprofit Organizations and Small Business Firms Under Government Grants, Contracts and Cooperative Agreements," and any implementing regulations issued by the awarding agency.

6. Clean Air Act (42 U.S.C. 7401 et seq.) and the Federal Water Pollution Control Act (33 U.S.C. 1251 et seq.), as amended—Contracts and subgrants of amounts in excess of $100,000 shall contain a provision that requires the recipient to agree to comply with all applicable standards, orders or regulations issued pursuant to the Clean Air Act (42 U.S.C. 7401 et seq.) and the Federal Water Pollution Control Act as amended (33 U.S.C. 1251 et seq.). Violations shall be reported to the Federal awarding agency and the Regional Office of the Environmental Protection Agency (EPA).

7. Byrd Anti-Lobbying Amendment (31 U.S.C. 1352)—Contractors who apply or bid for an award of $100,000 or more shall file the certification required by 49 CFR part 20, "New Restrictions on Lobbying." Each tier certifies to the tier above that it will not and has not used Federal appropriated funds to pay any person or organization for influencing or attempting to influence an officer or employee of any agency, a member of Congress, officer or employee of Congress, or an employee of a member of Congress in connection with obtaining any Federal contract, grant or any other award covered by 31 U.S.C. 1352. Each tier shall also disclose any lobbying with non-Federal funds that takes place in connection with obtaining any Federal award. Such disclosures are forwarded from tier to tier up to the recipient.

8. Debarment and Suspension (E.O.s 12549 and 12689)—No contract shall be made to parties listed on the General Services Administration's List of Parties Excluded from Federal Procurement or Nonprocurement Programs in accordance with E.O.s 12549 and 12689, "Debarment and Suspension" and 49 CFR part 29. This list contains the names of parties debarred, suspended, or otherwise excluded by agencies, and contractors declared ineligible under statutory or regulatory authority other than E.O. 12549. Contractors with awards that exceed the small purchase threshold shall provide the required certification regarding its exclusion status and that of its principal employees.

APPENDIX 2

SF-269

FINANCIAL STATUS REPORT
(*Long Form*)
(*Follow instructions on the back*)

1. Federal Agency and Organizational Element to Which Report is Submitted	2. Federal Grant or Other Identifying Number Assigned By Federal Agency	OMB Approval No. **0348-0039**	Page of pages

3. Recipient Organization (Name and complete address, including ZIP code)

4. Employer Identification Number	5. Recipient Account Number or Identifying Number	6. Final Report ☐ Yes ☐ No	7. Basis ☐ Cash ☐ Accrual

8. Funding/Grant Period (*See instructions*) From: (Month, Day, Year)	To: (Month, Day, Year)	9. Period Covered by this Report From: (Month, Day, Year)	To: (Month, Day, Year)

10. Transactions:	I Previously Reported	II This Period	III Cumulative
a. Total outlays			0.00
b. Refunds, rebates, etc.			0.00
c. Program income used in accordance with the deduction alternative			0.00
d. Net outlays (*Line a, less the sum of lines b and c*)	0.00	0.00	0.00
Recipient's share of net outlays, consisting of: e. Third party (in-kind) contributions			0.00
f. Other Federal awards authorized to be used to match this award			0.00
g. Program income used in accordance with the matching or cost sharing alternative			0.00
h. All other recipient outlays not shown on lines e, f or g			0.00
i. Total recipient share of net outlays (*Sum of lines e, f, g and h*)	0.00	0.00	0.00
j. Federal share of net outlays (*line d less line i*)	0.00	0.00	0.00
k. Total unliquidated obligations			
l. Recipient's share of unliquidated obligations			
m. Federal share of unliquidated obligations			
n. Total Federal share (*sum of lines j and m*)			0.00
o. Total Federal funds authorized for this funding period			
p. Unobligated balance of Federal funds (*Line o minus line n*)			0.00
Program income, consisting of: q. Disbursed program income shown on lines c and/or g above			
r. Disbursed program income using the addition alternative			
s. Undisbursed program income			
t. Total program income realized (*Sum of lines q, r and s*)			0.00

11. Indirect Expense	a. Type of Rate (*Place "X" in appropriate box*) ☐ Provisional ☐ Predetermined ☐ Final ☐ Fixed			
	b. Rate	c. Base	d. Total Amount	e. Federal Share

12. *Remarks: Attach any explanations deemed necessary or information required by Federal sponsoring agency in compliance with governing legislation.*

13. Certification: **I certify to the best of my knowledge and belief that this report is correct and complete and that all outlays and unliquidated obligations are for the purposes set forth in the award documents.**

Typed or Printed Name and Title	Telephone (Area code, number and extension)
Signature of Authorized Certifying Official	Date Report Submitted

SF-269 (continued)

FINANCIAL STATUS REPORT
(Long Form)

Public reporting burden for this collection of information is estimated to average 30 minutes per response, including time for reviewing instructions, searching existing data sources, gathering and maintaining the data needed, and completing and reviewing the collection of information. Send comments regarding the burden estimate or any other aspect of this collection of information, including suggestions for reducing this burden, to the Office of Management and Budget, Paperwork Reduction Project (0348-0039), Washington, DC 20503.

Please do not return your completed form to the Office of Management and Budget.

Please type or print legibly. The following general instructions explain how to use the form itself. You may need additional information to complete certain items correctly, or to decide whether a specific item is applicable to this award. Usually, such information will be found in the Federal agency's grant regulations or in the terms and conditions of the award (e.g., how to calculate the Federal share, the permissible uses of program income, the value of in-kind contributions, etc.). You may also contact the Federal agency directly.

Item	Entry

1, 2, and 3. Self-explanatory.

4. Enter the Employer Identification Number (EIN) assigned by the U.S. Internal Revenue Service.

5. Space reserved for an account number or other identifying by the U.S. Internal Revenue Service.

6. Check *yes* only if this is the last report for the period shown in item 8.

7. Self-explanatory.

8. Unless you have received other instructions from the awarding agency, enter the beginning and ending dates of the current funding period. If this is a multi-year program, the Federal agency might require cumulative reporting through consecutive funding periods. In that case, enter the beginning and ending dates of the grant period, and in the rest of these instructions, substitute the term "grant period" for "funding period."

9. Self-explanatory.

10. The purpose of columns, I, II, and III is to show the effect of this reporting period's transactions on cumulative financial status. The amounts entered in column I will normally be the same as those in column III of the previous report in the *same funding period*. If this is the first or only report of the funding period, leave columns I and II blank. If you need to adjust amounts entered on previous reports, footnote the column I entry on this report and attach an explanation.

10a. Enter total gross program outlays. Include disbursements of cash realized as program income if that income will also be shown on lines 10c or 10g. Do not include program income that will be shown on lines 10r or 10s.

For reports prepared on a cash basis, outlays are the sum of actual cash disbursements for direct costs for goods and services, the amount of indirect expense charged, the value of in-kind contributions applied, and the amount of cash advances and payments made to subrecipients. For reports prepared on an accrual basis, outlays are the sum of actual cash disbursements for direct charges for goods and services, the amount of indirect expense incurred, the value of in-kind contributions applied, and the net increase or decrease in the amounts owed by the recipient for goods and other property received, for services performed by employees, contractors, subgrantees and other payees, and other amounts becoming owed under programs for which no current services or performances are required, such as annuities, insurance claims, and other benefit payments.

10b. Enter any receipts related to outlays on the form that are being treated as a reduction of expenditure rather than income, and were not already netted out of the amount shown as outlays on line 10a.

10c. Enter the amount of program income that was used in accordance with the deduction alternative.

Note: Program income used in accordance with other alternatives is entered on lines q, r, and s. Recipients reporting on a cash basis should enter the amount of cash income received; on an accrual basis, enter the program income earned. Program income may or may not have been included in an application budget and/or a budget on the award document. If actual income is from a different source or is significantly different in amount, attach an explanation or use the remarks section.

10d, e, f, g, h, i and j. Self-explanatory.

10k. Enter the total amount of unliquidated obligations, including unliquidated obligations to subgrantees and contractors.

Unliquidated obligations on a cash basis are obligations incurred, but not yet paid. On an accrual basis, they are obligations incurred, but for which an outlay has not yet been recorded.

Do not include any amounts online 10k that have been included on lines 10a and 10j.

On the final report, line 10k must be zero.

10l. Self-explanatory.

10m. On the final report, line 10m must also be zero.

10n, o, p, q, r, s and t. Self-explanatory.

11a. Self-explanatory.

11b. Enter the indirect cost rate in effect during the reporting period.

11c. Enter the amount of the base against which the rate was applied.

11d. Enter the total amount of indirect costs charged during the report period.

11e. Enter the Federal share of the amount in 11d.

Note: If more than one rate was in effect during the period shown in item 8, attach a schedule showing the bases against which the different rates were applied, the respective rates, the calendar periods they were in effect, amounts of indirect expense charged to the project, and the Federal share of indirect expense charged to the project to date.

SF-269A

FINANCIAL STATUS REPORT
(Short Form)
(Follow instructions on the back)

1. Federal Agency and Organizational Element to Which Report is Submitted	2. Federal Grant or Other Identifying Number Assigned By Federal Agency	OMB Approval No. **0348-0038**	Page of
			pages

3. Recipient Organization (Name and complete address, including ZIP code)

4. Employer Identification Number	5. Recipient Account Number or Identifying Number	6. Final Report ☐ Yes ☐ No	7. Basis ☐ Cash ☐ Accrual

8. Funding/Grant Period *(See instructions)* From: (Month, Day, Year)	To: (Month, Day, Year)	9. Period Covered by this Report From: (Month, Day, Year)	To: (Month, Day, Year)

10. Transactions:	I Previously Reported	II This Period	III Cumulative
a. Total outlays			0.00
b. Recipient share of outlays			0.00
c. Federal share of outlays			0.00
d. Total unliquidated obligations			
e. Recipient share of unliquidated obligations			
f. Federal share of unliquidated obligations			
g. Total Federal share *(Sum of lines c and f)*			0.00
h. Total Federal funds authorized for this funding period			
i. Unobligated balance of Federal funds *(Line h minus line g)*			0.00

11. Indirect Expense	a. Type of Rate *(Place "X" in appropriate box)* ☐ Provisional ☐ Predetermined ☐ Final ☐ Fixed			
	b. Rate	c. Base	d. Total Amount	e. Federal Share

12. Remarks: *Attach any explanations deemed necessary or information required by Federal sponsoring agency in compliance with governing legislation.*

13. Certification: **I certify to the best of my knowledge and belief that this report is correct and complete and that all outlays and unliquidated obligations are for the purposes set forth in the award documents.**

Typed or Printed Name and Title	Telephone (Area code, number and extension)
Signature of Authorized Certifying Official	Date Report Submitted

SF-269A (continued)

FINANCIAL STATUS REPORT
(Short Form)

Please type or print legibly. The following general instructions explain how to use the form itself. You may need additional information to complete certain items correctly, or to decide whether a specific item is applicable to this award. Usually, such information will be found in the Federal agency's grant regulations or in the terms and conditions of the award. You may also contact the Federal agency directly.

Item	Entry
1, 2, and 3.	Self-explanatory.
4.	Enter the Employer Identification Number (EIN) assigned by the U.S. Internal Revenue Service.
5.	Space reserved for an account number or other identifying number assigned by the recipient.
6.	Check *yes* only if this is the last report for the period shown in item 8.
7.	Self-explanatory.
8.	Unless you have received other instructions from the awarding agency, enter the beginning and ending dates of the curent funding period. If this is a multi-year program, the Federal agency might require cumulative reporting through consecutive funding periods. In that case, enter the beginning and ending dates of the grant period, and in the rest of these instructions, substitute the term "grant period" for "funding period."
9.	Self-explanatory.
10.	The purpose of columns, I, II, and III is to show the effect of this reporting period's transactions on cumulative financial status. The amounts entered in column I will normally be the same as those in column III of the previous report in *the same funing period*. If this is the first or only report of the funding period, leave columns I and II blank. If you need to adjust amounts entered on previous reports, footnote the column I entry on this report and attach an explanation.
10a.	Enter total program outlays less any rebates, refunds, or other credits. For reports prepared on a cash basis, outlays are the sum of actual cash disbursements for direct costs for goods and services, the amount of indirect expense charged, the value of in-kind contributions applied, and the amount of cash advances and payments made to subrecipients. For reports prepared on an accrual basis, outlays are the sum of actual cash disbursements for direct charges for goods and services, the amount of indirect expense incurred,

Item	Entry
	the value of in-kind contributions applied, and the net increase or decrease in the amounts owed by the recipient for goods and other property received, for services performed by employees, contractors, subgrantees and other payees, and other amounts becoming owed under programs for which no current services or performances are required, such as annuities, insurance claims, and other benefit payments.
10b.	Self-explanatory.
10c.	Self-explanatory.
10d.	Enter the total amount of unliquidated obligations, including unliquidated obligations to subgrantees and contractors.
	Unliquidated obligations on a cash basis are obligations incurred, but not yet paid. On an accrual basis, they are obligations incurred, but for which an outlay has not yet been recorded.
	Do not include any amounts online 10d that have been included on lines 10a, b, or c.
	On the final report, line 10d must be zero.
10e, f, g, h, h and i.	Self-explanatory.
11a.	Self-explanatory.
11b.	Enter the indirect cost rate in effect during the reporting period.
11c.	Enter the amount of the base against which the rate was applied.
11d.	Enter the total amount of indirect costs charged during the report period.
11e.	Enter the Federal share of the amount in 11d.
Note:	If more than one rate was ineffect during the period shown in item 8, attach a schedule showing the bases against which the different rates were applied, the respective rates, the calendar periods they were in effect, amounts of indirect expense charged to the project, and the Federal share of indirect expense charged to the project to date.

SF-272

FEDERAL CASH TRANSACTIONS REPORT	OMB APPROVAL NO. 0348-0003

FEDERAL CASH TRANSACTIONS REPORT

(See instructions on the back. If report is for more than one grant or assistance agreement, attach completed Standard Form 272A.)

1. Federal sponsoring agency and organizational element to which this report is submitted

2. RECIPIENT ORGANIZATION	4. Federal grant or other identification number	5. Recipient's account number or identifying number
Name:	6. Letter of credit number	7. Last payment voucher number
Number and Street:	*Give total number for this period*	
City, State and ZIP Code:	8. Payment Vouchers credited to your account	9. Treasury checks received (*whether or not deposited*)

3. FEDERAL EMPLOYER IDENTIFICATION NO.	10. PERIOD COVERED BY THIS REPORT	
	FROM (*month, day, year*)	TO (*month, day, year*)

11. STATUS OF FEDERAL CASH *(See specific instructions on the back)*	a. Cash on hand beginning of reporting period	$
	b. Letter of credit withdrawls	
	c. Treasury check payments	
	d. Total receipts *(Sum of lines b and c)*	0.00
	e. Total cash available *(Sum of lines a and d)*	0.00
	f. Gross disbursements	
	g. Federal share of program income	
	h. Net disbursements *(Line f minus line g)*	0.00
	i. Adjustments of prior periods	
	j. Cash on hand end of period	$

12. THE AMOUNT SHOWN ON LINE 11j, ABOVE, REPRESENTS CASH RE-QUIREMENTS FOR THE ENSUING Days	13. OTHER INFORMATION	
	a. Interest income	$
	b. Advances to subgrantees or subcontractors	$

14. REMARKS *(Attach additional sheets of plain paper, if more space is required)*

15.	CERTIFICATION		
I certify to the best of my knowledge and belief that this report is true in all respects and that all disbursements have been made for the purpose and conditions of the grant or agreement.	AUTHORIZED CERTIFYING OFFICIAL	SIGNATURE	DATE REPORT SUBMITTED
		TYPED OR PRINTED NAME AND TITLE	TELEPHONE (*Area Code, Number, Extension*)

THIS SPACE FOR AGENCY USE

SF-272 (continued)

INSTRUCTIONS

Public reporting burden for this collection of information is estimated to average 120 minutes per response, including time for reviewing instructions, searching existing data sources, gathering and maintaining the data needed, and completing and reviewing the collection of information. Send comments regarding the burden estimate or any other aspect of this collection of information, including suggestions for reducing this burden, to the Office of Management and Budget, Paperwork Reduction Project (0348-0003), Washington, DC 20503.

Please do not return your completed form to the office of management and budget. send it to the address provided by the sponsoring agency.

Please type or print legibly. Items 1, 2, 8, 9, 10, 11d, 11e, 11h, and 15 are self-explanatory. Specific instructions for other items are as follows:

Item	Entry
3.	Enter Employer Identification Number (EIN) assigned by the U.S. Internal Revenue Service or the FICE (institution) code.
4.	If this report covers more than one grant or other agreement, leave items 4 and 5 blank and provide the information on Standard Form 272A, Report of Federal Cash Transactions - Continued.
	Enter Federal grant number, agreement number, or other identifying numbers if requested by sponsoring agency.
5.	This space reserved for an account number or other identifying number that may be assigned by the recipient.
6.	Enter the letter of credit number that applies to this report. If all advances were made by Treasury check, enter "NA" for not applicable and leave items 7 and 8 blank.
7.	Enter the voucher number of the last letter-of-credit payment voucher (Form TUS 5401) that was credited to your account.
11a.	Enter the total amount of Federal cash on hand at the beginning of the reporting period including all of the Federal funds on deposit, imprest funds, and undeposited Treasury checks.
11b.	Enter total amount of Federal funds received through payment vouchers (Form TUS 5401) that were credited to your account during the reporting period.
11c.	Enter the total amount of all Federal funds received during the reporting period through Treasury checks, whether or not deposited.
11f.	Enter the total Federal cash disbursements, made during the reporting period, including cash received as program income. Disbursements as used here also include the amount of advances and payments less refunds to subgrantees or contractors; the gross amount of direct salaries and wages, including the employee's share of

Item	Entry
	benefits if treated as a direct cost, interdepartmental charges for supplies and services, and the amount to which the recipient is entitled for indirect costs.
11g.	Enter the Federal share of program income that was required to be used on the project or program by the terms of the grant or agreement.
11i.	Enter the amount of all adjustments pertaining to prior periods affecting the ending balance that have not been included in any lines above. Identify each grant or agreement for which adjustment was made, and enter an explanation for each adjustment under "Remarks." Use plain sheets of paper if additional space is required.
11j.	Enter the total amount of Federal cash on hand at the end of the reporting period. This amount should include all funds on deposit, imprest funds, and undeposited funds (line e, less line h, plus or minus line i).
12.	Enter the estimated number of days until the cash on hand, shown on line 11j, will be expended. If more than three days cash requirements are on hand, provide an explanation under "Remarks" as to why the drawdown was made prematurely, or other reasons for the excess cash. The requirement for the explanation does not apply to prescheduled or automatic advances.
13a.	Enter the amount of interest earned on advances of Federal funds but not remitted to the Federal agency. If this includes any amount earned and not remitted to the Federal sponsoring agency for over 60 days, explain under "Remarks." Do not report interest earned on advances to States.
13b.	Enter the amount of advance to secondary recipients included in item 11h.
14.	In addition to providing explanations as required above, give additional explanation deemed necessary by the recipient and for information required by the Federal sponsoring agency in compliance with governing legislation. Use plain sheets of paper if additional space is required.

SF-272A

Public reporting burden for this collection of information is estimated to average 120 minutes per response, including time for reviewing instructions, searching existing data sources, gathering and maintaining the data needed, and completing and reviewing the collection of information. Send comments regarding the burden estimate or any other aspect of this collection of information, including suggestions for reducing this burden, to the Office of Management and Budget, Paperwork Reduction Project (0348-0003), Washington, DC 20503.

Please do not return your completed form to the Office of Management and Budget. Send it to the address provided by the sponsoring agency.

FEDERAL CASH TRANSACTIONS REPORT		OMB APPROVAL No. 0348-0003	
CONTINUATION *(This form is completed and attached to Standard Form 272 only when reporting more than one grant or assistance agreement.)*		1. FEDERAL SPONSORING AGENCY AND ORGANIZATIONAL ELEMENT TO WHICH THIS REPORT IS SUBMITTED	

2. RECIPIENT ORGANIZATION *(Give name only as shown in item 2, SF-272)*

3. PERIOD COVERED BY THIS REPORT *(As shown on SF-272)*

FROM *(month, day, year)* — TO *(month, day, year)*

4. List information below for each grant or other agreement covered by this report. Use additional forms if more space is required.

FEDERAL GRANT OR OTHER IDENTIFICATION NUMBER *(Show a subdivision by other identifying number if required by the Federal Sponsoring agency)*	RECIPIENT ACCOUNT NUMBER OR OTHER IDENTIFYING NUMBER	FEDERAL SHARE OF NET DISBURSEMENTS	
		NET DISBURSEMENTS *(Gross disbursements less program income received)* FOR REPORTING PERIOD	CUMULATIVE NET DISBURSEMENTS
(a)	*(b)*	*(c)*	*(d)*
		$	$
5. TOTALS *(Should correspond with amounts shown on SF - 272 as follows: column (c) the same as line 11h; column (d) the sum of lines 11h and 11i of the SF-272 and cumulative disbursements shown on last report. Attach explanation of any differences.)*		$	$

SF–270

REQUEST FOR ADVANCE OR REIMBURSEMENT				

<table>
<tr><td rowspan="3">REQUEST FOR ADVANCE
OR REIMBURSEMENT

(See instructions on back)</td><td colspan="2">OMB APPROVAL NO.

0348-0004</td><td colspan="2">PAGE   OF

               PAGES</td></tr>
<tr><td rowspan="2">1.
TYPE OF
PAYMENT
REQUESTED</td><td>a. "X" one or both boxes
☐ ADVANCE ☐ REIMBURSE-
                   MENT</td><td colspan="2" rowspan="2">2. BASIS OF REQUEST

☐ CASH

☐ ACCRUAL</td></tr>
<tr><td>b. "X" the applicable box
☐ FINAL   ☐ PARTIAL</td></tr>
</table>

3. FEDERAL SPONSORING AGENCY AND ORGANIZATIONAL ELEMENT TO WHICH THIS REPORT IS SUBMITTED	4. FEDERAL GRANT OR OTHER IDENTIFYING NUMBER ASSIGNED BY FEDERAL AGENCY	5. PARTIAL PAYMENT REQUEST NUMBER FOR THIS REQUEST
6. EMPLOYER IDENTIFICATION NUMBER / **7. RECIPIENT'S ACCOUNT NUMBER OR IDENTIFYING NUMBER**	8. **PERIOD COVERED BY THIS REQUEST** FROM *(month, day, year)* / TO *(month, day, year)*	
9. RECIPIENT ORGANIZATION *Name*: *Number and Street*: *City, State and Zip Code*:	10. PAYEE *(Where check is to be sent if different than item 9)* *Name*: *Number and Street*: *City, State and Zip Code*:	

11.   COMPUTATION OF AMOUNT OF REIMBURSEMENT/ADVANCES REQUESTED

PROGRAMS/FUNCTIONS/ACTIVITIES ▶	(a)	(b)	(c)	TOTAL
a. Total program outlays to date *(As of date)*	$	$	$	$ 0.00
b. *Less*: Cumulative program income				0.00
c. Net program outlays (*Line a minus line b*)	0.00	0.00	0.00	0.00
d. Estimated net cash outlays for advance period				0.00
e. Total (*Sum of lines c & d*)	0.00	0.00	0.00	0.00
f. Non-Federal share of amount on line e				0.00
g. Federal share of amount on line e				0.00
h. Federal payments previously requested				0.00
i. Federal share now requested (*Line g minus line h*)	0.00	0.00	0.00	0.00
j. Advances required by mouth, when requested by Federal grantor agency for use in making prescheduled advances 1st month				0.00
2nd month				0.00
3rd month				0.00

12.   ALTERNATE COMPUTATION FOR ADVANCES ONLY

a. Estimated Federal cash outlays that will be made during period covered by the advance	$
b. *Less*: Estimated balance of Federal cash on hand as of beginning of advance period	
c. Amount requested (*Line a minus line b*)	$ 0.00

SF-270 (continued)

13.	**CERTIFICATION**	
I certify that to the best of my knowledge and belief the data on the reverse are correct and that all outlays were made in accordance with the grant conditions or other agreement and that payment is due and has not been previously requested.	SIGNATURE OR AUTHORIZED CERTIFYING OFFICIAL	DATE REQUEST SUBMITTED
	TYPED OR PRINTED NAME AND TITLE	TELEPHONE (AREA CODE, NUMBER, EXTENSION)

This space for agency use

INSTRUCTIONS

Please type or print legibly. Items 1, 3, 5, 9, 10, 11e, 11f, 11g, 11i, 12, and 13 are self-explanatory. Specific instructions for other items are as follows:

Item	Entry

2. Indicate whether request is prepared on cash or accrued expenditure basis. All requests for advances shall be prepared on a cash basis.

4. Enter the Federal grant number, or other identifying number assigned by the Federal sponsoring agency. If the advance or reimbursement is for more than one grant or other agreement, insert N/A; then, show the aggregate amounts. On a separate sheet, list each grant or agreement number and the Federal share of outlays made against the grant or agreement.

6. Enter the employer identification number assigned by the U.S. Internal Revenue Service, or the FICE (institution) code if requested by the Federal agency.

7. This space is reserved for an account number or other identifying number that may be assigned by the recipient.

8. Enter the month, day, and year for the beginning and ending of the period covered in this request. If the request is for an advance or for both an advance and reimbursement, show the period that the advance will cover. If the request is for reimbursement, show the period for which the reimbursement is requested.

Note: The Federal sponsoring agencies have the option of requiring recipients to complete items 11 or 12, but not both. Item 12 should be used when only a minimum amount of information is needed to make an advance and outlay information contained in item 11 can be obtained in a timely manner from other reports.

11. The purpose of the vertical columns (a), (b), and (c) is to provide space for separate cost breakdowns when a project has been planned and budgeted by program, function, or

activity. If additional columns are needed, use as many additional forms as needed and indicate page number in space provided in upper right; however, the summary totals of all programs, functions, or activities should be shown in the "total" column on the first page.

11a. Enter in "as of date," the month, day and year of the ending of the accounting period to which this amount applies. Enter program outlays to date (net of refunds, rebates and discounts), in the appropriate columns. For requests prepared on a cash basis, outlays are the sum of actual cash disbursements for good and services, the amount of indirect expenses charged, the value of in-kind contributions applied, and the amount of cash advances and payments made to subcontractors and subrecipients. For requests prepared on an accrued expenditure basis, outlays are the sum of the actual cash disbursements, the amount of indirect expenses incurred, and the net increase (or decrease) in the amounts owed by the recipient for goods and other property received and for services performed by employees, contracts, subgrantees and other payees.

11b. Enter the cumulative cash income received to date, if requests are prepared on a cash basis. For requests prepared on an accrued expenditure basis, enter the cumulative income earned to date. Under either basis, enter only the amount applicable to program income that was required to be used for the project or program by the terms of the grant or other agreement.

11d. Only when making requests for advance payments, enter the total estimated amount of cash outlays that will be made during the period covered by the advance.

13. Complete the certification before submitting this request.

SF–271

OUTLAY REPORT AND REQUEST FOR REIMBURSEMENT FOR CONSTRUCTION PROGRAMS *(See instructions on back)*	OMB APPROVAL NO. 0348-0002		PAGE OF PAGES
	1. TYPE OF REQUEST ☐ FINAL ☐ PARTIAL		2. BASIS OF REQUEST ☐ CASH ☐ ACCRUAL

3. FEDERAL SPONSORING AGENCY AND ORGANIZATIONAL ELEMENT TO WHICH THIS REPORT IS SUBMITTED	4. FEDERAL GRANT OR OTHER IDENTIFYING NUMBER ASSIGNED BY FEDERAL AGENCY	5. PARTIAL PAYMENT REQUEST NO.

6. EMPLOYER IDENTIFICATION NUMBER	7. RECIPIENT'S ACCOUNT NUMBER OR IDENTIFYING NUMBER	PERIOD COVERED BY THIS REQUEST
		FROM (*Month, day, year*) TO (*Month, day, year*)

9. RECIPIENT ORGANIZATION	10. PAYEE (*Where check is to be sent if different than item 9*)
Name:	Name:
No. and Street:	No. and Street:
City, State and ZIP Code:	City, State and ZIP Code:

11.   **STATUS OF FUNDS**

CLASSIFICATION	PROGRAMS -- FUNCTIONS -- ACTIVITIES			TOTAL
	(a)	(b)	(c)	
a. Administrative expense	$	$	$	$ 0.00
b. Preliminary expense				0.00
c. Land, structures, right-of-way				0.00
d. Architectural engineering basic fees				0.00
e. Other architectural engineering fee				0.00
f. Project inspection fees				0.00
g. Land development				0.00
h. Relocation expense				0.00
i. Relocation payments to individuals and businesses				0.00
j. Demolition and removal				0.00
k. Construction and project improvement cost				0.00
l. Equipment				0.00
m. Miscellaneous cost				0.00
n. Total cumulative to date (*sum of lines a thru m*)	0.00	0.00	0.00	0.00
o. Deductions for program income				0.00
p. Net cumulative to date (*line n minus line o*)	0.00	0.00	0.00	0.00
q. Federal share to date				0.00
r. Rehabilitation grants (100% reimbursement)				0.00
s. Total Federal share (*sum of lines q and r*)	0.00	0.00	0.00	0.00
t. Federal payments previously requested				0.00
u. Amount requested for reimbursement	$	$	$	$ 0.00
v. Percentage of physical completion of project	%	%	%	%

12. CERTIFICATION			
I certify that to the best of my knowledge and belief the billed costs or disbursements are in accordance with the terms of the project and that the reimbursement represents the Federal share due which has not been previously requested and that an inspection has been performed and all work is in accordance with the terms of the award.	a. RECIPIENT	SIGNATURE OF AUTHORIZED CERTIFYING OFFICIAL	DATE REPORT SUBMITTED
		TYPED OR PRINTED NAME AND TITLE	TELEPHONE (*Area code, number, and extension*)
	b. REPRESENTATIVE CERTIFYING TO LINE 11V	SIGNATURE OF AUTHORIZED CERTIFYING OFFICIAL	DATE SIGNED
		TYPED OR PRINTED NAME AND TITLE	TELEPHONE (*Area code, number, and extension*)

SF-271 (continued)

Please type or print legibly. Items 3, 4, 5, 8, 9, 10, 11s, and 11v are self-explanatory. Specific instructions for other items are as follows:

Item	Entry

1. Mark the appropriate box. If the request is final, the amounts billed should represent the final cost of the project.

2. Show whether amounts are computed on an accrued expenditure or cash disbursement basis.

6. Enter the Employer Identification Number (EIN) assigned by the U.S. Internal Revenue Service or FICE (institution) code if requested by the Federal agency.

7. This space is reserved for an account number or other identifying number that may be assigned by the recipient.

11. The purpose of vertical columns (a) through (c) is to provide space for separate cost breakdowns when a large project has been planned and budgeted by program, function or activity. If additional columns are needed, useas many additional forms as needed and indicate page number in space provided in upper right; however, the summary totals of all programs, functions, or activities should be shown in the "total" column on the first page. All amounts are reported on a cumulative basis.

11a. Enter amounts expended for such items as travel, legal fees, rental of vehicles and any other administrative expenses. Include the amount of interest expense when authorized by program legislation. Also show the amount of interest expense on a separate sheet.

11b. Enter amounts pertaining to the work of locating and designing, making surveys and maps, sinking test holes, and all other work required prior to actual construction.

11c. Enter all amounts directly associated with the acquisition of land, existing structures and related right-of-way.

11d. Enter basic fees for services of architectural engineers.

11e. Enter other architectural engineering services. Do not include any amounts shown on line d.

11f. Enter inspection and audit fees of construction and related programs.

11g. Enter all amounts associated with the development of land where the primary purpose of the grant is land improvement. The amount pertaining to land development normally associated with major construction should be excluded from this category and entered on line k.

11h. Enter the dollar amounts used to provide relocation advisory assistance and net costs of replacement housing (last resort). Do not include amounts needed for relocation administrative expenses; these amounts should be included in amounts shown on line a.

11i. Enter the amount of relocation payments made by the recipient to displaced persons, farms, business concerns, and nonprofit organizations.

11j. Enter gross salaries and wages of employees of the recipient and payments to third party contractors directly engaged in performing demolition or removal of structures from developed land. All proceeds from the sale of salvage or the removal of structures should be credited to this account; there by reflecting net amounts if required by the Federal agency.

11k. Enter those amounts associated with the actual construction of, addition to, or restoration of a facility. Also, include in this category, the amounts for project improvements such as sewers, streets, landscaping, and lighting.

11l. Enter amounts for all equipment, both fixed and movable, exclusive of equipment used for construction. For example, permanently attached laboratory tables, built-in audio visual systems, movable desks, chairs, and laboratory equipment.

11m. Enter the amounts of all items not specifically mentioned above.

11n. Enter the total cumulative amount to date which should be the sum of lines a through m.

11o. Enter the total amount of program income applied to the grant or contract agreement except income included on line. Identify on a separate sheet of paper the sources and types of the income.

11p. Enter the net cumulative amount to date which should be the amount shown on line n minus the amount on line o.

11q. Enter the Federal share of the amount shown on line p.

11r. Enter the amount of rehabilitation grant payments made to individuals when program legislation provides 100 percent payment by the Federal agency.

11t. Enter the total amount of Federal payments previously requested, if this form isused for requesting reimbursement.

11u. Enter the amount now being requested for reimbursement. This amount should be the difference between the amounts shown on lines s and t. If different, explain on a separate sheet.

12a. To be completed by the official recipient official who is responsible for the operation of the program.The date should be the actual date the form is submitted to the Federal agency.

12b. To be completed by the official representative who is certifying to the percent of project completion as provided for in the terms of the grant or agreement.

CHAPTER 10

Evaluating Grant Programs

Grant writers and program managers often convince themselves that evaluation is something that occurs at the conclusion of a grant project or program. The reality is that the evaluation should be planned prior to even beginning implementation. As indicated in Chapter 5, evaluation planning begins during the program planning stage, often to meet funding agency expectations regarding evaluation in the grant application packet. After discussing evaluation as a core component of accountable governance, this chapter provides a succinct introduction to the two primary types of evaluation that funding agencies often expect. The first type is a simple process evaluation that considers whether or not the grant was implemented and carried out as indicated in the scope of work. The second type of evaluation is more elaborate and involves determining the effects of the program on particular outputs, outcomes, and impacts of interest to the funding agency.

Whether or not the funding agency requires an evaluation, grant recipients should be aware of the benefits evaluation can provide to program knowledge and organizational learning. Evaluations are particularly useful for programs that involve unique interventions, new methods, or otherwise innovative approaches to service delivery. From well-planned and appropriate evaluations, program managers can obtain useful information in determining which program components are working well and which program components are not.

WHY EVALUATE?

Government in the hollow state (Frederickson & Frederickson 2006) and government by proxy (Kettl 1988) are expressions used to convey the nature of modern governance in the United States. At their core is the shift of public good production from governments to the private and nonprofit sectors. Increasingly, the goods and services governments provide are produced elsewhere under contract, and agency managers become administrative specialists in contracting and performance management rather than in the substantive policy area of the agency's focus. "It is these [third-party] actors, not federal agencies or staff, who actually deliver the services to eligible individuals" (Radin 2002, p. 50).

No longer is it the case that public goods are produced by one government agency acting alone. Rather, it is much more common for joint production to be the norm. In such hollow state governance, the "logic of joint production, carried out to the extreme, refers to a government that as a matter of public policy has chosen to contract out all of its production capability to third parties, perhaps retaining only a systems integration function responsible for negotiating, monitoring, and evaluating contracts" (Milward 1996, p. 193). And Frederickson and Frederickson (2006) note that adding the word *grants* to *contracts* provides an apt description of some agencies.

As Beryl Radin (2002) notes, government programs are not all created equal, and a one-size-fits-all approach to accountability is not appropriate. Differences in grant forms (block, categorical, and formula grants) reveal different performance expectations, most notably of which is the degree of agency control over the program. Decisions about which grant forms are to be used are made during the policy design stage, when the federal government asks: (1) whether government should be involved, (2) what level of government should be involved, (3) for what aspects of the issue should each level of government be responsible, (4) what mechanisms should be used to carry out that responsibility (including grants, implementation requirements, and evaluation requirements), and (5) what rules will be used to allocate resources? (Radin 2002, p. 45–46).

In other words, government agencies (in this case the federal government) make conscious decisions about how to generate a desired policy impact, and who should be responsible in the U.S. intergovernmental system. These decisions are manifested in the grant form selected as well as in requirements for implementation and evaluation. Because the government agency is not directly producing the goods or services, but making grants to other levels of government, nonprofit agencies, and even private firms, evaluation is the only method the agency has to assess its performance with regard to the policy goals in question. Accountability includes management of the financial system from a process perspective, but from a policy and political perspective, the agency must also demonstrate that it is achieving the desired policy results through its grant making activities.

Radin (2002) sums up the need for evaluation quite succinctly: "When others—particularly state agencies—are involved in the crafting of a policy or program, they become part of the accountability system surrounding that effort" (p. 51). Grants are made to support congressionally determined purposes (Frederickson & Frederickson 2006, p. 51). Without evaluation, the granting agency is not able to ensure that federal policy objectives are met. Although there is an expectation of variance in program approach and implementation by different grantees, the key outcomes of interest can be assessed through the evaluation mechanism.

Under the Government Performance and Results Act, agencies are required to develop a mix of process, output, and outcome goals and measures for their programs. Performance measurement has been extended into the George W. Bush administration through the PART initiative, the Program Assessment Rating Tool. Through these efforts, federal agencies are expected to develop measures that reflect the policy goals their programs are intended to address. These goals are often integrated into grant application requirements and evaluation expectations. Grantees can expect to report data on those key variables of interest.

So, from a governmental standpoint, evaluation is an important mechanism to ensure accountability, both in program implementation (doing what you said you would do, when you said you would) and program performance (generating the expected program outputs), but also in the broader outcomes that reflect the policy goals under which the grant was established.

Non-governmental grants have similar expectations, but for different reasons. Foundations are not accountable to the public at large, but to their mission, and to directors who are charged with carrying out the mission. Foundations often still require evaluation as an accountability mechanism. They do so to ensure that the program was implemented as planned, but more important, because they are interested in the impact they made in the community. Foundations increasingly give for instrumental purposes, and evaluation is their way of assessing whether they were indeed instrumental in addressing the identified need.

Sometimes grants are given to try a new method, previously untested, that has significant theoretical merit. Evaluation in this case is most interested in determining whether the method works and how it compares to alternative methods and approaches. For example, the Robert Wood Johnson Foundation provided large grants to state Medicaid agencies to fund their Cash and Counseling Program—a human services program for individuals with developmental and other disabilities that was intended to enhance consumer choice for capable individuals by displacing traditional state case worker systems of support. Because of the theoretical merit of the idea and the conceptual appeal of "choice" in a nation founded on principles of freedom, the pilot program was thoroughly evaluated to determine whether it worked, how well, and how it compared to traditional programs in cost and outcomes. On the basis of evaluation results, the foundation expanded the program to more states through additional grants in subsequent years.

Although foundations do not have the same accountability requirements that face governments, they recognize the role of oversight in ensuring grantee performance. They also have a vested interest in the program's success and want to be sure that it is monitored to inform practice in the field and to publicize success when it is found.

EVALUATION BASICS

As indicated in Chapter 5, most grant writers and program managers are not skilled in evaluation methodologies. Students in public administration programs are exposed to statistical analysis experience and oftentimes receive training in evaluation design sufficient to enable them to design rudimentary evaluations. However, an evaluation result is only as good as the methodology used to produce it. Professional evaluators are knowledgeable about various methodologies that can be applied to improve internal and external validity and to increase the reliability of the measures to be utilized. For this reason, Chapter 5 suggests that evaluators be consulted during program design so that they could design an evaluation plan that coincides with key program activities and processes.

Various measures and various data collection efforts are necessary and important during program implementation to ensure successful evaluation results. Many of the measures evaluators need to assess a program's effectiveness must be collected at appropriate times during implementation and are very difficult to obtain if they are not collected when it is most convenient to do so. For example, participant information sheets could be used to collect information on various program components. This information could then be used to provide key demographic information that would enable evaluators to assess whether there are program differences that result from gender, age, or race. If these sheets are not collected at enrollment, it will not be possible to tell how participants differ from those prospects who elected not to attend or who dropped out during the program.

Professional evaluators are able to assess the key constructs of interest to program managers, or to the funding agency, and they are able to combine this knowledge with their knowledge of evaluation methodology to arrive at a sound approach that will provide answers to the key evaluation questions. The evaluation design depends entirely on its intended purpose, and simple evaluations may not require external expertise. But whether or not professional evaluators are utilized, it remains an absolute certainty that evaluation must be considered prior to and during program implementation, as well as after program implementation. This chapter continues with a discussion of the key purposes evaluations serve and follows with a discussion of methodologies and approaches that can be utilized to obtain the information of interest. The primary purpose here is to provide the reader with sufficient understanding to design and conduct a relatively simple grant program evaluation in either of the two most common evaluation formats called for by grant making agencies—process and outcome evaluations.

Two common categorizations are used to differentiate among evaluation types. The first distinction is between formative and substantive evaluation. This categorization relies on the purpose of evaluation to define the evaluation type, with the purpose of a formative evaluation being to inform program design. That is, to shape the program as it is being implemented with feedback about the effectiveness of various components. On the other hand, a substantive evaluation is intended to evaluate the substance of the program, or its outputs, outcomes, and impacts on key variables of interest. The second categorization utilized to distinguish evaluation types is that between the process and the outcome evaluation. This distinction considers the timing at which the evaluation occurs rather than its purpose, with process evaluation occurring during implementation and with outcome evaluation occurring after implementation is complete.

The terms *process* and *formative* are often used interchangeably because evaluations intended to affect program design tend to occur during implementation. In similar fashion, *outcome* and *summative* are frequently used to refer to the same type of evaluation—one that assesses evaluation results at the end of the program implementation, or at least the first cycle thereof. Recognizing that these terms are not technically identical, and that important distinctions exist among them, in this chapter I refer to evaluations only as process or outcome evaluations to minimize confusion.

The first evaluation type to be considered is the process evaluation. As already mentioned, process evaluations are intended to provide feedback to program administrators as the program is being implemented. Important program steps are assessed according to the timing and completeness of their implementation. The purposes of process evaluation are learning and continuous improvement, which help to ensure that problems are identified and corrected early so as not to negatively impact program outputs or the program's ultimate success. Process evaluation occurs in stages or phases, often by regular divisions of the calendar (monthly or quarterly), but more usefully by natural breaks in program activities. That is, an evaluator will collect program information at regular intervals predetermined in the program's implementation plan, and often described in the grant application scope of work. Problems will be identified, and potential solutions will be posited and provided to program managers for consideration and decision. Process evaluations document that the program was implemented, to what extent (fully, or with pieces missing), and whether it was on the desired time frame; they also look out for unexpected problems with implementation. Process evaluation is an important part of sound program management, whether grant funded or otherwise.

In the way of an example, if a program aims to recruit 30 participants to enroll in an adult education class, it is a reasonable expectation that 40 to 50 eligible participants need to sign up for the program to ensure sufficient attendance after attrition. A process evaluation of this example might examine when and where recruitment took place, how many eligible participants were identified, how many participants signed up for the program, and ultimately how many enrolled. If fewer than the desired number of participants (30) are enrolled, the evaluator will look back to the previous implementation steps to determine the cause and will further suggest a potential solution or solutions to correct the problem as soon as possible.

Outcome evaluation is not concerned with what happened and when. Rather, it focuses on what the program achieved in one full operational cycle. So, for a training program, from startup to completion of the training for the first cohort of students, an outcome evaluation would examine the results. Outcome evaluations consider the policy mechanism—the tool or tools used to bring about the desired results—to explain the outcomes of interest. They are concerned with assessing program effectiveness, and so tend to involve more specific measurement and often more sophisticated analysis. Common outcome evaluation approaches ask whether an outcome was produced or whether a condition improves or worsens as a result of the program. They examine the level of the outcome and its trend over time. It is also common for outcome evaluations to compare program effects to alternative program delivery methods or approaches to determine which is superior.

The challenge of outcome evaluation is to attribute the observed effects to the program itself, to the exclusion of plausible alternative explanations. For example, crime rates are observed to decline in a major metropolitan area. Police program managers are eager to claim credit for the decline as a result of enhanced police patrol services. However, crime also declines when national economic performance is positive and improving. To what extent is the change in crime rates the result of the program versus contextual conditions in the environment? These are the sort of questions outcome evaluations address. The more important it is to attribute the observed results to the program, the more sophisticated the evaluation model must be. I discuss evaluation designs used to achieve this goal later in the chapter. For now, it is enough to say that outcome evaluation seeks to determine the results or effects a program brings about, with the simple purpose of declaring it a success or a failure.

BUILDING BLOCKS OF EVALUATION: MEASURES AND RELATIONSHIPS

Before embarking on a journey into the specifics of particular evaluation types, it is necessary to develop an understanding of the key components of evaluations. This section provides an introduction to measures, methods, and their relationships to one another.

Let's begin by reviewing program theory, first discussed in Chapter 5. A program's theory is the relationship between inputs, including program activities, and specific outputs, outcomes, and impacts. There are usually one or more intermediate outputs that occur during a program implementation that are necessary, but not sufficient, to produce the outputs of interest as defined by program goals. Program theory explains how the pieces fit together in a logical fashion, working to bring about the desired results. For review, Figure 5.2 portrays the relationship among inputs, outputs, outcomes, and impacts. Figure 5.10 shows in greater detail the relationship among process or implementation goals, intermediate goals, and substantive/outcome goals. Because evaluation is intended to document what occurred and ascertain program performance, both absolute outcomes (effectiveness) and the cost of obtaining those outcomes (efficiency) need to be considered. As such, it is necessary to take inputs into consideration along with outputs and outcomes.

Inputs are any identifiable item that is utilized in the program. The most common examples are personnel and money. In grant programs, we often spend own-source finances as match, or we utilize in-kind contributions from various partners. To accurately depict the true costs of a program, these resources should be documented and included in any input assessment. At the broadest level, inputs can be expressed in monetary terms because all personnel are paid and all goods and services are purchased. Even volunteer time can be converted to a financial variable, as indicated in Chapter 4. So, with some work, it is usually possible to determine the absolute cost incurred to execute the program, including both grant and non-grant support. And such measures are useful in calculating the program's efficiency in a cost-benefit analysis.

However, dollar amounts are not very descriptive and do not adequately capture the nature of the program. So, outside a cost-benefit framework, it is more useful to characterize program inputs according to more descriptive categories, usually based on objects of expenditure. So, we could indicate the number of personnel involved, and the percentage of their time required to administer the program. The number of personnel hours required is a more meaningful input measure than the cost of such personnel. Likewise, a partner agency may provide free transportation to program participants to attend program activities. The value of the transportation can be computed, but it is more useful to know that 150 rides were provided, or 15,000 person-miles in free transportation were contributed. Everything that is used to implement and administer the program is an input and should be identified.

Some inputs are not contributed and do not have a financial variable but are nonetheless essential to program success. At the top of this list are the participants themselves. A public highway safety program will fail if there are no drivers. An adult education program will fail if there are no students. Thus, the program targets are also key inputs that should be documented. The value of policy targets is not as important as their characteristics. If a program intends to increase literacy, the program's success will depend on how well the participants can read and write when they enter the program. If they are all highly literate upon admission, they will still be literate upon program completion, but the program will have very little effect on their abilities. On the other hand, if the participants have very low literacy skills upon admission, they may achieve basic literacy by the program's completion, but the change in these participants' abilities would be significant. Program targets, whether people, organizations, or places, have important effects on program success.

The final group of inputs to consider is the program's mechanisms of change—that is, the specific policy approach that is used. Various inputs go into this element of the program, but it is their unique combination that reflects how the program works to bring about the results. In other words, the manner in which the other inputs are combined constitutes an input of equal or greater importance than the collective inputs themselves.

Outputs, as discussed in Chapter 5, are the direct and immediate results of the program activity. They are the products that result from a successful implementation. As noted earlier, there are often various intermediate outputs that are necessary, but not sufficient, to generate the outputs of interest. These preliminary and intermediate outputs form a logical chain of interaction that can be traced and evaluated, leading to an assessment of the program's performance during implementation. It is very often the case that one intermediate output is necessary for the following to occur. For example, participants must be recruited to participate in a program before it is possible to teach them, and they must attend classes to obtain the full benefit of the curriculum. So, although a course completion or a test score may be the ultimate output of interest, it is dependent upon preliminary process outputs along the way. This logical chain forms the program theory and suggests important nodes at which outputs can be measured. An explanation for why test scores are low or few graduates are produced can often be found in these preliminary process measures.

In that a program's outputs are dependent upon those inputs that are utilized, identification of a particular weakness along the way can be analyzed to determine whether the problem is a result of resource shortages or a result of the approach used. Inputs and outputs are directly related. Again, outputs are those things that a program generates directly and that can be clearly attributed to the program. Test scores and program graduates are useful measures of program performance, but they do not address the larger concerns in the policy area of question. Workforce development programs, for example, do not exist to confer degrees upon their graduates but to reduce poverty and increase local wages. Alternatively, they may exist as an economic development strategy to recruit firms with higher skilled workers. These broader policy goals are not outputs, but outcomes that the program seeks to affect.

Whereas outputs are the direct result of the program, outcomes are indirect at best. There is no guarantee that a program participant, having completed a workforce training program, will be able to obtain better employment, or that new employers will be recruited in the area. A given program may have a meaningful effect on the outcome of interest, but alone it is rare for any single program to be sufficient to bring about a desired policy impact. Broader conditions from the organization's operating context play very important roles in determining program success. Socioeconomic conditions such as recession or economic expansion, international migration, globalization, and various other factors clearly have impacts at the local level. A responsible approach for administrators managing innovative or unique programs is to attempt to isolate the effects the program has on these broader policy outcomes. That is where program evaluation comes into play. By eliminating possible alternative explanations, evaluation designs can determine whether the program is having any meaningful effect on these areas of interest.

Program evaluation seeks to understand, map, and measure the relationships between inputs and outputs, and subsequent outcomes and impacts. The tools of the program evaluator include understanding the program and its underlying theory, data collection, and analysis. A rudimentary program evaluation would simply identify each point at which an output is produced, whether preliminary or substantive, measure the outputs against a program goal or benchmark, and present charts and tables that reflect the program's progress. More sophisticated program evaluations seek to determine relationships among the variables.

So, for example, the cost per output could be computed, and simple linear regression could be used to assess the correlation between program outputs and broader outcome measures. Relationships between inputs and outputs can be compared in other ways. For example, participant characteristics were identified as an important input. In a program with a wide variety of participants across the dimensions of age, sex, and race, it is possible to measure the program's effects on different subsets of the target population. Again, simple linear regression can be used to determine whether the effect size is the same for individuals in different age categories or individuals of different genders and races. The specific comparisons that are made in any evaluation depend on the evaluation questions established prior to program implementation. To be clear, we should not evaluate simply for the sake of evaluation, but to answer important questions about the program, how it works, and its ultimate effects. These questions will address the important goals the program was intended to realize.

Constructs and Measurement

Previously, I discussed the various measures of importance to program evaluation including inputs, outputs, and outcomes. These measures are the foundation of evaluation constructs. A theoretical construct is a concept that you intend to measure, such as "quality of life," "literacy," "highway safety," or "client satisfaction." These broad conceptual constructs define the policy or program goals of interest and often correspond to the key outcomes the program is expected to produce. Constructs can be on either side of the statistical equation, however—as both independent and dependent variables. Constructs can also be input- or output-oriented in evaluation models. The theoretical construct is a broad conceptualization of the issue, what we might call a label for an issue of interest. In preparing to evaluate a policy or program, and in designing an evaluation, it is important to identify the program's core constructs, label them, and map the expected interactions between them. In essence, this is what program theory is all about.

Beginning with a map of constructs and their relationships, the evaluator must then *operationalize* the measures. That is, the evaluator must identify concrete measures that accurately and adequately reflect the construct of interest. Sometimes one operational measure is sufficient. At other times, constructs are broad and have many facets that require multiple measures to adequately represent them. For example, one theoretical (conceptual) construct is "socioeconomic need." Relevant operational measures might include poverty status, per capita personal income, unemployment, median household income, or participation in the national free or reduced school lunch program. The specific operational measure(s) selected will depend on the nature of the question and perhaps the locus of the program. For example, a program that addresses school children would be better represented by childhood poverty or participation in free lunch programs than by unemployment rates. Appropriately defining constructs and identifying measures takes time and skill. It is important to settle on measures up front because data collection takes time and can become expensive. A few good measures are usually preferable to a larger set of mediocre measures.

Figure 10.1 provides an overview of a possible conceptual model among several theoretical constructs. In this model, socioeconomic need is thought to reduce educational attainment. Greater educational attainment is expected to improve an individual's employability and earning

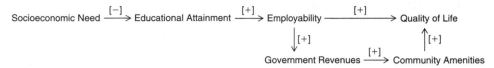

FIGURE 10.1　Relationship Among Conceptual Constructs

potential, which will improve the individual's quality of life and simultaneously increase local government revenues. The increase in government revenues leads to superior community amenities that in turn further enhance local quality of life. **Table 10.1** provides an example of a possible scheme of operational measures that could be utilized to capture each of the conceptual constructs. It is important to note that the unit of analysis changes from construct to construct. Socioeconomic need in this model is an individual variable, as are educational attainment, employability, and quality of life. Government revenues and community amenities, on the other hand, are not individual-level measures, but community measures. Many evaluations require measurement of constructs at different units of analysis. Depending on the program in question, evaluators may find any of the following to be appropriate units of analysis: individuals, groups, communities, organizations, cities, counties, states, and others.

TABLE 10.1　Operational Measures for
Key Contracts

Socioeconomic Need
　Personal income
　Poverty status
　Disability status
Educational Attainment
　Dropout status
　High school graduate or equivalent
　Years postsecondary education completed
Employability
　Education required in preferred profession
　Local unemployment rate
　Number of eligible positions within 30 miles
Government Revenues
　Local occupational tax receipts
　Local sales tax receipts
　Local property tax receipts
Community Amenities
　Acres of parks per square mile
　Number of public golf courses within city
　Square feet of public library space per person
Quality of Life
　Citizen satisfaction questionnaire

Collecting Data for Analysis

With a set of essential operational measures in mind, the next step is to collect the requisite data. Information used in evaluations can come from various sources. Among them are: (1) direct sources, through observation, interviews, or questionnaires, (2) archival data and other artifacts, and (3) indirect sources. Each source of information has its advantages and disadvantages. The exact method we use to collect data depends on the question to be answered, and for any situation, some options are preferable to others.

Direct sources of information include the participants themselves, or affected parties. Information collection need not be limited to participants; program staff can provide valuable information about the program, its operations, and its participants. Participant behavior can be observed directly by a trained observer and coded into a spreadsheet format. Alternatively, interviews with participants may yield more elaborate qualitative information from the participant's perspective. And to limit costs and time constraints, evaluators sometimes find questionnaires to be useful tools for collecting information directly from affected persons or organizations. Direct sources of information can be very accurate, but they are also subject to biases. Response bias occurs when respondents provide the answers they believe the examiner wants to hear rather than the true answer. For example, social desirability of some characteristics leads respondents to overreport them, such as having a library card. Weiss (1998) reports that in some subcultures, "being bad" is desirable, and negative aspects are overreported (p. 149). In such cases, it is advantageous to utilize an alternative measurement technique.

One option is to refer to archival data, also known as program artifacts. Although individuals may over- or underreport possession of library cards, the evaluator may be able to obtain records from the library that disclose actual library card distribution. Rather than questioning athletes about drug use, urine tests yield conclusive evidence that is not subject to bias. Nonobtrusive methods—methods that do not involve asking anyone anything—are preferable where possible and feasible. And as Weiss (1998) indicates, the wear on the tile in front of museum exhibits may be more telling than respondent surveys (p. 149). Archival data, such as registration forms, often contains information about personal characteristics that can be obtained more easily than issuing a questionnaire to the affected individuals.

Another option to help reduce response bias is the indirect approach to data collection. Indirect methods typically involve questioning someone other than the directly affected participant. For example, to determine the success of an anti-smoking program, staff may question the participant's spouse rather than the participant. Also potentially included in this category are data collected by other institutions, such as the census. Most public data are aggregated such that individual-level information is protected, but if your unit of analysis is a city, county, or community, government data may prove to be very useful.

When all else fails, or at least when the questions to be answered suggest their use, survey questionnaires can be quite useful for collecting original data regarding the key constructs of interest. In designing surveys, there are a few guidelines that should always be followed to enhance both construct validity and reliability. Twelve suggestions for designing successful surveys are provided in **Table 10.2.**

TABLE 10.2   Twelve Steps to Designing Successful Survey Instruments

 1. Use simple language; avoid jargon.
 2. Ask respondents only questions for which they should know the answer.
 3. Make each question as specific as possible.
 4. Provide definitions for any terms that may be unclear.
 5. Stay away from yes-no questions; more categories provide more information.
 6. Don't use double negatives in question phrasing.
 7. Don't ask double-barreled questions.
 8. Use working language familiar to the field being studied.
 9. Provide information to jog people's memory; reference events.
10. Ask only for first-hand information, not second-hand.
11. Be aware of and sensitive to cultural aspects; seek advice from group members.
12. Learn to deal with difficult respondent groups.

Adapted from: Weiss 1998, p. 141–142.

Without going into great detail on the design of questionnaires, let me suggest that anyone considering developing a formal questionnaire should consult a text on that subject, such as one of the following:

Fowler, F. J. 1998. Design and evaluation of survey questions. In *Handbook of Applied Social Research Methods* (p. 343–374), L. Bickman and D. J. Rog, Eds. Thousand Oaks, CA: Sage.
Sudman, S., N. M. Bradburn, and N. Schwarz. 1996. *Thinking About Answers.* San Francisco: Jossey-Bass.

That being said, I briefly highlight a few of the less familiar items on the list in Table 10.2. The charge to make each question as specific as possible means that asking broad and general questions will yield broad and general responses. So, rather than asking, "Do you like movies (yes/no)?" an evaluation question might read "Please indicate the number of times you have viewed each of the following types of movies during the past twelve (12) months: Westerns, Romantic Comedy, Horror, etc."

A good question provides superior information that directly informs the evaluation about the specific program goals. And, rather than asking how old someone is, you can ask a person "in what year were you born?" or "on your next birthday, how many years old will you be?" Ask questions to obtain specific information; if need be, specific information can later be aggregated into new categories. But questions with categorical answers can never be disaggregated to more specific data. It is a common mistake for individuals drafting questionnaires to lean toward categorical variables, such as "select the category that represents your age: 18–25, 26–34, etc." Asking a respondent's age is always preferable to asking the category of their age. An evaluator never knows when all the respondents may be in the 26–34 age range. If this is the case, then two categories might be preferable, such as 26–30 and 31–34. Again, these categories can be created through aggregation of more specific data, but the opposite is never true. Specific questions and specific answers will prove to be more reliable and more effective at capturing the construct of interest.

Another common mistake is the use of double-barreled questions. A double-barreled question is one to which the meaning of the answer cannot be distinguished because multiple factors are addressed. For example, "Please indicate the extent to which political support and popular support affect agency decision making." If this question were accompanied by a rating scale from 1 to 5, with 1 being little and 5 being a lot, no answer would be valid. It may be the case that the respondent finds political support affects decision making a lot, while popular support affects it very little. They were asked about two separate constructs in the same question, and it is not possible to separate their answers. Double-barreled questions are easy to spot once you know what to look for, but they are very common for first-time questionnaire writers. It is a good idea to read over your survey questions and ask yourself, "Will I be able to tell what the answer to this question means?" If not, you may need to rephrase the question or separate it into more than one part.

Once you have successfully developed your draft questionnaire, it is advisable to ask someone to read through it for mistakes and clarity. Then, you should ask one or more persons in the group to be surveyed to take a preliminary version of the survey with you or another evaluator present so that they can ask questions and highlight things that are not clear. Pilot testing can eliminate important errors that affect overall quality of the survey results. Treatment group members often possess specialized knowledge with which non-group members would not be familiar. In other words, the evaluator may be able to ask more specific survey questions of the group familiar with the concept than of the general population.

With data collection complete, using any combination of methods presented earlier, the evaluator should next turn to organizing the data in an analytic structure. Of course, to some extent, the structure informs data collection as well. If multiple groups are needed, or if information is needed at multiple time periods, data collection efforts may have to be continued after the next step. Once again, this highlights the importance of developing the evaluation plan prior to launching the program so that such kinks can be ironed out and data can be collected throughout program implementation as demanded by the evaluation design. The next section considers evaluation designs that are commonly used to measure program effects.

BUILDING BLOCKS OF EVALUATION: DESIGN

Evaluation design depends entirely on the question or questions to be answered and the level of confidence needed to satisfy concerns about the program's effectiveness. Many novice evaluators are attracted to the idea that a survey constitutes an evaluation. And surveys are often used in evaluations; however, surveys are often utilized to capture individuals' perceptions about a program or their own assessment of their knowledge skills and abilities. Starting with the presumption that evaluation requires a survey can lead to a survey being administered following the program. But the survey probably will not provide answers to key questions about program performance, and if this is the case, it would be a waste of time and money. Surveys are but one method that can be used, but evaluation does not imply that surveys must be used.

Earlier I discussed the fact that evaluation takes one of two primary forms, that of the process evaluation and that of the outcome evaluation. Each of these forms calls for a different evaluation design. Also remember that process evaluation is about program improvement—allow monitoring during implementation to identify areas that require attention because they have not been properly implemented or because proper implementation has not achieved the desired result. Process evaluations very rarely involve sophisticated statistical analysis, but rather rely on rich qualitative information about the program and what it has done. So, although data may be collected for process evaluation, they will probably be analyzed in simple ways to paint a picture of how the program has operated. With this information in hand, simple comparisons between expected and actual outputs can be made and an assessment of performance at each node can occur. Those areas that are performing well are noted, as are those that are not. Suggestions for correcting problem areas are made and sent back to program managers so that they can make adaptations to correct the problem as quickly as possible.

Outcome evaluations, on the other hand, seek to determine the program's impact. If the program is already known to work effectively, less sophisticated designs are required. In this case, we will simply seek to measure the program's outputs and, if applicable, its outcomes. These figures are then compared to our expectations based on the level of funding and the level of need in the area. But many programs are innovative, and their effectiveness is not yet known. In these cases, evaluation designs can become quite sophisticated in an effort to determine the program's true impact. As I mentioned previously, the evaluation design selected will depend upon the level of confidence we require that the program effects observed are the true effects of the program and not some alternative explanation. In statistics we talk about type I errors and type II errors; these occur when we obtain a false positive or false negative, respectively.

A false positive occurs when, in statistical terms, we reject the null hypothesis although it is actually true. In other words, we observe a difference where one does not exist. So, for example, if we were comparing two pills, one a pharmaceutical compound and the other a placebo, and our statistical analysis suggests that the placebo has a strong positive impact on the condition of interest, we would have experienced a false positive. In this case, it is easy to tell that the result is a false positive because one of our treatments was a placebo that should have no effect whatsoever. If we had been comparing two pharmaceuticals, however, we would not know the result was not valid.

A false negative occurs when we fail to reject the null hypothesis although it should have been rejected. In this case, we fail to observe a difference where one does exist. Using our pharmaceutical example again, when comparing a placebo to the pharmaceutical, our results show that there is no difference between a placebo and the drug. However, in reality the drug is effective at reducing the condition of interest. It should be apparent that type I and type II errors can lead to significant problems for researchers. Errors such as these could lead doctors to prescribe medicines that have no impact or to prescribe medicines that have serious detrimental effects on human health.

These error types are known, and evaluation design can be adjusted to correct for them. In the case of type I error, we simply set our models to produce results with lower probability of the error occurring. The p value in statistics, often referred to as the level of significance, provides this check. With p values of .05, there is a greater probability of type I error than with *p* values of .01 or .001. In the case of type II error, the solution is less certain because these errors' probability of occurrence is not known. However, larger sample sizes reduce the likelihood of their occurrence. Increasing the number of participants increases our confidence.

This discussion of error types is intended to communicate the risk that occurs when we conduct statistical analyses and accept the results as true. In some cases, programs have limited risks to humans or their targets more generally, and in these cases we can accept some degree of risk regarding the validity of our statistical results. But in other cases these risks are not acceptable, such as in the pharmaceutical examples earlier. We demand greater confidence for those programs that have real costs and impose real risks to program participants or innocent bystanders. Hall and Jennings (2008) suggest risk is important to consider in evaluating public programs and deciding what works and doesn't work. They consider best practices and the various methods that researchers have used to label and categorize practices. Program evaluation plays a central role in this task, and many programs that catalog best practices require stringent methodologies such as experimental designs that show the program works beyond a shadow of a doubt. Other methods of categorizing practices leave room for the possibility that a practice may be effective although there is not experimental evidence that this is the case. Hall and Jennings (2008) suggest that some programs need not have sophisticated experimental results to be categorized as a best practice because their risk of harm to participants is low and experimental designs are not always possible or cost-effective.

Just as best practices need not have stringent evidence of their effectiveness to be labeled best practices, sophisticated program evaluation is not always necessary to be able to state the program works. Nonetheless, if we require confidence that the results we obtain are true, then more sophisticated methods of analysis are necessary. In the following section, I present several common evaluation methodologies that can be used to assess program effect. I begin with simple designs and conclude with the more sophisticated approaches.

Single Group Designs

The simplest evaluation methodology is called posttest only. As its name implies, the posttest-only design involves taking measurements upon program completion. In assessing the program's absolute effect, this method is appropriate (**Figure 10.2**). However, the posttest-only design does not enable us to determine with certainty that the program had a meaningful impact. Most programs intend to create change, and a posttest measure alone is insufficient to measure change.

The second methodology most commonly used is the pretest posttest design. This evaluation design calls for measurement prior to the program and after the program (**Figure 10.3**). By comparing pretest scores to posttest scores, it is possible to determine how much change occurred during the program.

A variation on the pretest posttest design is the simple time series approach where measures are taken both before and after the program, but also at various intervals during the program. An interrupted time series approach takes several measures prior to the program

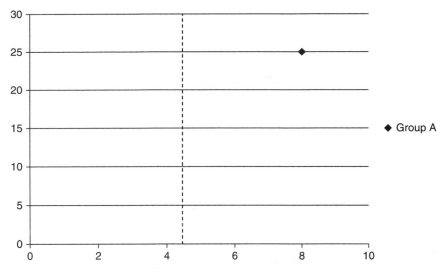

FIGURE 10.2   Single Group Posttest Only Design

and several measures after the program so that the trend before and after the program implementation can be assessed (**Figure 10.4**). The program serves as the interruption between the two time periods, hence the name. The usefulness of multiple measurements across time is that they enable the researcher to assess trends and patterns of change that may provide greater information than pretest and posttest scores alone. These methods enable the researcher to attribute the observed change to the program itself, though not

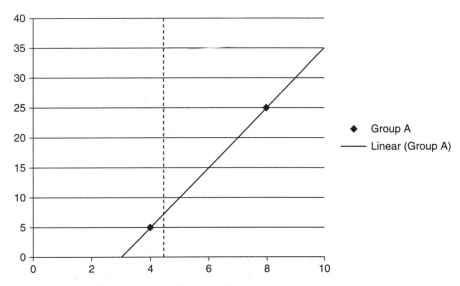

FIGURE 10.3   Single Group Pretest Posttest Design

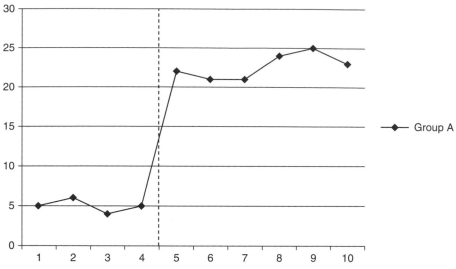

FIGURE 10.4   Single Group Interrupted Time Series Design

with absolute certainty. Various threats to validity make these designs problematic if we require our analysis to demonstrate the effect of the program beyond a shadow of a doubt.

Threats to Validity

A threat to internal validity simply means that there are plausible alternative explanations for the observed result; that is, conditions other than the program may have led to the results we observed. Because these threats to validity can potentially affect our evaluation results, they merit some attention here.

The most common threats to validity include changes in the participants, changes that depend on who is observed, and changes related to our methods of observation and measurement (Posavac & Carey 2003, p. 164–168). I consider each in turn. Changes that occur in participants take two primary forms; the first is maturation, and the second is history. Over time, individuals change; they mature, and that maturity can lead to differences in their performance. So, for example, an elementary school student naturally grows in cognitive ability very rapidly. A posttest score compared to pretest score will reveal the differences that result from the program, but also that result from the natural maturation of the student and her cognitive ability. Likewise, at the opposite end of the spectrum, it is common for elderly individuals to lose cognitive ability. If we evaluate a driving program for senior citizens that takes place over a 12-month period, our evaluation results comparing pretest posttest scores may reveal no change. The threat to validity resulting from maturation here is that the seniors' ability to drive actually decreased as their cognitive abilities decline over time, but that the program made up the difference. A simple pretest posttest design of the single group of individuals is insufficient to determine how much of the effect is the result of maturation and how much is a result of the program.

History, on the other hand, refers to specific events that take place between the time the individual is enrolled in the program and takes the pretest, and the time of the posttest. For example, in a workforce training program participants may be asked to disclose their hourly wage and employment status at the beginning of a program and again at the end. A worker may report a $10 per hour wage at the beginning of the program but only an $8 per hour wage at the end of the program. It would appear that the program was unsuccessful because the participant declined in wage rate. However, the individual's history may be to blame. The company for which he works at the beginning of the program may have closed down and the individual had to seek alternative employment. The program cannot be blamed for occurrences outside its purview. In fact, it may be the case that the individual was only able to obtain alternative employment because of the experience he attained during the program. It is always the case that an $8 per hour wage is preferable to no wage at all. Changes occur to participants as a result of many things outside the program's direct control. These changes are real threats to internal validity and should be taken into account when possible. It is usually not possible to control for these threats to validity using a single group design.

The second group of threats to validity regards who is measured. Selection bias occurs when participation is voluntary and individuals who elect to participate in the group differ from individuals who elect not to participate. Consider for a moment a program to help individuals stop smoking. In program design, we advertise the program to the community and as a result we recruit a group of 25 interested individuals. The individuals complete the program, and they are found to stop smoking at a rate of 50% as of 6 weeks past the program's conclusion. Selection bias in this example involves differences between those individuals who elected to participate in the program and those who elected not to participate. Individuals in both groups are smokers, but there may be differences in the groups that led to their decision to participate in the program. For example, program enrollees may have a stronger psychological will to stop smoking. Again, the single group design does not enable us to determine whether the effect is the result of the program or the result of the individuals' underlying psychological will.

Attrition is a second threat to validity that depends on who is measured. Attrition refers to program dropouts. Over the course of most programs conducted by public and nonprofit agencies, some individuals who were selected to participate inevitably stop participating at some point before the program concludes. It is usually the case that individuals who continue to participate in the program are different from individuals who stop at some point. To continue with the same smoking cessation program example, those individuals who drop out of the program may decide that they don't really want to stop smoking, or they may not have the same degree of psychological will as those who continue to participate. Once again, the single group design does not help us to differentiate the effects of the program and the effects that result from differences in the individuals we observe.

The third threat to validity regarding the individuals measured is regression toward the mean. Regression toward the mean implies that some individuals are predisposed to show improvements or declines in their performance. For example, if students are selected for a supplementary education program on the basis of previous test scores, and the lowest-scoring students are selected to participate, this group of students is most likely to experience improvement in their test scores naturally without the program's influence. Although it may well be the case that the program did have an impact, it is not possible to distinguish the program's impact from the students' natural progression upward toward their classroom averages.

The final group of threats to internal validity includes the measurement instruments themselves. Two examples include testing and instrumentation effects. These threats to validity imply that it is not just when we take our measurements that matter, and neither is it simply a matter of differences in respondents, but the tests themselves can also affect findings. Testing effects refer to individual responses that take place because they know they're being tested. Participants act in ways that conform to program expectations when they know they are being watched, for example, in a lab, and test results may be higher than if the these same participants were secretly observed in their natural habitat. Instrumentation effects, on the other hand, take place when respondents become familiar with the instrument used to collect the data, such as is the case when the same instrument is used for both the pretest and the posttest, or when the examiner becomes familiar with the observation and scoring process. In other words, the posttest goes more smoothly than the pretest, and the instrument itself affects the results.

With each of the aforementioned threats to internal validity, doubt is introduced as to whether it was the program or some external factor that caused the observed results. It is possible to develop designs that control for some of these factors. The trouble with more sophisticated designs is that they are more costly, more involved, and they take a great deal more time to administer. Returning to the premise with which this chapter began, that evaluation design depends on the questions to be answered as well as the required confidence in the evaluation result, sophisticated designs are not always necessary. The more sophisticated the design, the more we can learn about the program, but these designs may go above and beyond what is expected by grant making agencies and the level of knowledge required for everyday program management. Nonetheless, where greater confidence is demanded, designs are available. I turn now to evaluation designs that involve multiple groups, including comparison and control group designs.

Multiple Group Designs

The next group of evaluation designs helps to control for the various threats to internal validity identified earlier. Multiple group designs have as their basis the simple designs described previously: posttest only, pretest posttest, and simple time series. The difference is that these multiple group models utilize a treatment group that received the program alongside a second group of individuals or targets that did not. The use of a second group for comparison or control eliminates threats to validity because it enables evaluators to compare individuals who receive the program with those who did not, or with those who received an alternative treatment program. Differences in the individuals that create the threats to validity discussed earlier are eliminated because individuals in both treatment and comparison groups are expected to exhibit similar qualities. So, for example, individuals in each group would mature at the same rate. By then comparing the effects of the treatment group with the second group, we assume that maturation had the same amount of effect on each case and the resulting difference observed between the two groups is a result of the program alone. Likewise, on average a group of individuals can be expected to experience similar types of history-related events such as plant closures. Again, use of a second group enables us to isolate the effect of the program relative to these other concerns.

The posttest-only design is once again the simplest evaluation model because it involves measurement only after the program takes place (**Figure 10.5**). The addition of the second group helps us to address concerns regarding various threats to validity, but the formation of that group determines the extent to which this is true.

Three terms are regularly used to describe the groups that comprise evaluation designs. The first is the treatment group, or the group of individuals or other targets that receive the program in question. The remaining two groups include individuals who did not receive the program or who received some alternative program in the event we are comparing the effectiveness of two programs designed to have similar effects. These two groups are referred to as comparison groups or control groups. The difference between the two is that comparison groups are selected on the basis of their qualities so as to arrive at a group as similar as possible to the treatment group, with the only difference being that the comparison group did not receive the treatment in question. Comparison groups can be formed at any time during the study, including after the program has concluded in many cases.

Control groups, on the other hand, must be selected prior to program implementation. Control groups are formed by random assignment, meaning that a pool of potential applicants is randomly assigned to either the treatment group or to the control group. Randomization in this manner helps us to ensure that the individuals receiving the treatment are as similar as possible to those individuals who do not. Random control group designs are referred to as experimental designs, and they are the gold standard of evaluations because they eliminate most threats to validity and convey with relative certainty that the program

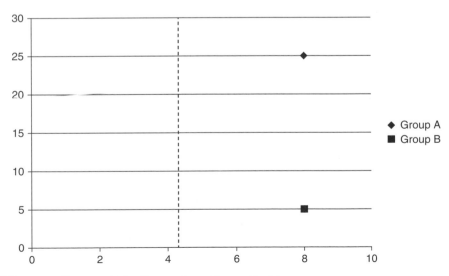

FIGURE 10.5   Posttest Only Comparison Group Design

has the effects observed. Random assignment has the additional advantage of making the results generalizable to the population from which the participants were selected.

Evaluation designs that rely on a comparison group are referred to as quasi-experimental because the approach utilized is the same as in the experimental setting, but without randomly selected groups. Random assignment is the factor in evaluation methodology that is used to determine whether or not the program should be classified as a best practice in many cases; however, experimental designs are not always appropriate or necessary (Hall & Jennings 2008). In many social programs, it is not appropriate to exclude any group from receiving the treatment in question, and in such cases it would be considered unethical to deprive comparison or control group members from the services to be delivered.

So, by comparing the results of the treatment group after the program is complete to the result of the comparison/control group at the same time, we are able to observe the differences among individuals who receive the program relative to those who did not. This particular methodology eliminates the need to take pretest measures because the comparison/control group members reflect the average score absent the program. A slightly more complicated design, the pretest posttest comparison group design allows the evaluator to determine not only the effects of the program, but also the effects of maturation, history, or other threats to validity (**Figure 10.6**). In other words, by examining change over time in the comparison/control group, we come to a better understanding of the relative impact of the program as well as plausible alternative explanations for the observed results in the treatment group.

As with the single group designs, the addition of multiple measurement points across time provides richer data that can be used to explain program impacts. The same holds true for multiple group designs, whether experimental or quasi-experimental. The addition of

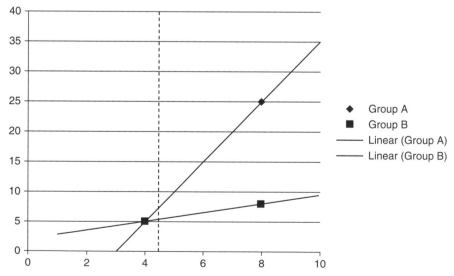

FIGURE 10.6   Pretest/Posttest Comparison Group Design

more measurement points enables the researcher to assess trends over time and how the trends differ between the two groups. An interrupted time series design with multiple groups can also be used. Several pretest measures could be taken prior to program implementation for both groups, after which the program is implemented for treatment group A followed by a second series of measures. The results enable us to determine the difference in not only the absolute results between the two groups, but also in the trends. In this example, if there are concerns for excluding eligible clients from the service, the second group could be given the treatment in a subsequent time period, after which an additional set of measures could be taken.

Interrupted time series analysis provides an opportunity to better understand how the program affects participants over time. **Figure 10.7** shows a program that has a slow initial impact that increases rapidly before stabilizing. If the program had been evaluated at only time period 6, its true results would have been underestimated. Other trends are possible. **Figure 10.8** shows a program that has immediate effects that remain stable over time. **Figure 10.9** exemplifies a program with a strong immediate impact followed by rapid decay. Finally, **Figure 10.10** shows a program that has a small initial effect, a gradual increase to a peak, and then a gradual decline over time. To demonstrate the example highlighted earlier, where both groups need to receive the treatment as soon as possible, a result like that observed in **Figure 10.11** is expected.

We have now discussed a variety of important components needed to organize and conduct a program evaluation. You will recall from the beginning of the chapter that there are two primary types of evaluation approaches—the process evaluation and the outcome evaluation. The remainder of the chapter discusses how to apply this background to evaluation designs of each type.

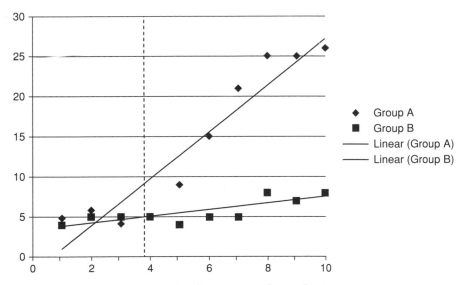

FIGURE 10.7   Interrupted Time Series Comparison Group Design

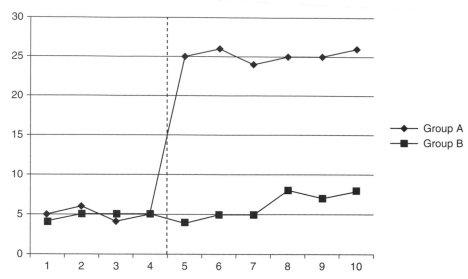

FIGURE 10.8   Interrupted Time Series Comparison Group Design: Immediate Stable Response

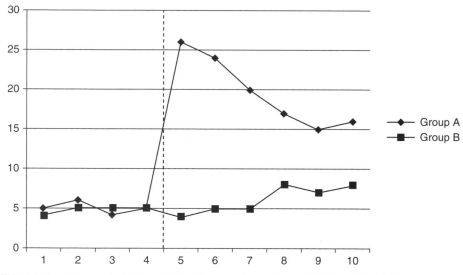

FIGURE 10.9   Interrupted Time Series Comparison Group Design: Rapid Decay

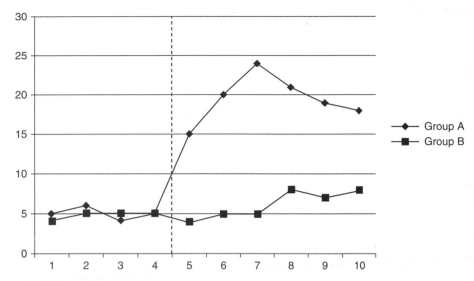

FIGURE 10.10   Interrupted Time Series Comparison Group Design: Gradual Increase and Decay

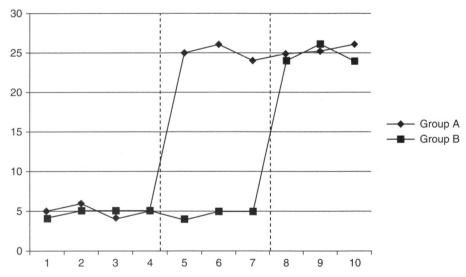

FIGURE 10.11   Interrupted Time Series Design with Treatment in Both Groups

DESIGNING THE PROCESS EVALUATION

Grant making agencies usually have a minimum expectation that process evaluation will be carried out by grantees because it provides them with evidence of program implementation. In other words, it shows that the money was spent according to the plan presented in the grant proposal. Process evaluation in this sense entails monitoring program activities, documenting them as they occur, and comparing activities to the time line and benchmarks established in the implementation plan provided in the grant proposal narrative. As mentioned in Chapter 9, reporting expectations vary by program and by grant making agency. However, it is customary for quarterly reports to be required. Programs of shorter duration may require more or less frequent reporting, depending on the funding agency. For example, many federal programs with a 1-year duration require only an interim report at 6 months and a final report upon program completion. So, how does one develop a process evaluation plan?

Process evaluations are usually dominated by qualitative analysis. There may be some data collection and analysis, but for the most part such data are presented in raw form without further analysis. In planning such an evaluation, you can follow several steps to facilitate the process (Table 10.3).

The first step in designing a process evaluation is to identify key project activities that will serve as indicators of implementation progress. So, for example, key project activities might include hiring staff, developing curricular materials, marketing the program, recruiting participants, conducting training sessions, assessing participant progress, and evaluating outcomes. Note here that outcome evaluation is a step in the implementation plan and can thus be used as an indicator of performance in the process evaluation. Alongside each of these indicators of progress toward implementation is a date or range of dates that can be used to assess the timeliness of implementation. Implementing the program to its fullest extent within the time period of funding is dependent upon the applicant's ability to carry out the steps in a timely fashion. So, the timing of implementation is as important as the implementation step in question.

The second step in designing a process evaluation entails linking each project activity to the date at which it is supposed to be initiated or completed. For example, training sessions may be conducted over a 6-month period, so the date of the first session and the date of the last session are important indicators. But before this step could take place participants need to be recruited. The project activities and implementation dates go hand in hand

---

TABLE 10.3   Simple Process Evaluation Design Steps

1. From the implementation plan, identify *key project activities*.
2. From the grant narrative time line, indicate *key progress dates*.
3. Identify *key indicators of project performance*, such as intermediate outputs. (Note: These should be apparent from the detailed workplan.)
4. Assign *responsibility for monitoring* the program activities identified.
5. *Describe the process* that person will use to collect and analyze the required information.
6. Indicate that these results will be *integrated into periodic reports* to the funding agency.

in determining the progress toward program implementation. Quarterly reports are generally intended to assess this progress, and these two steps will provide the information necessary for those reports. Of course, as indicated in Chapter 9, most grant reports require both technical and financial aspects. So, it is also necessary to monitor program expenditures that coincide with each activity. Financial expenditure should be commensurate with the activities that have taken place as described.

The third step of process evaluation is aimed at identifying key output measures that indicate successful implementation. The intermediate outputs are not the final goals of the program, but as we discussed previously they are necessary for the program to achieve its ultimate goals. So, looking at the list of project activities identified previously, the number of staff hired is such an output measure. More important than the number of staff is the quality of the staff. Remember that process evaluation is more qualitative in nature. It would be appropriate to describe the staff member that has been hired, his experience, and training. A second output would be the number of media announcements made in program marketing. A third output might be the number of individuals who have expressed interest in the program, followed by the number of applications received. Obviously, these outputs will not occur simultaneously. They occur in sequence as described in the implementation plan for the project. Evaluation is simply a task of comparing expectation to reality. So, if 30 program participants were expected, but only 10 applications were received, the applicant's process evaluation indicates a problem in program design or in the implementation strategy.

The remaining three steps are about describing how this process evaluation will take place. Who is responsible? For simple evaluations of this nature, it is common for program staff to carry out the evaluation function. So, the program manager may have responsibility for evaluation, or she may designate someone else on staff to carry out these responsibilities. A process should be in place to collect the information necessary to create the evaluation report, and the process should integrate the previous steps to demonstrate how they will be combined to provide program feedback and to generate reports. In writing evaluation plans of this sort, it is a good idea to make note of the due dates for progress reports, whether quarterly, monthly, or annually. The process described should indicate how the data will be collected, combined, and analyzed in advance of each report in a timely fashion.

The process evaluation described here is about generating reports to document program implementation for funding agencies. But process evaluation plays a larger management role necessary to ensure program success. In the broader sense, process evaluation is used as a mechanism to provide program feedback that will correct errors, suggest changes in implementation strategy, and ultimately improve performance. Any sound management plan would incorporate true process evaluation of this kind to demonstrate the applicant's ability to manage its programs. In doing so, it involves adding steps to the process described here. **Table 10.4** itemizes these additional steps.

The additional steps identified in Table 10.4 involve the agency's use of the data collected to inform program management. Step 5.1 communicates the agency's plan for comparing its goals and objectives to the outputs generated to date for each evaluation period. Step 5.2 indicates how the agency defines normalcy. We may expect 30 participants, but 29 participants would not indicate severe program dysfunction, and neither would 32 participants.

TABLE 10.4   Full Process Evaluation Steps

5.1. Describe how expectation and reality will be compared.
5.2. Describe what constitutes a problem for each date, output, or activity.
5.3. Identify the process that will be used to alert program staff and management to the problem.
5.4. Describe management's expected response to negative feedback.

So, for example, the agency might define a range of acceptability within which no change would be necessary, such as 28 to 32 participants. A second range might be identified in which minor program modification is required, for example 24 to 27 participants and 32 to 35 participants. Any number falling outside these two ranges would be considered problematic and require immediate and drastic program modification. Expectations can be based on quantities such as in this example, but they can also be based on timing. So, if our activity occurs a day later than expected, we would not define that as a significant problem. However, if the activity occurs 3 months late, we certainly would.

Step 5.3 indicates how the person charged with evaluating the program will notify program management and staff. Step 5.4 indicates how program management is expected to respond. It is obviously not possible to predict every contingency, so the steps are described generally. For example, "Upon receiving negative program progress reports, the program manager will call a meeting of the advisory commission within one week to discuss the identified problem and develop potential solutions. The recommended solutions will be debated, and the preferred approach will be implemented immediately." At this stage, the feedback mechanism has served its purpose and the program has learned from its mistake. And so we also continue with the initial list of steps by returning to the reporting mechanism.

Significant program problems should not be swept under the rug, but should be included in periodic program reports. This is particularly true if the funding agency is interested in whether or not the program design is effective. Hiding program difficulties may lead the funding agency to suspect that the program works as is and support future program proposals using the same approach. It is always advisable to report program difficulties as they occur to enhance program knowledge for the funding agency as well. And naturally, presenting difficulties as they occur prevents a surprise when the program ultimately fails to achieve its goals. Hopefully, of course, process evaluation will correct most deficiencies and success will result. The next section discusses preparing for the outcome evaluation—the substantive evaluation of program effects.

DESIGNING THE OUTCOME EVALUATION

In addition to process evaluation expectations, some funders will also be interested in determining the program's effectiveness. Even when the funding agency does not request an outcome evaluation, the grant recipient should be concerned with determining whether or not the program was effective. This is particularly true when the program of interest is innovative, unique, or a pilot test for a program that is intended to be more broadly implemented in the near future.

Outcome evaluations are not concerned with program implementation issues. Because they are conducted after the program has come to close, or at least after the first full program cycle has been completed, there is very little opportunity to influence implementation. The outcome evaluation seeks to answer the simple question, "Did the program work?" It may also ask, "How well did the program work?" Or "Did the program work better than the most preferred alternative?" In other words, program outcome evaluations are distinct from process evaluation in that the former seek to measure the outputs, outcomes, and impacts that are directly related to the program's goals and purposes. This function means that they are mostly concerned with data collection and analysis. Unlike the process evaluation model, outcome evaluations are most commonly data-driven and have quantitative analysis as their focus.

Just as with process evaluations, outcome evaluations can also be approached from a series of basic steps. Although the evaluation itself is conducted upon program conclusion, it is necessary to define the evaluation prior to program implementation. Clearly defined goals will aid program staff by giving them a clear direction regarding the program's purpose. Moreover, the evaluation design may suggest particular steps during implementation. For example, if a pretest posttest design is to be used, provisions will need to be made in the implementation plan to collect pretest data from participants. It is not possible to collect pretest data after the program has been completed, so it should be apparent how important it is to consider the evaluation methodology prior to program implementation. Rather than waiting until the program has been implemented to begin evaluation, it is always advisable to design the evaluation process up front. Table 10.5 presents the steps that constitute outcome evaluation planning and execution. Steps 1 through 7 are planning steps, whereas steps 8 through 10 are active implementation steps.

In following these steps to planning outcome evaluations, it is useful to refer to the earlier sections of this chapter related to measurement and design. For those individuals

TABLE 10.5   Outcome Evaluation Planning Steps

1. Define evaluation question(s) and hypotheses. (These may be absolute or relative/comparative.)
2. Consider the level of confidence necessary to demonstrate success.
3. Consider the resources available for evaluation.
4. Select an appropriate evaluation design.
5. Determine appropriate operational measures for each evaluation construct.
6. Identify appropriate methods of analysis.
7. Amend the implementation plan with activities necessary to provide evaluation data.
8. Collect program data and organize it in a performance management system.
9. Analyze program data.
10. Draw conclusions about program performance.

wishing to obtain additional information about program evaluation, it is recommended that they consult one or more texts that are specialized on the subject, such as the following:

Posavac, Emil J. and Raymond G. Carey. 2007. *Program Evaluation: Methods and Case Studies, 7th Edition*. Upper Saddle River, NJ: Prentice Hall.
Wholey, Joseph S., Harry P. Hatry, and Kathryn E. Newcomer. 2004. *Handbook of Practical Program Evaluation, 2nd Edition*. San Francisco: Jossey-Bass.
Patton, Michael Quinn. 2008. *Utilization-Focused Evaluation, 4th Edition*. Thousand Oaks, CA: Sage.

The American Evaluation Association (www.eval.org) has many resources that may prove to be useful as you develop evaluation skills. Also, the American Psychological Society has a web-based short course available that may prove beneficial to new evaluators as they prepare to develop an evaluation design (www.the-aps.org/education/promote/promote.html).

The first step suggests that proper evaluation questions need to be designed. Each evaluation can be assessed on the basis of its quality. However, there is no such thing as a good or bad evaluation. There are only good and bad evaluations relative to the questions being asked. Evaluation questions determine the appropriate approach to be used, the data to be collected, and the methods of analysis to be employed. Without a proper evaluation question it is not possible to design an effective evaluation. Evaluation questions may be broad and simple, such as, "Did participants develop new skills that enhance their employability?" Or alternatively, evaluation questions may be very specific, such as, "What underlying explanatory factors predict the participant's ability to acquire new work-related skills?" But generally speaking, the broad question of interest is, "Was our program effective, and how effective was it?" Effectiveness in this case depends on the policy goals that the program is intended to affect.

With an evaluation question or questions established, it is next necessary to ask what level of confidence is required of the evaluation findings. Is there a significant risk to human health? Is the program very expensive? Are there significant negative externalities that are expected to result from the program? If the answer to any of these questions is yes, then a higher degree of confidence is necessary and appropriate evaluation design will be necessary. However, if the answer to these questions is no, then sophisticated evaluation methodologies are probably not necessary, and their expense would not be justified. Again, the evaluation question and the evaluation's larger purpose are important to determining the appropriate evaluation methodology, but so is the level of confidence required.

In an ideal world resources would be abundant, and the appropriate methodology would be selected on the basis of the first two steps alone. Of course, if resources were abundant, there would be no need for grant funding in the first place. Limited organizational resources, including grant funds, often limit the availability of staff time and the funding necessary to conduct proper evaluations. Once again, if there are significant risks or concerns, every effort should be made to obtain the necessary funding because the evaluation will ultimately become a central component of the program. But if there are not significant risks, available resources will provide a constraint on the methodologies that can be utilized.

Generally speaking, external designs (those that use a randomly selected control group) are very expensive to conduct. Some cost savings can be accrued by using a comparison group study rather than the control group. Single group designs are obviously less expensive than either of these options, but they run the risk of providing results that are less useful because of the threats to internal validity discussed earlier. In similar fashion, each data point collected is an expense to the study. So, if resources are particularly short, it may be necessary to conduct a posttest-only evaluation. It is obviously true that pretest posttest measures are superior, but they add expense to the evaluation. The interrupted time series design, with its multiple data collection points, is more expensive still. Resource considerations also influence the type of data that can be collected. Surveys are generally expensive, though often not as expensive as individual interviews, focus groups, or utilizing expert observers. Most often archival data, such as agency records, can prove to be the least expensive to collect. Resource constraints have important effects on the evaluation design that we ultimately choose.

With these considerations in place, the next step is to select an appropriate evaluation design. The goal of this step should be to select the design that offers the greatest confidence in the expected results given the limitations of the program and agency resources. Once again, experimental designs are ideal but rarely necessary or justified (Hall & Jennings 2008). With an evaluation design in place, the evaluator must next break down each of the conceptual constructs that frame the evaluation into appropriate operational measures. And on the basis of the design selected, and the data expected to be available, given the initial evaluation questions, the evaluator will select methods of statistical analysis appropriate to obtain the answers desired. In the most simple evaluations, rudimentary comparisons may be used. As the designs become more sophisticated, comparison tests of group means, correlations, and regressions may also be used. The more complex the evaluation questions and the more confidence required that the results are valid, the more sophisticated these methods of analysis must be.

With the evaluation design complete, the only remaining step for planning purposes is to amend the original project implementation plan so that it conforms to the evaluation design that will be used to evaluate the project. Additional activities may be added, including assessments, pretests, and other data collection activities. These activities will involve additional personnel, and they may incur additional costs that also need to be budgeted. Thinking through the evaluation prior to program implementation improves the quality of evaluation that can be attained.

Steps 8, 9, and 10 are active evaluation steps that include collecting data, analyzing data, and drawing conclusions. The conclusions reached should provide answers to the evaluation questions of interest, and naturally, they should also tell us whether the program achieved its intended goals and objectives. In many cases, it will not be possible to measure the program's ultimate outcome so quickly after the program concludes. Moreover, the more time that passes, the less confident we can be that the outcome realized is the effect of the program versus other contextual factors. Most outcome evaluations conclude with a decision regarding the program's continuation. An outcome evaluation will generally present the conclusions accompanied by one of three recommendations: to continue the program as is, to terminate the program, or to continue the program with substantial modifications.

These 10 steps provide an overview to planning and executing an outcome evaluation, and they should provide guidance to program managers wishing to evaluate programs and to grant writers who are developing narrative descriptions for grant applications. In practice, outcome evaluations are often conducted by unbiased third parties referred to as independent evaluators. Independent evaluators are hired under contract to assess the program's goals, determine the program's progress toward those goals, and to make recommendations regarding the program. Independent external evaluators can offer an unbiased opinion of the program's performance because their recommendations are less likely to be biased by human considerations that would affect program employees or agency staff. In some cases, large organizations have an independent evaluation unit that is called upon to evaluate programs on behalf of other organizational units. The Government Accountability Office (formerly the General Accounting Office) is the federal government's evaluation unit, and it is called upon to assess other federal agency programs on a continuous basis. Although not purely independent, this is still preferable to outcome evaluation conducted by agency staff, who will desire to show their program in the best possible light.

The following section considers performance management systems and the important role they can play in program management, but especially in preparing for and conducting program evaluations.

Performance Management Systems

Performance management systems establish routines for collecting, coding, and storing information relevant to an organization and its program activities. Systematizing data collection is a sound way to ensure ongoing performance measurement, thus ensuring program decision making is continually focused on results and performance enhancement. Collecting data as you go enables regular reporting (such as quarterly grant reports) and facilitates both process and outcome evaluation by reducing the time spent searching for data when the evaluation is being prepared. The Urban Institute has been at the forefront of performance measurement and management for some time, and their publications provide sound resources for developing and implementing an organizational or program performance management system. The following resources may prove useful as you attempt to design and implement such a system in your organization:

Hatry, H. P. 1999. *Performance Measurement: Getting Results.* Washington, DC: Urban Institute Press.
Morley, E., S. P. Bryant, and H. Hatry. 2001. *Comparative Performance Measurement.* Washington, DC: Urban Institute Press.

CONCLUSION

This chapter introduces the important reasons for evaluating public programs, particularly programs funded by government grants. Two general approaches to evaluation, the process and the outcome evaluation, are presented and discussed. Finally, the logic behind evaluation is presented, with a discussion of measures, program theory, and evaluation designs to facilitate development of evaluations best suited to answering the questions of greatest importance to your grant program. The chapter concludes with an approach to developing evaluations of each type and a brief discussion of performance management systems and their usefulness in monitoring organizational progress and providing the data required by program evaluators.

REFERENCES

Frederickson, David G. and H. George Frederickson. 2006. *Measuring the Performance of the Hollow State*. Washington, DC: Georgetown University Press.

Fowler, F. J., Jr. 1998. Design and Evaluation of Survey Questions. In *Handbook of Applied Social Research Methods* (p. 343–374), L. Bickman and D. J. Rog, Eds. Thousand Oaks, CA: Sage.

Hall, Jeremy L. and Edward T. Jennings, Jr. 2008. Taking chances: Evaluating risk as a guide to better use of best practices. *Public Administration Review* 68(4): 695–708.

Hatry, H. P. 1999. *Performance Measurement: Getting Results*. Washington, DC: Urban Institute Press.

Kettl, Donald F. 1988. *Government by Proxy: (Mis?)Managing Federal Programs*. Washington, DC: Brookings Institution.

Milward, H. Brinton. 1996. Symposium on the hollow state: Capacity, control, and performance in interorganizational settings. *Journal of Public Administration Research and Theory* 6(2):193–195.

Morley, E., S. P. Bryant, and H. Hatry. 2001. *Comparative Performance Measurement*. Washington, DC: Urban Institute Press.

Patton, Michael Quinn. 2008. *Utilization-Focused Evaluation, 4th Edition*. Thousand Oaks, CA: Sage.

Posavac, Emil J. and Raymond G. Carey. 2003. *Program Evaluation: Methods and Case Studies, 6th Edition*. Upper Saddle River, NJ: Prentice Hall.

Posavac, Emil J. and Raymond G. Carey. 2007. *Program Evaluation: Methods and Case Studies, 7th Edition*. Upper Saddle River, NJ: Prentice Hall.

Radin, Beryl A. 2002. *The Accountable Juggler: The Art of Leadership in a Federal Agency*. Washington, DC: CQ Press.

Sudman, S., N. M. Bradburn, and N. Schwarz. 1996. *Thinking About Answers*. San Francisco: Jossey-Bass.

Weiss, Carol H. 1998. *Evaluation: Methods for Studying Programs and Policies, 2nd Edition*. Upper Saddle River, NJ: Prentice Hall.

Wholey, Joseph S., Harry P. Hatry, and Kathryn E. Newcomer. 2004. *Handbook of Practical Program Evaluation, 2nd Edition*. San Francisco: Jossey-Bass.

CHAPTER 11

Turning the Table:
It Is Better to Give Than to Receive

Through this point in our journey, this text has examined the composition of the grant making system, the process used to identify funding sources, how to apply for and secure funding, and how to manage grant funds once awarded, including the process of program evaluation. Many practitioners and students of public administration will, at some point in their careers, find themselves on the giving end rather than on the receiving end. State agencies often make grants or issue contracts. At other times, they manage federal grants by redistributing the money among applicants within their states or cities, as is often the case with Community Development Block Grant entitlement funds. Many nonprofit organizations make grants to local organizations for efforts that further their objectives. Some organizations make grants for specific purposes, such as studies or projects. And some of you may work for a foundation or a nonprofit organization that exists primarily to distribute funds to worthy applicants through grants, such as the United Way.

This chapter turns the table on these previous discussions by providing guidance about how to distribute funding to meet your organization's objectives. How should you go about selecting grant types? What conditions should you add to the award contract? What oversight mechanisms will you use? How will you go about determining awardees? Each of these considerations is examined in a three-phase framework that begins with preparation and planning and continues with the decision process and making the grant awards, and concludes with oversight and monitoring to ensure compliance with conditions and performance.

PREPARING TO MAKE GRANTS: THINKING THROUGH ACCOUNTABILITY RELATIONSHIPS

As you begin to consider how to go about distributing funds, it is important to recognize the accountability relationships and expectations you and your organization face. Are you accountable to government agencies at the federal or state level? Are you accountable only to your own constituents who pay the tax dollars that will be used to fund grant programs at the local level? Are you accountable to donors? Are you accountable to a board of directors? Or are you accountable to other members of your profession?

Accountability takes many forms, and each form suggests differing expectations for your performance in distributing funding. Public sector organizations usually have more stringent accountability expectations than do private or nonprofit organizations. Public organizations must maintain the public trust, and they are accountable to constituents for their use of funds, for the method used to equitably distribute them, and the outcomes of the projects that are funded. Private foundations and nonprofit organizations are accountable to their donors, trustees, and boards of directors. In these private settings, accountability for the use of funds, the method used to distribute them, and the outcomes are still relevant, but accountability requirements extend from the guidelines and restrictions established by a few individuals rather than the population at large.

Understanding to whom you are accountable and the expectations for your performance in distributing funding will suggest a series of steps that may be taken to ensure that accountability expectations are fulfilled. Koppell (2005) suggests that accountability has five dimensions that include transparency, liability, controllability, responsiveness, and responsibility. The first two, transparency and liability, are procedural in that they are required for the remaining three types to exist. In the case of government funding, transparency means following federal or state information laws such as the Freedom of Information Act and open meetings regulations. (Individuals interested in better understanding government transparency should consult the work of Suzanne Piotrowsky and David Rosenbloom.) There is no expectation of transparency in the case of private foundations. Public foundations, on the other hand, must disclose their finances to the Internal Revenue Service using Form 990. But private and nonprofit organizations do not have the same procedural requirements for transparency that apply to government funds.

For nonprofit organizations, the liability requirements associated with distributing grant funds simply require not violating any state, federal, or local laws, and not violating any contractual obligations through the funding decisions or actions resulting from the funded program or activity. In the case of government organizations, these same liability requirements exist, but so also do the specific requirements of the authorizing legislation that created the funding program. So again, liability is more explicit for government funds than for private funds.

Controllability refers to the ability of elected officials or boards of directors to determine what actions grant administrators take. In other words, administrative agents are expected to carry out the will determined and expressed by their political principals. Controllability is a dimension of accountability because it varies across settings and actors. The extent to which it is possible for principals to control their agents or subordinate employees differs from organization to organization and over time. In private organizations, an employer can exercise the threat of revoking an individual's employment. In public nonprofit organizations this is true, but such decisions are sometimes subject to approval by the board or an executive committee, diluting the threat. In other words, it is easier for a unitary authority to decide it is necessary to fire someone than for a decision-making body to come to majority agreement.

It stands to reason that controllability is even weaker in public sector (government) organizations. Individuals within the executive branch of government make hiring and firing decisions, but Congress often delegates program design and administration issues to the bureaucracy for implementation. One reason for delegated authority is the inability to arrive at a consensus on approach; another is the lack of technical expertise (Meier & Bohte 2007). Whatever the cause, expectations are not always clear. As a result, administrators have broader latitude to carry out their tasks. Democrats and Republicans cannot agree among themselves, and certainly not with each other, on many issues. The House of Representatives and the Senate do not agree in whole on many details, and further differences of opinion arise with regard to the president. The same case is true for state and local governments.

But when any single party has control over more than one institution, controllability increases because goals are more uniform and clear. For these reasons, controllability is weaker in public sector organizations than in private sector organizations. So, although the legal environment of public sector organizations is more constraining, and the resulting decisions still may be scrutinized, it is difficult for a political principal to enforce any particular decision. (This is what is referred to as the principal–agent problem.) The controllability–accountability relationship looks upward within the organization and is internal in nature. Controllability can be brought about through contract provisions and compliance enforcement.

Accountability relationships also extend downward and outward from the funding agency to affected constituents and stakeholders. This form of accountability is referred to as responsiveness, and it takes into account the fact that funding agencies are concerned about the needs of those individuals or organizations they seek to serve. Government agencies are plied by interest groups, or by agency constituents, who are seeking particularistic benefits in the form of funding, services, and so on. Grants provide an alternative to direct service provision for these agencies. Responsiveness relationships can become complex when there are multiple groups applying pressure for contradictory decisions or benefits. To be effective in this dimension, the funding agency should have clearly identified its stakeholders. To whom must it be responsive? Should it be responsive to its clients, to the population as a whole, or both? Does one group receive priority over another? Often some guidance can be found in the organization's mission statement or its authorizing legislation.

Over time, public agencies can become captured by interest groups through mutually reinforcing beneficial relationships among the agency, the interest group, and a congressional subcommittee (Birkland 2005). When this occurs, the primary interest becomes the one to which the agency is most responsive. As the environment changes, so do these relationships. So, although one interest or population group is most important today, it will not necessarily be as important in the next year or the next decade. Public agencies are responsive because they reap the political fallout if they are not. Congress can tighten budgets and increase oversight to bring about responsiveness in the desired direction. Organizations in the third sector (nonprofit organizations) establish their own missions, often through strategic planning and visioning processes (see Bryson 2004). The board of directors approves the mission, but it must be flexible as well, and as the environment changes, the organization must change with it to remain effective in addressing its goals (Hall 2007).

Responsiveness requires changing the organization's activities to remain closely aligned to the particular problem or need, often expressed by the public will in the form of complaints, social mobilization, lobbying, and activism. Nonprofits and governments differ in that government usually has a broader scope whereas nonprofits serve more narrow groups. Responsiveness may be more challenging for government agencies than for nonprofits, but this depends, of course, on the specific nature of the agencies and their programs.

Responsiveness has been found to positively influence citizen evaluations of government performance (Glaser & Denhardt 2000). Success on this dimension of accountability can be judged by stakeholder satisfaction or political support. For example, the 1996 national welfare reform legislation resulted from a shift in thinking about the nature of the problem. Whereas welfare had been a system to provide a safety net for less fortunate individuals, it had come to be perceived as wasteful and corrupt. Public thinking translated into political support and ultimately legislative change. Responsiveness can be enforced through solicitation of stakeholder feedback, through expert assessments, and so on.

Very closely related to the concept of responsiveness is responsibility. Responsibility refers to accountability derived from laws, rules, and regulations that determine the organization's purpose and eligible activities. In the case of nonprofit organizations, responsibility refers to their mission or an area of impact that the organization has selected to address. Environmental groups have a responsibility to the environment, and humane societies have a responsibility for animal welfare, as does the U.S. Fish and Wildlife Service. Responsibility is also an outward, or external, accountability relationship. Responsible organizations take ownership of a problem, or a particular range of affairs, and seek to bring about positive change. Success on this dimension of accountability can be assessed through evaluation and performance measurement to determine the extent of outputs generated and the degree of the problem persisting after the organization's activity. Naturally, the definition of success depends on the organization's perspective, so the measures chosen will determine the resulting perceptions of any change to the status quo. Responsibility can be enforced through evaluations, studies, and general attention to the environment.

It is a good idea to make a list of all of the accountability expectations that face the organization. These will usually be more involved and complicated for government agencies than for private nonprofit agencies because of government's responsibility for equal protection and equal rights. So, for example, federal grant money must not be used for discriminatory purposes, must protect the rights of people with disabilities, and so on. To prioritize these expectations, it may help to distinguish between mandates and expectations. Determining all of the organization's constraints and expectations up front facilitates developing a grant making operation that maximizes the extent to which accountability goals can be accomplished.

Once the expectations and requirements are identified, it is possible to determine whether policies and procedures need to be developed to help the organization to remain accountable during the preparation phase, the decision phase, or the award management phase. Before continuing, take a few moments to consider the importance of each phase to ensuring your organization's accountability.

The preparation phase is the time to think about how the grant will be administered, its type and form, any conditions that may be required, any legal requirements or constraints, and any process requirements. If there are transparency rules or laws that apply to your organization, you must ensure that the process allows for these mandates to be enforced. If there are legal constraints on what your organization can and cannot do, they must be considered to limit the risk of liability. What are the expectations expressed in the mission or authorizing legislation? These determine the scope and shape of the program and any conditions on the award. Does the organization wish to induce grantee spending as well? This influences the selection of matching requirements. Is there an expectation of fairness? If so, what procedures need to be in place to ensure equity? And of course, what format should the application take? This depends on the number of applications expected as well as the type of information required. Should it be open response, or should you develop and use a standard application form? In short, a well-thought-out process better prepares the grant making organization to achieve its desired goals and remain accountable in every way possible.

The second phase, the decision process, is centered on the approach taken in evaluating proposals. A transparent organization (that is, one that must disclose the results of its evaluation and decision process) will not want to be caught with its pants down by a disgruntled applicant seeking feedback. A sound decision process, to maintain equity, needs to have a clear set of rules and procedures. What should be done with applications received after the deadline? What about applications that do not conform to the application requirements? Who will evaluate the proposals? If you wish to be responsive and responsible, you might elect to use a peer review system of the applicants' peer group who understand the problem and acceptable approaches to countering it. If your donors or board have clear expectations about eligible types of programs, you may not wish to delegate this control to external reviewers. Or if you do, you may have to write strict criteria for eligibility. How will the awards be prioritized? Which factors are most important, and how should they be weighted? And will you negotiate the scope of work or make funding decisions outright?

The award management phase extends your organization's reach beyond its walls and into the field where the programs are being implemented. If you are concerned with liability, you may include various conditions for award, such as prohibited activities and expenditures, in the grant award contract to transfer liability to the recipient organization. If you want to ensure responsibility, you may require and enforce an outcome evaluation as part of the award, or you may conduct an audit or outcome evaluation independently. If you want to remain responsive, you may wish to provide opportunities for the applicant to amend its scope of work to better address the problem in the target population or area as it changes.

Will you require reports? If so, how often? Reporting burden enhances program accountability to a point, after which it only enhances administrative burden with declining marginal returns. And of great significance, will you provide funds up front or on a reimbursement basis? The former option limits your administrative costs, but it provides opportunity for waste and abuse. Various mechanisms can be used to bring about oversight, such as audit requirements, field visits, and so forth. The extent to which these tools are utilized will depend on your trust in the grant recipients and the forms of accountability to which your organization is most sensitive.

These three phases constitute the framework of a typical grant making operation. Some programs are one-time events, rising and falling with a pool of available funds. Others are recurring, such as from a stream of endowment revenue at a foundation. And sometimes, even the recurring program cycles undergo amendment to bring the program into sync with the agency's goals, mission, and preferred strategies. Each step in each phase can be used to bring about greater accountability. However, each additional requirement and step adds complexity and cost to the administration of the grant program. Some elements may be sacrificed to maximize direct spending on the program rather than technical administration of the grant award process. The specific dimensions of your organization's or program's accountability requirements determine the extent to which you adopt various accountability-enhancing requirements, and their specificity.

Brown and Potowski (2003) evaluate government contracting with an emphasis on the forms of capacity required to manage contracts effectively in three phases: feasibility assessment, implementation, and evaluation. They find that past experience with contracting, and particularly dissatisfaction with prior contracting experiences, lead local governments to invest in greater contract management capacity (Brown & Potowski 2003, p. 159–160). They also find that greater contracting transaction costs, brought about by increases in the use of contracts or the complexity of the contracts, lead to more investment in contracting capacity. What lesson can we draw from this finding? Simply, governments tend to invest in contract management capacity once they learn how challenging it can be on their own. The pitfalls of poor contract management can be avoided by investing in the appropriate capacity prior to undertaking a significant contracting burden such as grant programs often entail.

Proper attention to the planning process through the three phases of grant management identified can prepare a grant making organization by highlighting areas where greater capacity is needed. Legal assistance may be required, evaluation expertise may be helpful, but sufficient program and administrative staff to monitor and manage the program should be in place prior to attempting a full-scale grant program implementation. Just like direct service delivery, grant programs have costs; sufficient capacity to manage a program depends on the nature and scale of the program. As Donald F. Kettl (2002) puts it, "Government strategies, especially grants and contracts, do not manage themselves. Rather, they require the cultivation of new skills to specify program goals, negotiate good contracts, and oversee the results" (p. 162). The better prepared a program, the better it will be managed, and the better managed a program, the better are the results that can be expected. With that in mind, let us now explore the key considerations that comprise each of the three phases of grant administration.

PHASE ONE: PLANNING AND PREPARATION

The first phase, planning and preparation, includes seven steps that are necessary to design an effective grant program (**Figure 11.1**).

Selecting the Grant Type

From the discussion in Chapter 1, you should have an appreciation for the differences in grant types: formula (non-categorical), project (categorical), or a hybrid of the two (block). The key question to ask in preparation for this stage is: "What is the organization's purpose in making grants?" At the broadest level, this means determining whether your purpose in giving is expressive or instrumental. That is, do you want to provide general financial assistance to the organization without conditions or strings, or do you have some more specific

STEP	DESCRIPTION
1	**Select Grant Type**
	—Expressive vs. instrumental
	—Categorical vs. non-categorical
	—Conditional vs. unconditional
2	**Select Eligibility Requirements**
	—Individual vs. organization
	—Public vs. private
	—Nonprofit vs. for-profit
	—Specific organization types (e.g., universities)
3	**Develop Program Description and Guidelines**
	—Mission and purpose
	—Eligible activities
	—Expected components
4	**Select Conditions for Award**
	—Matching requirements
	—Direct program-related conditions (e.g., serve only rural populations)
	—Indirect management conditions (e.g., audit and reporting)
	—Eligible expenditures and cost items
5	**Establish Application Procedures**
	—Deadline and submission procedures
	—Forms and format (e.g., application forms, page limits, font size)
	—Response components (key questions that must be addressed)
6	**Develop Forms**
	—Cover sheet or application summary sheet vs. no summary form
	—Budget forms vs. no budget form
	—Application form with preformatted space for response vs. open-ended response
7	**Establish Management Responsibility and Procedures**
	—Time line of key activities (notification of receipt, review, decision, notification, negotiation)
	—Project responsibility (management and administration roles assigned)
	—Develop review process (continues with phase 2)

FIGURE 11.1   Planning and Preparation Steps

instrumental purpose that will require conditions? In other words, do you support organizations or projects? From this general question, attention should turn to the scope of giving. Does the organization have broad giving purposes, or a few specific areas? And are the organization's goals specific or general in each program area? The answers to these questions will inform every remaining detail required to construct a grant making system.

If the purpose is expressive, a check may be written for the desired amount without any need for further conditions or controls. For an agency like United Way, a formula can be established to distribute funds across the eligible agencies. If the purpose for giving is even the least bit instrumental, however, as a funding agency, you will want to develop a process that includes accountability-enforcing mechanisms in the manner associated with project grants.

With the general purpose in mind, what is the purpose of the specific program? If you are passing through federal block grant money, the purpose is predetermined for you in the federal authorizing legislation. And if you are granted entitlement money, it will be your responsibility to ensure that it is redistributed to purposes that fall within those eligibility requirements. If you are administering the charity of a local philanthropist, you may have a broader mission such as "community development" or "arts and education programming." If you have discretion to form more specific funding guidelines, it may be advantageous to do so—it will depend in large part on how much funding you have available and how much competition exists for it. It may also be helpful to think in terms of your funding objectives. For example, if your objective is to improve literacy, that focus is more specific than is general education funding. If your objective is to promote faith-based social services, that focus is more specific than are "religious purposes" or "social services" alone. The more specific are your goals, the better you can frame your proposal guidelines to limit the number of uncompetitive proposals received.

Selecting Eligibility Requirements

Eligible recipients must be determined before issuing a request for proposals to ensure that the funding agency receives requests only from those entities it is willing to fund. Some granting agencies make grants directly to individuals, although most do not. Some also fund corporations to perform research or some other service. However, it is most common to limit the pool of eligible recipients to nonprofit agencies and government agencies whose mission is not to earn a profit, but to provide a valuable public service. And in some cases, it is even necessary to limit the eligible recipients to a particular organization type, often defined by its purpose. Universities are a subset of nonprofit organizations that are commonly selected as eligible recipients for grant programs. But depending on your organization's purpose, you may select any number of eligible organization types, such as tourist commissions, animal welfare agencies, state highway departments, and so on. The key is that you identify those types of organizations that have the capacity to execute and implement the projects you are interested in funding. This list of organizations, or the limitations on organization type if you opt for a more general description, should be included in the request for proposals so that non-eligible applicants will be dissuaded from submitting an application.

Determining Program Description and Guidelines

In preparing to issue a request for proposals, it is necessary to develop a concise program description that communicates your organization's goals and the intended purpose or mission of the grant program. The mission and purpose will help potential applicants to determine whether their mission and goals are a good match with your program's intent. If your purpose is to fund a particular activity in several locations, then you should describe the eligible activity in the program description and clearly communicate that the funding will be provided for only that activity. If you are interested in funding a variety of possible activities within a particular policy area, then your program description can be broader. It is often easier to identify activities that are not desired than those that are. In other words, applicants responding to a request for proposals can be very creative in designing new programs to address old problems. Rather than specify particular programs or activities that you would fund, and stifle this potential creativity, it is often easier simply to say, "We do not fund . . ." The same principle applies to eligible organizations. So, for example, you may desire to specify that funding will not be made available to public schools, or to groups with religious affiliations, or to some other organizational subset.

In developing the request for proposals, it is also necessary to identify the components you expect any applicant to provide in its proposal. Are you interested in knowing the extent of the problem in the target area? Are you interested in the applicant's planned approach? Are you interested in the applicant's management capacity? Is there a need to provide an outcome evaluation for this project? Does the time line matter? Would it be useful to have background information on the applicant organization? In truth, most of these components are usually helpful in making funding decisions, but the value of each component declines as the number of components increases. In other words, lengthy proposals are more difficult to read and take longer to evaluate. So, it is very important to identify which components are most important and require that each applicant provide a response. Sometimes these take the form of a general description, and other times they take the form of a specific question. Which particular form you elect to use for your request for proposals depends entirely on your goals and purposes.

The most common elements required in a grant proposal include an executive summary, introduction to the area and organization, a definition of the problem and description of need, a description of the planned approach (including program activities, the management plan, and the implementation plan), a description of the organization's capacity and experience as they relate to the problem, a spending plan, and an evaluation plan. Again, you may not elect to utilize each of these sections, and you may label them differently. In some cases, you may elect to ask very specific questions rather than rely on the applicant's open-ended response.

Selecting Conditions for Award

The next question is whether you are satisfied to be the sole supporter of the project or whether you want to leverage your resources to maximize your impact. This question gets at the notion of financial conditions in the form of matching requirements. If you want to leverage your investment for maximum impact, then you will want to add matching requirements. The extent of matching required will determine the amount of impact possible. Keep in mind, however, that many small organizations have limited resources, or they wouldn't be seeking your assistance. So, by placing extremely stringent match requirements on funding, you may be inadvertently excluding a deserving group of organizations that would benefit most from your assistance. The use of in-kind match requirements as a substitute for cash matching helps to soften this condition. Once you have determined whether or not to use matching requirements, you must determine the type (in-kind or cash) and the proportion. Common proportions are 25% and 50% of total project costs, but these expectations vary widely across programs. It is important to specify whether your match requirements are computed as a proportion of the grant amount or of the total project cost to avoid applicant confusion.

Non-financial conditions can shape the range of activities that applicants may pursue. These are considered direct program-related conditions. For example, program-related conditions might include a requirement that at least 60% of program participants meet federal poverty guideline criteria; another might be that the beneficiaries must be rural residents. Program-related conditions help to ensure that the funds are used in the manner most compatible with the funding organization's goals and objectives. Opting for more conditional grants can be useful in causing the recipients to adopt particular policies or program features. Non-financial strings may be used, but as with financial strings, they can have the effect of turning away would-be applicants that are not willing to sacrifice their local values for your organization's preferences.

Non-program-related conditions, or indirect conditions, involve management activities that the grant recipient is expected to fulfill. For example, the applicant may be required to complete an annual audit of its consolidated financial statements. Another common condition is the use of reporting requirements on program activities and spending. Administrative conditions of this nature are intended to ensure that the program is managed effectively and to reduce the likelihood of serious program failure.

The final set of conditions that should be considered are eligible costs. The aforementioned conditions will help to ensure that the applicant, if awarded a grant, does not engage in undesired activities. In other words, without reporting requirements or audit requirements a grant recipient could engage in the activities described in the scope of work with few limitations on its spending. Of course, if the granting agency is not interested in limiting expenditures, such conditions would not be advisable. However, most funders understand that expenditure on luxury items enhance the quality of life within the institution without having any observable impact on the problem of interest or the targeted beneficiaries. So, it is very common for funding agencies to limit expenditures on, for example, alcoholic beverages, laptop computers, color printers, and other items that, although possibly desirable, do not further the program's interest. Your task will be to identify categories of expenditure that are not allowable or specific items that are not permissible. Many nonprofit foundations limit administrative expenditures (indirect or overhead costs) because they are interested in the program's direct support and not in support of the institution performing the work. Expenditures of this nature are usually capped at some reasonable level, such as 10% of program expenditures, although some organizations forbid them entirely.

Establishing Application Procedures

In preparing the request for proposals, you must also provide information to potential applicants about the program deadline for application submissions and submission procedures. How should you go about determining an acceptable deadline? For many organizations, the deadline may be insignificant. However, for most organizations, whether governmental or nonprofit, funding is issued on the basis of an annual budget. So, to allocate funds during the budget year, it is necessary to receive, review, and fund applications during the period for which funding authority is available. If your fiscal year ends on June 30, then you must make funding decisions prior to that date. And if you intend to expend funds during the period of budget authority, then you will probably want to look closer to the beginning of the fiscal year to make awards.

For example, if you plan to make grants during the fiscal year, you may wish to make awards effective July 1. You will probably want to make funding announcements at least a month in advance to provide recipients with sufficient time to prepare to implement the program. On this calendar, you would need to make award notice no later than June 1. And so you would want to require sufficient time between the receipt of applications and the date of planned notification for proposal review and evaluation, for example, on April 1. So, the structure of your deadline decision will depend upon three factors: when you need to spend money, how long you think it will take your organization to review the applications received, and your estimate of an appropriate amount of time for applicants to review the program announcement and develop a responsive application.

Submission procedures also depend on your plans for evaluating proposals. Do you want to receive piles and piles of paper documents? If so, do you want to bear the burden of photocopying these documents yourself, or would you prefer to shift the expense to the applicant by requiring multiple copies at submission? It is increasingly common for grant applications to be submitted electronically, either through a web-based portal or through electronic mail to a dedicated address. The advantage of electronic submission is that the proposal can be stored electronically without taking up storage space, and it can be transmitted efficiently and rapidly from person to person. So, if you intend to send proposals to volunteer peer reviewers in distant locations, then an electronic format may be preferable.

Whatever the case, you must specify the location to which applications must be sent, whether a web portal, e-mail address, or a physical address. In the case of physical addresses, many organizations utilize different addresses for mailing than they do for parcel delivery; if this is the case for you, and you are willing to receive applications in either fashion, then you should provide both addresses. When must proposals be received? Organizations have handled this question differently as well, with some opting for a receipt deadline and others preferring a postmark deadline. Again, in either case, you must specify one or the other. To be fair to all applicants, it is usually preferable to specify a deadline for receipt rather than postmark. And to this end, it is also advisable to specify the time by which proposals must be received.

In issuing a request for proposals, you should always provide very specific proposal format requirements. For example, if you plan to receive proposals on paper, then you may wish to restrict applicants to only black and white to prevent applicants with color printers from obtaining a comparative advantage in the review process. You should specify a maximum number of pages, minimum font size, line spacing, and margin size in addition to paper size. Applicants can be very creative at finding ways to include more information within an established page limit, and such formatting requirements prohibit them from including a disproportionate amount of information compared to other applicants on the threat of disqualification.

Should you create an application form? Should your entire application be form based? If you are providing funding for a very specific activity, such as spaying and neutering stray animals, the process of which varies little from place to place, then you may elect to ask the necessary questions on a standard form to prevent applicants from submitting unnecessary information that will add to your review time and expense. On the other hand, you may prefer an open-ended response that provides a more adequate description of the target area, the problem, and the proposed procedure. But even in this case, there will be certain standard information that you will require from each applicant. In these cases, you may elect to utilize an application form to provide this basic information while still allowing for an open-ended narrative response to the award factors.

The elements that are commonly included on an application form may include contact information, the organization's official name and employer identification number, a description of the targeted service area, an estimate of the budget request for the proposed program, and so on. Forms help to consolidate information into a readily accessible and understandable format, and the data may be entered into a database for management purposes. Application forms, by organizing information into a standard format, save time and expense in application review.

Earlier, I indicated that you should consider general areas that each application should address, which may be limited to a few specific questions. That description was intended to focus attention on the application contents, particularly as they relate to the program description. But another set of key questions must also be considered for inclusion. If there are any specific requirements that you expect a recipient to fulfill, then those questions should be asked clearly and concisely. So, for example, you may be interested in whether the applicant has requested funding from any other source. This question is not directly related to the program, but it may still be important in your decision, so on the application form or as a program description requirement you may ask the applicant to disclose approved or pending funding requests from other sources. Once again, the nature of the specific questions depends entirely on the nature of your goals and expectations and may be quite varied from organization to organization or program to program.

Developing Forms

As mentioned previously, you may elect to utilize a cover sheet to standardize the information received from various applicants, or you may allow applicants to provide information in their own format. Although developing an application form may be a seemingly cumbersome task, it can be a valuable use of time for the savings it generates during application processing and review. Again, if you are providing funding for a very specific purpose or a very specific activity, then you may elect to utilize an application form with preformatted space to respond to each question. The use of such space limitations restricts applicants to providing only that information that is important to you, and it forces them to provide a concise response.

Budget forms might seem unnecessary for those of you who are already engaged in organizational budgeting activities. We become accustomed to a particular budget format with specific categories, and perhaps through bounded rationality we expect most of the world to use such a standard budget format. In reality, many grant writers do not engage in organizational budgeting activities, and they often do not share the same aggregation of cost items by budget category or even the same set of categories. To standardize the financial information received in grant applications, it is advisable to develop a simple budget form to which each applicant's proposed spending plan must conform. You may need to provide a description of the categories you utilize to ensure that each applicant provides the same information in the same format.

Chapter 4 in this text is based on the federal government's standard budget categories, which provide a sound framework. But if your organization utilizes a different set of standardized categories, then it is probably to your advantage to utilize that budgeting system. If you plan to analyze budgets using ratios or other techniques, a standardized format is essential. For example, you may find after reviewing a number of proposals that some applicants request an inordinate amount of funds for travel. If you are concerned about frivolous trips detracting from more relevant program activities, then you may elect to compute the percentage of program expenditures allocated to travel and deduct points for those budgets exceeding a certain percentage.

Develop a Program Time Line

As indicated previously, your time line for requiring applications to be submitted depends on your plan for expenditure. Likewise, most program activities can be mapped out on the basis of your spending plan. It's a good idea to map out key activities that must take place upon receiving a pool of grant applications according to some fixed time goal. So, you may wish to provide applicants with a notice that their application has been received within one week, which would correspond to a specific date. You should also set target dates for beginning and completing the review process, for making funding decisions, for notifying applicants that their award has been approved, and for negotiating and executing any necessary contractual documents.

A sound management plan will have considered each of these activities in advance and made preparations for carrying them out. Each task should be assigned to a responsible staff member who will be accountable for seeing that the goals are met in a timely fashion. With all of these components in place, our attention turns to developing a review process to be utilized in evaluating the proposals received. Because you will want to provide prospective applicants with information about your process and procedures in advance, information about the review process will need to be incorporated into the request for proposals. The following section provides information regarding this essential activity.

PHASE TWO: A DECISION PROCESS FOR SELECTING AWARD RECIPIENTS

With the first phase well thought out, it may be tempting to issue a call for proposals and solicit applications. This would be unwise, however, because the elements of the remaining two phases shape the nature of the conditions that will apply, and thus hold potential to alter the program description and factors for award. The phases are iterative in this manner and must be considered in concert before beginning grant program implementation. The second phase, developing the review and award process, includes seven additional steps that are necessary to design an effective process for receiving, reviewing, and prioritizing grant applications (**Figure 11.2**).

STEP	DESCRIPTION
1	**Decide How to Deal with Non-Compliant Applications**
	–*Discard vs. maintain*
	–*Maintain as-is vs. require modifications*
	–*Notify non-compliant applicants*
2	**Determine the Nature of the Review Process**
	–*Establish phases of review: preapplication, threshold, technical, budget*
3	**Decide Who Will Review Applications and Make Award Decisions**
	–*Agency staff vs. review by applicant peers*
	–*Volunteer peer review vs. paid review*
	–*On-site review vs. off-site electronic review*
	–*Split review: some components reviewed by agency staff, others reviewed by peers*
4	**Prioritize Rating Factors and Establish a Procedure for Scoring Applications**
	–*Equal weights vs. priority weighting*
	–*Assign point distribution to factors/subfactors*
	–*Establish distinct scoring for applicants representing different classifications (e.g., new vs. return)*
	–*Descriptive comments: use vs. non-use; specific comments by factor vs. general summary comments*
5	**Decide Whether Negotiation Will Be Considered**
	–*Negotiate budget vs. keep budget as-is*
	–*Negotiate scope of work vs. maintain scope of work as-is*
	–*Allow amendments to scope of work and budget prior to award documentation*
6	**Draft Boilerplate Contracts**
	–*General applicability vs. project specific*
	–*Include conditions vs. no conditions*
	–*Include performance clauses vs. no performance clauses*
7	**Decide On a Payment and Announcement Approach**
	–*Outright payment up-front vs. periodic installments*
	–*Cash basis vs. reimbursement basis*
	–*Notify by telephone or in writing*
	–*Notify awardees first or last*

FIGURE 11.2   Steps for Developing a Review and Award Process

Dealing with Non-Compliant Applications

In the course of administering grant programs, you will find from time to time that one or more applicants fail to abide by the submission requirements established. What should you do with these applications? As a general rule, you should have determined this and included your decision rule in the request for proposals so that applicants will be prepared for the ramifications of their actions. What is the appropriate action to take? Should the application be disqualified, or should it be allowed?

Failure to follow rules in a simple grant application is usually an indication that an applicant will find it difficult to abide by the conditions of award, so it may be advantageous to disqualify the application and exclude the applicant from consideration for funding. Of course, if the discrepancy is minor, such as inclusion of color tables when you specify black-and-white, exclusion may be a bit extreme. The key is that you should establish a set of standard rules to follow in evaluating each application. Such a heuristic-based decision process ensures equity and fairness to all applicants, especially those who followed the rules. It also will reduce the decision time required to evaluate applications for compliance when they are received.

If you expect very few applications to be submitted in the first place, then excluding those applications with inconsistencies may limit your potential application pool and also limit the potential of the funding organization to realize its goals. In this case, you may elect to notify applicants with application irregularities and request an immediate modification. Although this may seem unfair to those who are able to follow the rules, it is fair in that it provides the same opportunity for all applicants. If you elect to disqualify applications that fail to meet your criteria, then you should notify those applicants immediately in writing so that they will not continue to anticipate an award decision.

Working Out a Suitable Review Process

The nature of the review process you establish will depend, once again, on your specific goals, but also on your preferences for handling applications. Preapplications can be required, as indicated in a previous chapter, to provide an estimate of the number of applications that may be received or to serve a gate-keeping function to limit the number of complete proposals that must be reviewed. It is customary for very long applications for very complex programs to use these requirements whereas other programs do not. However, if you find that the management function the preapplication serves is helpful to you, then you may elect to utilize it.

How many steps will you use to review proposals? Only one? Generally, at least two phases are required to maximize efficiency during the review process. The first, a threshold review, provides an opportunity to review the application for consistency with the eligibility requirements specified in the request for proposals. If the applicant is not eligible, if the activities are not eligible, or if the amount requested exceeds the maximum amount, an application may be disqualified without further review. Threshold review eliminates the need for time-consuming technical review of the application and saves time and expense.

Technical review, the second phase, is all we generally think about when we discuss reviewing grant proposals. The technical review considers each of the factors for award that were identified and assesses the quality of the applicants' proposals. Budget review provides a final possibility that may be distinct from the technical review. Budget review will assess whether the amount requested is suitable for the proposed activities and whether any particular financial conditions are met.

Who Will Decide and How?

Who will review the applications that you receive? The two most common choices are agency staff and external peer reviewers. Each has its advantages and disadvantages. The use of agency staff permits greater control over the funding process, and it can be internalized and managed efficiently. But agency staff may be somewhat isolated from the problem or from practice in a particular field. In this case, it is advantageous to use peer reviewers that represent the spectrum of applicants present in the pool. Peer reviewers are more difficult to manage in that they are not subject to direct agency control, they have the potential to add expense and time to the review process, and they detract from the agency's control over funding decisions. However, an applicant's peers are closest to the problem and practice, and they will be able to provide a valid assessment of whether a proposal is an acceptable approach in the field. Peer reviews also allow agency staff to concentrate on program management and administration without dedicating large amounts of their time to the proposal review process.

If you elect to use peer reviewers, you must also decide whether to compensate them or not. Paid grant reviews have the advantage of stimulating response more quickly and effectively, but they do add considerable expense to the review process. Voluntary reviews, on the other hand, depend on the altruistic motives of the reviewers to participate and provide feedback in a timely fashion. Of course, they are less expensive.

If you use peer review, whether paid or unpaid, you must also decide whether to hold the review on-site or off-site. On-site review at the agency ensures timely response by peer reviewers because they make themselves available for a finite time. On-site review is also helpful because teams of peer reviewers can interact and discuss proposals as they develop their scores and rankings. Off-site peer review can make communication more difficult and it can be more difficult to enforce timely proposal evaluations, but such reviews do not entail the additional expense of travel and lodging. In this electronic age, it is possible to facilitate communication in such a way that replicates face-to-face discussion of proposals through instant messaging, teleconferences, and other electronic means, but these mechanisms are not true substitutes for face-to-face communication.

As indicated earlier, peer review shifts control over funding decisions outside the agency. So, it is possible to shift blame for funding outcomes to the peer review process. In some political circumstances, this might be advantageous. One way to preserve control, while also shifting some blame outside the agency, is to split the components of review into multiple parts. Some components of the proposal, such as the program narrative, can be reviewed by peers outside the agency, while technical components such as the budget may be reviewed in-house.

Establishing a System for Scoring Applications

Utilizing the key components of the program description identified previously, a systematic process must be developed for scoring proposals to ensure that each proposal is evaluated according to the same standards. You may elect to itemize each of these components and assign each an equal weight, but it is customary to assign greater weight to those components with higher priorities. So, for example, if there were 10 components to the proposal, you may assign 10 points to each for a total of 100 points. Alternatively, and more commonly, simple sections on background, need, and organizational capacity are allocated fewer points, while sections such as the program description and the implementation plan receive greater weight in the evaluation process.

Once all of the program components have been identified, a total number of points should be allocated across the factors. It is also acceptable to identify specific subfactors within each award factor, and then allocate each factor's points across its subfactors in a similar priority weighting. Naturally, you should double-check your math to ensure that the total number of points allocated sums to the total available in each factor, and then the total points awarded across the set of factors sums of the total points available for the proposal.

You may find that some award factors require different scales for different applicant classifications. For example, if you have an interest in the applicant's capacity and experience, then applicants that have previously received an award from your program will have an advantage over those that have not. In this case, you may simply reallocate points, or you may require altogether different responses from applicants of different types.

The final decision you should make pertains to the nature of comments to be provided. Public agencies often must adhere to a higher standard of transparency and equity, so they must be prepared to document their efforts in writing and be criticized. Detailed comments provide evidence of a thorough review process and document the reasons for which the application was denied funding. Private funding sources, on the other hand, rarely have to provide a justification for their decisions, and extensive comments are not necessary. Providing extensive comments can be helpful if those comments are succinct and clear. It may be advantageous to provide comments according to each subfactor that has been identified and allocated points. Organized comments in this fashion could prove to be useful in deciding between two equally scored proposals in the funding margin.

The most effective comments are those that are well organized, so efficient reviews may require development of a standardized score and comment form. Comments are particularly important if you plan to provide feedback to applicants to assist their future grant seeking efforts. When applicants request comments on their denied proposals, they are looking for documentation of errors and omissions or weaknesses in their application that they can use to improve future applications.

Negotiating Award Provisions

Once scoring is complete and a simple quantitative prioritization of proposals has been developed, it is possible to start with the application obtaining the highest score and make grant awards to each successively lower score until there is no remaining funding. It is highly likely that this process will result in a mismatch between total funding requests and the total amount of funds available. And in this case, it may be necessary to request budget reduction amendments from some proposals selected for award in order to be able to fund one additional proposal. Of course, this tactic has the negative effect of reducing funding for a project with an excellent proposal. Alternatively, the residual funding may be withheld and rolled into the future year funding. You must decide whether to negotiate applicant budgets or to accept them as submitted. The question here is essentially whether the reduction in expected benefits of selected proposals targeted for budget reductions outweighs the expected benefits of the additional proposal.

It is also necessary to consider the applicant's scope of work for potential amendment prior to executing an award agreement. For example, a team of peer reviewers may give a proposal a very high score while failing to notice that a key program element is not permissible under the eligible activities. Agency staff must then decide whether to fund the proposal or disqualify it. Obviously, if the proposal is exceptional, then it makes sense to delete the ineligible activity and provide funding. But these decisions must be made in advance, and policies and procedures should be established for negotiating changes to the budget and the scope of work.

A closely related subject is whether to allow applicants to amend their own budget and scope of work prior to executing award documentation. The time elapsed between submitting an application and an award decision can have significant impacts on budget estimates, and an immediate amendment may better reflect the program to be implemented than the initial application. For example, skyrocketing gasoline costs can have a dramatic impact on transportation expenses. A budget for a program that is heavy on travel would need to reflect increased travel expenses by decreasing planned travel. Although you may elect to allow or disallow scope of work or budget amendments prior to executing award agreement, it is customary to permit changes that do not substantively change the nature of the planned program and that do not alter the total grant funding request.

Documentation: Contracts and Conditions

In preparing to issue grant awards, proper contractual documents need to be developed. If you will be making general awards, then your contract should specify conditions common across all funded projects. If, however, you will be making awards for programs that are complex and specific, it may be necessary to seek legal assistance in drafting unique contracts for each award. In either case, it will be necessary to seek legal assistance to ensure that liability is transferred to the grant recipient, to provide for enforcement of any program-related or administrative conditions, and to provide recourse in the event those expectations are not met. In other words, contracts become an enforceable mechanism for providing accountability. Any conditions that were important enough for you to itemize, such as eligible activities and expenditures, should be important enough to merit mention in your contractual agreements. Contracts should document conditions and provide relief when they are not met, through program funding suspension or termination of the grant agreement.

Increasingly, governments in the hollow state are relying on performance contracts to ensure quality and timeliness of services provided. For example, transportation agencies issue contracts with conditions that reduce the amount of payment for each day a major construction project is past the agreed completion date. You may wish to utilize performance clauses in grant award contracts to provide tighter control and accountability over grant recipients. You will also want to provide rules for terminating the agreement altogether if necessary; this is addressed in the final phase.

Making Announcements and Issuing Payment

Before making funding announcements, you should decide how you will provide funds to the successful applicants—by check up front, by periodic cash installments, or by reimbursement of expenses on a periodic basis. The advantage of reimbursement is, again, that greater control can be exercised over recipients and their activities. Ineligible expenses can be denied for reimbursement. So, if you have strong accountability expectations, such as liability, you may need to utilize a reimbursement basis. If you want to prevent the ills that face many recipients when they receive lump-sum transfers, such as overspending, you may wish to divide the award into periods, distributing equal amounts each month or quarter. And if your purpose is purely expressive and you do not wish to exercise any control or monitoring, you may provide up-front payment. The only consideration remaining is responsiveness to applicant needs. Many small organizations will not have adequate resources to implement the proposal unless the funds are provided in advance of program activities. It may be necessary to provide special treatment for such circumstances.

Once you have determined how to provide funds, announcements can be made. You must decide whether to notify successful and unsuccessful applicants at the same time or whether to notify them separately. Notifying awardees as soon as possible may provide more time for planning and preparation in anticipation of implementation. It may be best to hold off on notifying non-recipients until after awards have been executed in case one or more applicants decide not to accept the funding. Although rare, this does happen from time to time.

And finally, how you choose to notify recipients depends on your preferences, your familiarity with the applicants, and the sheer number of awards. Telephone contact is a personal approach that can prepare applicants to receive award documentation, but most of us have learned not to put faith in a promise until it is provided in writing. If you opt to notify recipients in writing, depending on the payment approach you adopt, you may save time and postage expenses by including the check or the contractual paperwork and instructions with the award notice. A reminder of reporting expectations and deadlines should also be included.

PHASE THREE: MANAGING GRANT AWARDS

The third and final phase of grant administration entails eight additional considerations that will shape the nature of the grant management process from award to closing (**Figure 11.3**). As with the second phase, there are elements of management that will affect the program description and guidelines, so the three phases should be considered iterative, each requiring thought and decision prior to beginning program implementation.

Assigning Responsibility for Management

With awards made, attention turns to grant management. Unlike management from the recipient's standpoint, which entails implementation and adherence to conditions required by the grant making agency, managing a portfolio of programs as a granting agency requires organization and administrative skill. Receiving and reviewing technical and financial reports, issuing payment, and processing amendments and dealing with other concerns of grant recipients can be time consuming and challenging. Grant making is not

STEP	DESCRIPTION
1	**Assign Responsibility for Management Components** *—Program officers vs. technical specialists (or combined)*
2	**Establish Applicant Reporting Requirements** *—Technical reports* *—Financial reports* *—Periodicity (annual, semiannual, quarterly, monthly, etc.)*
3	**Audit Requirements** *—Require independent audit of program expenses vs. no audit requirement*
4	**Evaluation Requirements** *—Implementation evaluation (completeness)* *—Process evaluation (project management)* *—Outcome evaluation (program learning)* *—Should evaluations be conducted by applicant, grantor, or independent evaluators?*
5	**Establish and Enforce Sanctions of Non-Compliance or Non-Performance** *—Cease and desist orders vs. project continuation* *—Project amendment vs. project termination* *—Receivership by the granting agency: technical assistance vs. no assistance*
6	**Prepare Procedures for Terminating Awards** *—Contract provisions with time limits for notice vs. termination without time limits for notice* *—Time limits for expense reimbursement after termination* *—Return of unused grant funds: plan for enforcement; plan for reallocation*
7	**Establish Sanctions on Future Applications by Delinquent Awardees** *—Disqualification from future application vs. no disqualification* *—Future qualification with conditions vs. no conditions for qualification*
8	**Establish a Performance Management Process** *—Report on cumulative grant program performance across applicants* *—Identify weaknesses and strengths to shape organizational policies and procedures* *—Feedback evaluation results into program design to promote policy learning* *—Disseminate grant program accomplishments and program knowledge to relevant actors*

FIGURE 11.3   Steps to Effective Program Management

easy; nor is it easier than direct service provision—it's just a different type of specialized work.

The first step in effective management is to assign management responsibility to agency staff. This can be done by function, such as to program officers (substantive matters) and technical specialists (financial or legal matters), or by region (west/east, urban/rural, etc.), or by programs in alphabetical order. If there are many awards, then responsibility will be divided in multiple directions. A solid structure is necessary to coordinate all of these components. Program staff may have expertise on service delivery matters, but may be weak on financial reporting. Technical specialists may have accounting skills but lack specific program knowledge. Responsibility should be assigned so as to maximize efficiency and effectiveness.

Oversight and Compliance: Reporting Requirements

What reports will you require of applicants, and how often? Generally, there are two types of reports expected, though they may be combined under one umbrella. The technical report is the document that describes, in the program manager's words, activities that have taken place and provides a general assessment of project progress. Financial reports provide documentation of expenditures and are often accompanied by requests for reimbursement (if the award is so administered). These reports are generally expected on a periodic basis, with quarterly being the most common. Monthly reporting often leaves too little time to realize meaningful change; annual reporting provides insufficient detail.

In the case of very short awards, such as 3 to 6 months, only a final report may be required. Medium-term awards up to a year in duration might require a report at 6 months and a final report at closing. Longer awards generally require quarterly reports as well as a comprehensive final report at closing. The periodicity and report format you choose depend on the length and amount of the award and your particular accountability enhancement goals.

Audit Requirements

Audit requirements are probably not necessary for small awards because there is little room for corrupt activities, and large expenditures on unapproved items would be difficult to conceal. On the other hand, large awards provide more opportunity for such activities and may demand external audits of the program account and/or the organization's consolidated financial statements to ensure the sanctity of the reported expenditures. Audits provide stronger assurance of financial accountability.

Evaluation Requirements

Whether you require an evaluation depends almost entirely on the nature of the program and your goals regarding program knowledge and dissemination. For a better description of evaluation, you should refer to Chapter 10. An implementation evaluation simply compares the scope of work to reality to assess the completeness of program implementation. This evaluation goal is generally achieved through regular reporting and a final report of program activities. Process evaluation may be required, or at least expected, to ensure management capacity during implementation. If you lack confidence in your grant recipients or want to further dissuade corruption or ensure that report content is valid, you may choose to schedule annual site visits to some or all grant recipients.

Managers with a plan for assessing program progress and making program adjustments on the fly to maximize performance will be more responsive and responsible to the problem, and they will achieve greater results than do those who implement strictly according to the initial proposed plan with no intermittent reality checks. Outcome evaluation seeks to determine the program's results and has a general purpose of providing accountability for results and performance. Outcome evaluation can link program activities to the realized outcomes to make some determinations about which programs or activities are most effective at addressing the problems. This knowledge promotes program learning and can lead to best practices in the field.

Whether the evaluation activities should be conducted by the applicant or by an independent third party depends on these goals. Generally speaking, implementation is best assessed by the program manager or the program officer in the granting agency. Process evaluation is best conducted internally by those closest to the action. Outcome evaluation is generally left in the hands of an independent professional to avoid potential bias in findings that comes with self-evaluation by the agency—the desire to present oneself in a more appealing light. Also, sound methodologies require expert knowledge to produce valid and reliable results, and such knowledge is often only available from evaluation professionals.

Sanctions for Non-Compliance and Non-Performance

When you observe, as a program officer, that a particular awardee is not performing according to expectation, steps should be taken to correct the problem. Generally, non-compliance with conditions may exist, but non-performance may be more common. In some cases, the appearance of non-performance is not because of a lack of good-faith effort, but the result of intervening circumstance. Close interaction between program officers and program managers is necessary to determine which is the case.

When an applicant proves unable to meet the conditions of award, it may be time to consider amending the scope of work significantly and writing off early efforts, or terminating the project. Generally, the lack of good-faith effort results in termination whereas other problems lead to hands-on retooling of the scope of work to better fit the applicant's abilities and local conditions. Program officers may visit and assist the recipient in examining the problems and their causes and help to produce a viable solution through direct technical assistance.

Essentially, the program falls into receivership until it is back on track. You must determine when a cease and desist order is called for in your organization and grant program. These decisions usually require discretion on the part of program officers, but your accountability expectations may call for strict adherence and project termination.

Terminating Awards

To execute a cease and desist order, your contractual provisions in the award document must expressly describe the conditions under which it may occur and the process for executing it. Generally, this means that the grant making agency identifies a series of conditions under which it may terminate the agreement "for cause." That is, your agency has a justifiable reason for terminating the agreement. These provisions are generally broad for those with the money to ensure that their interests take precedence over those of the awardee. The second component is usually a time frame for notice prior to the termination taking effect. Generally speaking, 30 days notice is acceptable to allow the grantee to discontinue the program activities. Longer or shorter periods may be applied depending on your organization's goals.

It is customary for any expenses incurred prior to the notice to be reimbursable, and generally expenses incurred between the time of notice and the effective date of the termination are also allowable for reimbursement. If you paid grant funds in advance, it will be more difficult to recoup unused funds from the recipient. In these cases, it may be necessary to seek relief in a court of justice with jurisdiction over the contract. And of course, a plan should be in place to utilize any unused or returned grant funds, either through subsequent awards, new programs, or rollover into the following year's program budget.

Delinquency: Creating Sanctions on Future Application

You should develop a system to document applicants that have been delinquent on past grant awards from your organization so that they can be handled appropriately in future grant competitions. In most cases, organizations that are, or have been, delinquent on an award are disqualified from participating in future competitions. This requirement should be expressed in the request for proposals to substantiate any disqualification decisions on these grounds. In some cases, the disqualification is permanent; in others, it is in force for a fixed number of years or until the delinquency is resolved. You may wish to avoid outright disqualification in favor of specific conditions under which a delinquent applicant may be considered for funding.

Performance Management for Grant Administration

The final, and perhaps most important, step in managing the portfolio of grant programs is the process in place to monitor performance across the system. Because you are not providing services directly, you must rely on the outputs and outcomes of your grantees to measure your impact on the identified problem. Certainly, you could measure the efficiency of the grant making operation, but these process (or intermediate) outputs are not the real purpose behind the grant program. You should plan to prepare a report on the cumulative outcomes across all funded grant programs at least once a year to fulfill your accountability expectations to your superiors, whether administrative executives, political principals, citizens at large, or donors. The variety of programs may make it difficult to use uniform performance measures, but measures can at least be categorized and summarized to demonstrate program effectiveness.

This process should reveal strengths and weaknesses in your established policies and procedures for grant administration. Careful attention to problem cases, complaints, and kinks in the application and review process can highlight areas where changes should be considered. Most programs, even in the rule-laden federal system, undergo revision and modification on an annual basis. Your programs will likely be no different as you experiment with better ways to administer your grant programs from year to year.

If you use outcome evaluation as suggested, then across your portfolio of awards, some activities will prove to be more effective than others are. This knowledge and information can be reintegrated into program design to promote program learning. That is, as you find programs that work, you may add requirements to restrict eligible activities to those that are effective, or at least to avoid those that are not effective. Policy learning can lead to improved results in future program years if the information obtained is analyzed and integrated into program design. This knowledge can extend well beyond the granting agency for which you work if you expend some program funds not only on grants, but on reporting your performance, results, and findings to relevant actors in the field of interest. Stakeholders in other funding agencies, nonprofits, and governments will be able to draw on your experience to improve practice beyond your organization's immediate sphere of influence.

CONCLUSION

This chapter provides a discussion of the web of accountability expectations and relationships that face grant making agencies. These relationships are integral to each decision made about your grant program in the planning and preparation, review and award, and management phases of your grant program. Key steps are identified so that you, as a grant maker, can think through and plan your activities to maximize these accountability expectations in advance. The result should be a more streamlined grant making process that functions smoothly and realizes superior performance in the areas of importance to the agency and its stakeholders.

This text presents the entire grant making enterprise from several perspectives intended to improve management and performance from various angles. Chapter 1 provides a close look at the system as a whole, how grants work, and how the system has changed over time. Chapter 2 presents an approach to effectively search and select programs that are closely matched to your program needs and organizational characteristics. Chapter 3 continues by presenting an approach to managing complex relationships in grant seeking within the organization and in the context of a network of partners collaborating to generate public good. Chapters 4 and 5 present an approach to developing program budgets and application narratives, while Chapter 6 attends to the necessary forms and documents that accompany most applications. Chapter 7 provides guidance on submitting grant applications, and Chapter 8 reveals the inner workings of the grant making decision process. Chapter 9 turns the focus from effective seeking and application to the practice of managing grant awards once received. Chapter 10 reviews the basics of program evaluation as it relates to grant programs in particular, highlighting the important management role evaluation plays in program performance and success. This concluding chapter looks at grant making from the perspective of a grant making agency to reveal the complex decision-making process that forms the basis of all the requirements with which grant seekers must contend during both grant application and management. As a result of this endeavor, whether student or practitioner, you should have a sound understanding and appreciation for the grant making enterprise with an improved ability to seek, receive, manage, or even make your own grant awards in search of greater public value.

REFERENCES

Birkland, Thomas A. 2005. *An Introduction to the Policy Process: Theories, Concepts, and Models of Public Policy Making, 2nd Edition.* Armonk, NY: M. E. Sharpe.

Brown, Trevor L. and Matthew Potowski. 2003. Contract management capacity in municipal and county governments. *Public Administration Review* 63(2): 153–164.

Bryson, John M. 2004. *Strategic Planning for Public and Nonprofit Organizations: A Guide to Strengthening and Sustaining Organizational Achievement, 3rd Edition.* San Francisco: Jossey-Bass.

Glaser, Mark A. and Robert B. Denhardt. 2000. Local government performance through the eyes of citizens. *Journal of Public Budgeting, Accounting, and Financial Management* 12(1): 49–73.

Hall, Jeremy L. 2007. Implications of success and persistence for public sector performance. *Public Organization Review* 7(3): 281–297.

Kettl, Donald F. 2002. *The Transformation of Governance: Public Administration for the Twenty-First Century.* Baltimore: Johns Hopkins University Press.

Koppell, Jonathan G. S. 2005. Pathologies of accountability: ICANN and the challenge of "multiple accountabilities disorder." *Public Administration Review* 65(1): 94–108.

Meier, Kenneth J. and John Bohte. 2007. *Politics and the Bureaucracy: Policy Making in the Fourth Branch of Government, 5th Edition.* Belmont, CA: Wadsworth.

INDEX